# DATE DUE

| JE 607 | | | |
|--------|--|--|--|
| | | | |
| | | | |
| | | | |
| | | | |
| | | | |
| | | | |
| | | | |
| | | | |
| | | | |
| | | | |
| | | | |
| | | | |
| | | | |
| | | | |
| | | | |
| | | | |
| | | | |
| | | | |

DEMCO 38-296

# A HISTORY OF THE AUSTRALIAN ENVIRONMENT MOVEMENT

Lake Pedder, Kakadu, Fraser Island, Green Bans, forests, urban pollution—environmental issues have been at the forefront of Australian politics since the 1960s. This book traces the development of the environment movement in Australia from the first visionaries who pressed for preservation of native fauna and for sanitation in cities to a mass social movement that challenges the most powerful interests in society.

The authors examine the social bases and traditions which contributed to the rise of an environmental ethic in the late nineteenth century and show how the environment movement evolved as a social movement, becoming a sophisticated actor in the political process and developing a coherent philosophical direction. Decades of activism produced recognition that environmental issues are interconnected with many others, such as the ANZUS alliance, Aboriginal land rights, civil liberties and social justice.

DREW HUTTON is a lecturer in the School of Humanities at Queensland University of Technology. He is the editor of *Green Politics in Australia* (1987).

LIBBY CONNORS is a lecturer in Australian history at the University of Southern Queensland. She is a co-author of *Australia's Frontline* (1992) and has contributed to two edited books on Australian colonial history. Both authors are prominent members of the Australian Greens at state and national levels.

# A HISTORY OF THE
# AUSTRALIAN ENVIRONMENT
# MOVEMENT

DREW HUTTON
LIBBY CONNORS

CAMBRIDGE
UNIVERSITY PRESS

TE OF THE UNIVERSITY OF CAMBRIDGE
Street, Cambridge, United Kingdom

UNIVERSITY PRESS
CB2 2RU, UK   http://www.cup.cam.ac.uk
40 West 20th Street, New York, NY 10011–4211, USA   http://www.cup.org
10 Stamford Road, Oakleigh, Melbourne 3166, Australia

First published 1999

Printed in Australia by Brown Prior Anderson

Typeset in New Baskerville 10/12 pt

*A catalogue record for this book is available from the British Library*

*National Library of Australia Cataloguing in Publication data*
Hutton, Drew, 1947–
A history of the Australian environment movement.
Bibliography.
Includes index.
ISBN 0 521 45076 4.
ISBN 0 521 45686 X (pbk).
1. Green movement – Australia – History.
I. Connors, Libby, 1960. II. Title.
363.7050994

ISBN 0 521 45076 4 hardback
ISBN 0 521 45686 X paperback

# Contents

# Abbreviations

| | |
|---|---|
| AAAS | Australasian Association for the Advancement of Science |
| ACF | Australian Conservation Foundation |
| ACTU | Australian Council of Trade Unions |
| AOU | Australasian Ornithologists Union |
| CALM | Department of Conservation and Land Management (WA) |
| CART | Citizens Against Route 20 (later Citizens Advocating Responsible Transport) |
| CESS | Campaign to End Sewage Smells |
| CNFA | Coalition for a Nuclear-Free Australia |
| CROPS | Concerned Residents Opposing Pulp Mill Siting |
| CSIR | Council for Scientific and Industrial Research |
| CSIRO | Commonwealth Scientific and Industrial Research Organisation |
| DURD | Department of Urban and Regional Development |
| EIS | Environmental Impact Statement |
| ESD | Ecologically Sustainable Development |
| FIDO | Fraser Island Defence (later Defenders) Organisation |
| GBRC | Great Barrier Reef Committee |
| GBRMPA | Great Barrier Reef Marine Park Authority |
| HEC | Hydro-Electric Commission |
| IUCN | International Union for the Conservation of Nature |
| LPAC | Lake Pedder Action Committee |
| NCC | Nature Conservation Council (New South Wales) |
| NDP | Nuclear Disarmament Party |
| NF&FPC | Native Fauna and Flora Protection Committee (RSSA) |
| NP&PAC | National Parks and Primitive Areas Council |
| NPAQ | National Parks Association Queensland |
| NPWS | National Parks and Wildlife Service (NSW) |

POOO      People Opposed to Ocean Outfalls
RAOU      Royal Australasian Ornithologists Union
RATS      Residents Against Toxic Substances
RSSA      Royal Society of South Australia
STOP      Stop The Ocean Pollution
SWP       Socialist Workers Party
TNFAG     Terania Native Forest Action Group
TWS       The Wilderness Society (previously Tasmanian Wilderness
          Society)
VNPA      Victorian National Parks Association
WLPSA     Wild Life Preservation Society of Australia
WPSQ      Wildlife Preservation Society of Queensland

# *Preface*

In early 1980 I attended a talk by a young academic on 'The New Militarism'. The speaker turned out to be Drew Hutton. As Ronald Reagan and Margaret Thatcher reinvented the Cold War he was presciently attempting to re-engage the vestiges of Queensland's anti-Vietnam War and anti-uranium movements against the new threats to peace. At the time I was on the fringes of Queensland's civil liberties and anti-uranium movements, unsure of how to express my sense of political indignation. Soon after Drew founded a local branch of the War Resisters' League and when the British aircraft carrier HMS *Illustrious* darkened Brisbane skies as its huge bulk filled the arch of Brisbane's Gateway Bridge, he was in a canoe on the Brisbane River along with Ian Cohen and Eleri Morgan-Thomas and other members of the Brisbane Peace Fleet as I looked on from the safety of the accompanying river bank protest. While Greenpeace was making international headlines with its protests against environmental and human destruction both east and west, Drew was incorporating peace studies into his teaching and into Brisbane local politics. In 1985 Drew stood as a Green candidate for mayor and the first of what was to become hundreds of local residents rang him to seek help over an inappropriate development next door to her suburban home. Dredging of the river, clearing of urban bushland, destruction of wetlands, loss of low income housing to urban gentrification, the ruin of heritage streetscapes by new freeways – the list of campaigns was extensive. It was Drew's complaint to Queensland's Criminal Justice Commission over the illegal disposal of toxic liquid waste which probably brought him the most state-wide attention. Here was irrefutable proof of the failure of various levels of government to manage industry with dire consequences for the state's waterways and from a political channel that was difficult for the powers that be to ignore.

Drew and I married in 1986 and I was also involved in many of these campaigns. Our lives have not been an unbroken succession of conflicts; there were periods of retreat for family, study and work reasons and periods of accommodation when group representatives sat down with government or industry to resolve environmental conflicts. To people who do not share our sense of moral protest, the breadth of these activities will seem an inexplicable jumble of causes, the bandwagon or rent-a-crowd image so over-used by unfriendly politicians and media commentators. For those of us directly involved, however, these activities were not an expression of unthinking militancy. Even when causes were seemingly thrust upon us because of their immediacy there was a growing sophistication in movement responses as our practical understanding of how political processes operated was refined and our articulation of grievances improved.

In this sense our personal history intersects with a wider national history for our specific local causes were repeated in many different settings around the country and elsewhere too activists were learning from their own successes and failures and eagerly appropriating new strategies from others. This book is an attempt to explain the pattern of historical development of the environment movement in Australia. Its internal logic has been dominated by the responses of Australian governments, by the emergence of new threats but most decisively by the ways in which campaigners learn from one another, borrow each other's successful strategies and try to avoid one another's mistakes.

We know that writing this book while teaching full-time and remaining active in many campaigns nearly drove various staff at Cambridge University Press to the limits of their patience as we repeatedly stretched deadlines to the utmost. We want to begin with our thanks to them, especially to Phillipa McGuinness who in 1993 was sympathetic to the idea of the history of the environment movement but never expected it to be still hanging over our heads so many years later.

In a book about the importance of grassroots political activity to our national life it would be wrong not to acknowledge the groundwork that goes into such a production as this. We are most grateful to the kind assistance we received from librarians and archivists at the Battye, La Trobe, Mitchell, News Ltd, Australian Consolidated Press, National, John Oxley, Fryer and Southern Queensland and Central Queensland University Libraries and the Noel Butlin Centre Archives and Tasmanian Archives Office. The courtesy we received from these librarians is a tribute to their professionalism. In comparison our obligations to the many volunteer and underpaid office workers at regional and state conservation councils around the country who assisted us are even greater. They not only helped us with records and recommended interviewees but allowed us to take up precious time on overworked photocopiers in under-resourced offices. The Australian Conservation xi

Foundation is owed a special debt for giving us access to its records at the Noel Butlin Archives Centre as is Louise from Habitat who helped us with photographs. We also wish to thank our respective universities, Queensland University of Technology and the University of Southern Queensland, for providing us with funding to undertake this research and also the School of Humanities at Griffith University (in particular its head, Mark Finnane) and the Department of Government at the University of Queensland (particularly Ralph Summy) for supporting each of us for spells as visiting fellows while we were working on this project.

Many people who have been active in the movement gave up valuable time to be interviewed for this project. It was wonderful to finally meet people whose names had become so well known in environment movement circles and a great privilege to hear their recollections of events. We are very grateful to everyone who agreed to be interviewed. A full list of their names appears in the bibliography but there are two caveats that need to be noted. We were not able to interview every leading environmental campaigner of the past few decades and so there are some regrettable omissions of environmental 'leaders'. Those whom we were able to speak to will not necessarily agree with the approach we have taken in this book. That is a feature of most writing projects but philosophical diversity is a particularly strong feature of social movements.

Social movements are the combined actions of hundreds of people who work towards common goals most of the time without even knowing one another. Although we have both been involved in social movement activity in Queensland for over 20 years, and with the formation of the Australian Greens at the national level for almost a decade, we know that as active members or as academics we do not 'own' the Australian environment movement. No one can own a social movement – not a particular organisation, nor any number of charismatic individuals, nor the academics who analyse it. Or perhaps it is more correct to say that everyone who participates in social movement activity owns the movement. For this reason we want to dedicate this book to all those hundreds of supporters who have worked behind the scenes in campaigns around the country but whose names do not make it into this book. The strength of the movement nationally resides in the personal convictions of hundreds of Australians who individually do not receive public recognition but who collectively have changed the way Australians relate to their environment. So we dedicate this book to everyone who has ever been prepared to take a public stance in defence of the biological integrity of this planet and of our own little neck of the woods.

LIBBY CONNORS

Darwin

Ranger
Uranium
Mine

Jabilu
Uraniu
Mine

Kakadu World
Heritage Area

The Kimberleys

● Noonkanbah

NORTHERN
TERRITORY

Shark Bay

WESTERN
AUSTRALIA

SOUTH
AUSTRALIA

Perth

South-East Forests

Stirling
Ranges

0          500

kilometres

Significant Campaign Sites

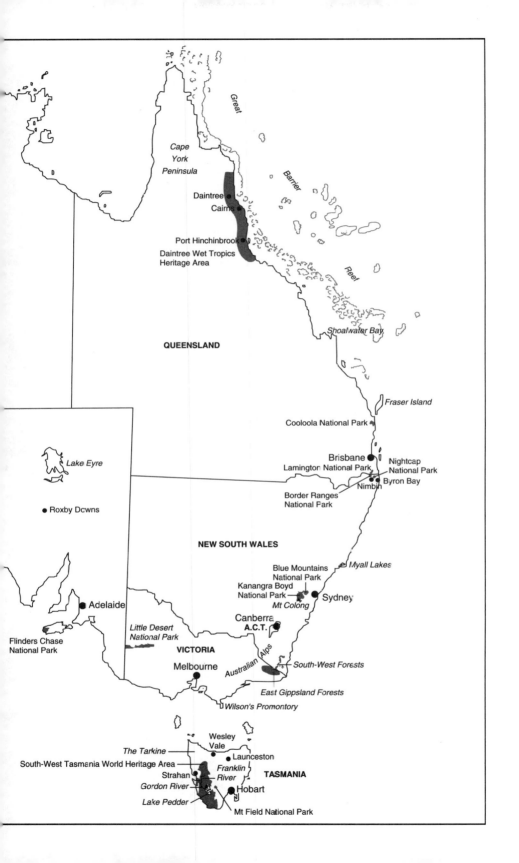

Great Barrier Reef

Cape
York
Peninsula

Daintree

Cairns

Port Hinchinbrook

Daintree Wet Tropics
Heritage Area

QUEENSLAND

Lake Eyre

Roxby Downs

Adelaide

Flinders Chase
National Park

Shoalwater Bay

Fraser Island

Cooloola National Park

Brisbane
Lamington National Park
Border Ranges
National Park

Nightcap
National Park
Byron Bay
Nimbin

NEW SOUTH WALES

Myall Lakes

Blue Mountains
National Park
Kanangra Boyd
National Park
Mt Colong

Sydney

Canberra
A.C.T.

Little Desert
National Park

VICTORIA

Melbourne

Australian Alps

South-West Forests

East Gippsland Forests

Wilson's Promontory

Wesley
Vale

The Tarkine

Launceston

South-West Tasmania World Heritage Area

Franklin
River

TASMANIA

Strahan

Gordon River

Hobart

Lake Pedder

Mt Field National Park

# Introduction

In 1990 Australia's Dr Bob Brown, the leader of the campaign to save the Franklin River in Tasmania's south-west from a hydro-electric dam, won the Goldman Award, the world's largest environmental prize and regarded by activists as the environmentalists' equivalent of the Nobel. Three years later John Sinclair was a recipient for his work in campaigning to protect Fraser Island. In winning these international awards, they joined the prestigious ranks of a small number of environmental campaigners from around the world who have been so acknowledged, including Dai Qing, the famous Chinese poet, dissident and environmentalist who endured imprisonment in her fight to try and prevent the mammoth Three Gorges Dam on China's Yangtse River.

By international comparison, Australia's environment movement has been enormously successful. In the late 1980s, environment movement organisations claimed to have 300,000 members Australia-wide—more than all the members of political parties combined. The environment movement could probably have claimed, as the peace movement in the mid-1980s did, to be larger on a *per capita* basis than its counterparts in the rest of the Western world.[1] Its strength has inspired a number of international environmental campaigners to make regular visits; Petra Kelly first toured in 1977 as part of the campaign against uranium mining and made several more visits in the 1980s before her untimely death;[2] and Professors David Bellamy and David Suzuki continued to draw large crowds in the 1990s.

Internationally known spokespersons and personalities are an example of the contemporary environment movement's transnational character, yet this movement can only be understood and interpreted through localised studies. Particular ideas and problems might have a global audience, but they have to be received and acted upon at the

1

local and national level. No amount of research into the contradictions between global economic growth and environmental degradation can have any impact without a carrier and interpreter of these ideas at the national level. Consequently, the environment movement is affected by material conditions as well as the constraints and opportunities of national political culture. The Australian movement has been part of the broader global environment movement, but it developed in response to local problems and was shaped by Australia's particular economic and political landscape.

Australian political culture has been particularly fertile ground for environmental protest. Over 200 years ago Alexis de Tocqueville, the French sociologist and politician, interpreted protest movements as the politics of hope. People first must have some expectation of their rights before they will object to and protest against attempts to inhibit or restrain what they have always taken for granted.[3] For many years Australian national history has been dominated by the formative influence of the labour movement which mobilised in the 1890s and produced the Australian Labor Party, Australia's oldest political party and one which continues to dominate our political landscape. Since the 1970s feminist historians have emphasised the effect of the women's movement on national development. Furthermore, no narrative of Australian history has been able to overlook the enormous impact of the peace and anti-conscription movements which have periodically altered government policy and have greatly affected Australian national and international outlooks. The environment movement has been generally overlooked as a participant in this national history except when its more obvious disruptions, such as the left-wing Green Bans of the 1970s and the blockade of the Franklin River, are acknowledged. Yet as early as 1981 the historian Geoffrey Bolton first charted the tensions between resource development—which has been central to national political formation—and protection of the environment. Even geography's influential contributions to the field in the 1970s and 1980s were seen as marginal to the national historical discourse; Heathcote interpreted environmental consciousness as a product of cultural dispositions rather than a cause, while J. M. Powell's extensive work on the history of environmental management had the effect of reducing the field of historical conflict to a problem of administration or bureaucratic struggle.[4]

We argue that the environment movement as a social movement was a factor in Australian historical development long before the Green Bans of the 1970s. The Australian conservation movement existed alongside the labour, women's and peace movements of the late nineteenth century; it continued to exist, albeit in quiescent mode, in the years after World War II, right up to the 1960s. Then it rapidly remobilised and transformed itself until, by the 1996 federal election, John Howard as leader of the coalition (conservative) parties would insist that 'We're all Greenies now.' The Australian environment movement has provoked conflict over resource development, and this engagement in political debate has affected Australian attitudes and values concerning the environment and become a significant factor in bureaucratic and institutional development. This book is an attempt to understand the historical development of the environment movement as a social movement. Our main concern is to establish its historical lineage, and the causes of particular mobilisations and of its periodic changes in strategy. An understanding of this dynamic, we believe, is crucial to a full explanation of shifts in Australian cultural and political attitudes towards the environment.

Assessments of the strength of the environment movement by those who oppose it and by those who participate in it vary widely. The same 1996 election which saw John Howard win government also witnessed an unusual event in Australian politics when Pauline Hanson won a seat as an independent in the federal parliament's lower house, the House of Representatives. Hanson had been disendorsed by the Liberal Party during the course of the election campaign for making racist statements. A popular support base gathered around the controversial member of parliament, who began to articulate a residual hostility to the success of the progressive social movements of the past thirty years. Not only was the Aboriginal movement attacked as being 'an industry', but 'special interests' were accused of having too much influence in federal policy-making. Hanson's views of the strength of Australia's progressive social movements stand in marked contrast to those of their supporters. Even during periods which, with the benefit of hindsight, we know were times of expansion, activists' writings are marked by pessimism, by the sense of always fighting against the tide, always feeling on the margins.

It was the need to put these campaigns into perspective and to assess realistically the movement's current fortunes that were our *personal* motivations in attempting this history. We have been active in the movement for many years, but we reject the suggestion that such a bias negates the value of this interpretation. Leading European intellectuals such as Herbert Marcuse and Alain Touraine who have contributed to the development of social movement theory have also been active participants in social movements. As green activists we are no different from European scholars who have written histories of their national environment movements despite their partisan involvement.[5] In many respects our view as insiders was invaluable, allowing a better understanding of processes and conflicts that would not be apparent to outsiders. Our motivation has never been to celebrate the movement—

in fact it was the faltering of the movement's fortunes in the early 1990s that first stimulated our interest in the topic. The intention has been to chart its processes in order to better understand the strengths and limitations of social movement activity.

## Social Movements

The theoretical assumptions that underpin this account are those of social movement theory. This field is well known to political scientists and sociologists but less familiar to Australian historians. Its literature extends back more than 100 years, but it was substantially revised in the 1970s in the light of the student movements of the 1960s and the expansion of human rights and peace and environment protests in the 1970s. Among the most important assertions made by the new generation of social movement theorists are that protest movements are historical actors and that they create a historical dynamic. Alain Touraine argues that social institutions and social orders are born out of social movements and not the reverse, as is so often assumed.[6] Those sociologists who emphasise the internal diversity of movements, such as Alberto Melucci, are wary of this claim, doubting that political change is their main orientation.[7] Nonetheless, they all concur that protest movements affect norms by producing counter-ideologies which challenge the status quo and transform institutions; this symbolic challenge contributes to our understandings of how new discourses are generated and adopted.[8]

### Characteristics

Despite the extensive sociological literature, social movements are notoriously difficult to define. They elude traditional historical narratives because they are not formal institutions. They do not have precise beginnings and ends, and their boundaries cannot be delineated accurately. One of their defining characteristics is a fluid structure which includes individuals, formal organisations, official memberships, and a much wider circle of non-affiliated supporters. They appear at times to be very small and weak in terms of institutional status, with no public visibility; yet they have proved to be capable of generating wide support, far beyond their organisational size. Formal organisations may go into periods of decline, and some collapse altogether; but as new threats appear, social movements can remobilise, generating new groups and supporters with impressive force and rapidity.

*Instrumental Goals*

The definitive features of social movements were extracted in the process of sociological debate in the 1980s. The largely US-based resource mobilisation approach emphasises the instrumentalist and strategic logic of collective behaviour; the European action/identity school focuses on the normative dimension, specifically the anti-systemic values that unite diverse groups of people. The major elements of these two influential schools were brought together in a unitary definition by a number of theorists in the mid-1980s and these were summed up by Alberto Melucci as consisting of solidarity, sustained conflict, and breaking of system limits.[9] More recently, Sidney Tarrow defined the basis of social movement activity as contentious collective action 'by people who lack regular access to institutions, act in the name of new or unaccepted claims, and behave in ways that fundamentally challenge others. [This activity] produces social movements when social actors concert their actions around common claims in sustained sequences of interaction with opponents or authorities.'[10]

*Expressive Identity*

Social movements are not simply pressure groups, but a series of organisations and a series of events which are unified by solidarity or a shared identity. The basis of this solidarity is interpreted broadly by different scholars: from Tarrow's 'common claims' to 'knowledge interest', which is the very specific term used by Jamison, Eyerman, Cramer and Laessoe to designate the cognitive plane in which movements form their collective identity.[11] But since movements by nature are broad and encompassing and lack any unitary disposition, it would be wrong to interpret this in too narrowly instrumentalist or too narrowly ideological a way.[12] Social movements articulate a moral critique of society, and it is this expression of moral protest which is a principal component of actor identity.[13] Movement supporters may disagree with particular goals and have widely divergent ideological and philosophical positions, but a shared sense of moral outrage builds participant identity, commitment and solidarity.

However, as Jean Cohen argues, an expressive identity is not sufficient to define a social movement. A context of struggle is also fundamental.[14] Movement actors express their identification with the movement in many ad hoc ways, from membership of formal organisations and involvement in movement activities through to occasional participation in movement events. Outside these domains, individuals may be in accord with the movement's goals; but this does not necessarily make them part of the movement. In fact, the expression of a lack of identity with movements, even while agreeing with their goals, has become part of popular discourse—the refrain of 'I'm not a feminist but ...' symbolises the way in which audience and participants distinguish themselves.

*Movement Boundaries*

The distinctions are more problematic at the level of production of knowledge. Movement analysts who focus exclusively on philosophical underpinnings or the development of movement ideologies tend to place too much emphasis on the role of intellectuals and scientists. Since the goal of social movements is to change the normative base of society and to question the governing logic, they tend to produce intellectual ferment and increase critical reflexivity, rather than the reverse. A scientist who is engaged in environmental science research is not necessarily an 'environmentalist' in the protest movement's sense of the term. The boundary that divides the social movement from bureaucrats employed to implement policy resulting from the demands of the movement is also a shifting one. This has been a particularly vexing question for the women's movement as leading feminists have moved into positions of authority in the state system, earning the label of 'femocrats',[15] but it is also an issue for the environment movement, given the extensive environmental industry that operates in both government and business spheres. A scientist or a bureaucrat may share the movement's values and even contribute to the development of new cultural models and understandings but, unless they have engaged in contestation, they are not part of the movement. However, those intellectuals and bureaucrats who publicly or covertly assist movements in their conflicts are clearly identifying with, and temporarily becoming, movement actors. Historically there have been a number of such personalities and they have usually been widely acclaimed for their influential role.[16]

Engagement in conflict helps to define movement boundaries in respect of other related groups as well. Indigenous peoples, for example, are not automatically part of the environment movement. Traditional cosmologies may share many attributes of ecological consciousness, and indigenous lifestyles are usually far more environmentally sensitive than those of industrialised societies, but without the element of contestation they do not constitute movement protest activity. Indigenous resistance, on the other hand, is clearly a form of social protest; environmental desecration may be one of the triggers for indigenous struggle, but it is not usually the main issue and is contingent on other priorities. Indigenous movements have their own internal culture, values, protest styles and agenda, which constitute a distinct social movement; they are separate from, but often prepared to cooperate with, other progressive movements.

### Self-limiting Radicalism

Social movements cannot exist without contestation, but they are not the sources of social breakdown and chaos that their opponents imagine them to be. Although nationalist movements in particular may be taken over by revolutionary organisations,[17] a distinguishing feature of post-1960s Western social movements has been their rejection of revolutionary aims. This characteristic was first conceptualised by Alain Touraine in his study of the Polish Solidarity movement,[18] and further articulated by Jean Cohen in her analysis of contemporary movements. Although movement actors seek to expand civil society and to reorganise 'relations between economy, state and society', their goal is not state power. Cohen argues that contemporary activists not only value democracy and plurality, but also recognise the failures of the New Left and its descent into revolutionary Marxism. By contrast, the post-1960s movement actors 'interpret their actions as attempts to renew a democratic political culture and to reintroduce the normative dimension of social action into political life. This is the meaning of self-limiting radicalism.'[19]

Fighting within the perimeters of liberal democracy has internal and external strategic advantages. Lacking a unifying ideology, and with participants who insist on their own autonomy, movements cannot impose the discipline on their constituents that a revolutionary challenge would require. Operating within the system's own terms also saves movements from the marginalisation of revolutionary sects. A campaign that does not confront authorities directly with demands for radical restructuring protects movements from state repression. No matter how radical individual activists might be in their personal beliefs and philosophy, they end up fighting the system on its own terms.

### Anti-systemic

Although movements refuse a revolutionary challenge, they are nonetheless anti-systemic in their orientation. Movements annoy authorities because their demands cannot be easily met within existing institutional arrangements. Modern social movements 'do not engage in frontal assaults on states', Roberta Garner argues, but they do erode state power: 'They seep into all institutional structures, transforming their practices and mentalities.'[20] Social movements do not appear to be radical because they simply appeal to fundamental moral values—peaceful relations, the integrity of the environment, the right to equality and participation, and so on. It is the interpretation that modern society is betraying, or incapable of implementing, these values that allows their message to penetrate and to become an urgent priority. Social movements challenge the internal logic of social structures by insisting that their practices are threatening to, or even the antithesis of, these values.[21] This struggle inevitably becomes a battle for the control and production of information, as well as a struggle over the aims of society. Social movements take on a prophetic function in their efforts to invest the social and political worlds with new meanings and to test prevailing assumptions. Their sustained emphasis on the contradictions that govern social, political and economic domains has heightened the reflexivity of the modern era.[22]

### Historical Conditions for Social Movement Activity

#### A Material Problem

Social movements are a response to an objective problem, but it is clear that material conditions are not a sufficient explanation for their existence. Three factors act as a catalyst for the rise and persistence of a social movement—there must be a material problem, a social base prepared to respond to this problem, and a strong but open state with a political culture that permits extra-parliamentary activity.[23] As Ferdinand Muller-Rommel and Thomas Poguntke comment, most of the theoretical work overlooks the significance of the material problems that social movements strive to address, but this is because new stimuli do not necessarily produce a social movement reaction.[24]

#### Generational Radicalism

Since F. Parkin's 1968 study of the British peace movement, theorists have drawn a connection between middle-class radicalism and movement participation, but this does not explain why the middle class is more likely to respond in some historical situations than in others. Other social categories which are highly represented in movements are those outside the labour market, such as the unemployed, students and retirees.[25] The distinguishing features which attracted attention in the aftermath of the student movement, however, were the youthfulness and high educational attainments of protesters; theorists began to point to age demographics as a feature of alternative politics. Pakulski argues that there may be historic experiences that radicalise particular age cohorts, rather than attributing a rebellious sentiment to the young generally.[26] The advantage of this interpretation is that it also helps to explain other characteristics of social movements, such as their tendency to arise periodically in recurring waves. Brandt notes that what are sometimes termed 'new' social movements actually have their precursors in the Romantic movement of the late eighteenth and early nineteenth centuries and the Progressivism of the late nineteenth and early twentieth centuries. He categorises them as reactions 'to far-reaching thrusts of modernisation', but whether they may be linked 'to the long waves of accumulation cycles' is still inconclusive.[27] Since technological development and higher levels of investment in research and education are consequences of the accumulation cycle, this argument offers a number of explanatory insights. Educational expansion in the latter part of the nineteenth century after a period of sustained growth created new avenues of social mobility for the brightest of the working class—and, for the first time, middle-class females—who moved into the new scientific fields. Technological innovation requires a critical and reflective technocratic class whose social expectations are raised in the process of their training. In the Australian context the impact of the ideas and personnel of this new middle class on the women's movement at the beginning of the twentieth century has been analysed,[28] but its influence on the other progressive movements is less clear. The 1960s expansion in tertiary education similarly followed a period of sustained growth and was intended to lay the groundwork for the space and computer age. Much larger numbers of young people were affected, and their social expectations were significantly higher than those of their parents. Whether their radicalisation was cognitive, a product of their critical training, or a reaction to the socio-political blockage of the 1970s economic downturn and their ultimately peripheral socio-economic status is debated by sociologists.[29] Whatever the cause, the formative values of these radicalised generations remain after individuals have withdrawn from militant activity; new issues can trigger renewed mobilisation.

*An Open State*

The third factor that is essential for social movement development is a state prepared to countenance mass protest.[30] In Western democracies such as Australia, the state is strong enough to permit a great deal of extra-parliamentary protest and associational activity; but the level of openness of the state is not a given, even in liberal democracies. In times of emergency, such as war, civil liberties are often formally suspended; while during the Cold War, public anxieties were exploited to such an extent that political rights were culturally and unofficially prohibited. In

times of such sociopolitical blockage, social movements may contract
to organisational maintenance and the promotion of only those aims
that are institutionally acceptable. Informal repression, in contrast to
totalitarian states, is not sufficient to block social protest permanently,
however: a new generation of political agitation can reopen and expand
the cultural space of civil society, enabling the mobilisation of new
movements.[31]

### Movement Trajectories

#### Connecting with Political Power

The nature of the state is one factor in the rise of social movements and
it also influences the way they develop. Social movements are not social
clubs or sub-cultures. They form because they feel threatened by some
aspect of the dominant culture; individuals feel powerless to do
something about this through accepted channels and so they link up
with like-minded others to work for significant changes in public policy.
This also usually requires substantial changes to attitudes and values in
the community at large. Consequently, all social movements attempt to
link with political power, because this is the main way to achieve changes
in public policy. Therefore, it is possible, as some writers do, to over-
emphasise the desire by social movements to maintain their autonomy
and cultural values over their political goals.[32] They certainly attempt to
maintain their independence from governments and political parties
but, at the same time, their ultimate aim is to make themselves redund-
ant by having such a profound impact on the mainstream culture that
their program becomes part of that mainstream.

#### Problems of Incorporation

However, the movement's goals will not be met by becoming incorporated wholly by government, especially if the government does not
implement that program to an extent that the movement finds
acceptable. Movement activists can then find much of their time taken
up with routine administrative tasks—responses to government discussion papers, impact assessment studies, representation on government committees—so that they have little time for other things, like
organising more proactive campaigns and maintaining their grassroots
base. An adroit government using just the right amounts of incremental
reform, spin-doctoring, and funding of groups can sometimes neutralise
a movement's ability to mount campaigns against that government's
unwillingness to introduce serious reform. Another possibility is that
the movement might be faced with strong resistance to its demands;

consequently, it collapses altogether or goes into a latent phase. Alternatively, if the material conditions that caused its formation remain potent, and especially if the movement is not concerned only with a single issue, then activists will probably consolidate the movement and wait for better times. A social movement is, therefore, likely to go through cycles of partial incorporation with consequent demobilisation, followed by a remobilisation if the initial threat remains obvious.

This is a process that is familiar to peace movement historians, and it is also a well-known characteristic of the histories of feminist and indigenous movements. Australian peace movements tend to mobilise large numbers quickly when there is a war or a threat of war, and then demobilise even more quickly when the war, or the most objectionable aspect of Australia's participation, ends. The movement then reverts to a latent phase in which core activists with strong philosophical commitments maintain key functions. The Australian indigenous movement made strong connections with political power on several occasions, only to be blocked by the political influence of opposing forces. The most notable of these was Prime Minister Bob Hawke's move to introduce uniform land rights legislation in the early 1980s, a move that was abandoned because of pressure from the mining industry. Instead of becoming demoralised and demobilising, however, the movement retained an impetus strong enough to absorb the reversal, consolidate, and wait for more promising times. A movement that has developed a more comprehensive perception of its objectives and expanded horizontally to link with a broader coalition of groups is much more capable of withstanding these difficult times than a unidimensional movement.[33] The development of more holistic objectives, like maintaining biodiversity or achieving ecologically sustainable development, has helped the environment movement through its most recent downturn in fortunes.

## Counter-movements

Social movements can also run into difficult times as a result of provoking counter-movements. Once a social movement becomes influential, its opponents must either work for an accommodation with it or seek to undermine it. Therefore, those determined to support patriarchy, exclusive pastoral landowner rights, or unrestrained resource use will often mobilise their resources to prevent any further gains by feminists, indigenous people, and greens, respectively. This usually involves the adoption of tactics similar to many used by the social movements themselves; they will even, at times, form industry front groups or support grassroots organisations.[34]

*Movement Culture*

As social movements mature, they also develop internally. Despite the importance of connecting with political power, it is still important for movement participants to feel a sense of collective identity. This is achieved through the creation and manipulation of certain symbols; the communications established through rallies, newsletters and common campaigns; the work of those who maintain networks; and the actions of charismatic leaders. Activists experience that sense of identity at a number of levels—their local group, the networks they belong to, the campaigns they are involved in. Collective identity is mostly developed through campaigning, by engaging in contestation with opposing forces and developing a sense of solidarity. The cultural style developed by participants then is reflected in the movement's meeting procedures, organisational features, interpersonal relations, and forms of communication. However, those movement actors who present themselves in public forums often make an effort to separate their personas from the cultural life of the movement. It is possible, for example, for campaigners to combine a strong utopian philosophical commitment at the personal level, characteristic of many others in the movement, with a level of hard-headed pragmatism in campaigning that is anything but utopian. They realise that short-term gains are essential, not only for the movement's desired outcomes but also for maintaining morale and enthusiasm among participants and supporters.

## Methodology

The application of these theoretical insights to a historical project presents a number of methodological problems that have affected the approach of this book. The ad hoc nature of social movement events makes reconstructing them particularly difficult. Since formal membership of organisations is only a partial indicator of movement activity, how can the historian do justice to past participation? Melucci refers to *submerged* networks that contribute to group solidarity and may only become apparent when a particular issue brings the group into open conflict with authority. As movements develop, they grow horizontally: groups and individuals involved in similar issues discover their affinity and link up; but again this may not happen in public and may be a product of friendship and social networks.[35] As a structural feature of movement organisation and development, Mario Diani has used networks as an interpretive framework for the Italian environment movement. This produced a study grounded in detailed empirical evidence, yet it narrowed the definition of the Italian environment movement in controversial ways; for example Diani concludes that, despite environmental protest on pollution issues in Italy in the 1970s, there was no environmental movement until the 1980s.[36] Our study takes evidence of environmental protest as proof of movement activity, and tentatively infers from associational links and biographical data that networks did in fact exist although they have never been documented. This is not controversial for the period after 1960, for which we have been able to interview participants, but is speculative for the movement before this time. Similarly, when movements go into a latent phase and periodically withdraw from overt contestation, this does not necessarily mean that they no longer exist. Historical evidence of movement continuity in the latent phase is also difficult to reconstruct—the difference between latency and death becomes a matter of historical judgment.

In contrast to Diani's structural approach, Jamison, Eyerman, Cramer and Lassoe in their history of the environment movements of Sweden, Denmark and the Netherlands used ecological consciousness for their analytical interrogation. Clearly environmental consciousness is heightened and developed as a result of social conflict. As new issues come to the fore, both movement activists and the public become more sensitive to movement values and ideas. However, historical evidence of heightened consciousness may be as illusory as the movement's submerged networks. The dilemma is that the self-limiting radicalism of social movements and their preparedness to contest authority on its own terms affect movement language and rhetoric. A leaflet's utilitarian language or a poster's simple aesthetic appeal is not a fair indicator of ecological philosophy because it is directed at a non-movement audience. No matter how sophisticated movement 'knowledge interest' may have become, activists are forced to channel their long-term aims into more mundane goals and specific campaigns that will connect with non-participants. Consequently, movement artefacts often express instrumentalist goals rather than deep ecology.

Recourse to internal sources and movement ideologues does not necessarily resolve the problem. While they may reveal clear philosophical underpinnings, the diversity within movements makes it difficult to judge how widely they can be assumed to apply. In practice, ecological consciousness may become as narrow and restrictive an interpretive framework as networks. Jamison in his study of the Swedish environmental movement, for example, defines the most advanced form of ecological consciousness as incompatible with incorporation into Swedish social democracy; since the Swedish social democrats adopted much of the movement's agenda and won support from many environmentalists in the 1980s, he concludes that the identity of the

Swedish environment movement had disintegrated despite the apparent strength of environment organisations.[37] In this sense, systems ecology and its penetration of ecological consciousness can become as blunt a measure as the purity of working-class consciousness became for historians assessing the strength of the labour movement.

In our experience, philosophy has never become a major source of conflict within the Australian environment movement. While there has been tension between urban environmentalists and nature conservationists and philosophical differences among deep ecologists, resource conservationists, animal rights exponents and many others, these have never been the main preoccupations of environmental activists. Many in the Australian movement are thankful they have been spared the debilitating disputes, between so-called deep ecologists on the one hand and social ecologists (represented by Murray Bookchin) on the other, which have been part of movement politics in the United States, or the raging arguments between *Fundis* and *Realos* in German green politics. The main battles were over strategy—should the movement continue to lobby politely or take to the streets, use non-violent civil disobedience or sabotage, give 'brown' issues or 'green' issues priority, involve itself in government policy or maintain its independence? In the 1980s and 1990s leading Australian environmentalists shared remarkably similar philosophical understandings and assessments of ecological limits but argued bitterly over short-term strategy and directions. Certainly, personal philosophical differences can fuel these debates but such differences do not necessarily exclude activists nor immobilise the movement more than temporarily. Clearly, there is little to be gained by a history which labels and dismisses sections of the movement on the basis of their philosophical purity. Consequently, our periodisation of the movement is derived neither from philosophical development nor from structural attributes, but from changes in the strategic direction of the movement.

The largest methodological hurdle to developing this framework was the artificiality of writing a national history of a social movement. The horizontal, loose, informal nature of a social movement had to be managed by selecting issues and campaigns and giving priority to those of national significance. Reducing diversity to a representative core is always a problem of historical narration, but the localism of much environmental activity forced us to be particularly discriminating. Australia's federal political structure, which makes most environmental issues the responsibility of the states, added to the difficulty of selection. Our assessment of 'national' campaigns is based not simply on the level of government to which they appealed, but on those that had the most impact on activists and on internal movement structure and organisation. (Local activists watch interstate campaigns with interest and can usually call on state and national networks.) A second criterion was impact on public consciousness and the development of public policy. We have also endeavoured to illustrate the variety of issues that Australian environmentalists have campaigned on, as well as the movement's base around the country.

### Outline of this Book

Our emphasis is on those campaigns that we believe best characterised the strategic directions of the movement in its different phases because our central hypothesis is that the movement developed in response to two main factors—the appearance of new threats, and the success or failure of past campaigns. The different phases are covered in five parts.

Part I attempts to show the breadth and depth of environmental movement activity in Australia in the nineteenth and early twentieth centuries and to explain its moderation in contrast to the contemporary movement. It argues that Australia has experienced two major waves of environmental activity, and it seeks to illustrate the continuity between the first and second waves in issues, backgrounds of participants, and value concerns. In contrast to the mass mobilisations of the contemporary movement, however, the pattern of the first wave was four serial and thematic mobilisations, and these are explored in Chapters 1 and 2.

Part II begins with a discussion of the routinisation and partial institutionalisation of the first-wave movement by the 1950s. When the Australian environment came under new threats from a boom in foreign investment in the 1960s, neither the established institutional framework of government nor the largely assimilated movement was capable of responding effectively; this resulted in a number of environmental conflicts that rapidly remobilised and renewed the movement. The most important of these campaigns, beginning with the Great Barrier Reef and ending with Lake Pedder, exemplify these conflicts and are the basis of Chapter 3.

Part III traces this new generation of environmental activists as they broke through the incorporation that had rendered the movement ineffective by borrowing partly from traditions of left-wing and working-class struggles, and mobilising publicly around environmental issues. In these campaigns the movement expanded, linked up with other movements, developed more powerful collective identities, and used the disruptive influence of mass protests to try to force governments to accept its programs. Chapter 4 combines an analysis of urban and anti-nuclear campaigns as well as the change in leadership in the movement,

while Chapter 5 deals with the fights for wilderness preservation, beginning with the Fraser Island campaign and ending with the struggle to
stop the damming of the Franklin River in South-West Tasmania.

In the aftermath of the success of the Franklin campaign, the prospect of influence with the federal government resulted in a new
direction for the movement in the mid-1980s. Part IV studies the
development of a more professional movement, one that relied less on
good-hearted, adventurous spirits and more on sound administrators,
skilful lobbyists and thorough researchers in organisations that often
resembled traditional bureaucracies more than the grassroots. It is in
this period that the post-1960s movement becomes most institutionalised. Nevertheless, the movement always had its anarchists, direct
actionists and counter-culturists, and Part IV acknowledges the tensions
between the different tendencies. It finishes with the 1990 federal
election, where the influence of green organisations was strong enough
to be a vital factor in Labor Party victory. Chapter 6 looks at forest and
wilderness campaigns, Chapter 7 the urban environment and pollution,
and Chapter 8 green politics.

Part V consists of one chapter which looks at the difficult times
encountered by conservationists once the forces threatened by the
movement's influence began to counter-attack in a concerted and more
skilful manner. The greens had few influential friends in the Keating
government and even fewer in the Howard government after March
1996. Consequently, the level of incorporation of the movement,
combined with the Coalition's reluctance to take environmental reform
seriously, forced the movement to reassert its autonomy, learn from
experience, remobilise, and find new ways to connect with political
power as economic globalisation, free-market economic policies and
worsening global environmental indicators presented even greater
challenges.

The legacy of the Australian environment movement at the institutional and cultural level has been considerable. It has never been
as institutionalised as the labour movement, but it has won some
important concessions nonetheless. Although we conclude that it is
currently reflecting on a downturn in its fortunes, we also argue that it
will be a force in any new political settlement in the decades ahead.

# PART I

# The First Wave: 1860s to World War II

> It takes few pages to define and defend the concept of
> social movement, but it should take many years for
> sociologists to disentangle various components of com-
> plex social and cultural actions, and to identify the
> presence of social movements in collective behaviour
> which has many more components.[1]

Lacking a sense of its own history, the contemporary environment
movement has been slow to claim its past. This historical amnesia
enabled the movement to view itself as distinctly new and offering
radical critiques and original solutions. It added to the sense of excite-
ment and vitality that marked the movement in the 1970s and 1980s.
This newness was utilised by the movement's opponents to try to dismiss
it as a fad, opportunistically riding on a fashion of protest without any
appreciation of the long-standing basis of many resource disputes in this
country's history.[2] The short-term view also had the disadvantage of
limiting understanding of the way protest movements operate, their ebb
and flow and their long-term contribution to social development.

This part seeks to establish the continuity of the contemporary
movement from its nineteenth-century origins.

In a post-colonial world, claiming one's past has become fraught with
danger. The dilemma is evident in current writing on the Australian
women's movement. In the late 1980s and early 1990s two important
pieces of work helped to bury the 1970s antagonism to the first-wave
women's movement. By placing nineteenth-century women's defence of
the family, social purity and temperance in its social and political context, Marilyn Lake and Katie Spearritt reconstructed the oppositional
nature of the early Australian women's movement. Victorian era
feminists lost their puritanical conservatism and could once more be

understood as trail-blazers asserting their rights against the dominant values of their day.[3] Since that time, however, Lake's work on white feminists who sought to extend their concern for women's rights to indigenous women has recast the early women's movement as 'domination ... at the heart of an emancipatory project' and its activists as missionaries.[4]

Similarly, work on early environmental thought has emphasised its role as a product of the imperial mission,[5] and a popular case study of two nineteenth-century Melbourne conservationists has pointed to their gender, racial and militarist prejudices.[6]

The oppositional nature of past protest has to be seen relative to its own time. Social movements begin by criticising one aspect of the dominant ideology, but as they mature and establish affinity with other groups fighting battles against similar authorities, broader social criticism develops. The reflexivity of social movements is one of the key factors in undermining hegemonic ideas, but this does not happen overnight. Systemic analyses evolve in the process of struggle. Activists in earlier mobilisation phases upheld the discriminatory practices of their day, even while adopting an oppositional stance from within an imperialist hegemony. They opened up the debates and the political spaces that contemporary social movements now occupy.

Reclaiming the environment movement's past also has to be done in the face of scepticism from the social scientists and historians of Australian environmental politics. Although some social scientists acknowledge the continuity of environmental ideas from last century to the present, they argue that first-wave environmentalists were merely a technocratic elite; that they only ever operated within traditional political channels; and that they failed to present any institutional challenge to the political culture of their day.[7] Specialist historical studies have also been harsh in their assessments of early environmentalists. A history of Victoria's national parks system argues that early conservationists lacked the unity of a symbolic universe, and consequently did not constitute a social movement until they developed an 'institutional order' in the 1940s.[8] Similarly, R. B. Walker doubts that New South Wales campaigners constituted a movement until the interwar period when they developed an ecological consciousness, while a study of Tasmania's Scenery Preservation Board only credits early activists as a 'proto-movement'.[9] Even Verity Burgmann's study of political protest dismisses the early conservation movement on the grounds that it failed to seek social transformation, placing it outside the boundaries of social movement activity.[10] Such criticisms suggest a narrow interpretation of what constitutes social movement activity and a failure to appreciate the historical context of early environmentalist activity.

This part uses the criteria for defining social movements discussed in the Introduction to trace the boundaries of the early Australian movement. It examines the ways in which campaigners of the late nineteenth and early twentieth centuries responded to the material conditions of their day, participated in and interpreted the international environment movement's concerns in the Australian context, developed networks, and articulated an anti-materialist critique of industrial society's destructive tendencies. Successful connection with political power resulted in the development of new institutional arrangements—not just the national parks that became their most celebrated achievement, but also forestry departments, nature study in schools, and colonial and state intervention in urban public health, urban parklands and town planning.

This definition enables us to draw clear distinctions between movement and non-movement environmental opposition. Although the earliest resistance to European destruction and degradation of the landscape came from Aborigines, their struggle was over more than the natural resources of this country.[11] The insurrectionary nature of their struggle against European invasion placed them well outside the bounds of a self-limiting social movement. Their continuing resistance has its own counter-cultural style, values and language that also place it outside the contemporary environment movement.[12] This part does not appropriate the indigenous struggle, which is a distinct indigenous social movement with its own history. Aboriginal opposition to environmental degradation is only covered where the two social movements worked alongside one another, as they did in the 1970s and which is discussed in Part III.

The political strategies of early conservationists showed little variation, largely relying on traditional lobbying and public meetings. When blocked, they tended to retreat to educating the public on environmental values; but they also developed campaigning techniques that are still used by the modern movement. Early campaigns never developed the mass scale of their contemporaries, the labour, women's or peace movements, and this has contributed to their historical invisibility. Yet the conditions of Australian development provoked a number of anxieties that fed a series of largely sequential mobilisations around environmental issues that sustained environmental opposition until World War II.

The intellectual context of these mobilisations was progressivism, the reform movement which was highly influential in the United States under President Theodore Roosevelt and also inspired the environment movements of Western Europe and the British dominions. Hence we have William Selway, chair of the Field Naturalists Section of the Royal

Society of South Australia, addressing the society's annual meeting in 1909 on 'that far-seeing and true statesman, President Roosevelt'. Selway's passion was preserving native forests. More than a decade later another Australian environmentalist in another state was summoning Roosevelt's name as first president of the US Playground Association to endorse a different aspect of the environment movement, park reservations.[13]

In William Lines's history of the Australian environment, however, progressivism is reduced to national efficiency and technocracy, which carry only negative environmental connotations, and the name of Gifford Pinchot (1865–1946), the great American bureaucrat and forester, is intoned as proof of this phenomenon.[14] Yet progressivism also supported a large popular environment movement in the United States, of which Pinchot represented only one wing, albeit a very powerful one. Prior to his forestry career, Pinchot had linked up with the conservation movement, presenting himself to the great nature preservationist, John Muir, as an acolyte.[15] Even when Pinchot set up his own community organisation to support his political platform of utilitarian resource conservation, he found that its social base soon subverted the organisation's goals—his economic assessments of resources were replaced by judgments of their moral benefits, efficient resource use by a commitment to nature protection and anti-materialist values.[16] This was because progressivism encompassed much nobler goals than mere technocratic utilitarianism. It fed contemporary radicalism with a mistrust of *laissez-faire* economics, monopolistic business and materialism, and so inspired the women's, peace and labour movements of the era as well.

Progressivism rested on a faith in both human rationality and human subjectivity. It was both technocratic and romantic, and the greatest source of romantic inspiration was nature. It represented romantic virtues of joy and freedom and authentic human experience as well as scientific interest in human origins and evolution. At their worst, these latter notions fed the obsession with race and racial ideas that were readily adopted by Australian social movement activists and imperialists. Ideas about living close to the soil and nature also encouraged belief in the superiority of rural life—another value shared by both the left and right of Australian politics.[17] At its best, however, progressivist nature worship produced the rational and aesthetic enjoyment of nature that united and inspired Australia's first-wave environmentalists.

Progressivism also fed the nationalism of the decades leading to World War I. A nation's greatness could be judged by the scale of its resources, both human and material, and a wise government could be recognised by its marshalling of them. This intellectual framework had contradictory implications. Such views, on the one hand, endorsed the natural wonders of a country as a symbol of a nation's greatness and justified the protection of these wonders in *national* parks. They also affirmed appreciation of the nation's natural resources and opposed selfish and wasteful use of them in favour of sound scientific management. Wise resource use and nature protection were thus two strands of early conservation that capitalised on nationalistic pro- gressivism. On the other hand, the mastery of those resources by human scientific and technical skills was doubly praised. Progressivism thus enabled the early conservationists to exploit nationalist sentiment as part of their persuasive repertoire at the same time as it endorsed large publicly funded engineering feats—dams, irrigation schemes, bridges, railways—that accelerated environmental degradation.

The language of progressivism emphasised human and national benefit, in contrast to the ecocentrism of today's environment move- ment, which rejects human-centred evaluations of the natural world. This emphasis has contributed to the reluctance on the part of social scientists to define early conservationists as part of the environment movement. To understand first-wave conservationists, it is necessary to place their struggle in historic context and to understand their fight on their terms. The young scientists, foresters, engineers and architects who led the movement had to debate nineteenth-century development on its own terms. Again and again we find them arguing for the economic usefulness of protecting birds, national efficiency goals for preserving our native forests, the recreational value of national parks, and the public health benefits of sanitation and pollution controls. Undoubtedly, utilitarianism was a value shared by many of their sup- porters; but in the personal writings of early environmentalists we also find a more profound basis for their activities. 'The wild birds do not belong to us to treat as we like,' Dudley Le Souef of the Australasian Ornithologists Union declared in 1907.[18] As early as 1871 Ferdinand von Mueller was promoting ideas of intergenerational equity in an emotional defence of native forests, 'I regard the forest as a heritage given to us by nature, not for spoil or to devastate, but to be wisely used, reverently honoured, and carefully maintained.'[19] The bushwalkers of the early twentieth century took these ethical arguments further towards the ecocentrism of today. In early 1941 Arthur Groom went bushwalking 'while at the other side of the world great mechanised armies fought in savagery with the amazing inventions of industry. The deduction to be drawn is obvious,' he wrote. 'Civilization had lost much of the counterbalance to be found in the primitive things of Nature ... Many millions have lost sight of the fact that man was created in a primeval wilderness.'[20] For Bernard O'Reilly, the philosophy of the nature-lover made 'the voice of the grey thrush in your shrub more desirable than the purr of a thousand-guinea motor car in your garage; ... beetles more interesting than bonds, and sunsets more desirable than securities'.[21] They not only used the language of their day, but appealed to those moral values which they felt Australian society had betrayed and corrupted. 'The earth is the Lord's and the fulness thereof' one contributor to *Emu* quoted, pointing out that 'Man has not created even the humblest of the species of birds, mammals, or fish that adorn and enrich this earth.'[22] Like contemporary social movements, they used the language of moral protest to awaken Australians to the loss of their natural world.

The social base and the main carriers of progressivist ideas were the young and highly educated. Like their counterparts of the 1960s and 1970s, they were a product of a 'radicalising historical sequence'.[23] When the economy's demand for a technically literate workforce extended secondary and tertiary education for the baby-boom generation, it unwittingly provided the social base for the 1960s radical social movements. This was not the first time society had extended access to public education coinciding with a period of rising social expectations. In the 1870s the Australian colonies had introduced free, compulsory and secular schooling, and enabled partial access to secondary and tertiary education through scholarship systems. By the 1890s young women had finally won access to some university courses. This education offered the hope of social mobility and aspirations for social improvement which fed the social movements. The result was the rise of a technically educated middle class, trained in health sciences, engineering and biological sciences, which invigorated some of the royal societies and triggered the formation of new nature societies and clubs. These groups provided a vehicle for political activism for members of the new middle class who had previously been excluded from the political process; these groups might also partly explain women's relatively high profile in the environment movement even in the nineteenth century.

Many of the environmental activists of early this century were the beneficiaries of the new educational opportunities; their involvement in the new nature clubs and scientific bodies brought them into contact with one another and with a broader social base, which was the necessary leaven for political mobilisation. The social and professional networks that supported this activism can be detected around the personalities of von Mueller, John Sulman, David Stead and Myles Dunphy, among others. Between them their social contacts included journalists, scientists, politicians, labour activists and feminists.

The Australian colonies' geographical and political separation prior to Federation meant that conservationists had to muster support within their own colonies. Even after the Commonwealth of Australia was formed in 1901, the states relegated only limited and precise powers to the Australian government, so that conservationists continued to direct most of their efforts to state-level administration of matters such as land. Consequently, it is necessary to try to chart developments in each colony (later state) because it is simply not possible to assume that what happened in Melbourne or Sydney applied elsewhere. Many of these campaigns could fill their own book: some of them have already been covered in postgraduate theses, organisational histories and academic sources. What this part offers is a social movement context for these diverse campaigns from around the country.

Chapter 1 outlines the social base for two movement streams. Firstly, there is the scientific societies' efforts to secure national parks in the face of extensive species loss by the 1890s. Secondly there is the campaign for regulated resource exploitation, the wise resource use concern that emerged from the acclimatisation societies of the 1860s and 1870s but which did not become urgent until imperial demand for Australian hardwoods increased in the 1880s. These two themes are linked by overlaps in personnel and timeframes. The chapter begins by discussing the institutional context of colonial science and outlines the involvement of the scientific societies in nature conservation campaigns colony by colony, before moving to the struggles over wise resource use and the fight for new institutional arrangements to regulate Australia's natural resources.

As the scientific movement wound down, the railway age brought a new group of actors to the cause: bushwalkers, who relied on the railways for weekend leisure. The outdoor recreationists generally developed a broader movement base than the scientists, and among their affiliations were the urban parks groups. The bushwalkers focused on national parks campaigns but the urban parks and playground groups were part of an older environmental concern, the public health of the cities. Chapter 2 looks at both these streams and their mobilisations up to World War II.

# CHAPTER 1

## *Professors, Learned Assessors*

The year 1908 was a busy one for Australian wildlife supporters. In March the president of the Linnean Society of New South Wales gave a passionate address on the need for bird protection. 'It is hard to speak in terms of calm moderation on the subject of the protection of our native birds. Enthusiasm is liable to be looked on with suspicion,' Mr A. H. S. Lucas began. 'But the point is that everyone who studies the useful work done by our beautiful feathered friends inevitably becomes an enthusiast for their protection.' The Linnean Society resolved to write to other societies around the country in order to co-ordinate their appeals to government on the issue.

Independently, the Australasian Ornithologists Union had chosen a similar course of action. It had keenly followed international events. At its past two annual conferences the presidents had given addresses on developments in bird protection in the United States and Europe. In July 1907, President Dudley Le Souef represented the union at the International Zoological Congress in the United States; the following year, Colonel Ryan, a past president, was endorsed by the Commonwealth government to represent Australia on the matter of the destruction of Australian birds before a committee hearing of the House of Lords. The union had written to the prime minister, Alfred Deakin, in July 1907 and had intended to follow this up with a deputation from its annual conference of 1908 which was to meet in Melbourne, then the seat of the federal government.

Victorian conservationists were also fired up over the issue. Like the Linnean Society and many other animal protectionist groups around the country, they were frustrated by inadequate state laws that were poorly enforced and easily circumvented by traders of feathers and bird skins. Professor Baldwin Spencer and the Victorian Advisory Committee re Fisheries and Game Acts also sought a meeting with the prime minister. They wanted Deakin's leadership to secure national uniform bird protection laws. In the end the two groups co-operated so that 'a powerful deputation, representing all the ornithologists' societies in Australia waited upon the Prime Minister' on 4 August 1908.[1]

Deakin, successful politician that he was, praised the group's dedication to a cause that was of enormous economic benefit to the country. But he also understood that, for this audience, the issue was more than just a matter of birds' economic usefulness; it was, he acknowledged, a matter of 'humanitarianism'. The language of ecocentrism had not yet been invented and so Deakin had to express the idea that birds had a right to exist irrespective of human wants in the moral terms of his own day. Deakin was knowledgeable on the issue and sympathetic, but the Australian Constitution did not give him the powers to impose animal laws on the states. Since the main demand for plumage was for women's fashions, his solution was firstly to appeal to women directly for 'womanly pity' could achieve 'at once what the Government could not do for many years to come'. Secondly, the federal customs powers gave him power to prohibit imports of bird plumes; it would require new legislation to control exports of birds and he would take the matter up with the customs minister.

So the bird protection groups had to double their campaigning efforts in 1909. They continued with their public education strategy; they resumed their lobbying of state governments for better enforcement and protection, and now added the federal minister for customs, Frank Tudor, as a target for their attention. On 30 August 1910, another deputation met with Tudor; he promised to do what he could to stop 'the wholesale murder of birds', including amending the Tariff Bill to give the Commonwealth powers to prohibit certain exports. When New Protectionism and tariff policy were reviewed by a Commonwealth commission during World War I, the protection of Australian bird life and the conservation of native forests were among the commissioners' concerns.[2]

The ornithologists' campaign presents a challenge to the standard interpretations of Australian history. For many years, historians gave pride of place to the labour movement for its successful incorporation of industrial goals into the framework of federal policy in the formative years of the Commonwealth. The effect of the peace movement too, active against the Boer War at Federation and vocally opposing the militarism of Australian society, has been acknowledged as part of these radicalising decades. In later years, feminist historians have shown the extent to which the women's movement also moved the debate and influenced the Deakinite settlement that would determine the

parameters of Australian political life for the next seven decades. This
'settlement', also referred to as the Australian Settlement, facilitated
national growth and prosperity by using industry protection to provide
workers with award wages and manufacturers with a competition-free
internal market. Other sectors of the white community were accom-
modated by national loyalty to empire (and imperial preference trade
arrangements) and a racist immigration policy that kept Australia white
and its culture anglomorphic. It was a uniquely Australian version of
what is referred to elsewhere in the Western world as the 'Fordist
accumulation model'.[3] The environment movement, however, was
assumed not to have had an impact before the early 1970s: yet here was
a coherent national campaign by numerous independent bird and
scientific societies actively brokering environmental rights as part of the
national protection of the tariff system.

The prominent role of scientists in these efforts to influence government policy was no coincidence. Scientific interest and fascination with
the Great South Land had begun even before white settlement, and all
early European expeditions included scientists. Their role in facilitating
and encouraging British imperialism traditionally has located them with
the forces of destruction of the environment. Recently, however,
international scholarship has begun to reassess the relationship between
Western imperialism and environmental concern. Richard H. Grove
argues that, despite the connections between imperialism and Western
science, the relationship was not without its internal contradictions.
Colonial expansion brought Western science into contact with other
cosmologies and epistemologies, reawakened Western utopian beliefs
concerning a Garden of Eden, and provoked anxiety about survival and
climatic change, all of which promoted environmental concern among
colonial scientists. Furthermore, the impact of plantation economies on
the ecology of tropical island possessions from as early as 1600 provided
measurable evidence of species loss and land degradation for the
scientists to use to argue against colonial policies.[4]

European settlement of Australia came in the wake of this Enlighten-
ment science and as part of an expansionary industrial capitalism which
asserted its dominance over all other life forms, its technocratic values
challenging those of non-industrial societies at home and around the
world. The cultural counter-movement of romanticism rebelled against
this hostility to the natural world and, although individual scientists and
adventurers were inspired by the romantic movement,[5] the earliest days
of Australian colonial society were not as receptive to environmentalism
as they were to other British reform movements such as evangelicalism.[6]
Passionate concern for the natural world came to be regarded as an
oddity within white society. Alexander Chisholm, an avid field naturalist

and birdwatcher and a key figure in Australian conservation circles in the first half of the twentieth century, expressed his frustration in his autobiography at those who probed him as to how he had come to be such a nature-lover. For him, the real mystery was how so many Australians had lost what he believed was a natural human attribute.[7]

The first nature-lovers and field naturalists on the fringes of European society did not provide a collective challenge to colonial progress. Their position on both a racial and geographical frontier highlights the contradictory elements of colonialism. The earliest naturalists encouraged relations with tribal peoples because of their detailed knowledge of the location and seasonal availability of plant species and habits of fauna. Sometimes Aboriginal lore and assistance inspired admiration and sympathy from the Aborigines' white companions. At a time when the rest of the white community was at war with the Nyungar, Georgiana Molloy, an avid field collector at Swan River, was granted certain intimacy and affection by Battap who had assisted her in the bush.[8] The explorer and scientist Count Strzelecki was even more exceptional, arguing forcefully for the rights of Aboriginal Australians,[9] but for the most part colonial relationships were not challenged even by those who shared an environmental sensibility. Aboriginal people were useful guides and field assistants to early Australian naturalists, whose contributions to imperial science would unwittingly lead to further economic expansion and degradation of the very landscapes that both Aborigines and nature-lovers cherished.

Nonetheless, these contradictions between professional scientific interest and rapidly disappearing habitats and species did eventually stir the colonial Australian scientific community. As an interest group it was the scientists, amazed at the uniqueness of the environment that they found themselves in and sensitive to its vulnerability, who were the first to call for the protection of special areas and species. When they began to agitate for environmental protection, they did so from a range of public scientific societies and with a surprisingly wide and popular social base.

### The Scientists

The first scientific society, the Philosophical Society of Australasia, was formed in New South Wales in 1821; the younger colony of Van Diemen's Land was not far behind, establishing its own society at the start of 1830.[10] These first scientific societies were often small and elitist and, as Finney has shown, as faction-ridden as the colonial society from which they sprang. Their significance lies only in the fact that they represented the first organised commitment to serious study of the

Australian environment and the dissemination of this information. As well as publishing their papers, the colonial press was keen to report the activities of early scientific societies owing to the appeal of natural history which had enjoyed popularity with the British public since the 1750s and which continued to grow throughout the nineteenth century.

### The Social Base of Scientific Conservatism

The great demand for specimens from Australia provided the first amateur scientists and nature-lovers with an income as natural history collectors. Alongside collecting was the important work of illustrating, and the attention to detail required by both was often accompanied by sensitive appreciation of the natural landscape. The combination of art and nature study made collecting a respectable field for genteel women, so the involvement of women with environmental interests has a long and remarkable precedent. Elizabeth Gould worked in collaboration with her husband John Gould in Van Diemen's Land and the Swan River region in the 1830s, although their famous work *Birds of Australia* was not published until 1848, some eight years after Elizabeth's death.[11] The Goulds stand out among the early collectors: John Gould was one of the first scientists to warn that Australia's large mammals were in danger of extinction and he made a plea for protection of native animals and for a ban on exotic flora and fauna.[12] At about the same time as the Goulds were visiting Australia, Georgiana Molloy was 'botanising' and making detailed studies of Australian native plants in Western Australia, and Louisa Meredith arrived in Van Diemen's Land and commenced her lifelong interest in Australian wildflowers. The Port Phillip District (later Victoria) also had its female collectors and botanical artists. A Miss Roadknight from Geelong sent specimens across Bass Strait to Ronald Gunn in Launceston, so that by 1842 he had sufficient material to publish an article on the Geelong flora. The process was repeated again and again in the Australian colonies, with the wives and sisters of pastoralists gathering local specimens and making natural history notes for male botanists working far away in colonial museums and acclimatisation societies, and even sometimes for Kew Gardens and British societies. Only occasionally do women make it into the scientific record in their own right. The Royal Society of South Australia mourned the passing of Jessie Hussey in March 1899, for she had been one of their 'most active and enthusiastic workers', with a number of international correspondents. In New South Wales, Caroline Atkinson gained recognition as a naturalist for identification of plant species new to Western science and for her illustrations of native plants and animals. A pastoralist and bird illustrator, John Cotton, initially sought the support of one of his daughters to colour his etchings but later encouraged her to draw Australian flowers instead. Cotton's granddaughter, Ellis Rowan, was to make this family's most popular contribution to the natural history of Australasia with her extraordinary quests to paint the wildflowers, birds and insects of the region; they were popularised at the turn of the century through her writings and art exhibitions.[13]

The contribution of these women was to the appreciation of the Australian natural environment rather than any active part in protecting it, and this appreciation was highly individualised. Georgiana Molloy's love of the wildflowers of Western Australia and her rambles through the bush in search of them gave her life a personal meaning that set her apart from her wealth-seeking neighbours.[14] Ellis Rowan, when well into her sixties, went into unmapped territory with the assistance of local guides to capture native birds for her paintings, but would insist on releasing the birds afterwards.[15] A Miss Chewings of Kent Town, South Australia, bequeathed £7000 towards the 'cultivation' of the trees and bird life of inland Australia in 1916, although it is unlikely her wishes were carried out.[16] Minard Crommelin, who worked for wildlife preservation in New South Wales, donated her private land to the University of Sydney for a biological research station.[17] Only Louisa Meredith, who publicised cruelty to animals in her colonial writings, has achieved any notice for her commitment to conservation causes.

The involvement of these women was in part the product of the pre-professional era of science. The nineteenth century was a time for the amateur in science, in which the self-taught could still make their mark through diligent fieldwork. Scientific activity and interest was prolific from the 1850s onwards,[18] although scientific calls for preservation and conservation did not become strong until the last decade of the century. This social base for science was important grounding for some of Australia's first conservation activists. Neither Alec Chisholm nor David Stead, two men who played leading roles in the conservation movement in the early twentieth century, had university training. In their youth, Chisholm in Victoria and Stead in New South Wales had joined natural history associations which had included both scientific members and amateur nature-lovers. Australian scientific knowledge was still in its cataloguing phase and it was possible for amateurs to publish good fieldwork studies in scientific journals, although professional biologists were asserting the difference between theoretical and experimental biology and populist natural history.[19] This popular base contributed to the particular cultural style of the movement. Tom Griffiths has noted the distinctive dress style and totemic paraphernalia of the late-nineteenth-century field naturalists.[20] The opening comments from the president of the Linnean Society about the public reaction to the commitment of the nature-lovers give a sense of the cultural boundary that divided movement participants from mainstream audiences.

By the 1880s Europeans encircled the entire continent, although their hold was still tentative in some areas in the north where Aboriginal resistance persisted for another four decades or more. In the south, urbanisation and industrial capability were expanding rapidly. Diminishing 'pristine' areas for scientific study disturbed the naturalists of the late nineteenth century, whose concern for environmental preservation increased witn settler impact. The naturalist and president of the Royal Society of South Australia, Professor Ralph Tate, elaborated on the problems facing the biologist in his presidential address of 1891:

> the reliance which can be placed on the naturalness of any species in an Australian locality is ... every day becoming less. If there is to be an exhaustive and accurate record handed down for future use in science of the indigenous distribution of species on any large area of the earth's surface—which looks likely enough to be an essential condition of success in solving the more complex problems of natural science that will come before our successors—it would scarcely be going too far to say that it must be made in Australia; and it is absolutely certain that if it is to be made it must be made at once.[21]

While Professor Tate encouraged his members to take up fieldwork with some urgency, other scientists called for the preservation of natural areas as a national priority.

Calls upon colonial governments were enhanced by the wide public participation in science and nature study. Few popular scientific societies were as fortunate as the Zoological Society of Victoria in 1857, and its successor organisation the Acclimatisation Society of 1861, which had a newspaper proprietor and editor, Edward Wilson of the *Argus*, as an enthusiastic founding member.[22] Nonetheless, the colonial presses were usually keen to report the activities of early scientific societies. Almost all local natural history societies contributed articles, and sometimes reports of activities, to their regional newspapers. The popularisation of interest in the natural environment was aided by talented writers within the field of natural history. In New South Wales, Caroline Atkinson often contributed nature columns to the *Sydney Morning Herald*, and at the turn of the century Charles Barrett, a leading Victorian naturalist, ornithologist and journalist, publicised nature study through newspaper articles and books. Barrett acknowledge his debt to Donald McDonald, who began contributing nature columns to the *Argus* in 1881, but Barrett in turn developed his own following. A series of nature articles entitled 'Our Bush Hut on Olinda', by three men who called themselves 'the Woodlanders', influenced a young Alec Chisholm. The men were Thoreau enthusiasts and named their weekend hideaway Walden Hut. 'The whole series ... had a warm impact on my fifteen-years-old consciousness,' recalled Chisholm, 'especially when set against life in a factory.' One of the Woodlanders was Charles Barrett, and Chisholm followed him into a career in journalism and ornithology some years later, contributing nature columns and feature articles to Sydney and Brisbane papers.[23] A sympathetic audience was being cultivated for the emerging nature protection movement.

The movement's organisational base extended beyond the cities and into provincial centres. After less than three decades of white settlement, a small community such as Rockhampton boasted a thriving Natural History Society, which had a representative on the executive council of the Australasian Association for the Advancement of Science, and an active group of local botanists, ornithologists and collectors, some of whom were members of international and intercolonial scientific societies.[24] At the turn of the century Toowoomba supported a science committee as well as a Field Naturalists Club operating prior to World War I. In the 1880s the regional Victorian centres of Geelong, Bendigo and Ballarat all supported field clubs devoted to the study of natural sciences.[25] By the 1930s north Queensland also supported a naturalists' club which had come into existence in the midst of a political debate over the extensive clearance of rainforest on the Atherton Tablelands.[26]

### Formal Organisations and National Park Campaigns

Regional interest was merely a reflection of what was happening throughout the Australian colonies. By the 1890s, every colony sustained a royal society or a natural history society or both. Western Australia's organised scientific conservation was perhaps the shakiest. A Western Australian Natural History Society was formed there in 1891 with the governor, Sir William Robinson, as patron and the premier, Sir John Forrest, as president. Forrest's involvement seems odd, given his family connections with land, timber and mining interests, but as a young surveyor he had contact with the botanist Ferdinand von Mueller and he collected botanical and geological specimens on his extensive expeditions, which had earned him election to the Linnean Society of London in 1882. His wife Margaret was also an enthusiastic painter of Western Australia's wildflowers and shared a painting expedition with Ellis Rowan (another friend of von Mueller's) to the north-west of the colony in 1889.

After correspondence from the South Australian national parks campaigner, A. F. Robin, the Natural History Society successfully applied to
have an area of 65,000 hectares between Pinjarra, North Dandalup and
the Bannister River proclaimed as a flora and fauna reserve in 1894. The
ambiguity of Forrest's position as premier and supporter of economic
development and as nature conservationist soon came to the fore. After
requests to cut timber from the reserve, Forrest recommended its
cancellation in 1898. The Natural History Society objected. Bernard
Woodward, secretary to the society and director of the West Australian
Museum, called for the area to be declared a national park; he was
supported by the then governor, Sir Arthur Lawley, and Anglican Bishop
Charles Riley, a society member. But in 1911, after long-term pressure,
the state government revoked the flora and fauna reserve and converted
it to a timber reserve. Scientific conservation was by no means dead in
the west, however. In 1910, a wilderness supporter, J. G. Hay, became
secretary to the Natural History Society and began to campaign for a
national park in the Stirling Ranges. New scientific societies had also
formed with conservation goals. The express object of the Mueller
Botanical Society was to preserve the natural flora of the colony, and
Forrest as patron again promised government support for the protection of specific plants and trees. In 1903 the Mueller Botanical
Society broadened its interests and it eventually evolved into the Royal
Society of Western Australia in 1914. These groups, with support from
Woodward, were successful in lobbying for a number of nature reserves.
By 1925 there were 143,000 hectares of 'Class A' reserves, including the
Stirling Ranges National Park, which could only be alienated by act of
parliament. During the period between the two world wars, scientific
organisations were active in campaigning for native fauna and flora
protection.[27]

Queensland's Royal Society had been established in 1883. It had
evolved from the Queensland Philosophical Society, which had been
founded in the colony's separation year of 1859. The motivation for
the name and organisational change had come from the Reverend
J. E. Tenison-Woods, an eminent scientist with intercolonial contacts
who visited Queensland in 1878.[28] The changes he urged were symptomatic of the growing professionalisation of science throughout the
Australian colonies, with increasing intercolonial contact and ex-
changes, and a growing number of government-appointed scientists
and science positions within the universities. Queensland did not yet
have a university, but the tensions between the professional biological
scientists and the amateur field naturalists that have been described
by Colin Finney for the southern colonies were also evident in
Queensland.[29]

For all the concerns about raising biology above the non-theoretical standards of natural history, it was the Field Naturalists Section of the Royal Society which was the most popular and informal. The populist field naturalist clubs and societies contributed a grassroots social base for professional science which was politically useful in its lobbying of governments for more resources, and in particular for calls for preservation of flora and fauna and reservation of lands; thus it is not surprising to find scientific members of the Royal Society as leaders in the naturalist clubs.[30] The Queensland Royal Society and its members were instrumental in the first campaigns for national parks in Queensland, although it was the Queensland branch of the Royal Geographical Society which led the way under the personal leadership of two key members, R. M. Collins and Romeo Lahey.

Collins was of the old middle class. From one of the oldest pastoralist families in Queensland, he inherited the family grazing property on the Albert River in the shadow of the McPherson Ranges. At the age of thirty-five, he undertook a world tour with his brother; they visited California in 1878, where he learnt of Yellowstone and the national park campaign for Yosemite. On his return to Queensland, he maintained contact with American national park supporters inspired by their example, he began to press for a national park along the McPherson Range. In 1896 he was elected to the Queensland parliament, and in the same year he read a paper to the Royal Geographical Society outlining his ideas for a national park in the south-eastern highlands of Queensland. After Collins became president, the society committed itself to promoting the idea to the government.[31] In 1903, J. T. Bell, another member of one of Queensland's oldest pastoralist families and also hailing from a grazing property south of Brisbane, became minister for lands. Collins lobbied him on the national parks idea and in 1906 Queensland's first national parks and state forests legislation was passed. A small area on Mount Tambourine was declared a national park two years later and landholders' support for reservations at Cunningham's Gap and the Bunya Mountains led to the creation of those national parks soon after. But Collins was getting nowhere with his proposal for the McPhersons, owing to local objections.

Collins was now in his late sixties; as he tired, the cause was taken up by a younger Royal Geographical Society member, Romeo Lahey, who promoted a much grander national park. Lahey's father owned one of Queensland's largest sawmills, operating in Canungra in the beautiful Gold Coast hinterland. Romeo Lahey was born in 1887 and grew up on the edge of a wilderness that was constantly being pushed further back into the McPherson Range. In his adult years he was described as 'seldom ... without a scratch or a cut on his head, a relic of his wallaby-like habit of hopping in and out of any jungle from Cape York to Sydney'. Lahey did not explore the depths of the McPhersons until Easter 1908, but the beauty of the upper Coomera River moved him. 'The idea of those glorious falls being destroyed by selection higher-up filled me with an intense determination to have them kept for people who would love them, but who did not even dream of their existence,' he recorded in his diary. In 1911 he began his engineering studies at the University of Sydney, but persistently maintained his lobbying for a national park in the McPhersons from there. His strategy involved convincing not only the state government but also local shires and residents. He wrote to local newspapers, debated with local councillors, and took a petition door-to-door. On one of his trips to the range, he took photographs of the area's scenic wilderness which he used to illustrate newspaper articles and public talks in the district. Romeo Lahey was an ardent grassroots campaigner, and his lobbying letters also show that mistrust of vested interests that was the hallmark of progressives. His fear was that self-interested local councils would oppose a national park which rightly belonged to 'the people', the 'higher court' to which he urged the government to listen. On the eve of the historic Queensland elections of 1915, he chased politicians from 'city to country and from country to city'. He wrote to the US forestry department and, like Myles Dunphy, the great New South Wales wilderness campaigner, he was interested in the Aboriginal heritage of the region and proposed Aboriginal names for the park. In true progressivist fashion, Lahey envisioned his national park agitation as a matter of national duty. In June 1915 Labor won the elections. In the final days of his campaign, Lahey wrote to the new minister urging a quick decision 'as I want to get away to Europe to my next duty, but cannot leave this one unfulfilled'. After twenty years of lobbying and Lahey's intense seven-year campaign, the area was finally gazetted Lamington National Park in July 1915; Lahey enlisted in the AIF. Sadly R. M. Collins did not live to see the park: he had died in 1913.[32]

In early 1916 the Royal Society joined with the Royal Geographical Society, the Field Naturalists Club and the Institutes of Surveyors and of Local Government Engineers to sponsor a public meeting at the state library in order to form an advisory body for the national park and to lobby the government for scientific management of the park. Representatives of these professional groups not only wanted preservation of the unique flora and fauna, closed seasons, and eradication of all pests: they also wanted to be the management body for the park. While the minister was prepared to listen to their scientific advice, he was not prepared to relinquish departmental control.[33] Although the scientific fraternity had taken a back seat to the young Romeo Lahey and his grassroots campaign, they played a significant lobbying role in defence of their own scientific and professional interests. Their relationship with government was subsequently important in safeguarding the national park from later threats of roads, timber-getting and grazing.[34]

The earliest scientific associations in New South Wales did not survive the colony's social and political fluctuations. In 1866, however, the Royal Society of New South Wales was established, and it too became a forum for concern about human degradation of the Australian environment. R. B. Walker argues that scientific societies in New South Wales had no conservation objectives in their early years, yet individual members used the societies to raise issues and they led the earliest animal protection campaigns.[35] The Reverend William Clark, for example, addressed the society in 1876 on the disastrous effects of forest clearance. Eccleston du Faur, then a surveyor for the New South Wales government, was elected a fellow of the Royal Society in 1873, and took the opportunity to promote environmental approaches to understanding climate patterns. As chairman of the society's Geography Section, he urged exploration expeditions to Antarctica to gather information on the polar icecap's impact on Australia's weather. However, it was the Zoological Society of New South Wales which made the first, very limited, moves for animal protection. In 1881 the Zoological Society succeeded in convincing the New South Wales government to pass the Bird Protection Act to protect songbirds; a number of amendments over the years extended protection to native species.[36]

The Natural History Association of New South Wales, first mooted in 1880, did not get under way until 1887, but by 1888 its popularity was strong with an enrolment of 348. This group attracted young amateurs, including a young David Stead who joined in the 1890s.[37] Stead's self-developed interest in natural history aroused his concern for the future of native fauna in Australia. From 1900 he tried to awaken interest among the public for protection of wildlife, publishing articles in the *Sydney Morning Herald* and trying to convince the Naturalist Society to take up the cause. Although Stead was part of a group that agreed there was an urgent necessity for protection of native animals, his efforts met with little organisational success until 1909. In that year the Swedish Consul-General, Count Birger Morner, resigned from the Royal Zoological Society of New South Wales in protest over poor management in an affair which became public. Morner transferred his support to Stead, who called a public meeting in 1909 to form a special organisation to campaign for wildlife protection. Fifty people, including many professional members of the Zoological Society, immediately joined, and the Wild Life Preservation Society of Australia was born.[38]

The first scientific societies of Van Diemen's Land foundered on factional problems similar to those of early New South Wales. The liberal Governor Franklin was not only patron of the Tasmanian society, founded in 1839, but also personally funded the publication of the society's journal. His wife, Lady Jane Franklin, was an enthusiastic supporter who attended meetings, used her personal contacts to distribute the journal, organised construction of a museum for the society, and upon her departure bequeathed the rental income from one of her properties to support it. However, colonial factionalism continued to plague the society even after the Franklins had left the colony, and by the late 1840s it had merged with the Royal Society of Tasmania. From this period the Royal Society not only became the centre of science in the colony: it also became the first scientific society in Australia to call for flora and fauna reserves, and continued to be a forum for promoting national parks throughout the century.[39] By 1890 Tasmania had a number of small reserves; the most popular was the Russell Falls area near Mount Field, which had been declared in 1885. There was renewed agitation for preservation of special regions as national parks by the society in the 1890s, and these calls were supported by ornithologists as well as by the Tasmanian Field Naturalists Club after its formation in 1904.[40]

The Victorian scientific community was also organised early in the colony's history with the Philosophical Institute, later the Royal Society of Victoria, forming in 1855.[41] However, it was the populist wing of the scientific organisations that led the way in terms of early moves towards conservation. The Field Naturalists Club of Victoria was formed in 1880 and elected Frederick McCoy, professor of natural science, as its first president. Like field clubs in other colonies, it was made up of a few professionals but mostly of committed enthusiasts; over the years its members included distinguished professional biologists and active early conservationists, among them Ferdinand von Mueller, Charles Barrett and Alec Chisholm.[42] The popularity of natural history and fieldwork extended beyond the capital, with Victoria sustaining naturalist clubs in provincial towns.[43]

The activities of the Field Naturalists as a voluntary organisation are remarkable for their leadership and persistence in pressing for conservation measures since the 1880s, when they included 'the preservation and protection of the fauna and flora indigenous to Australia and its environs' among their founding objects.[44] J. B. Gregory, A. H. Lucas and Thomas Hall took leading roles in the club's campaign for the preservation of Wilson's Promontory as a national park. Baldwin Spencer, professor of biology and president of the Royal Society of Victoria, was brought into the campaign to address public meetings and write letters to the editor. The Field Naturalists and the Royal Society also won the support of other scientific and professional organisations, such as ornithologists and the Victorian branch of the Royal Geographical Society, for their campaigns. They finally succeeded in having the promontory temporarily reserved in 1898, but this was only a partial victory; Baldwin Spencer then took up the leadership of the campaign. Further conferences and meetings of scientific organisations were convened, including a public meeting at which the governor of Victoria, Sir John Madden, presided, adding his prestige to the campaign.[45] The government finally agreed to a permanent reservation in January 1905, although concerned scientific bodies had to maintain political pressure before they achieved the appointment of a ranger and they were unsuccessful in securing control by trustees. By 1916 local and scientific groups had secured nine national parks. Other campaigns waged by the Field Naturalists included the reservation of Alfred National Park, which was declared in late 1925, and of Sperm Whale Head (now Lakes) National Park, which was granted in 1927.

Although the role of professional scientific groups declined, the Field Naturalists Club continued to campaign on nature preservation issues in the period between the two world wars. In 1936 the club organised a meeting with other natural history societies and voluntary organisations to discuss interstate and overseas developments in regard to national parks and to reinvigorate the Victorian campaign. More than forty-three groups attended the meeting and agreed to the formation of a group to fight for preservation legislation. By the 1940s the Field Naturalists Club had a permanent sub-committee to fight for nature conservation, the National Parks and National Monuments Sub-committee.[46]

Of the various royal societies, the Royal Society of South Australia (RSSA) displayed the greatest commitment to conservation issues. The society had began life in 1853 as the Philosophical Society of South Australia, changing its name in 1876. In 1883 a Field Naturalists Section was established, and it was this section of the society which led the way in lobbying for conservation measures. The Field Naturalists were the populist arm of the RSSA, holding joint functions with the Boys Field Club and ornithological associations, and were proud of their high rate of female participation. In the late 1880s, A. F. Robin, secretary of the Field Naturalists Section, began lobbying for a system of national parks as a means of preserving indigenous plants and animals. The Field Naturalists set up a permanent sub-committee, the Native Flora and Fauna Protection Committee, which led the campaign to have Belair Park declared a national park. Robin was secretary and Samuel Dixon was chair for twenty-three years, followed by Edwin Ashby and Captain White. The sub-committee lobbied, wrote letters, pamphlets and newspaper articles, and liaised with other interest groups and politicians to protect native birds and animals and to create national parks and forest reserves. Samuel Dixon's commitment to the cause of environmental protection was spelt out in an address to the RSSA in 1892, in which he summed up the disastrous effects of European cultivation on the natural environment throughout the country. The effects on the native vegetation he declared to be a 'national loss'. The problems for the scientist were great, since 'in few spots can the botanist now discover the specimens of the peculiar and lovely flora for which it was celebrated, when first settled; ... the loveliest district of Australia has now become commonplace and comparatively uninteresting to the botanist'. He concluded with a statement of the urgency of the situation: 'the preservation of our indigenous flora whilst looked upon as a fad by the ignorant and unthinking, is really in its cumulative effects one of great national importance'.[47]

The RSSA is an excellent case study of a progressive political organisation at the turn of the century. Its leadership was dominated by dedicated professionals who were involved in various worthy causes. The medical doctor Joseph Verco, for example, was vocal on urban sanitation and public health; Captain White the ornithologist was a critic of 'the march of civilisation' and an advocate on Aboriginal issues, who worked with the churches in the 1920s to secure an extensive Aboriginal reserve; and both were active on fauna and flora preservation. The RSSA was also able to draw upon an amateur support base and worked co-operatively with other progressive organisations such as trade unions and the Australian Natives Association. This association was the vehicle for a number of patriotic and progressive causes in this period, and it became a useful ally in several conservation campaigns around the country. After a tough three-year fight, the RSSA finally won the campaign for Belair National Park when the government dedicated it as a public recreation ground in December 1891. The success of the RSSA's campaign had been secured by extending beyond its own disciplinary sections and scientific contacts to community groups such as the Trades and Labour Council and local friendly societies—actions which are typical of the horizontal and alliance-building features of social movement development. It also sought to broaden its appeal by including arguments about the recreational values of national parks in its submissions.

Within a few years, however, the RSSA found that the playground function of the park was dominating all other goals, particularly those of conservation of flora and fauna. The Field Naturalists then turned their attention to securing the western end of Kangaroo Island as a nature reserve, and raised the matter at an intercolonial level through the

Australasian Association for the Advancement of Science (AAAS) in 1892. For over two decades their campaign for the declaration of Flinders Chase reserve focused on the protection of rare fauna. The Cape Borda Lighthouse Reserve was proclaimed in 1907; continued pressure from the Fauna and Flora Committee (with support from the Australian Natives Association) secured additional lands in 1910. 'We hammered so hard that the Minister promised to introduce a bill into Parliament,' Captain White recorded, but the final act was not passed through the South Australian parliament until October 1919, when Flinders Chase was finally created.[48]

All these societies and associations operated independently of one another, but they established good intercolonial communication and informal networks. Government-appointed botanists and museum curators in the various colonies maintained extensive networks with collectors in the regions, but ordinary members also developed associational links with one another. The role of Ferdinand von Mueller was particularly important in this respect. Although he was appointed Government Botanist of Victoria in 1853, his fascination with Australian plant species took him on travels around the continent, providing him with an opportunity to meet fellow botanists in other colonies. He was also an indefatigable letter-writer and maintained a voluminous correspondence with fellow enthusiasts. Baron von Mueller's influence is particularly important, given his leadership on matters of preservation. His foremost conservation concern was the protection of Australian forests; he campaigned for them on more than just scientific grounds, developing utilitarian, ethical and intergenerational arguments. He also campaigned strongly for flora and fauna reserves.[49]

Intercolonial scientific links were formalised towards the end of the century with the formation of the Australasian Association for the Advancement of Science in 1888. The success of this new association was a landmark for the growing body of professional scientists throughout the colonies and the furtherance of their interests, but this prestigious new body also contributed to growing scientific concern with conservation issues. At its first general meeting the group established its Protection of Native Birds and Mammals Committee.[50] Ferdinand von Mueller's commitment to conservation also stamped the association. When the annual conference was held in Melbourne in 1890, von Mueller was made president. His inaugural address as president made a plea for conservation measures; subsequent meetings in different colonial capitals became forums for the promotion of particular conservation causes in each colony.[51] At the first meeting in Hobart in 1892, for example, members called for nature reserves to be declared from Schouten Peninsula to Coles Bay, and the following year for the

Freycinet Peninsula to be declared 'Tasmania's National Park'.[52] At
the same meeting South Australian members put the reserve at Cape
Borda in their home colony on the conference agenda.[53] In 1893 the
association asserted the need for government-funded reserves in all
colonies.[54] This continued to be an organisational interest throughout
the twentieth century.

### Fauna Protection Campaigns

Scientists were active in other areas besides national park reservations.
Ornithologists joined the demands for flora and fauna protection to
highlight the threats to Australia's native birds. Early beliefs concerning
Australian birdlife were as misconstrued as any concerning Australian
natural history. Alec Chisholm recounted how, in his boyhood in rural
Victoria, boys frequently robbed birds' nests and scalped the native
honey-eaters and parrots, but they were reprimanded only when they
attacked introduced sparrows, which were esteemed by local farmers as
destroyers of insects and reminders of 'the old country'. Similarly, the
first bird protection legislation in New South Wales initially protected
only introduced birds and songbirds, and the pattern was similar in
other colonies.[55]

By the late nineteenth century, economic growth had created an
expanding middle class with the consumer power to participate in new
clothing fashions and tastes which were wreaking havoc on the world's
birds and furred animals. From the 1880s on, the growth in demand for
Australasian plumage (bird-of-paradise and lyrebird skins were particularly prized) and furs to decorate European fashions led to large-scale
slaughter of Australian birds and marsupials. The scientific societies had
regularly raised issues of bird and animal protection, but the assault of
the expanding plumage trade towards the end of the century prompted
ornithological interests to form their own specialist groups. The
Tasmanians formed an ornithological society in 1888; South Australia
had a Bird Protection Society active in the 1890s, as well as an
ornithological association formed in 1899. A group of Victorian bird-
lovers formed the Bird Observers Club in 1905. The club had an explicit
commitment to the protection of native birds but membership was
exclusive. Although the seventeen-year-old Alec Chisholm had been
invited to join on the basis of his newspaper articles on birds, in 1906
the group voted against allowing women to attend meetings and against
increasing membership to thirty. In spite of the attitudes of the
Victorian club, bird-watching, like field nature studies, was popular in
this period as part of the growth in outdoor recreation.[56]

The colony-based organisations lobbied their governments over
improvements to existing game laws and extensions of closed seasons.

They were aided in this work by sympathetic journalists and nature columnists, who regularly decried the reckless shooting of birds and removal of their eggs, and by local papers publicising the closed seasons and the species under legal protection. Female columnists vented their moral outrage against the women who purchased feathered and fur-trimmed clothing, urging a consumer boycott to end the cruel trade. These columnists were by no means uninfluential. Mary Gilmore wrote upon the subject for the *Australian Worker*, while 'Johanna', the *Bulletin*'s correspondent, 'declared that any woman who wore feathers torn from a brooding bird should be compelled to change her gay attire for prison garb'.[57] By 1901 the South Australians had succeeded in convincing their government to pass a new Bird Protection Act which they had assisted in preparing; New South Wales also passed new legislation which extended protection to more native birds. New state laws could not be effective, however, when different states not only had different periods for their closed seasons but also protected different species. Enforcement of the acts was difficult: bird and animal skins illegally trapped in one state were easily sold and exported from another.

Aware that skin traders were evading state laws, Samuel Dixon of the Royal Society of South Australia wanted the Australian Natives Association to take up the issue of 'so thoroughly patriotic a work' as national uniform protection laws. By the time of Dixon's appeal, another bird body had already formed to take up this mantle. The previous year a group of ornithologists who had been regularly holding informal meetings decided to launch the Australasian Ornithologists Union (AOU), a national body with both scientific and protection objectives. Later granted the royal title, the union encompassed both professionals and amateurs committed to a national campaign against the feather and fur trades in Australia.[58]

The campaign against Australia's bird and feather trade was probably the first organised environmental activity to pierce the Australian consciousness about a particular environmental threat. It was also significant, for this campaign was not based on preserving potential recreation areas, nor was it of direct utilitarian benefit to most Australians (although the bird-lovers always led their arguments with calculations of the value of birds as destroyers of insect pests): it was about the imminent loss of native species, some of which had become national icons.

Australian sensitivity on the issue was heightened by the inter-national conservation movement and scientific lobby. The International Ornithologists Conference in London in 1905 called on the federal government to protect Australia's birds from yet another threat, the international oil trade, which was boiling down seabirds, including Australian penguins and muttonbirds, for their oil.[59] The Tasmanian commissioner of police estimated that over 2.5 million muttonbirds had been sold through Launceston markets from 1904 to 1908.[60]

In 1906, Colonel Charles Ryan as president addressed the AOU on the need to go beyond 'a few preliminaries and suggestions' for bird protection and to start promoting 'something more practical'. Professionally Ryan was a leading surgeon but he had inherited a love of ornithology from his grandfather, John Cotton. The passion was shared by his famous sister, Ellis Rowan, who contributed illustrations to *Emu*, the official publication of the AOU; and by his cousins the Le Souefs, noted zoologists who were all founding members of the AOU although their residences were scattered from Perth to Sydney.[61]

Ryan's speech invigorated the ornithologists' campaign for national protection measures, which gathered momentum. Three months after meeting with Alfred Deakin in 1908, the AOU succeeded in convincing the state governments to support a meeting of government representatives and ornithologists to discuss moves towards more uniform bird protection laws. It was hosted by the Victorian government in November 1908. Although New South Wales declined to attend, the meeting drew some influential wildlife supporters. Western Australia delegated Sir John Forrest (now MHR for Swan, temporarily without portfolio) and Queensland was represented by E. W. Archer (MHR for Capricornia), whose family property, Gracemere, was the first bird sanctuary in central Queensland. The meeting decided against preparing model legislation for the states, but it did call for, among other things, Commonwealth legislation to complement state protection laws, an end to the introduction of exotic birds, and all states to institute a bird day in schools.[62]

The defeat of the strategy of national animal and bird protection laws did not radicalise the movement. There were still other means of asserting influence to be tried, and this obstruction of the federal tactic sent conservation campaigners in two complementary directions. The first was a renewal of the push at the state level and an expansion of the agenda to include native mammals. The second was to improve public education strategies. Two important new bird and animal conservation groups were formed in the wake of the limited outcomes of the federal meetings. David Stead and the Wild Life Preservation Society of Australia have already been discussed; the other group to form in 1909 was the Gould League of Bird Lovers, which was established first in Victoria and subsequently in New South Wales and Queensland, and belatedly in Western Australia.

Over the next three decades the bird groups and the Wild Life Preservation Society continually lobbied for improved legislation to protect birds and animals. The assault on Australia's mammals was as horrific as that on the birds. The American Museum of Natural History cited 5.8 million Australian furs traded in the period 1919–21. The extent of the fur trade disturbed scientists, who predicted the demise of Australian mammals; as a result, Australia was inundated by scientific and commercial collecting expeditions in 1921–22. The fear was not unfounded, given the pending demise of the thylacine. Conservationists did achieve some improvements, with a new act in Queensland in 1921 and amendments in New South Wales in 1930. Bird and animal field clubs discovered how weak government commitments were when the Queensland government, under political pressure from growing unemployment figures, rescinded its protection of koalas and possums in 1927. Wildlife groups from around the country protested against the decision; interstate newspaper editorials as well as the *Brisbane Courier* condemned the government's action, to no avail. In one month over one million possums and over half a million koalas were killed by hunters for their skins—an onslaught from which the koalas have never fully recovered. The political uproar contributed to the defeat of Labor at the Queensland state elections of 1929.[63] Still the federal government failed to intervene, although the Victorian government passed amendments in 1930 which prevented game killed in another state from being sold in Victoria. This was fortunate timing: later that year the Lang government in New South Wales, for similar reasons to Queensland, allowed an open season on possums. Protests initiated by the Wild Life Preservation Society and joined by the RAOU, field naturalists, zoologists and bushwalkers succeeded only in having licences restricted to the unemployed. The result was the killing of more than 800,000 possums for their fur in a two-month period.[64]

## Partial Incorporation

As conservation groups generally met governmental resistance, they began to put more emphasis on education. The rediscovery of the work of John and Elizabeth Gould by bird conservationists in the 1900s inspired the name of the group, but their motto—'education is more potent than legislation in furthering the cause of conservation'— reflected an optimistic faith in the face of governmental deferrals and inaction. Given the resistance to the introduction· of professional biology to the university curriculum, it is not surprising that education departments at the turn of the century were slow to incorporate science teaching in the schools.[65] A young schoolteacher and member of the Royal Society of South Australia, W. Catton Grasby, led the way by introducing the study of natural history through 'object lessons' and field study in South Australian schools in the late 1880s and 1890s. Catton Grasby founded the Boys Field Club, which by the 1890s had

involved about 1500 boys in its excursions and camps, and whose objects
were 'to encourage the practical study of natural science' and 'to
provide healthful recreation'.[66] Although Australian public schools had
taken to Arbor Day with enthusiasm in the 1890s, nature study was still
not an official part of the curriculum, and Catton Grasby's approach was
radical. His work influenced Victorian educators Charles Long and
Frank Tate, the latter being that colony's first director of education and
a keen ornithologist.[67] The Victorian Education Department led the way
in supporting the Gould League, and in 1909 incorporated an annual
bird day into the school curriculum to foster appreciation and protection of Australian birds. The Gould League and Bird Day were taken
up by New South Wales the following year, and had also been adopted in
Queensland by World War I. The league had some influential and
committed supporters: among them were Alec Chisholm, David Stead
and his partner, the biologist Thistle Harris (later Thistle Stead), in New
South Wales; and Henry Tryon and John Shirley in Queensland.[68]
In Western Australia its formation was delayed by a lack of support
from the state education department, which refused to endorse it until
1939. In the meantime its supporters there established a junior wing of
the Western Australian Naturalists Club.[69] In Queensland the league
changed its name to the Nature-lovers League. In New South Wales a
Junior Tree Wardens League was formed in the 1930s, which merged
with the Forest League in 1949 and eventually combined with the Gould
League in the 1960s to promote environmental education generally.
Whatever the name changes, the education orientation showed that the
movement was embracing more acceptable institutional goals.

The ornithologists continued to join campaigns for national parks
and nature reserves and sanctuaries, but as the union approached its
twenty-fifth anniversary it displayed the first signs of an organisation
whose processes were becoming institutionalised as the efforts of its
earliest enthusiasts wound down. In 1924 members of the central
Queensland bird society organised the annual conference of the Royal
Australasian Ornithologists Union (RAOU) in Rockhampton,[70] a conference which was notable because the conflict between the organisation's scientific and preservation goals came to a head. This internal
conflict was minor compared with the machinations of the US conservation organisations, which had mobilised earlier and drew greater
mass support than their Australian counterparts. By 1926 the famous
Audubon Association, for example, had an income of more than
$US250,000 and a paid full-time administrator.[71] Many of the US con-
servation organisations were the beneficiaries of huge grants from the
gun lobby, with a vested interest in maximising wildlife game reserves.
Between 1929 and 1931 the Audubon Association earned an income of

$US50,000 by 'renting' one of its bird sanctuaries to fur trappers who were using birds as baits; when some members objected, they were dismissed by the association as 'zoophiles', triggering an internal struggle that lasted several years until a new committee reformed its processes.[72] While the RAOU had no large donors to compromise its work, it did have self-interested collectors and ornithologists with narrow scientific goals. At the 1924 annual general meeting a coterie of South Australian members, who were in favour of hunting birds for their private skin and egg collections, stacked the state branches with their nominees. Respectable ornithologists around the world had denounced the traffic in skins and eggs; the RAOU's official position was that birds should be killed only for limited scientific purposes and such specimens should be donated to public institutions. Having been outmanoeuvred over the election of officers, the congress had to pass resolutions condemning indiscriminate collecting of birds and their eggs and reaffirming the conservation policy.[73] It was ironic that the RAOU, which had had such success in leading a national conservation campaign, was suffering from internal disruption by members whose own environmental commitment was limited. Having fought off the rearguard action, the RAOU continued to lobby governments over native fauna reserves, customs laws on the export of native animals, and conservation laws generally.[74]

## Utilitarians

Scientific organisations had specific professional interests at stake in their lobbying for environmental protection, but they used diverse arguments from ecology to utilitarianism to further their aims. At times their interests coincided with those of groups advocating improved resources use. In fact, amateur botanists were more likely to be attracted to acclimatisation societies and horticultural clubs in the middle to late nineteenth century than to the more elitist royal societies. Traditionally the acclimatisation movement has been viewed by historians and con-servationists as the antithesis of the modern environmental movement.[75] Historically, the acclimatisation societies are known for the introduction of exotic species that became noxious pests, and for their general disdain for the indigenous environment. Yet one of their primary objectives was efficient and wise resource use, and they experimented on both indigenous and introduced species to achieve this end.

Colonial ignorance about the indigenous flora and fauna, and about what the indigenous climate could sustain, contributed to the scientism of the early movement. The enthusiasm for scientific knowledge was understandable when so much about the Australian environment was still unknown and government support for botanical research was slight. Colonial governments eager to reap the benefits of gold discoveries appointed geologists on large salaries, but there was less support for biological research. The first Colonial Botanist was appointed in Victoria in 1853 and in the same period the Universities of Sydney and Melbourne were founded, but such positions could not meet the demand for information. In 1897, a resident of north Queensland wrote to the *Queenslander* newspaper bemoaning the lack of state funding for research into the properties of native timbers, which were cut down 'as if they are of no commercial value, and were fitted only to make the billy boil'. The few Colonial Botanists who were employed in the latter half of the nineteenth century were not only under-resourced but also found their positions were not secure. In Victoria in the 1870s Ferdinand von Mueller, the colony's botanist since 1853, lost the directorship of Melbourne's Botanic Gardens because of dissatisfaction with his management of the gardens for scientific, rather than ornamental, purposes. In Queensland Walter Hill also exercised joint duties of colonial botanist and director of the Brisbane Botanic Gardens from 1855 to 1881. His successor, F. M. Bailey, was retrenched in 1893 in the midst of government cutbacks; after public outcry he was rein-stated some months later, but with a reduction in salary of more than 40 per cent.[76]

This lack of state support also explains why early conservationists so often resorted to bureaucratic solutions and why criticism of their failure to secure strong regulations is anachronistic.[77] Whole areas of life were still only weakly regulated in this period. Effective indus-trial legislation to protect workers, for example, was still being debated in the 1890s, so it is not surprising that little attention was given by politicians to effective animal protection and resource conservation. Environmentalists had to argue for public management and invent state structures to regulate and protect resources at a time when even simple appointments such as that of the Colonial Botanist had to be defended.

Colonial ignorance about indigenous flora and fauna and the limits of the climate, and the under-resourcing of biological research by the state, led to the founding of acclimatisation societies in the eastern colonies in the 1860s. They existed in provincial centres as well as the capital cities, with small informal clubs and groups, some linked with botanical gardens.[78] Community-based but, like the royal societies, supported by influential residents and amateur and professional scientists, the acclimatisation societies played an important role in public education and political pressure.

*Some Early Campaigns*

However misguided its motives by today's standards, the Victorian Acclimatisation Society fought one of the earliest political campaigns for land reservation, a campaign which has some interesting similarities with modern campaigns. In 1861 the society sought the reservation of Phillip Island for acclimatisation purposes. After two years of deputations and submissions to the Department of Crown Lands and Survey, they won a partial reservation, and they began turning the island into a wildlife sanctuary in anticipation of further reserves. But such activities were not a priority for bureaucratic decision-makers: in 1866 the department announced land sales for the island, despite vocal objections from the society. Acclimatisers launched a new campaign, targeting members of parliament and raising questions about whether decisions on land use should rest solely with departmental officers. Their anti-bureaucratic spirit was a reaction against the limited utilitarianism of the Lands Department, which recognised only water, timber and mineral reserves for current use and otherwise promoted maximum land sales. In late 1867 the society's parliamentary champion died; the following year the department proceeded with its first land sales on the island without any recourse to parliament.[79]

While the Victorian society put most of its efforts into introducing exotic species, its members were not totally dismissive of the value of indigenous fauna. They attempted to introduce emus to Phillip Island, and their vice-president Ferdinand von Mueller had promoted the benefits of eucalyptus among his acclimatisation and botanical contacts all around the world.[80] Native flora and fauna were taken much more seriously by local natural scientists in central Queensland. The two O'Shanesy brothers, John and Patrick, who arrived in Rockhampton in 1864 and 1866, had trained as 'scientific gardeners' and were part of von Mueller's extensive network of collectors. John O'Shanesy—who on arrival in the colony had worked for the Botanic Gardens in Brisbane— set about proving that oats, maize and lucerne could all be grown in central Queensland. Such interests have resulted in acclimatisation societies being uniformly condemned in the twentieth century for their introduction of so many inappropriate exotic species to the Australian environment. However, the O'Shanesys, like many of their contemporaries in the acclimatisation movement, shared the vision of a democratic yeomanry working family-sized agricultural plots. Their ideal was to develop a sustainable agriculture that could support more than a peasant social system or the feudal-style, large-scale grazing enterprises that had become the Australian staple by the mid-century. These ideas were promoted by Patrick O'Shanesy in his publication

*Contributions to the Flora of Queensland*, based on his expeditions and fieldwork around central Queensland. His reports emphasised regions suitable for agricultural settlement and, although they dismissed the brigalow scrub as 'cheerless waste', were not hostile to the indigenous environment. At times Patrick was poetic about the wilderness he found himself in, and his overriding concern in the book was 'to stimulate the colonists generally to a lively interest in the flora of their adopted country, by showing that it is replete with a vast number of economic and industrial plants, which are worthy of our greatest attention'. He promoted a native citrus that had a lime-like fruit, and the medicinal properties of eucalypts; he argued that native grasses were far superior to introduced species, and campaigned for planting of valuable timber trees as a matter of urgency for the sake of future generations.[81] The O'Shanesys were probably influenced by another leading proponent of the value of indigenous species in the Rockhampton district, Anthelme Thozet, a professional botanist who had left France for political reasons and made his way to the Canoona gold rush of 1858. Thozet was another of von Mueller's many collectors, and in 1867 he sent an impressive collection of 350 items including various specimens of edible roots, tubers and fruits from central Queensland via Melbourne for the Paris Exhibition.[82] Thozet published the catalogue to his exhibition collection and made a note in his introduction that has now become part of popular wisdom: 'Our pioneer explorers and travellers, in passing through trackless paths previously untrodden by the foot of the white man, ... often die of hunger although surrounded by abundance of natural vegetable food in the very spot where the aborigines easily find all the luxuries of their primitive method of life', he wrote, also urging further interest in 'the practical resources of our Flora'.[83] Despite their failings, not all advocates of the acclimatisation movement were insensitive to the values of the Australian environment.

In fact, Australia's first national park proclamation has been attributed to the work of New South Wales acclimatisation advocates. The original goals of the Zoological Society of New South Wales when it was formed in March 1879 centred on introduction and acclimatisation of exotic birds and animals. One of its leading figures, Walter Bradley, lobbied the government for support and was promised land for acclimatisation purposes. In April the New South Wales government proclaimed 7300 hectares, later doubled to 15,000 hectares, at Port Hacking, 22 kilometres south of Sydney, as the National Park. Its planned uses were for recreation, zoos and fairgrounds and, while destruction of native flora and fauna was subsequently prohibited, exotic species were introduced into the park. Much of the Zoological

Society's time and effort, however, went into its zoo, originally at Moore Park; its internal development makes an interesting contrast to the RAOU. When David Stead helped form the Wild Life Preservation Society in 1909, he attracted a number of leading zoological members, pointing to the limits of that society's concerns; but by 1917 when Bassett Hull, a committed ornithologist and conservationist, was in his second year as president of the Zoological Society, protection of native animals was listed as its second aim. In the years between the two world wars, it attracted a number of members noted for their conservation commitments, such as Neville Cayley, Launcelot Harrison, William Froggatt and Alan Marshall. Despite the internal developments of the Royal Zoological Society, responsibility for the National Park was vested in trustees, whose limited utilitarian approach soon led to conflict with conservationists with broader aims. As early as 1902, the trustees' cavalier attitude to their parklands had offended the government botanist, who argued unsuccessfully for ministerial control over national parks. Between 1890 and 1920 the trustees alienated part of the park through land swaps; they considered opening a coalmine within its boundaries during World War I; and they allowed a private company to erect a sawmill and fell timber within the park's boundaries. The last activities outraged David Stead and the Wild Life Preservation Society, and their opposition resulted in the intervention of the government and qualification of the authority of the trustees.[84]

### The Role of David Stead

In his professional life, David Stead was much more sympathetic to the goals of wise resource use which motivated acclimatisation advocates. Stead was the epitome of progressivist environmentalism. Born in 1877, the son of a house-painter, he left school at the age of twelve to take up an apprenticeship to a stampmaker, but achieved recognition and social mobility as a scientist and conservationist. His love of nature and bushwalks led him to join the New South Wales Naturalists Society as a teenager and to undertake a course in zoology at the Sydney Technical College. By 1900 he had had several scientific articles published by the prestigious British Linnean Society, and in May 1902 his expertise in ichthyology won him appointment as scientific assistant to the director of the New South Wales Fisheries Commission. His famous daughter, the novelist Christina Stead, parodied him as being 'part of the Huxley-Darwin reasonable-rational nature-agnostic mother-of-all-things-fresh-air-panacea eclectic-socialist universal-peace-manhood-suffrage-and-vegetarianism of the English breed'. But in kinder moments she

also recalled the passion and enthusiasm for the natural world that her
father conveyed to her through his wonderful stories

> about the first Australians and their corroborees ... of Krakatoa and Mauna
> Loa ... Captain Cook's travels, Charles Darwin's voyages ... and extinct
> monsters ... that used to roam the mud swamps ... The stories went 'on and
> on, night after night'. They left her with a feeling of wonder and excitement,
> a curiosity about 'men and nature', and a sense of the equality of all
> creatures—black people, white people and coral insects alike.[85]

His interests were universal extending from botany to geography, town
planning and forestry. He was a friend of David Starr Jordan, the internationally renowned ichthyologist and president of Stanford University,
who shared his passionate belief in 'the good of nature, fresh air and
exercise, education and democracy'; and of the poet and labour activist,
Mary Gilmore. He was a pacifist and a socialist, who joined the New
South Wales branch of the League of Nations Union and in 1936
founded and chaired the International Peace Campaign.[86]

Stead had been promoting the great variety of edible fish available in
New South Wales,[87] and when in 1914 there was a shortage of fish for
sale in Sydney, he proposed a scheme for a state-run deep-sea trawling
industry. The Labor government of William Holman was sympathetic,
and Stead was sent overseas to purchase trawlers and to investigate
canning and distribution methods. The following year, while war was
being waged on the other side of the world, he was appointed manager
of the State Trawling Industry. Since 1868 a number of New South Wales
Fisheries Acts had attempted to police harvesting of marine resources
to prevent wastage.[88] Stead's approach continued in this vein of optimal
use of fish resources, rather than protection *per se*, with the state government playing a leading role in management and distribution of the
catch. He was politically naive, however, and his vision of rational and
equitable management of fish resources pitted him against private
shipping interests. The war blew out running costs and Stead came
under personal attack by the conservative opposition who accused him
of overfishing. He lost his job in early 1920, despite a royal commission's
praise of his efforts. He was neither the first nor the last enlightened
bureaucrat urging sustainable state management of an industry to be
removed from his post in interwar Australia.

### Campaigns for the Forests

The longest campaign for wise resource use originating in the nineteenth century was that of the forests, and it was an event of the
international environment movement which triggered Australian

developments. In 1864 the American G. P. Marsh published *Man and Nature*. His book marked a turning-point in attitudes among naturalists that was as radical as the effect of Rachel Carson's *Silent Spring* a century later. Marsh's theme was the destructive effects of human domination of nature, and his ideas about the damage caused by forest clearance were popularised in the Australian colonial press of the 1860s.[89]

The indefatigable Ferdinand von Mueller took up the cause of the forests with passion. In a lecture on forest culture delivered in 1871, he urged practical measures such as the establishment of local forest boards and used utilitarian, ethical, aesthetic and public health arguments for preservation. He ended his address with a moving tribute to forests and to intergenerational obligations: 'I regard the forests as a gift, intrusted to any of us only for transient care during a short space of time, to be surrendered to posterity again as an unimpaired property, with increased riches and augmented blessings, to pass as a sacred patrimony from generation to generation.'[90]

In New South Wales von Mueller's arguments were taken up by the Reverends W. B. Clarke and William Woolls before the Royal Society in 1876.[91] In Queensland the Acclimatisation Society began raising questions about forest clearance in 1870 and its continued pressure resulted in a parliamentary inquiry into forest 'conservancy' in 1875.[92] Even mining surveyors concerned about the depletion of timber supplies for mine props in deep-lead mines began urging practical conservation measures in Victoria;[93] numerous royal commissions were held or promised in the various colonies, but still no concrete outcomes were achieved. In South Australia, the forest resource was meagre; the combined efforts of Robert Schomburgk, the curator of the Adelaide Botanical Gardens, G. W. Goyder, the surveyor-general, and Heinrich Krichauff, a member of parliament, compatriot and friend of von Mueller, resulted in the establishment of a department of woods and forests in 1882 and the appointment of John Ednie Brown as conservator of forests soon after.[94] During the next three decades the RSSA continued to campaign for forest protection, additional forest reserves, and foresters to manage them, not only for South Australia but also for the Commonwealth.[95] The full onset of the age of railways and the consequent shift in the scale of imperial demand for Australian hardwoods in the 1880s forced other colonial parliaments to take the question of sustainable forestry seriously.[96]

The appointment of paid officials was the first step towards rational assessment of forest resources and systematic management, but it did not mean that the issue of sustained yield had been won. The first bureaucrats found themselves fighting the conservation battle against the entrenched interests of diverse forest users. George Perrin's term as

an early conservator of forests in Victoria has been characterised as one
of 'interminable bureaucratic wranglings, personality clashes, real and
perceived economic troubles' and one without 'any strong popular
support'. It required yet another royal commission, which reported in
1901, and the formation of a community pressure group, the National
Forests Protection League, in 1903 before the Victorian parliament
found the political will to pass the Forest Act of 1907.[97] Walter Gill, who
had replaced Brown in South Australia, complained to the AAAS in
1894 of his lack of power to defend the forests against parochial
interests:

> when an experienced forester in a State forest in these colonies decides that
> enough timber has been cut and decides to reserve the rest the timber-getter
> gets up a memorial and secures the aid of the local Parliamentary
> representative, who depicts in moving tones ... the tragic circumstances of
> hardship ... and the result is that the faithful servant of the State takes a 'back
> seat' ... while the sawyer or splitter gratifies his own self-interest at the State's
> expense.[98]

This was the economic climate in which those trained in the new
biological disciplines would wholeheartedly embrace the progressivist
ideology of rational decision-making by professionally trained experts.

The struggle for bureaucratic management was by no means over:
attacks on professional foresters continued. After enticing John Ednie
Brown with a higher salary to become New South Wales's director-
general of forests in 1890, that colony abolished his position altogether
in an economy drive three years later. Forestry Acts were finally passed
in New South Wales in 1909 and 1916, which established permanent
forest reserves and a Forestry Commission. These achievements were
reinforced by the formation of a community group, the New South
Wales branch of the Australian Forest League, in 1915.[99]

In Western Australia, where the industry was based on hardwoods for
export milled by large companies, a conservator of forests was finally
appointed in 1895. For the next twenty years appointees to the position
struggled to have all forestry operations placed within the one department. In 1916 the government appointed 31-year-old Charles Lane-
Poole to the position of conservator. Professionally trained and with
forestry experience in South Africa and Sierra Leone, Lane-Poole set
about establishing a training school for forestry staff, and drafted a
forests bill for Western Australia that was regarded as a model by his
peers. He was finally given control over a Forests Department in 1918,
but his struggle to establish 'sound forestry methods' was thwarted by
opposition to the implementation of his Forests Act of 1919 and the
government's granting of extraordinary concessions to a large timber

company. In 1921 he was forced to resign, following disagreement with the government over the granting of leases and concessions over more than 200,000 hectares to a single company for a ten-year period.[100] Lane-Poole went on to become forest adviser and then inspector-general of forests for the Commonwealth government, where his defence of the Australian forests continued. His reports criticised the undiscriminating land settlement practices of state governments which resulted in wholesale felling of forests. In a presidential address to the AAAS conference of 1926 he attacked the states' land policies and their failure to support sustainable forestry.[101]

Queensland's forestry legislation was late but promising. A public meeting organised by the Acclimatisation Society in Brisbane in 1873 had heard several papers on the need for forest management, including one by the pastoralist John Jardine, who argued in favour of the superior value of indigenous tree species and against the introduction of foreign flora.[102] After sustained lobbying by the society and much political backtracking, three decades later, in 1906, the State Forests and National Parks Bill was introduced to the Queensland parliament. Soon after, the Bunya Mountains and a small scenic reserve at Mount Tambourine were declared national parks upon the recommendations of the inspector of forests, who declared that their special values were more important than their timber.[103] Forestry officials were moving ahead of their political masters and public opinion, however. The Queensland director complained of the needless destruction of forest timber around Atherton in his report of 1908–09, and other forestry advocates complained of the public's excessive faith in plantations.[104] Two decades later the director of forestry was still fighting to maintain a scientific policy based on sustained yield and forest regeneration, not against millers big or small, but against governments intent on northern development and closer settlement.

In the 1920s the Queensland Lands Department made plans for the opening of massive rainforest lands in the north for closer settlement; they were vigorously opposed by the new chairman of the state's Provisional Forestry Board, E. H. F. Swain, who had responsibility for both national parks and state forests. Harold Swain, like his contemporary Lane-Poole, was a professionally trained forester. Although his father, a struggling flour merchant, was politically conservative, Harold and his older sister Muriel were exposed to the idealism of the times through their academic and professional studies. Muriel gained a university degree and in 1900 became the first woman to be appointed to the position of clerk in the New South Wales public service. She became active in the Public Service Association as well as in a host of other feminist, peace, philanthropic and scientific causes. Harold, born in

1883, never completed a tertiary degree but was appointed the first cadet forester in the New South Wales Department of Lands. His training brought him into contact with J. H. Maiden, the government botanist who had urged reform of the National Park Trust. In 1916 Harold also undertook a six-month forestry course at the University of Montana in the United States, becoming an enthusiastic supporter of business management in forestry in the process. Since the US Forestry Service, under the influence of foresters such as Aldo Leopold, was also pioneering ideas of primitive wilderness in national forests in this period, it is tempting to see this link as significant in terms of his subsequent conflict with the Queensland government. Whatever the source, Swain worked closely with Queensland's foremost national parks campaigner, Romeo Lahey.[105]

Swain argued that any vacant Crown lands in the north with stands of marketable timber should be declared either state forest or national park reservations. He also commenced reafforestation programs, established a forest products division to research the properties and economic uses of local timbers, and developed professional training for forestry staff. Yet Swain's visionary work received no acclaim from his employer. He was working in a system that was doubly weighted against him. Firstly the bureaucratic chain of command made him directly answerable to the Lands Department, the very department promoting closer settlement in the north. Secondly the Labor minister for lands was none other than Tom Foley, a northern-based large-scale timber supplier. After years of friction with Labor administrations, the conservative Moore government (1929–32) decided to resolve the disputes surrounding 'Swainism' by appointing a royal commission. Its report in 1931 was hostile to Swain and the forest service. 'Queensland needs no forestry science for present requirements,' it declared. 'There is abundance and enough timber for all. Business or commonsense management, and not science, is the first requisite.' It dismissed Swain's nurseries for threatened species, reafforestation, and other silviculture programs. The report even cited one timber merchant who had submitted to the commissioners that 'a much higher order of intelligence and skill is required to successfully cultivate ... a banana or a papaw tree than ... a Hoop Pine or a Blue Gum Tree'.[106] In a state where northern development was bipartisan policy, even a change of government could not save Swain. Percy Pease became Labor's new deputy premier and minister for lands; he was a former Cairns timber merchant and another promoter of northern development.[107] The new Labor government of 1932 discontinued the northern reafforestation programs; sacked the forestry board, replacing it with a sub-department of forestry; and terminated Swain's employment,[108] marking another major defeat for a professional bureaucrat arguing for a utilitarian policy of scientific yield.

In an economic environment of short-term exploitation and of political ascendancy over rational planning, it is not surprising that foresters came to rely on easily cultivated exotic pine plantations. These met with opposition from within professional forestry circles in the 1930s, especially where native eucalypts were removed for them,[109] but met popular, or at least political, expectations in terms of guardianship of public resources. At a time when even the basic utilitarian principles of natural resource management were under attack, professional foresters were forced into the vanguard of the conservation struggle. Scientific and acclimatisation groups had forced the public debate in the late nineteenth century, and even succeeded in having Arbor Day introduced into colonial schools in 1890.[110] However, governments continued to give in to vested interests which resisted systematic regulation, and in response new specific pro-forest preservation groups formed to defend professional forestry. Under this political regime, depression and war were probably the saving factors for Australia's southern forests, until they were beset by the next production onslaughts of the 1960s and a very different campaign was required to defend them.

The stream of the environment movement that emphasises wise resource use exemplifies the willing incorporation of social movements so that their goals and values will become part of the mainstream. The forest campaign persisted over several decades because the first government responses could not meet the movement's expectations. When new institutional arrangements were finally created, however, they became susceptible to internal redirection away from the original bureaucratic goals—a process which is common to attempts to regulate powerful resource industries. Regulatory capture of forestry departments by the 1970s would cast them as the enemy of the environment movement that had helped to create these departments, an issue that is discussed in Chapter 5.

*Movement Boundaries: Soil and Water Conservation*

The moral message at the heart of the wise use campaigns was that the country's natural resources are a common good that should not be squandered for private interest or be exploited at the expense of future generations. At another level, however, efficient use of resources is simply good business practice and readily adopted by private enterprise. As primary producers joined the community groups advocating wise resource use, these two goals coalesced. When oppositional core values are diluted, such community groups show all the signs of becoming incorporated and the movement's identity is weakened. This dilemma— industry lobby or social movement—is evident in two other major resource issues, soil and water.

Although there is a perception that land and soil issues have never been part of the Australian conservationists' vocabulary,[111] concern about soils has been long-standing. Official concern probably dates from the much-quoted 1803 proclamation of Governor King banning unlicensed tree-clearing along the Hawkesbury River because it had caused the loss of 'many acres of ground'.[112] Subsequently, self-governing colonies were reluctant to take any action, although the gentleman scientist Count Strzelecki was warning of land degradation in the 1840s.[113] Advocates of forest conservation had argued for the need to protect water catchments from siltation since the 1870s. In 1892 Samuel Dixon of the Royal Society of South Australia decried the advancing 'sandwaves' which resulted from overstocking in that colony.[114] His scientific concern was matched by Victorian field naturalists, but action on the erosion of farming land and the degradation of semi-arid zones awaited the arrival of agricultural scientists employed by all colonial governments by 1900.[115]

Soil and water conservation were two areas where the early movement walked a fine line between oppositional values and incorporation. Within both fields there were those who argued for state intervention to protect the common good and also for catchment protection rather than dams.[116] These campaigns were also supported by the more enlightened among primary producers. In many respects, soil and water conservation were merely an extension of government support for primary producers. The irrigation schemes of the first half of the twentieth century, for example, tended to be driven by government visions of rural development in which railways and water would fulfil the promises of closer settlement.[117] Government embracing of dams took the initiative on water conservation out of the hands of the movement. Yet there was identifiable conservation movement influence among some of the professionals who made up the soil and water conservation authorities which were formed in the interwar period. Like the foresters Lane-Poole and Swain, bureaucrats such as Baldur Byles of the Commonwealth Forestry Bureau and Sam Clayton of the New South Wales Soil Conservation Service have been extolled as exemplars of utilitarian conservation.[118] Bureaucrats promoting conservation values in the face of self-interested landholders test definitions of the boundaries of the movement. As Bolton has noted, the bureaucrats and scientists promoting rural resource protection came up against the 'scepticism of the practical farmer',[119] although it was not as big an obstacle as that of

the politician, especially in Victoria where Country Party administrations resisted bureaucratic intervention.[120]

The cause of soil conservation was boosted by the invitation to a
young English scientist to investigate two farming-related problems in
Australia in the 1920s and 1930s. Francis Ratcliffe was employed by the
Council for Scientific and Industrial Research to investigate the attacks
of flying foxes on Queensland orchards, and by scientists in South
Australia who wanted a scientific survey of the extent of the 'drifting
sands' of the semi-arid grazing lands. The sensitive account of his travels
around the country was first published by the young scientist in 1938 as
*Flying Fox and Drifting Sand.*[121] Ratcliffe's systemic approach was excellent
science and his book was enormously popular; but his work was the work
of a good government scientist, not a social movement activist. Ratcliffe
later moved to Australia and became the founder of the Australian Conservation Foundation in 1965; it is here that his ecological sensibility
becomes part of movement history.

Ratcliffe's work no doubt did have some effect on the reluctant
Victorian government. Eventually the combined pressure of agricultural
scientists, surveyors, engineers and members of the Water Commission
forced the adoption of a part-time Soil Conservation Board for that state
in 1939. This limited success was supported by the publication in 1942 of
*Australia's Dying Heart*, about the extensive problem of soil erosion
throughout the inland, by Jock Pick, a man whose background was
described as 'a life spent on the land'.[122] The campaign had been a hard
one but the enlightened farmers, bureaucrats, scientists and academics
who had been pressing the issue were successful in achieving a political
shift. After World War II the Victorian government recognised soil
erosion as 'the greatest long-term threat to the prosperity of the state';[123]
soil conservation legislation was passed in South Australia, New South
Wales, Western Australia and Victoria.[124]

### Counter-moves: The Isolation of Thomas Griffith Taylor

A lone voice raised another issue of resource sustainability which would
confront primary producers and governments head-on. It was the
question of the continent's carrying capacity in terms of population and
farming.

As part of the inducements for British investment in the 1920s, Australian governments committed Australia to Empire First trade arrangements, which guaranteed markets, and to population growth and land
development schemes to promote development. Enthusiastic business
and political supporters dreamed of an Australian population of more
than 100 million, while in the short term one lobby group called for 'a

million farms for a million farmers' to promote prosperity and, more importantly, to ward off Australian fears of invasion from the Asian north. Governments found plenty of supporters for the rhetoric of 'boosterism'; the slogan 'Men, money and markets!' summed up the popular panacea for the country's economic woes and national insecurity.

There was at least one bureaucrat in the small Commonwealth public service of this period who doubted the feasibility of such schemes and dared to challenge the mainstream value of national development. Before World War I the Commonwealth Weather Service was allied to the Intelligence Branch within the Department of Home Affairs. Thomas Griffith Taylor was appointed to the service with the title of Weather Service Physiographer in 1909; a tertiary-educated (Sydney and Cambridge Universities) and promising young scientist, he was expected to undertake research in the national and imperial interest. During and immediately after World War I, Griffith Taylor began publishing a number of papers that explored the climatic limits to agricultural settlement of the Australian continent. For him, scientific study of Australia's weather proved that new agricultural settlements were unlikely to succeed, and that the established pattern of settlement more or less matched the continent's environmental limits. In 1921 Griffith Taylor moved into academia, where he continued to publish his research and attempted to popularise his ideas on the physical limits to population growth in Australia. In his academic capacity he called for a national resource atlas to be compiled, and in 1923 he gave the presidential address to the AAAS on 'Geography and Australian National Problems'.

Despite his scientific credentials and his prestigious background as a member of Scott's Antarctic expedition of 1909, Griffith Taylor soon found that his emphasis on the aridity of Australia, rather than dreams of unlimited growth and prosperity, lost him many supporters. In 1921 the Western Australian education authorities banned his textbook because of its assessments of the arid lands; this contributed to the momentum of the personal campaign against him. In 1924 his national and imperial opponents, with Commonwealth funding, organised a tour by Arctic explorer and adventurer Vilhjalmur Stefansson to discredit Griffith Taylor's arguments. Stefansson, who had already advocated human settlement of the Arctic lands, confidently pronounced Australia's deserts also capable of sustaining greater human and animal populations. Griffith Taylor's stance had been an isolated one and in 1928 he gave up the fight, leaving the country to take up a chair in geography at the University of Chicago.[125] The grandiose immigration and agricultural schemes had limited success, for the most part foundering on the economic instability and finally depression of the 1930s.

## Scientific Incorporation

The impact of imperial expansion from the 1880s had provoked a number of experts and bureaucrats to try to manage and stem the onslaught against the environment for purely practical and utilitarian purposes. With the achievement of the first national parks and state legislation for flora and fauna protection, however, the scientist stream of the movement began to decline. There were still scientific groups involved in preservation issues in the interwar period but, as Chapter 2 will show, the lead role was taken over by other groups. The pattern of mobilisation of the utilitarians was similar. Their campaign grew from the 1870s but, even after new bureaucratic structures were created in the World War I era, the foresters in particular had to persist with their campaigns. The new state-level bureaucratic structures resulting from the movement's efforts had surrendered within a few decades to control by the resource industries that they were supposed to regulate.

These two streams were linked by the new training that many of their supporters shared, as well as by a professional desire to see their new scientific skills appropriately incorporated into government policy. Although they had a grassroots base in the field naturalist and horticultural clubs of the nineteenth century, they had not had to resort to noisy demonstrations. In the period between Federation and World War I, the combined effects of the new Commonwealth, the agitation of several social movements and the rise of the Labor Parties temporarily prised open Australia's political structures and allowed conservationist scientists to influence new institutional arrangements. They succeeded in gaining royal commissions and government inquiries by winning the patronage of influential personalities, by lobbying, and by persistence.

The impact of such enlightened self-interest should not be under-estimated. The community groups such as the Gould societies or the forest protection organisations that were the legacy of these first preservationists and conservationists were at least partially institutionalised by virtue of their relations with government and industry by the 1930s. Nonetheless, they brought about the community education and the shift in values which are fundamental components of good social movement activity. They taught Australians to love their fauna and to value forests, but a number of contradictions remained. When an idealistic John McCabe became involved in the newly formed Capricorn Conservation Council, based in Rockhampton, in the early 1970s, he repeatedly found himself having to re-educate older members of the council. They tended to view pine plantations and dams as exemplars of conservation[126]— the new generation would have to re-educate Australians about good conservation that was also good ecology.

Another group of Australians would react to the new incursions of industrial and imperial expansion from a more romantic position— the bushwalkers, recreational users and adventurers benefited from new technological developments such as the railways, but also keenly felt how limited Australia's wildlife and wilderness places had become. The urban participants in the first-wave movement are the subject of Chapter 2.

# CHAPTER 2

# *Sane Citizens and Sanitarians*

As nationalist and industrial efficiency goals took over public debates on conservation, the moral protest of the scientists and acclimatisers dissipated. However, two other streams of the early movement were also issuing an ethical challenge to Australian society as they protested against the commercialisation and industrialisation of urban life. For the bushwalkers, nature was a solace, a sanctuary where people could find their true selves away from the crass materialism of the city. For the urban reformers, however, equilibrium could be cultivated by removing the worst excesses of urban life: the cesspools, the crowded streets, the pollution of waterways, and the cruelty and violence of the urban lifestyle. These two groups mounted campaigns independently of one another, although by the 1920s they had come to acknowledge the affinity of their causes. The bushwalkers, like the field naturalists before them, developed their own cultural identity within the movement. All four streams of the early movement tended to draw their social base from the new middle class, but the distinctive recruiting grounds for these two streams were the cities.

## Adventurers

The difficulty of separating the different streams of interests which have contributed to the conservation movement is apparent when we seek the origins of recreational interest groups. Australia's earliest European bushwalkers, mountain climbers, cavers and boating enthusiasts were British imperial adventurers. We now appreciate the extent to which the first European discoverers merely followed the pathways of Aboriginal Australians and their total dependence on Aboriginal guides, but to their contemporary supporters their feats were inspirational tales of

61

heroism and tragedy. Colonial life represented more than the means of self-improvement and economic exploitation: to the imperial centre, it summoned up imaginative worlds of the faraway and the opposite—the discipline of industrial life juxtaposed with the indiscipline and freedom of the 'unsettled lands' of the imperial periphery. The Australian colonies, as much as any other outposts, represented the exotic and wild and mysterious places of the world.

Following in the footsteps of the first surveyors and European explorers, some of the early governors traversed their colonial territories to contribute to scientific and geographical information, to acquaint themselves with their districts, and also for invigoration and escape from administrative responsibilities. Both Charles La Trobe at Port Phillip and Sir John Franklin in Van Diemen's Land already had reputations for travelling and exploring before their appointments to the Australian colonies. La Trobe, a lover of botany and natural science, had published accounts of his ramblings in Europe and the Americas, which he undertook for pleasure and his personal quest for the 'picturesque'. Although it was not part of his expected duties as superintendent at Port Phillip, he undertook ninety-four journeys around south-east Australia during his fifteen-year colonial appointment. Sir John and Lady Jane Franklin also undertook expeditions through the wildest parts of Tasmania, including the rugged south-west during Sir John's term of office. Jane Franklin's journeys were regarded as extraordinary for a woman of her class, and her mainland travels added to her reputation.[1] While these vice-regal travellers commented with awe on the beauty of their surroundings, they did not envisage a time when such vast areas would be in need of preservation. They were, however, contributing to the tradition of the British elite's interest in the wilds of Australia which continued well into the twentieth century.

Many of the governors and regal visitors who followed shared their love of roaming about the Australian wilderness. Lord Lamington, governor of Queensland from 1895 to 1901, participated in R. M. Collins's expedition to the McPherson Range in 1897 as part of Collins's campaign to have the plateau declared a national park.[2] Excursions to the wild and scenic parts of Queensland became part of the vice-regal itinerary for distinguished British visitors. As a journalist, Alexander Chisholm recalled accompanying another Queensland governor, Sir Matthew Nathan, along with Sir Arthur Conan Doyle (described by Chisholm as a 'keen conservationist'), the Prince of Wales and Lord Louis Mountbatten, on various trips in the 1920s to impress upon them the importance of Queensland's rainforests and wild places.[3] Also part of this tradition were two expeditions to the Great Barrier Reef in the period between the two world wars. E. F. Pollock, Fellow of the Royal

Geographical Society and councillor of the Royal Zoological Society of New South Wales, led a group of about thirty men and women from Sydney on a combined nature study expedition and holiday to the Bunker and Capricorn island groups in late 1927. In 1928–29 a group of eighteen British scientists sponsored by the Royal Society of London spent ten months conducting research near Port Douglas.[4]

Colonial expeditioners were often ambivalent in their environmental attitudes. Although Lord Lamington had been enlisted by R. M. Collins as part of his campaign to protect the McPherson Range, Lamington's main recollection of the trip forty years later was the dying cries of the koala that he had shot,[5] for hunting was just as much a part of the experience of the wilds. Elliott Napier used his account of the 1927 reef expedition to praise the unique wonders of the reef, its importance as a national asset and the need for a scientific research station based in its waters, but also argued for better exploitation of its commercial values of fishing and tourism.[6] Despite mixed motives, elite support added prestige and gave important moral support to some of the early calls for recreational national parks across the country. Eccleston du Faur, the colonial surveyor and geographer who had supported expeditions to find Leichhardt and to study Antarctica, enjoyed his own personal explorations through rugged country near Sydney; these inspired him to press for the preservation of Kuring-gai Chase, which was declared a national park in 1894.[7] Like the media celebrities of the late twentieth century, influential personalities helped in winning popular endorsement and sometimes provided scientific authority for national park proposals.

### The Social Base of the Outdoor Movement

The idea of the colonial adventure—of expanding the boundaries of Western knowledge and accomplishment through great feats of human endurance—galvanised the entire community in the three decades preceding World War I. One did not have to be an imperialist to be affected by the romance and bravery of the genre of adventure tales, fictional and non-fictional, which flooded the Australian markets in these years. The amateur bird-watchers and ornithologists, the field naturalists and boys' natural history clubs were part of this romantic progressivist sentiment which looked on the boundaries of knowledge and on the boundaries of civilisation with new eyes in the search for inspiration and individual and national renewal. The popularity of these clubs and societies and their quest for outdoors experience place them as much within the category of romantic adventurers as within the scientific interest group. The artist Ellis Rowan similarly overlaps these two categories. Her quest to find and record every Australian wildflower and her delightful paintings of native birds, insects and butterflies were of botanical interest. Her published writings of her travels as a single white woman in the wilds of northern Australia and New Guinea were heroic adventure.[8] A little later, E. J. Banfield's writings, based on his life on Dunk Island in north Queensland, also contributed to the popularisation and romanticisation of the Australian wilds.[9]

This literature found an enlarged audience as a result of the economic changes of the late nineteenth century. Rapid urbanisation, improved literacy, and successful industrial campaigns for reduced working hours and annual holidays were influencing work and leisure patterns. Even more important were the technological developments which led to improved transport and communications. By the 1890s Sydney had a population of half a million people and a direct rail link to National Park, which had its own station inside the park grounds. Between 1880 and the 1920s each of the Australian capital cities had developed rail lines to open spaces and scenic spots on the city fringes which were thronged by city workers on weekends. Bicycles had also come within reach of working-class pay packets and a cycling craze swept Sydney in the 1890s.[10] The fictional and non-fictional colonial writing from the late nineteenth century was now reaching a mass Australian audience with limited opportunity to enact its own outdoors experiences away from the stresses of civilisation and industrialisation.

Much of the adventure literature of the period was explicitly imperialist, militaristic and male-oriented, emphasising bravery, stoicism in the face of hardship, loyalty, and manly resourcefulness and independence—all of which inadvertently contributed to the groundswell that led to the Great War. It was not militarism but the sense of adventure and personal pride in achievement that motivated a youthful Myles Dunphy to establish the Mountain Trails Club in Sydney in 1914. 'Why read about the fine achievements of people with plenty of "pep" and only wish for the same opportunities?' Dunphy recorded in his journal in 1919. This was not the first walking club in New South Wales. The Warragamba Walking Club had been founded in 1895; it organised popular walking tours which used the roads, with tourist accommodation for longer trips. The goal of Dunphy's club was to get away from the roads and cities and into the 'rough country'. This was not only a more satisfying nature experience but tested one's resourcefulness and self-reliance. The Mountain Trailers were proud of their bushcraft, and they designed specialist equipment for travelling and camping in the wilds. They also embraced the mateship and egalitarian values of the period; membership of the club was by invitation and for males only. For its first fourteen years the club had fewer than twenty members, and Myles Dunphy often referred to his bushwalking companions in his writings as the 'bush brotherhood'.[11]

Yet their social status was definitely new middle class. Myles Dunphy was the son of a socialist-leaning draper. At the age of sixteen he commenced work as an assistant draughtsman and undertook evening studies in architecture for the next nine years. After finishing his architecture studies, he was offered part-time teaching at the Sydney Technical College, becoming a full-time lecturer in 1922. Most of the Mountain Trailers had similar backgrounds in architecture, art teaching, engineering and private business. Dunphy's comment on the professional background of his 'bush brotherhood' was that 'they helped to keep it on an even keel, well-trimmed as regards ideas'.[12] While his writings display a keen romanticism, Dunphy also incorporated the rationalism of his age. Bushwalkers, he wrote, 'produced nothing to profit Government except a kind of sane citizenship in the Australian democracy'.[13] Bushwalking in the wilderness was good for the mind, the soul, and the country.

### The Leadership of Myles Dunphy

As a true romantic, Dunphy disliked the commercialisation and industrialisation of the towns and cities; his copious journals and letters testify to the sensitivity of his observations of the natural world. For him, the true human experience was that of the wilderness. Early on in his bushwalking career, he and his mate Bert Gallop misjudged a trek through uncharted country and, weakened and hungry, made their way to a township. Dunphy reflected on this experience in his journal:

> What we endured, no one but ourselves will ever really know. . . . But I, at any rate, never did regret that plug. Did we not see great things? Did we not adapt ourselves to nature itself—the Bush? We did not pit ourselves against it, for it would have broken us, sure thing. Did we not for a short time live the life which every man is intended for? And above all, did we not come to know our land a little better, even if under the hard task master Experience?[14]

In this passage, as much as in his lyrical descriptions of scenic beauty, Dunphy was harbinger to the contemporary bushwalking movement. He was a product of the age in which he lived but he sifted out the physical and natural enjoyment, the romantic and aesthetic values, and built them into a conservation philosophy which was to mark Australian bushwalking.

His sensitivity to the wilderness experience was apparent in his maps and feature names. In 1968 the New South Wales Geographical Names Board reviewed his names for the southern Blue Mountains. They recommended seventy-nine feature names, whereas Dunphy had used 168, including Aboriginal descriptors, poetic and standard terms from features such as rock, cone, crag, knoll, hillock, tor, dome and saddle to deeps, fissure, ravine, crevice.[15] Dunphy objected, arguing that the board's nomenclature would 'flatten his Wild Dog Mountains out of recognition', and he won. His dedication to the national parks and wilderness cause was unmatched; he spent hours compiling maps to accompany his park submissions to the government and hours more creating them for bushwalkers.[16]

In the days before the term 'bushwalking' had entered the popular vocabulary of Australians, the leadership of Myles Dunphy and other members of the Mountain Trails Club in organising popular recreational walking groups was central. In 1922 three new clubs had opened, including the Bushlanders which was the first in New South Wales open to women, and Dunphy was involved in all of them. As public interest in bushwalking and the demand for access and information to New South Wales's spectacular wild scenery increased, members of the Trails Club formed a new group in 1927, the Sydney Bush Walkers, which was open to the general public and facilitated the sharing of maps and information. Ten of the twelve founding members of the new club were also Mountain Trailers and their commitment to nature conservation was embodied in the new club's goals: they included 'to establish a definite regard for the welfare and preservation of the wildlife and natural beauty of this country' and 'to help others to appreciate these natural gifts'. By 1934, the growth in new walking clubs, such as the Coast and Mountain Walkers,[17] resulted in the founding of the New South Wales Federation of Bush Walking Clubs; it also had conservation as one of its main objectives and Myles Dunphy also played a part in it.[18]

Dunphy had been developing a vision of a Greater Blue Mountains National Park since his earliest bushwalks in the area with Bert Gallop in 1914, but for other walkers new park initiatives were not a priority while there were accessible bushlands near Sydney. In April 1931, however, a party of Sydney bushwalkers led by Alan Rigby was hiking through Grose Canyon; they discovered that a scenic portion of land at the junction of the Grose River and Govett's Leap Creek had been leased, and that the lessee intended to clear it. Rigby was outraged, and convinced the Mountain Trails and Sydney Bush Walkers Clubs to take action. The campaign was based on raising funds to buy back the lease and then return the area to the Lands Department for public recreation. It became known as the Blue Gum Conservation Campaign, and was significant for its successful garnering of support from community groups with similar interests, such as the Wild Life Preservation Society, the Parks and Playground Association of New South Wales, the Town Planning Association, the Australian Forest League, and the Tree and Flower Lovers. It was the first public conservation activism in New South Wales since the Wild Life Preservation Society campaign to prevent timber getting and other abuses of National Park in 1921–22.[19]

With only two large national parks, a small reservation in the Blue Mountains and some cave reserves, the increasing popularity of outdoor recreation put a strain on the available parklands and the need for wilderness areas became more apparent. According to Myles Dunphy, in the 1920s and 1930s the railways department had to appeal to the bushwalking clubs 'to divert some of their programmed walks and members to the Northern Line to ease the weekend stress' on the Illawarra line to National Park. Public access to Crown lands was on sufferance; while governments were open to reserving lands for recreational use for sporting clubs and playing fields, bushwalkers wanted primitive areas in which roads, car access and other development would not be permitted.[20] When bushfires swept through the bushlands near Sydney, the limited area available for recreation was made even more apparent. In 1932 representatives from the Sydney Bush Walkers, the Bush Tracks Club, the Coast and Mountain Walkers and the Mountain Trails Clubs met to plan for more parklands; the result was the formation of the National Parks and Primitive Areas Council (NP&PAC), an independent body dedicated to campaigning for the reservation of scenic, natural bushland for conservation and recreational purposes. Maurice Berry was elected chair and Dunphy was secretary; their first proposal was Dunphy's Blue Mountains National Park plan. During the next two decades the bushwalkers achieved a number of important reserves, including parts of the Greater Blue Mountains National Park which were declared by increment. Not all the parks were the work of Myles Dunphy and the NP&PAC; the gazettal of the Bouddi Natural Park was instigated by Marie Byles through the Sydney Bush Walkers and the Federation of Bushwalking Clubs in 1934.[21] Dunphy's maps and the NP&PAC's careful research of proposed park boundaries, their lobbying of senior bureaucrats and their public campaigning nonetheless raised public awareness of nature conservation and park issues. In 1934, as part of the Blue Mountains campaign, Dunphy and the NP&PAC prepared a supplement to the *Katoomba Daily* which promoted their ideas for a park incorporating tourist development and primitive areas as well as promoting conservation values generally. The activist core of the bushwalkers had to educate the public, other conservation bodies and the authorities about environmental matters and about 'the public's moral right to the use of Crown lands for bushland recreation'.[22]

While Dunphy was prepared to achieve his national park goals by beavering away at bureaucratic decision-makers, he also initiated new methods to reach his bushwalking constituency. In 1933, as part of his campaign to have land south of National Park declared a primitive area, the Sydney Bush Walkers distributed a handbill and petition at all the train stations abutting the region, as well as at other gathering points for bushwalkers such as Paddy Pallin's camping equipment shop in George Street. It succeeded in gathering more than 4600 signatures in just four weeks, and the land was eventually added to National Park.[23]

### Women's Involvement

The involvement of Marie Byles in the national parks campaign was no mere coincidence. The 'new woman' of the 1920s and 1930s was active in the bushwalking movement, to the surprise of the men who had founded the movement and grown up with the notion of outdoor adventure and frontiering as male pursuits. In December 1920, when access to the newly created Lamington National Park in Queensland's southern highlands was still difficult, Alec Chisholm was guiding a noted entomologist and the secretary of the Queensland Naturalists Club through the region when their paths crossed with those of two young female hikers. These women had come up from Sydney after reading about the region in a southern newspaper, much to the astonishment of their fellow wilderness seekers (in fact, Chisholm himself had written the article!).[24]

One of the most important identity aspects of the bushwalking conservation movement was the wilderness experience. Endurance bushwalks that lasted several days during which walkers had to rely on their own skills became part of the cultural bonds of the movement. Just as the field naturalists had their own symbols of identity, the knapsack and walking shoes identified the bushwalkers and the camping gear shop was their informal meeting ground. The language of Myles Dunphy's 'bush brotherhood' might resonate with images of Australian masculinity, but the bushwalkers emphasised the spiritual, scenic and character-building aspects of their bush experiences. This was a culture that women also came to share. The new woman was a significant part of the bushwalking movement's social base.

The evolution of women's involvement in bushwalking had not been an easy path. When Ethel Luth with two female friends set off on a bushwalk through Victoria's southern highlands one autumn day in 1909, the sight of young women on a walking trip was so rare that news of their venture travelled ahead of them; locals came out to greet them and to invite them into their cottages. As 'sleeping out for girls was "not done" in those days', the party had had to organise their accommodation beforehand and their Edwardian dresses were sent on ahead of them in a dress basket. By the end of the week the women had walked through snow and sunshine and covered over 250 kilometres. The following year the Melbourne Amateur Walking and Touring Club, whose membership was restricted to men, held its first Ladies Day for members' wives, relatives and 'lady friends'; it was not until 1922 that the Melbourne Women's Walking Club was finally launched. The new club relegated the MAWTC to 'the Men's Club' and bravely, given Victoria's climate, overcame notions that women should not sleep outdoors.[25]

New South Wales produced female bushwalkers whose feats earned them similar legendary status to that of their male counterparts. Dorothy Butler and Marie Byles enjoyed some outstanding treks, both in Australia and overseas. Byles's family background was progressive, but her love of bushwalking and mountain climbing took her to Asia where she discovered Eastern philosophy and Buddhism. She was born in 1900 to parents who were Fabian socialists and pacifists; her mother was a committed feminist. Her brother, Baldur Byles, had a career in that quintessential progressivist conservation cause, professional forestry. At the University of Sydney, study under the radical young Keith Duncan—whose agenda, according to one student, was 'The Reform of the Universe'—confirmed Marie's idealism. She studied law and became the first woman to be admitted as a solicitor in New South Wales in 1924. Besides her legal career, she was active in the women's movement; but her recreational outlet was bushwalking. Even this became a cause when she decided to campaign for the reservation of bushland on Pittwater in the 1930s, which became Bouddi National Park. She had joined the Sydney Bush Walkers and was the first editor of the *Bushwalker* in 1937. Her love of mountain climbing took her to New Zealand in the 1920s, and in 1928 she successfully scaled Mount Cook. In the 1930s she travelled to Asia and went mountain climbing in South China. Returning to Australia in the midst of the international tensions that led to World War II, she became active in the peace movement. Although injury later inhibited her mountaineering, she continued her annual trips to Mount Kosciuszko and her love of bushwalking was undimmed.[26]

The Queensland bushwalking community had some remarkable female participants too. Cyril White, appointed Queensland government botanist in 1917, was noted for his leadership of excursions for the Queensland Naturalist Club. He married Hattie Clark, who was herself a keen field naturalist and hiker, and was affectionately remembered for making her way to field outings on her motorcycle.[27] Despite professional scientific leadership, the Queensland Naturalists Club was

a community group with active female members, and a large party that
included several women camped at Lamington Plateau in late 1921.[28]
Irene Longman was perhaps the most remarkable of the women associated with the outdoors movement in Queensland. She married Heber
Longman, an avid field naturalist who was later appointed director of
the Queensland Museum, and whose early work she had assisted. She
listed walking as one of her recreations, was involved in the Parks and
Playgrounds Association and worked for the protection of native flora,
but her political achievement of being the first woman elected to the
Queensland parliament and her social welfare campaigns have overshadowed her environmental connections.[29]

In 1936 another young woman was about to discover that her passion
for bushwalking could not be divorced from commitment to national
parks. In the far south, young pianist Jessie Wakefield joined the Hobart
Walking Club. Eight years later she married a fellow member, Leo
Luckman, and the two of them played leading roles in the Tasmanian
bushwalking movement, exploring the most remote parts of the state,
developing new routes through difficult terrain, pioneering the club's
skiing activities, and shouldering executive responsibilities. Jessie was
one of the club's most outspoken conservationists and organised the
opposition to alienation of parts of Mount Field National Park and seal
culling on Macquarie Island in the 1930s.[30]

### Campaigns outside New South Wales

The impact of the bushwalking organisations on conservation goals
outside New South Wales was uneven. Victoria's first two national parks,
small areas at Fern Tree Gully in 1882 and Tower Hill in 1892 were set
aside on the grounds of public recreation. A request from the Bright
Alpine Club, supported by the local progress association, succeeded in
1898 in reserving the first part of what was to become Mount Buffalo
National Park. In late 1908 a coalition of interests had formed the
Victorian National Parks Association to promote more reservations
for national parklands, but it was short-lived. After World War I the
popularity of bushwalking in Victoria increased enormously. In 1934, in
response to the growth in bushwalking organisations, the Federation of
Victorian Walking Clubs was formed with an explicit commitment to
conservation; in the late 1930s it led protests to the government over
grazing in national parks and the need for primitive areas.[31]

In Queensland too there is considerable evidence of the growing
interest in bushwalking. While young Romeo Lahey was still trying
to interest the state government in his national park idea for the
Lamington Plateau, a party from the Railway Office Touring Club in

1911 went by train and tram to Beaudesert and Christmas Creek and then walked to the summit, the first of many walking parties who would explore the region. In the 1920s and 1930s among the increasing numbers of walkers and tourists who came to explore the southern highlands was the journalist Arthur Groom, whose dedication to the region soon approached that of Romeo Lahey.

When Arthur Groom first visited the McPhersons in 1927, he had just arrived from inland Australia. The shock of discovering sub-tropical jungle after his time in the dry west was immense and he became an immediate convert to the national parks cause. He recalled his first visit to the region:

> As I walked and scrambled through the Lamington National Park, sometimes with others, more often alone, I could but marvel at the contrast and grandeur, the concentration and beauty, the immense power and fertility of the soil, the tremendous variety of plant life, set aside in perpetuity for the benefit and enjoyment of the people. What foresight and vision! What great national outlook had been responsible?

Groom remained in the region lovingly exploring the mountains and writing articles on the area for the *Queenslander* and the *Brisbane Courier*. Three years later, when Lahey decided it was necessary to set up an organisation especially to campaign for national parks, he sought him out. Groom recalled their first meeting in Brisbane, when they sat in his old Ford car outside the boxing stadium in Charlotte Street, 'talking enthusiastically and cross-firing opinions, questions and answers, and finding we were both idealists of the obstinate type'. At a crowded public meeting in April 1930 they formed the National Parks Association of Queensland (NPAQ), with Lahey as president, Groom as secretary, and a strong committee of leading citizens, avid bushwalkers and scientists. Its first aim was to preserve national parks 'in their natural condition' and to secure new park areas.[32]

Some of Queensland's most indomitable bushwalkers were associated with Lamington Plateau and the NPAQ. Bernard O'Reilly's feats entered popular consciousness as a result of his persistent search for, and eventual rescue of, the survivors of the Stinson plane crash in the McPherson Ranges in 1937.[33] The NPAQ's regular field outings contributed to the development of recreational bushwalking in Queensland, and in the 1930s and 1940s the association felt obliged to remind its members that it was not a hiking or mountaineeering organisation and that these pursuits were secondary to its goal of protection of national parks.

One of the most remarkable treks in the association's history was made by Arthur Groom in the winter of 1931. He was helping to prepare

a camp outing for 200 people and, to finalise arrangements with the
property owner, completed a 112-kilometre walk through mountainous
country from O'Reilly's guest-house to west of Mount Lindesay. The
most extraordinary aspect was that most of it was done at night and in
just over twenty-four hours. Groom began his journey at twenty minutes
to midnight on the coldest night of the year:

> The moonlight on this cloudless, brilliant, and breathlessly still night had
> stolen down through the dense mass of domed foliage, and had filled the
> forest with its glow, so that all those living things not bewitched into
> immobility could move in cautious silence and wonder at it all, while the rest
> of the world slept. I was one of those living things, acutely conscious that I was
> perhaps the only human out of doors for many miles around. I walked out of
> the jungle and down open hill-sides, crossed murmuring streams, and went
> over mountain after mountain ridge, with a rapidity only possible by good
> physical condition and the crystallizing coldness of the night.[34]

Groom's journalism captures not only the physical achievement but the
communing with nature and the spiritual satisfaction that became the
hallmarks of bushwalking conservation.

The NPAQ had some important successes in the 1930s: additional
sections of the border ranges, the Glasshouse Mountains, parts of
Stradbroke Island, Tully Falls, Bellenden Ker, Herbert River Gorge,
Eungella and the Chillagoe caves in the north of the state all achieved
national park status following proposals developed by NPAQ. Girraween
and Carnarvon Gorge were also under discussion in this period. One of
their most important proposals started with a meeting of representatives
from the Great Barrier Reef Committee, the Field Naturalists, the Royal
Australasian Ornithologists Union (RAOU) and the Central Queensland Bird Protection Society in July 1931 to discuss the creation of
national parks for the islands of coastal Queensland. As a result national
parks were proclaimed in the Whitsunday island group in 1936, and
other unalienated islands were gazetted in the early 1940s.[35] Not all their
campaigns were won this easily. The NPAQ also had to fight a number of
defensive campaigns to protect national parks against plans for roads,
timber cutting, damage caused by military training in World War II, and
excisions for tourist developments. Even Lamington was not necessarily
secure. By the mid-1930s, Arthur Groom was already concerned about
population pressures in south-east Queensland affecting his beloved
national park, and he began to articulate his vision of the Scenic Rim—
a parkland of the entire McPherson Range from Point Danger on the
Pacific, inland to Cunningham's Gap, a wilderness of world standard.
He delivered the first drafts of his proposal to state and federal governments in 1941, but the plans would not come to fruition for another
half-century.[36]

Organised recreational bushwalking in South Australia was in a similar position to Queensland in the 1920s. Within the scientific societies which led South Australia's early conservation campaigns were individuals who had reputations as intrepid travellers. One was ornithologist Captain White, who (often accompanied by his first wife) undertook expeditions to Alice Springs, Cooper Creek, Darwin and the Nullarbor Plain between 1913 and 1922, using several modes of transport. After World War II another veteran conservationist and rambler, Warren Bonython, returned to Adelaide and commenced some of his marathon bushwalks around remote parts of the state. The Adelaide Bushwalkers supported calls for increases in national park reserves after World War II, and in the interwar period recreational interests had achieved some important conservation gains. The state government passed a National Pleasure Resorts Act in 1914 which reserved a number of small scenic areas near Adelaide. These parks were not the large primitive areas demanded by bushwalkers in the eastern states, but flora and fauna were protected. Concerned about the loss of the mallee lands which were increasingly being cleared for cultivation in the 1920s, and in particular the loss of habitat of the mallee fowl, Edwin Ashby, a veteran national parks campaigner and a former chair of the Royal Society's fauna and flora protection committee, began to press for a reserve of mallee scrub in the Murray region. Aware of the government's lack of interest in ecological arguments, Ashby resorted to resource use arguments—he even proposed the potential domestication and commercialisation of the mallee fowl—but his main argument rested on the potential of the mallee as a picnic spot and recreational area. In 1938, the South Australian government reserved the first part of what was to become the Ferries–McDonald Conservation Park.[37]

In Western Australia too recreational interests met with some conservation success. A lone woman, Frances Brockman, campaigned for the protection of the Margaret River Caves as a tourist attraction after the Lands Department reserved them in 1892. Later Winthrop Hackett of the Acclimatisation Society lobbied to have the area from the caves to the coastline declared a nature reserve.[38] But without an active national parks movement to defend primitive areas, park developments in Western Australia were dependent on the attitudes of local park boards. The lack of a community group fighting for national parks convinced Major Whittell, a member of the Western Australian Naturalists Club, of the need to take up the national parks cause, and in 1949 the Naturalists Club set up a Committee on Fauna and Flora Protection. The committee argued for the need for centralised control of national parks within a single department or authority, limits to

tourist facilities within parklands, and a management policy committed
to retaining areas in their natural state. Even without a broad national
parks movement prior to World War II, the community mood within
Perth was against development within parks, at least as far as the city's
large King's Park was concerned. Although sporting developments had
been allowed within the park's grounds from the turn of the century,
the park's board committed itself to a policy of flora preservation and
refused all applications for development. When in the 1950s the board
attempted to rescind this policy to allow a city council project, it met a
wall of resistance, including that of the state parliament which passed an
act to protect the flora values of the park. Other parks were dependent
on the goodwill and good sense of their board members: in the case of
many of the parks around Perth, this meant the leading bureaucrat
from each of the Premier's and Lands Departments, who made up the
State Gardens Board first formed in 1920. Owing to government
stringency, the board committed itself to a policy of no development in
parks, arguing that 'they need no embellishment beyond being made
available and, in some cases, restored to their pristine and natural
charm'.[39] Whether this was enlightened bureaucratic management or
pragmatic adjustment to funding constraints, the decision was consistent with the mood of the outdoor recreational movement of the
1920s and 1930s.

The bushwalking movement in Tasmania conformed to the stronger
pattern of eastern Australia, perhaps influenced by mainland bushwalkers who visited the island. Prior to the formation of the Hobart
Walking Club in 1929, individual bushwalkers had influenced the
establishment of some reserves. In 1914 the government botanist,
Leonard Rodway, and Herbert Nichols, a Hobart judge and politician,
who were both keen bushwalkers and had spent many years enjoying
rambling about the Russell Falls reserve area, proposed extending the
reserve to include Mount Field. Their appeal combined with recreational interests from as far away as Melbourne who were concerned
about timber-cutting in the area and overuse by visitors. In early 1914, a
group of diverse interests—representatives from scientific, patriotic and
tourism organisations—came together to form the National Park
Committee to fight for a national park of 9000 hectares, protected by
legislation, for the Mount Field area. In 1915 the new Labor
government agreed to proclaim a Russell Falls–Mount Field National
Park of 11,000 hectares and passed the Scenery Preservation Act to
reserve additional areas of natural beauty, scenic or historical interest.[40]

The national parks cause was to be boosted by the formation of the
Hobart Walking Club. The club modelled its rules on the Melbourne
Walking Club and consequently its objectives included a commitment to

promote the preservation of flora, fauna and natural scenery. Individual members played a direct role in the establishment of several of Tasmania's national parks. The club's founder and first president, E. T. Emmett, made direct representations in favour of Cradle Mountain–Lake St Clair National Park, which was gazetted in 1922. Then in 1933–34, after a party from the club had scaled Frenchman's Cap, they decided to join the moves to have this region protected; it was finally proclaimed in 1941.

As well as these gains, the club was forced into a number of defensive protests to protect conservation values. During the 1930s they successfully worked with fauna conservation groups (including some from the mainland) to stop commercial exploitation of seals on Macquarie Island, forcing the Tasmanian government to revoke a permit that it had issued to a Melbourne businessman. Lobbying to protect the integrity of Mount Field and Cradle Mountain–Lake St Clair National Parks was less successful. When the Hydro-Electric Commission proposed to dam Lake St Clair's outlet in the 1930s, the club took up the defence of the lake's beaches and inshore islets, but they were lost when the bushwalkers were defeated and the lake's level was raised.[41]

## The Promotion of Romantic Wilderness

Despite these disappointments, the bushwalking movement of eastern Australia increasingly played a leading role in conservation campaigns from the 1920s. The success of the bushwalking conservation movement was partly built upon the growth of the tourism industry, although the pattern was uneven across the country. The private sector was still small and relied on provision of infrastructure by government. For the most part infrastructure meant the vested interests of the railways departments. The railways were crucial to the development of the early outdoors movement, enabling city-dwellers to access the scenic bushland beyond the city limits; at the same time the leisure movement was also important to the railway departments, providing revenue for weekend operations and lines to low-density, outlying regions. In Tasmania, with only a small resident population and the most developed tourism sector in the country, the state government appreciated from an early stage the need for tourism to make the railway system economically viable. Fearing that private tourist agencies were favouring private coaches over rail, the state government took public control of Tasmania's tourist associations in 1914, establishing the Tasmanian Government Tourist Bureau which was to be run by the state's Railways Department.[42] There were thus strong financial reasons for the Tasmanian government to preserve scenic national park areas as tourist attractions, which it

commenced by passing the Scenery Preservation Act of 1915. It also
affirmed these linkages by appointing the new director of the tourist
bureau to the Scenery Preservation Board. The appointee turned out to
be a keen promoter of Tasmania's natural beauty, committed to further
expansion of the state's national parks; he was E. T. Emmett of the
Hobart Walking Club, a man who had a personal love of exploring
Tasmania's remote mountains and rivers.[43]

The most important contribution made by the railway departments
and the burgeoning tourism industry was through the railway maga-
zines, photographs and posters which were designed to promote rail
journeys to scenic places. These early marketing techniques assisted the
bushwalking and national parks cause by reinforcing and disseminating
a romantic and desirable image of Australia's bushlands. Once again
Tasmania led these developments by several decades, and this success
can be partly attributed to John Watt Beattie, state government photographer and a great lover of Tasmania's wild and beautiful places. In
many respects, of Australia's many founding conservationists, it is
Beattie who comes closest to the spiritual wilderness philosophy of
American John Muir. They were both Scottish-born but fell in love with
the landscape of their new lands and argued passionately for their
protection. Beattie's romanticism was expressed through his landscape photography. In the 1880s and 1890s he trekked through some
of Tasmania's most wild and rugged places carrying photographic
equipment weighing more than 27 kilograms. In later life he recalled
how 'nothing gives me greater delight than to stand on the top of some
high land, and look out on a wild array of our mountain giants. I am
struck dumb, but oh, how my soul sings.' Like Muir, he sensed the divine
in nature. In 1898 he undertook a trip through the rugged west coast,
ruefully anticipating the loss of wilderness when

> the solitude of the beautiful country would be broken by the shriek of the
> locomotive ... for what lover of nature can stand unmoved and contemplate
> her glories swept away by the tide of utilitarianism, the axe and the horrid
> sulphur fumes. Heaven grant that we may be able to retain many solitary
> places in this beautiful island of ours where nature in all her grandeur will
> reign supreme, and where sulphur fumes, and axes and jam tins will be
> forever unknown.

He gave papers before the Royal Society of Tasmania based on his
photographic expeditions to remote parts of the state, and endorsed the
society's calls for national parks. In 1899 the state government used
several of Beattie's landscape photographs for a series of postage stamps
to promote Tasmania's scenery nationally and internationally.[44]

The iconic value of the illustrations produced by new photographic
technology was quickly seized upon by conservation advocates. Beattie

was perhaps the first to use lantern slides to convince his audience of the beauty of remote areas and the need for their protection; he was followed by many other campaigners who appreciated the promotional value of the lantern slide to their campaigns. This approach was used by the Hobart Walkers Club in their campaign for Lake Pedder in the 1950s,[45] and by The Wilderness Society in the 1980s. The role of the sublime wilderness and wildlife photography in the modern conservation movement has its origins in the late nineteenth century.

### Moral Cause

For the nature conservationists of the early twentieth century, being outdoors and part of nature was not just a pleasurable recreation but a morally ennobling activity. From whichever stream of the movement, conservationists shared a progressivist faith in the national and personal benefits of nature worship. For Catton Grasby, open-air natural history lessons were intended to teach skills, and to develop students' powers of observation and reasoning as well as an appreciation for the wonders and beauty of nature.[46] For Frank Tate, the purpose of nature study was 'the fact, the meaning of the fact, and the wonder and the beauty of the fact'.[47] Thistle Harris, as secretary of the Tree Wardens League, defined children's appreciation of their native flora as part of developing their civic responsibility.[48] Outdoor recreation was believed to be a means of rational amusement for adults and for children. These ideas were central to the philosophies of both David Stead and Myles Dunphy, New South Wales contemporaries whose personalities clashed but who were both committed to conservation causes. Stead was dedicated to 'imparting to the community a love of nature and through that, a belief in goodness and justice'.[49] Dunphy was more utilitarian in his summation of the goals of bushwalking; in a journal entry he listed 'full application of all the senses, cultivation of faculty of observation, powers of endurance and self-reliance ... justify existence by appreciation of open air, life and rational way of living and by spreading the doctrine'.[50]

Thus, as well as the physical benefits of enjoying outdoor recreation, the nature conservationists of the early twentieth century also believed that there were mental, and even moral, benefits to be derived from this experience of nature. It was these aspects of the outdoor recreation groups that linked them closely to the last major interest group to fight for environmental rights, the public health and amenity advocates. Closely associated with urban environmentalism, this stream is usually seen as the weakest strand of the Australian conservation movement and often overlooked. Yet it is clear that urban groups were active at the turn

of the century and that the nature conservationists frequently looked to
them for support for their wilderness and fauna campaigns.

## Urban Reformers

Anxiety about physical and moral health was a product of conditions in
Australia's urban centres in the mid-nineteenth century. As colonial
governments progressively granted municipal status to each of the
capitals between 1838 and 1859, any power for overall planning was
significantly diminished and regulatory controls were weakened. These
problems of urban management were exacerbated by rapid population
growth and by local governments elected on restricted gender and
property franchises. The electoral system guaranteed the endorsement
of councillors with vested interests in favouring commercial priorities
over the public good. As colonial populations expanded, especially
during the boom of the 1880s, a plethora of small local councils were
proclaimed in the metropolitan regions, multiplying the administrative
units responsible for local infrastructure. At a time when the introduction of new technologies for urban transport and power required
greater regional co-ordination, parochial rivalries and demarcations
increased. The deterioration of the urban environment was rapid and
extreme. The absence of any communal system of drains and sewerage
or of regulation of noxious trades resulted in the pollution of ground,
water and air by human effluent, industrial and animal by-products,
smoke, and dust. Accounts of Australia's capital cities in the nineteenth
century emphasised the stench, the fouled pathways and foetid
waterways. Under these conditions disease was readily transferred and
epidemics of tuberculosis, scarlet fever, diarrhoea, diphtheria and
typhoid fever regularly swept the cities and towns in the second half of
the century. The most vulnerable were children under five. Infant
mortality in the urban centres was high. In the industrial suburbs of
Brisbane and Sydney in the 1870s and 1880s infant mortality
approached one in every two births—47 per cent in parts of Brisbane
and 46 per cent in parts of Sydney.[51] These rates were up to three times
higher than in the bush or in the United Kingdom for the same period.

   These material conditions were the catalyst for a number of individuals to become active in response to the social and environmental
problems that the cities created. Churchmen campaigned against the
inner-city slums on moral grounds; labour activists objected to the
state of working-class housing and suburbs; engineers, architects and
doctors protested against inadequate sanitation and building controls.
The 'problem' of Australia's nineteenth-century cities triggered extensive public debate on the themes of public health, social welfare,

temperance and morals, and urban pollution. Environmentalism was a central element of Victorian thinking and was drawn upon to explain this range of human and social problems which were encompassed by the catchcry of sanitarian reform.

### The Pollution Problem

Leading members of the medical profession focused on the specific issue of urban pollution; they were supported by community groups which formed to agitate on public health matters. The colony of Victoria had the Australian Health Society, founded in 1875 by the feminist and preacher Martha Turner, 'to educate public opinion' on sanitation issues. Although there were six medical men on the society's executive, it had a strong female membership and the organisation was affiliated with the Ladies Sanitary Association of Britain. The Tasmanian Women's Sanitary Association, although active more than a decade after the Victorian group, was probably in the same tradition.[52] The Health Society attempted to appeal to the broader public with talks in working-class suburbs as well as meetings specifically for women on matters of household and city hygiene. In 1887, when a severe typhoid outbreak gripped Melbourne, its membership reached 360.[53] Public agitation was also strong in New South Wales, where the problems of sewerage, housing, manufacturing wastes and water figured prominently in the press; they peaked in 1875, when a board was appointed to investigate the combined problems, and rose again in the mid-1880s in the face of inaction from the colonial government. The Sanitary Reform League attracted prominent New South Wales citizens in the 1880s, at a time when some local residents were doing battle with owners of noxious industries at the municipal level.[54] Brisbane too had its residents' associations opposed to nightsoil dumping and polluting industries in their areas. Dr John Thomson of the Central Board of Health led the city's medical profession in protests over government failure to control urban pollution. When the Intercolonial Medical Congress met in Melbourne in 1889, during the city's worst outbreak of typhoid, it used the occasion to condemn Melbourne's 'contaminated water supply, defective drainage, and improper disposal of nightsoil'.[55] These combined forces were successful in placing these matters on the political agenda of all colonies, as demonstrated by the numerous inquiries, reports, royal commissions and select committees on sewerage, water supply, noxious trades and sanitary conditions between 1860 and World War I.[56]

Stalling effective reform was an array of political and economic interests which has always made urban environmental problems difficult to resolve. There was political opposition from municipal councils who were not prepared to relinquish control of local matters to central authorities, and from central authorities who were not prepared to enforce controls despite their powers. One member of the Queensland parliament, the Hon. W. Wood, declared in 1866 that 'he could not see why, if the inhabitants of a town chose to be dirty, the Ministry should step in to prevent them'. Despite the complaints and appeals of medical men and the petitions of Brisbane residents about Brisbane's sanitation, two decades later the conservative politician McIlwraith gutted the colony's Health Act because he was 'of the opinion that the conservation of the public health should not be the function of central government but should be left entirely to the local bodies elected by the ratepayers'.[57] McIlwraith was allied with Queensland's pastoral and financial interests and perhaps, like his counterparts in other colonies, sought to protect from regulation the 'burgeoning trade in hides, tallow and meat' which was a major contributor to urban pollution.[58] Businesses resisted relocation; when they did agree to move away from densely populated areas and waterways, they opposed regulation of their methods, construction and outfalls. Residents' groups which objected to industry in their area on grounds of public health and amenity were opposed by the employees who feared job losses. Given the evidence concerning work and factory conditions in this era and the impact of poorly regulated industries on the surrounding working-class suburbs, one of the most misplaced alliances was surely that between the noxious traders and their employees. Yet there were instances in Melbourne and Brisbane when workers defended their industries against interference from the urban campaigners, dismissing criticisms of suburban pollution as class prejudice against working-class areas.[59]

Also splintering the political will for reform was the ambivalent attitude of the community. While residents disliked the smells and stenches and feared they might be the next household to be visited by the fevers and disease, ratepayers were reluctant to pay for the required infrastructure for a regional system of water supply and sewage disposal. Reformers were also divided over solutions for sanitation problems. In New South Wales, Chief Justice Sir James Martin prophetically opposed the sewerage system planned for Sydney because of concerns about the pollution of Sydney's beaches. Similarly, Queensland's first board of health opposed the introduction of sewerage in the 1870s because of concerns about turning the colony's tidal rivers into 'main sewers'.[60] Consequently it took four to five decades of political agitation for these fundamental problems of urban pollution and planning to be resolved.

*Animal Protection*

A trip from Melbourne to Geelong by steamer was like sailing down a sewer, wrote Louisa Meredith in 1861, but her horror at the pollution of the Yarra River was matched by her disgust at the mistreatment of domestic animals in the city environment. Cruelty to animals, Meredith wrote, was 'a moral pestilence throughout the land'.[61] Nineteenth-century urban life was heavily reliant upon animals, and by the 1870s industry had escaped the animal cruelty laws as effectively as it had escaped pollution controls. Sheep, pigs and cattle were held in filthy pens and yards for up to a week, often unfed and diseased, awaiting slaughtering. Cutting inflicted great suffering as it was carried out while some animals were still alive. Oxen hauled huge loads, horses pulled cabs, carriages and buses, and milking cows were kept in unhygienic conditions within city boundaries.[62] Effluent from animal pens, offal from slaughter yards and animal carcasses ended up in the waterways, along with the other detritus of nineteenth-century civilisation. Although the degraded treatment of animals was not restricted to the urban environment, it assaulted the senses there, along with noise, odour and visual pollution. Exploitation and cruelty to animals were part of the 'mental pollution' of the city which reformers like Meredith sought to clean up. A bad environment was believed to contribute to weakened physical and moral health and in turn produce a meanness of spirit in the city-dweller. Animal protectionists sought to reverse the process—educating people for kindness would raise their character, which in turn would elevate the whole community. Societies for the prevention of cruelty to animals were formed in each of the eastern colonies in the 1870s and in Western Australia in 1892.[63] As in the sanitarian reform groups, women were prominent in the animal protection organisations.[64] For Louisa Meredith, our treatment of dumb creatures was a trial and test of our own hearts. Animal protection was the epitome of nineteenth-century environmentalist ideology, resting on the belief that human surroundings affect temperament, morals and actions, and vice versa. Although some of its supporters also called for habitat protection for native animals, its main contributions, like the animal rights movement a century later, were to assert the rights of animals and to challenge human relationships with other species.

*Open Space*

If cruelty to animals diminished the humans who daily witnessed it, the mean and narrow alleys of the inner city slums, bereft of open space and fresh air, were also believed to be harmful to residents' physical, moral and mental health. There were a number of responses to this social and environmental problem. In Melbourne in the 1870s public campaigns in defence of parkland were vehement. When the Victorian minister for lands and agriculture decided to excise portions of Melbourne's Royal and Albert Parks for land sales in 1875, he provoked an uproar. A public meeting supposedly attracted 10,000 protestors and when the government pressed ahead with the sales, the auctions were disrupted by noisy demonstrators. In 1881 when the government wanted to build a road through another Melbourne park and excise sections of Edinburgh Gardens, public anger finally forced a backdown.[65] Others focused their concern on child welfare rather than environmental reform, like Dr Philip Muskett who proposed filling a barge with children from the inner city and towing it out to sea each day to ensure that they had some fresh air. This proposal is not altogether different from that of the New South Wales politician, Richard Arthur, who founded the Sunshine Club in 1924 to organise picnic holidays for slum children. While the city environment degraded its inhabitants, it was believed that fresh air, open space, exercise and the natural environment had the power to uplift the individual. By the turn of the century new organisations to promote urban parks were active. Some groups, like the Parks and Playground Associations which were formed just prior to World War I, agitated for open space in the city for children's play areas and playground equipment for structured recreation. Others, like the National Fitness Councils established in the 1930s, argued for reservations of urban land for sporting activities to improve health through physical training. While these groups lobbied to improve cities through the provision of public space, they also developed direct links with nature conservationists and supported their campaigns for national parks.[66] Although their language echoed the moral concerns and class fears of their day, these groups clearly saw themselves as part of a broader nature preservation movement.

By the turn of the century sustained public pressure in the face of public health crises had resulted in the development of rudimentary administrative machinery to deal with the basic problems of urban water and waste. The Victorian government had appointed Dan Gresswell as medical inspector to the new Victorian Board of Health and James Mansergh as sanitary engineer; in Sydney the outbreak of bubonic plague forced the New South Wales government to give consulting engineer George McCredie extraordinary powers to clean up the harbour, wharf frontages, and affected suburbs. In the wake of the 1919 Spanish influenza epidemic, the Commonwealth also established a department of health with expertise in industrial hygiene and sanitary engineering. The basic sanitarian message was becoming incorporated into new departments and government policy.

*Town Planning*

These developments released urban conservationists from immediate pollution problems, enabling them to address bigger questions of town planning. This change in direction was exemplified by a public meeting co-organised by George Taylor in 1909. Taylor, a former cartoonist for the *Bulletin* in the 1890s, was an *art nouveau* builder, draftsman, and building industry magazine publisher. The meeting attracted leading working-class activists and middle-class reformers of the day, such as Billy Hughes, Octavius Beale, J. D. Fitzgerald, T. R. Bavin and John Sulman; it called for a 'greater Sydney'. Its outcome was the Royal Commission for the Improvement of Sydney and its Suburbs, which acknowledged the need for unified urban planning. Taylor became disillusioned with the royal commission, but he proved his commitment to the issue by helping to establish an institute of local government engineers in 1909 and the Town Planning Association of New South Wales in 1913. Some of the goals of the association were to press for building and planning controls, parks and playgrounds, and anti-pollution measures.[67]

The catchcry of the town planning movement was the Garden City and it had talented and enthusiastic supporters around the country. The leading national figure was John Sulman, an architect and former president of the British Architectural Association who migrated to Australia in the 1880s. In 1890, he presented a paper to the second conference of the Australasian Association for the Advancement of Science on the duty of the state to restrict the rights of private property owners for the sake of public health. In fact Sulman had been involved in establishing the Australasian Association for the Advancement of Science (AAAS) in 1887 and consequently it had an Architecture and Town Planning Section a quarter of a century before the popular town planning movement began to gather momentum around the country.[68]

As Australian urban reformers increasingly turned their attention to problems of housing, traffic, and parks and playgrounds, they sought inspiration from overseas where these same questions were provoking similar community movements. In 1912 a Melbourne physician, James Barrett, attended the American Medical Association Congress where he heard US President Woodrow Wilson speak on the social duty of medics in 'the great ameliorating movements' of the day. The following year he was in London, where he observed the development of the Garden City Movement. He returned to Australia determined to push Melbourne's public health beyond Dan Gresswell's reforms, arguing that the public board of health should include an engineer and an architect as well as doctors, and that it should address a diversity of issues that affect the urban environment, from town planning to smoke abatement and food supplies. He promoted these ideas through public lectures in which he expanded on the need for town planning. In 1914 he helped to form the Victorian Town Planning and Parks Association. This new group amalgamated Victoria's first National Parks Association (of which Barrett had been secretary) and an urban group, the Anti-Slum Committee. It was committed to improved housing, retention of urban open space, protection of flora and fauna in permanent reserves, and 'all things allied ... to the provision of healthy and reasonable surroundings of people during work and leisure'.[69] In December, Barrett sailed for Egypt as a doctor with the AIF, but he returned to Australia after the war with his commitment to community service undimmed. In the interwar years he served as president of the Victorian Town Planning Association, and continued to promote the need for city playgrounds and national parks, arguing on ecological, aesthetic, utilitarian and humanist grounds. Barrett viewed Australia's problems from an ecological perspective; under his leadership the Town Planning Association had a sub-committee dedicated to nature and heritage protection, and he committed the organisation to supporting a number of national park campaigns as well as initiating their own park proposals.[70]

Australians also had direct contacts with the British and European Garden City movement, and a Perth representative attended the Imperial Health and Town Planning Conference in 1913. The following year the secretary of the International Garden Cities and Town Planning Association, C. C. Reade, toured Australia and New Zealand; in the wake of his visit the South Australian Town Planning and Housing Association was formed in 1914 and the Western Australian Town Planning Association in 1916. Enthusiasm for the movement was strong enough to enable two Australasian conferences on town planning to be held during the war, in 1917 in Adelaide and in 1918 in Brisbane.[71]

Although a third conference planned for Sydney in 1920 did not eventuate because of a lack of government financial support, the movement was by no means dead. The greatest success was Walter Burley Griffin's win in the design competition for the new national capital in 1912. Unfortunately his commitment to making the natural landscape central to his planning and architecture was not imitated by state authorities outside Canberra, and the best town planning ideas were left to private initiative. Burley Griffin developed the Sydney suburb of Castlecrag around native bushland and reserves. Richard Arthur established a project to help build cottages for returned servicemen at French's Forest and, under John Sulman's influence, went on to sponsor the planned suburb of Matraville. Another Sulman supporter, real estate agent Richard Stanton, developed the suburbs of Haberfield and Rosebery. In 1915 Sulman, with support from J. D. Fitzgerald, developed Daceyville as a garden suburb. The movement continued to range beyond style and aesthetics—George Taylor, for example, took the opportunity to study urban waste disposal during an overseas tour in the interwar period.[72]

The movement faltered with the retirement of Sulman and the 1930s depression and war. By the end of World War II, governments were forced to establish statutory planning authorities in the face of mounting housing, industrial and traffic demands. By then rapid development and growth threatened to obliterate significant colonial heritage sites, which became the new focus for urban concern and triggered the formation of state-based National Trusts in the 1950s.[73] The achievement of more than seventy years of urban environmentalist activity was twofold: it established the principle that industry and speculators did not have unrestrained rights—residents had the right to be protected from harmful urban pollution; and it helped to establish the administrative machinery required to regulate and control this pollution.

Like their parks and fitness colleagues, urban planners viewed themselves as part of a wider environment movement and had networks and memberships of organisations in all streams. Walter Burley Griffin was a member of David Stead's Wild Life Preservation Society, while Stead was also a part of George Taylor's network. In Queensland Dr Tom Price, a good friend of Alec Chisholm's, campaigned on public health issues in his town of Toowoomba, submitted a garden city plan for the new industrial suburb of Darra to the 1918 Town Planning Conference, had associations with wildlife protection dating back to 1909, and also campaigned for the creation of additional national parks among the border ranges of Queensland. In Victoria, the Town Planning Association had a section devoted to the national parks cause and a president, James Barrett, who also presided over the playground associations. Barrett was described by a contemporary as 'a pioneer in all the things that one could think of by which the human race might be bettered and improved', and in 1925 he edited the first book on Australian conservation; all four streams of the Australian movement— national parks, wise resource use, fauna and flora protection, and city parks and playgrounds—were incorporated into the text.[74]

### Four Streams, One Movement

In 1902 the Queensland novelist Rosa Praed published *Fugitive Anne: A Romance of the Unexplored Bush*. The novel resonates with contemporary social concerns: the heroine runs away from a brutal husband, finds refuge in the Australian bush with her Aboriginal companion, and falls in love with a Danish scientist who had come to Australia to study the native tribes and indigenous fauna.[75] Despite the prominent position Praed gives to her heroine's love of the bush and her scientist-hero, later historians, sociologists and geographers have downplayed the significance of the Australian environment movement at the beginning of the century.

Yet participants at the time clearly believed they were a part of a movement. The South Australian Native Flora and Fauna Protection Committee had been reporting on new developments in the fauna and flora 'movement' from 1891. *Emu* magazine reported on 'the international movement for the proper protection of birds', and the AOU described itself as a leader in 'the movement of bird protection'. Myles Dunphy wrote of the 'bushwalking conservation movement', Arthur Groom of the 'National Parks movement'.[76] So while there was no mass mobilisation to bring the four streams together—biological preservation, resource conservation, national parks and urban issues —early environmentalists defined themselves narrowly by their own specific causes.

Within the four streams, however, there were patterns of growth, consolidation, resolution of demands or failure, followed by withdrawal to organisational maintenance or disbandment, typical of social movement development.

The political impact of urban issues in each of the colonies indicates that the sanitarian campaigners were beginning to raise public awareness of sanitation and public health from the 1870s, and that the reformers had to sustain public pressure until effective bureaucratic processes under the leadership of experts were institutionalised in the first decade of the twentieth century. As improved regulatory mechanisms were put in place, leadership of the urban movement fell to the town planners; their influence peaked during and immediately after World War I before they retreated to narrow professional concerns in the 1930s.

Sustainable resource use groups, such as the acclimatisation societies, formed in the 1860s and linked up effectively with the scientists in the 1870s to push the public debate on forests (see Chapter 1). Even after the issue of bureaucratic management of state forests had been won, the emasculation of the forestry departments forced the formation of new defensive groups, but the capture of the departments by development interests continued. The resignation of Lane-Poole, the removal of David Stead and Harold Swain, and the campaign against Griffith Taylor marked the decline and retreat of utilitarian resource conservation by 1932.

Scientists were more successful in other fields of conservation. Between 1880 and World War I they led the movement for national parks, despite tentative organisational beginnings in some colonies and regions. Their most successful political intervention was convincing the federal government to use customs powers to control the export of Australian fauna and avifauna. The partial political resolution of fauna protection triggered new groups such as the Wild Life Preservation Society and the Gould League, determined to push for greater protection and public awareness of native birds and animals.

In the 1920s these two groups worked with recreational interests, who from this period on assumed leadership in conservation, centring their efforts on the defence of existing parklands and the promotion of new ones. They successfully mobilised around bushwalking and field naturalist interests in the interwar period, providing the framework of Australia's national park system until their campaigns were disrupted by World War II.

The limitations of first-wave conservationists were consistent with the material conditions in which they were operating, rather than any failure to understand ecological limits. When Dudley Le Souef told the annual conference of the AOU in 1909 that 'Queensland and Western Australia do not need sanctuaries nearly as much as the other States mentioned, they being so much more sparsely populated',[77] it was because the ecological threat was simply not of the same magnitude as it would be sixty years later.

While there was no mass mobilisation of conservationists under the environmental banner, they did not operate only at the elite level of national and state politics. From the last quarter of the nineteenth century, when the scientific societies and field naturalists underwent a revival, Australian popular attitudes to nature were turned on their head. One rainy day in 1916, Norbert O'Reilly, newly enlisted in the AIF, was home on his final leave before sailing for France. Norb was a bushman; his father had been a drover and pioneered the family's selection in the Blue Mountains; his younger brothers, sisters and mother would go on to pioneer a new selection from sub-tropical jungle on the McPherson Range in Queensland. While his mother and father farewelled him, his younger brother, thirteen-year-old Bernard, raced off in the rain up the range behind the town of Megalong to gather waratahs for Norb to take away with him. By the time of World War I, the notions that rare native animals had a right to protection and that the public had a right to national parks had become widely accepted. Love of Australia's native environment had come to be a crucial element of Australian patriotism, so that Norb, standing 185 centimetres tall in his manly digger's uniform, could accept a bunch of wildflowers from his young brother as a memento of home and country.[78]

Although the role of environmentalists was secondary to that of the labour and women's movements, they too were the brokers of the Australian settlement. The first-wave conservation movement not only

successfully intervened in national political life, it also achieved that
other criterion of successful social movement activity: it changed the
culture and values of Australian attitudes to the environment. When
environmentalists of the 1960s and 1970s provoked moral outrage over
mining in national parks or pollution of waterways or the slaughter of
Australian native animals, they were building on the legacy of more than
a half-century of environmental activism. As a result of these first-
wave campaigns, Australians had come to believe that the sanctity of
national parks, healthy cities, and protection of native animals were
their birthright.

# PART II

# The Second Wave Builds:
# World War II to 1972

The first-wave environment movement declined substantially in the aftermath of World War II. The material problems to which the movement is a response remained, but two other factors required for successful social movement mobilisation were diminished.[1]

Firstly, the social base of the movement had dissipated. The scientists and professionally trained resource managers who had been such an influential component of the early movement were now incorporated into the bureaucratic structures of the movement's making. The other important movement recruiting ground, the outdoor recreation groups, were suffering a temporary decline in numbers as growing car ownership and weekend driving trips rivalled traditional bushwalking.

The other factor was the restriction of legitimate spheres of citizen action that the Cold War engendered. Feminists and peace movement supporters in Australia found themselves increasingly isolated as their social criticism was interpreted as communist subversion.[2] The politics of domesticity created an unfavourable environment for social movement activity.[3] National park and bushwalking groups did not disappear—in fact some new associations were formed—but they restricted themselves to narrow park goals and defence of prewar gains.

The economic growth and technological developments of the postwar period were creating new environmental problems, however, and when the revived agenda of the international environment movement reached Australia, a growing number of Australians was receptive to its message. The most dramatic events of the international movement in this period were pollution crises that affected Western industrial centres in the 1950s and 1960s. In 1962 the American writer Rachel Carson published *Silent Spring*.[4] Carson was a trained marine scientist who in the postwar period became increasingly disturbed about the widespread application of new synthetic pesticides, especially DDT. Her book was not only a wonderful piece of nature writing but also an attack on the chemical industry and the collusion of 'independent' scientists with chemical companies which were a major source of research funding. *Silent Spring* chronicles the impact of DDT on the food chain and the disastrous effects of bioaccumulation; Carson's spring was silent because of the destructive effects of organochlorines on bird life. The book's great achievement was its ability to reach a popular readership. It was on the *New York Times* best-seller list for thirty-one weeks in 1962;[5] it triggered a public debate on pesticides that reached right around the world. As if to confirm the nature of the threat that Carson had outlined, in 1964 the world witnessed the deaths and incapacitation of Japanese who had eaten mercury-contaminated fish from the Agano River.[6]

The pollution threat was reinterpreted by Australian activists to suit the differing material conditions that operated here. The new investment pressures in Australia were not so much from the chemical industry as from expansion of resource extraction industries. It was the threat of pollution to the Great Barrier Reef by oil exploration that triggered the first major campaign in Australia since the 1930s. There were four other major struggles that would rebuild and remobilise the Australian movement as a force in national politics.

The remobilising of the movement was a painful process both internally and externally. The structures that first-wave conservationists had fought so hard for—the advisory committees, forestry departments, park boards and so on—were to prove inadequate against the resource demands of powerful overseas companies and powerful state authorities. Nor were governments as open to polite deputations and the well-researched lobbying that had been a feature of early Australian conservationists' strategies. No amount of letter-writing was going to convince a government willingly to forgo investment dollars or to risk being perceived as anti-development. The closure or inadequacy of traditional institutional processes led to the radicalisation of conservationists. The old protest forms and strategies of the first-wave movement would have to be jettisoned. The only strategy left to environmentalists was to take their moral arguments to the general public. They would have to educate the Australian people through direct appeal, and debate with governments not in private meetings or in the corridors of parliament but in the public space of civil society.

These developments were as painful for the movement as they were for the governments of the day. Old movement supporters, committed to listening politely to government 'experts', found their methods angrily rejected at noisy meetings. The failure of governments to protect the public good led to an anti-bureaucratic sentiment among the modern movement that was alien to some first-wave movement supporters who had had to fight for rational decision-making by experts against political opportunism. Now state facilitation of industry would make bureaucracy an enemy of the movement.

Even the language of the old movement was rejected. 'Conservation' and 'preservation' were inadequate concepts when dealing with chemical contamination or ocean pollution. The new activists, influenced by United States debates, began to identify themselves as 'environmentalists'. This term, however, failed to encapsulate complex inter-relationships and was soon challenged by the more abstract notion of ecology.

The speed with which this internal revolution was effected was a product of a new 'radicalising historical sequence'. A new generation was revivifying the movement's social base; their political values and moral frameworks were a product not just of their own experience of environmental conflict but also of modern reflexivity. They would learn from the failures and successes of other contemporary movement actors.

Chapter 3 begins with a review of movement activity in the period from World War II to the early 1960s that emphasises the extent of the incorporation of the movement. It then discusses the development of political strategy in five campaigns that were waged in the eastern states and the interaction of these campaigns with Australia's only nationwide conservation organisation in this era, the Australian Conservation Foundation. These campaigns affected movement development around the country and raised the environmental consciousness of Australians, who were also made aware of the limits of the federal political structure.

# CHAPTER 3

# *Old Meets New*

The lesson Australia's labour and women's movements learned from World War I was that government would try to use a national emergency to prevent social policy reforms. In World War II these movements were determined to use the emergency to their own advantage. In offering the federal government their full support, the social movements exacted some promises about involvement in postwar reconstruction. The peace movement fared least well in wartime politics. Although Prime Minister Curtin indirectly acknowledged the strength of anti-conscription sentiment, the peace movement was undercut by his historic compromise which extended the definition of compulsory military service for home defence. The trade unions tested public sympathy by pressing their demands even at the height of crisis in 1942, but also contributed plans for postwar reconstruction. The demand for women's war work presented the women's movement with a historic opportunity. In 1943, in the middle of the war, ninety-three women's groups came together in the Women's Charter Conference to draw up a plan for women in postwar Australia.[1] If the personal response of the Queensland National Parks Association's Arthur Groom to the war were typical, the conservation movement responded with less confidence, reflecting its place in the shadows of these larger movement mobilisations. In the aftermath of Dunkirk, Groom reflected that

> The whole National Park idea was to a certain extent in the melting-pot. What would emerge? Were National Parks to be considered unnecessary luxury during war-time? So much of the old goodwill had gone into service ... Was it essential that the remaining civilians should have holidays while others were being blasted to bits elsewhere, starved, tortured, murdered, and were suffering physical and mental illness?[2]

Groom's last question was rhetorical—his own personal belief was that wilderness had become essential to counterbalance the negative effects that industrial civilisation produced, of which war provided the most extreme examples. Many national parks around the country did become degraded as a consequence of the war—some because they were used for military training, others through the direction of state funds and management to more urgent priorities. However, national planning for postwar reconstruction also provided the conservation movement with an opportunity to influence postwar outcomes; Arthur Groom prepared his scenic rim proposal for the Queensland–New South Wales border and submitted it to several state and federal departments in May 1941.[3]

### The First Wave Ebbs

The war did not demobilise Australia's social movements but encouraged them to defer their plans. The late 1940s were marked by an activism and idealism in which the conservationists shared. In Victoria, Ros Garnet re-established the Field Naturalists Club of Victoria's nature conservation committee under the title of the National Parks and National Monuments Sub-Committee. In the 1920s as a young man, Garnet had spent his summer holidays touring Victoria by bicycle and camping out at night. As his love of Victoria's natural environment developed, he often spent his weekends in the Dandenongs or walking, cycling or catching the train to other bushland areas further afield. In 1941 his love of natural history and his commitment to conservation stimulated him to join the Field Naturalists Club of Victoria. In 1946 the club convened a conference to discuss the rehabilitation of Victoria's national parks and from that Garnet's sub-committee compiled a report on the national parks system.[4]

From there, things moved slowly. Further conferences were held; the government acknowledged the importance of parks legislation but could not enact it. Finally, in 1952 the Victorian National Parks Association (VNPA) was formed to press specifically for legislation to protect the parks. This was no radical organisation. Fewer groups were involved in its founding than had been involved in national park campaigns in the 1930s; the minister for agriculture launched the new group; and its goals were defensive. Having won the parks before the war, the movement had to struggle to defend their integrity with legislative protection. In the end the Victorian National Parks Association won—not because of vigorous campaigning, but because the government acknowledged the need to rehabilitate the parks in the lead-up to the Olympic Games to be held in Melbourne in 1956. The government invited submissions from the association for parks legislation, and in 1957 appointed its president to be the first director of the National Parks Authority. The association had reached its goal of institutionalisation of national parks into Victoria's political processes.[5]

This pattern of reinvolvement, followed by disappointment and at least partial institutionalisation, was also evident in Tasmania. The Hobart Bushwalkers were forced almost immediately into a campaign to prevent the alienation of more than 2000 hectares of high-quality woodland from Mount Field National Park for logging by Australian Newsprint Mills. It became the most important struggle of the Tasmanian conservation movement to that date, a campaign in which patriotic and conservation groups joined with the government's own Scenery Preservation Board to defend Tasmania's national park system from forest exploitation. An action committee was formed, petitions raised, and letters sent to unsympathetic newspapers—the excision was, after all, for hardwood for newsprint. When the government introduced a bill to override its own Scenery Preservation Board, the public debate erupted inside parliament. The legislation was sent to a Select Committee of Inquiry to which the Field Naturalists, Hobart Walking Club, Australian Natives Association, Country Women's Association, and Scenery Preservation Board made objections. After this three-year struggle, the government proceeded with the excision in 1949.[6] It was a gloomy outcome for the conservation movement in a year that marked a turning-point towards the conservatism of the Cold War both internationally and nationally.

Yet in 1954 the club successfully submitted a proposal to the Scenery Preservation Board for the proclamation of Lake Pedder as a national park. The Lake Pedder proclamation in 1955 highlights two interesting developments that would affect the movement in the coming years. Firstly, the remote lake became an issue for outdoor recreationists because the Aero Club of Southern Tasmania was able to land passengers and supplies there in the summer.[7] Postwar prosperity and technology were diversifying people's leisure habits in ways that were about to rekindle enthusiasm for outdoor adventure; by the late 1950s caving, mountaineering, snow-skiing and canoeing were resurgent, and new specialist clubs were being formed. These groups were not founded on the conservationist ethic of the original bushwalking clubs of Australia's south-eastern states but, when their places of recreation came under threat from new development proposals in the 1960s and 1970s, many of them were to become radicalised and active in the wilderness preservation cause. Secondly, the readiness with which the board approved the park, even when it knew the Hydro-Electric Commission had developmental interests in the south-west, suggests it was prepared to allow national parks to be revoked in the aftermath of the Australian

Newsprint Mills excision.[8] For the conservation movement, the easy gain lulled it, and the community, into a false sense of security.

The great postwar achievement in New South Wales was the passage of the Fauna Protection Act in 1948. This legislation finally had an emphasis on habitat protection after years of lobbying for such an approach by the Wild Life Preservation Society. It also required a Fauna Protection Panel to be established to recommend new fauna reserves. The panel illustrated the dilemmas of incorporation for social movement activists. Committed to seeing the goal of fauna conservation carried into action, a movement representative sat on the panel only to discover that implementation for the legislation was under-resourced and unsupported by other government agencies. Allen Strom represented the Wild Life Preservation Society and the Sydney Bushwalkers on the panel, which had no field staff before 1954 and a battle on its hands with the Lands Department for any piece of land it nominated for a faunal reserve. The panel's response to these stringencies was to try to win public support by establishing local community flora and fauna societies. The Fauna Protection Panel also organised a nature conservation conference in 1955, providing a secretariat and chairman, and out of this the Nature Conservation Council of New South Wales was created. The Nature Conservation Council began to raise the issue of national parks legislation for the state and in 1957 a new group evolved, the New South Wales National Parks Association, which brought together the bushwalking and nature conservation streams of the movement under the first presidency of the veteran bushwalker Paddy Pallin. Government-facilitated societies were symptomatic of the growing incorporation of the movement in the 1950s. Conservationists became used to working alongside government employees and with agendas set by governments. Allen Strom regarded the stimulation of local groups and the indirect establishment of the Nature Conservation Council as among the most successful outcomes of the Fauna Protection Panel. Yet the dilemma of institutionalisation was to be personally experienced by Allen Strom. By the 1960s he was Chief Guardian of Fauna for the state and chair of the Fauna Protection Panel. His successes were not necessarily regarded warmly by government—Lands Minister Tom Lewis regarded him as a 'fanatic'—and his position was abolished under the new National Parks and Wildlife Act of 1967.[9]

The Victorian movement was probably more incorporated than any other state because of the large role played by resource conservation groups. In the aftermath of a royal commission into the 1939 bushfires, a Save the Forests Campaign was developed to educate the public on the benefits of forests. The campaign comprised a number of government bodies, municipal councils and government departments. District committees were established to promote forestry and undertake local tree-planting. In 1951 the campaign transformed itself into the Natural Resources Conservation League, a non-profit company with a commitment to all forms of natural resource conservation. With government backing, the league grew to be one of the largest and best-funded of Victoria's conservation groups.[10] Locating the league within a social movement framework is difficult. The league essentially played a public education role for government authorities, although events in the 1960s would see it involved in one of the period's most important campaigns.

The extent of demobilisation was evident in the movement's lack of response to Australia's hosting of the British nuclear tests off the Western Australian coast and in Central Australia from 1952 to 1963. No doubt the isolation and stigma that befell peace activists of this period was noticed.[11] In this era of unofficial censorship, attacks were not just ideological in content but assumed all sorts of gender and sexual smears. Rachel Carson did not publish *Silent Spring* until 1962, but the weight of this politically charged and intolerant atmosphere still weighed heavily on her. With scientific credentials, middle-aged and leading a quiet personal life, she appeared an unlikely target for a smear campaign. But the world was still in the grip of the Cold War and riddled with ideological fears. Carson was accused of trying to sabotage the American food production industry. One chemical group spent a quarter of a million US dollars ridiculing her as 'a hysterical fool'. Another representative of the industry was even more bitter in his use of sexual politics: 'I thought she was a spinster ... What's she so worried about genetics for?' Her publisher was targeted, and sponsors withdrew support for a television documentary. Even the *Audubon Magazine* was threatened with legal action if it published excerpts of her book. Scientists and professionals with a background in the chemical industry who were also members of conservation organisations protested against the US environment movement's support for the book; one prominent member of the wilderness organisation the Sierra Club resigned over the issue.[12]

In Australia, environmentalists attest to the personal impact of Rachel Carson's book,[13] but this did not translate into immediate practical campaigns. In the early 1960s the movement continued to pursue only narrowly defined goals. Even in the cities, where modernisation was beginning to have a dramatic impact on the urban landscape, the movement politely raised its voice mainly over the destruction of historic buildings. The National Trusts began to form in the various states in this period—Sydney, not surprisingly, was the first and the other states followed throughout the 1950s, with Tasmania and Queensland last in 1960 and 1963 respectively.[14]

The bigger questions of technological impact were not seriously addressed by the movement in this period; in fact, science had never been as glamorous and exciting as it appeared in the twenty years after World War II. Scientists were in demand, and they withdrew from movement organisations. Many of the scientific groups which had originally been involved in conservation issues before the war retreated to narrow professional concerns. The break between professional and amateur was stronger than ever. In 1959 the Field Naturalists Section of the Royal Society of South Australia left the society to form an autonomous organisation. In New South Wales, in the midst of a number of conservation battles that had dominated public debate around the country, the president of the Royal Zoological Society of New South Wales felt compelled to reformulate the society's policy position on conservation. Noting that the society's constitution committed it to faunal conservation, he nonetheless proposed 'that council agree that it should not associate itself with any public protest on a conservation problem except when it is capable of making a specifically zoological contribution'.[15] Scientists working for government were under pressure to conform to industry facilitation goals. In 1952 a young scientist from Western Australia, Graham Chittleborough, found himself ordered from a whaling station for his insistence on recording accurate measurements of undersized whales. He was fortunate: although his employer, the Council for Scientific and Industrial Research, would not confront the Australian Whaling Commission over the issue, it did give him personal support.[16] The relationship of other outspoken scientists to their employer, the Commonwealth Scientific and Industrial Research Organisation (CSIR's successor organisation), was not so smooth. Dr Peter Springell, who was forthright on a range of environmental issues, found himself transferred around the country. But not many scientists made the connection between their research and social commitment. When A. J. Marshall published *The Great Extermination* about the destruction of Australian fauna in 1966, it was a landmark book for Australians, simply because so few scientists were prepared to stand up and point out such truths in the postwar period.[17] According to CSIRO scientist Len Webb, in the mid-1960s there was only a small network of environmentally committed scientists across the country.[18] Whereas at the turn of the century it had been in their professional interests to support government infrastructure for basic environmental management, the professional interests of scientists were now closely linked to private industry and industrial growth. When a new generation of environmentalists took up the challenge of conservation, they not only had to withstand Cold War attacks from politicians and business, and isolation from a timid mainstream Australia: they had to do so with the

support of only a handful of principled scientists and the actual hostility
of many professional scientific organisations.

## Turbulent Cross-Currents

The reception of Carson's critique of the chemical industry is a
reminder of the difficulties of social movement politics during the Cold
War. It was a courageous individual who chose to fight for any political
campaign. The same forces which impelled a dying Rachel Carson into
the public arena were also at work in Australia. Postwar economic
growth fuelled by a surge of foreign investment, particularly in the
mining sector, along with rapid technological development, caused
'progress' to intrude into new and once remote places across the
continent. Land development schemes, mining of coastal sands, of
marine environments and of public reserves, the flooding of Lake
Pedder for energy production, noise, air and water pollution—whole
new areas were under threat and environmental degradation suddenly
appeared insidiously in the lives of urban Australians.

The population growth and technological advances which brought
prosperity were a double-edged sword for government and industry.
Postwar developments in marine technology facilitated off-shore oil
drilling, but also produced the aqualung and underwater photography
used by the French environmentalist Jacques Cousteau, both of which
popularised scuba-diving and snorkelling. Motor vehicles set back the
bushwalking organisations briefly in the 1950s, but by the 1960s they
contributed to the resurgence in outdoor recreation, bringing more
and more people into direct contact with national parks. Perhaps the
most important contradiction of the period was the expansion of
secondary and tertiary education to increase the numbers of technical
and managerial personnel for industrial growth. The recipients were the
baby-boom generation; their education in critical thinking was intended
to advance utilitarian science but they were inadvertently radicalised by
the demands of the war in Vietnam. They were offered the temptations
of a technological wonderworld, from the mythical glamour of James
Bond's gadgetry to the spectacular achievements of the moon landings.
But for those in north Queensland who had to deal with the reality of
strontium residues in milk from French nuclear testing in the Pacific, or
had to fight to save rainforests from army proposals to test defoliants
for use in Vietnam, or could not avoid the evidence of the industrial
pollution of Cockburn Sound, those photographs from the lunar missions were likely to evoke quite different emotions. For veteran
campaigner Len Webb, the ability to look at the earth from the outside
was 'to see it as a very small and very lonely planet in space ... a finite

spaceship'. Geoff Mosley, a relative newcomer to the Australian conservation movement, believed that the view of the earth from the moon, 'more than all the propaganda used by the conservation groups, made people aware that for all practical purposes the earth's resources are finite'. For Milo Dunphy, who took over his father Myles's leadership role in New South Wales in the late 1960s, the desolate moonscape meant that 'we will now look on our own planet with a new tenderness, a greater love, ... with a greater reverence'.[19]

### Campaign for the Reef

One of the beneficiaries of new underwater technology was a north Queensland beachcomber, Noel Monkman. His first underwater explorations took place in the Pacific soon after World War I with a pair of goggles made by Tahitians using coconut husks. 'My God, the beauty,' he recalled over half a century later. 'You were underwater so you couldn't shout for joy. But you wanted to, at the wonder of it. That *gorgeous* blue world!' He came to Australia and moved to Green Island in 1929 when it was still uninhabited. His underwater photography of the Great Barrier Reef was to be shown around the world and by the early 1960s he was concerned about the threat to the reef from tourists and tourist operators whose quests for souvenirs were depleting the accessible reefs of shells and corals. He had passionately explained his fears to a visiting journalist: 'It doesn't belong to you, it ... doesn't belong to any living person. It doesn't belong to our unborn children. None of us own it. We're only privileged to see it. *Not* to take it away, *not* to sell it. We're caretakers, and that's all.' Just as great a threat was mineral exploitation of the reef. In 1963 Monkman made contact with the newly formed Wildlife Preservation Society of Queensland (WPSQ).[20]

The WPSQ was formed in 1962 with the goals of educating the public on conservation issues and publishing a magazine on wildlife. The student movement and anti-war movement had not yet begun to politicise large numbers of young people. When the poet Judith Wright, her friend and wildflower artist Kathleen McArthur, and the Gold Coast naturalist David Fleay decided to set up the organisation, they had to weather accusations of being cranks and the sense of being lone battlers against a tide of progress. But the need for a new community organisation to fight environmental issues in Queensland forced them into the fray. Contact with Noel Monkman alerted them to the environmental problems facing the reef, and they began to formulate the idea of a great marine park. Their approaches to marine biologists and zoologists were rebuffed and, although they had about 100 members in their first year, none of them were qualified biologists. Two crucial contacts in the early years ensured WPSQ's survival as a conservation organisation. Vincent Serventy, a Western Australian wildlife expert, active in conservation organisations on both the east and west coasts and with 'a flair for publicity', took on the editing of *Wildlife* magazine, ensuring its success. Then a trained ecologist who had been working in far north Queensland offered his services. Dr Len Webb, committed personally and professionally to ecology, provided invaluable expertise in rainforest ecology to the movement's forest campaigns in the 1970s and his dedication inspired younger activists. Wright immediately recognised his value, and WPSQ in her words 'seized on him and made him a vice-president at once'. As a CSIRO scientist, his expertise and independence were an essential counter-balance to the scientific organisations which threw their weight behind development schemes.[21]

Len Webb's other immediate contribution to WPSQ was his numerous contacts among sympathetic individuals in north Queensland, one of whom was John Busst. An artist, Busst had studied under Justus Jorgensen at Montsalvat near Melbourne before the war and came to live on the island of Bedarra from 1941 to 1957; but then, as the islands were invaded by tourists and pleasure boats, he moved to the mainland at Bingil Bay near Innisfail. Busst was crucial to the development of the Great Barrier Reef campaign which, along with the protection of the Cooloola Coast north of Noosa, became WPSQ's two preoccupations for the next decade. When journalist Patricia Clare met Busst, she felt that the pro-development forces, 'the apostles of the new technology', had struck the 'wildest bad luck ... as they moved in to exploit the Great Barrier Reef there was waiting for them ... a graduate of Montsalvat—a graduate who was not simply a romantic artist but John Busst, at once a man of emotion and a wickedly cool organizer'. To Judith Wright, Busst was 'our indispensable spokesman, contact with politicians, diplomat and tactician, as well as friend'.[22] Poets and artists with a growing groundswell of community support worked to save the Great Barrier Reef in what became a national campaign, involving the courts, state and federal governments and multinational oil companies.

The first large-scale exploitation to come to the attention of WPSQ was in mid-1967 when a sugarcane farmer applied to mine Ellison Reef off Innisfail for limestone for agricultural use. The Innisfail branch of WPSQ at this stage had a cash account with the sum total of five dollars, but John Busst was determined to oppose the application in the Mining Wardens Court, personally bearing the legal costs. The society looked to the Great Barrier Reef Committee (GBRC)—a scientific committee established in 1922 with the goal of scientific inquiry and a stated aim 'to protect and conserve the reef'—to provide expertise and moral support in opposing the mining application. The committee had no official government status but it operated the sole research station, Heron Island, in affiliation with the University of Queensland, the state's only university in the 1960s.[23]

The GBRC did not oppose the mining application; moreover, the University of Queensland argued that Ellison Reef was 'a dead reef' and by implication not worthy of preservation. This was patently untrue to those who had swum and dived on the reef, but WPSQ had difficulty obtaining biological evidence to counter it. Australian marine research was underfunded, while geological research had the financial backing of international mining corporations. Furthermore, geologists were a significant component of GBRC membership. The GBRC would not oppose 'development' of the reef. Very early in the campaign these tensions split the amateur conservationists and scientists. Dr Bob Endean, a well-known expert on the crown-of-thorns starfish, who was a member of the WPSQ council as well as chair of GBRC, withdrew from WPSQ over the Ellison Reef controversy. Even worse, the GBRC effectively blocked the Australian Academy of Science from entering the debate.[24]

Marginalised by the scientific community as hotheads, the WPSQ had to fight developmental interests almost single-handedly and produce their own independent scientific evidence at the same time. Fortunately, a group of marine science postgraduates, which included a young Eddie Hegerl, had just formed the Australian Littoral Society,[25] and they were prepared to assist the campaign. Using his remarkable organisational skills, John Busst managed to get them and scuba-diving equipment to the reef to undertake an underwater survey in the final days before the Mining Wardens hearing. The only fully qualified marine scientist WPSQ could draw upon to give evidence was Dr Don McMichael, the newly appointed director of the Australian Conservation Foundation (ACF). Founded in 1965, the ACF was the first nation-wide conservation body and the one with the most prestige, so it inevitably became involved in the movement conflicts of the period. Although at first hesitant, McMichael arranged leave from the foundation and WPSQ arranged his flight to Queensland. The society promoted the hearing as a test case for mining and oil drilling of the reef. It generated enormous public interest and increased awareness over the reality of threats to the reef. Queensland's system of mining courts is notoriously biased in favour of mining interests, but in a rare outcome the mining warden opposed the application for mining Ellison Reef. It was WPSQ's first victory, but the members were still feeling overwhelmed. Rumours of large-scale oil-exploration permits for the reef reached them daily.[26]

In September 1967 the Queensland government leased over 20 million hectares of the Great Barrier Reef for oil exploration. There was no avenue for individual legal objections; even if there had been, it would have been impossible to fight them one by one. Judith Wright was overseas in early 1968 when the extent of the leases became public knowledge. She switched her itinerary to include Morges, Switzerland, the headquarters of the World Wildlife Fund (WWF), to press it for support. The head of WWF, was horrified but cautious. Jurisdiction over the reef was an internal matter for Australia. In the UK, Peter Scott from WWF urged Wright to press for protection of small areas within the reef. While this was one step better than the Great Barrier Reef Committee— which in the face of this onslaught stuck to its policy of 'controlled development'—it was not satisfactory for Wright and the Wildlife Preservation Society. 'What good would be a marine national park in which pollution rode through on every tide?' she asked. As far as the 'amateurs' inside the movement were concerned, the reef as one whole ecological system had to be protected in its entirety. John Busst's dream was to press for land national parks bordering marine national parks as well, but conservationists were on their own in fighting for such a vision. WPSQ needed a political solution and John Busst came up with their first strategy.[27]

During Busst's years on Bedarra Island, among the visitors he had entertained was an old school friend, Harold Holt, who loved scuba-diving the warm reef waters. In January 1966 Holt had become prime minister and Busst began to lobby him furiously, whenever he could get the chance to talk to him. At one stage during the Ellison Reef case, Busst spent six days at the Prime Minister's Lodge with the Holts, but the prime minister was up and at Parliament House by 6 a.m., often not returning until 3 a.m. the next day. Busst took to sitting next to him at lunch and dinner, but there were always many distractions. In desperation, Busst got on a Melbourne-bound plane with Harold Holt, determined to get some uninterrupted time with him. An exhausted Holt promptly fell asleep; Busst unceremoniously woke him up and finally won his support. In December 1967, however, the prime minister disappeared while swimming off the coast from his Victorian holiday home. With Holt's drowning, a saddened and disappointed Busst turned to other senior federal politicians who fortuitously took holidays in north Queensland. The following year the new prime minister, John Gorton, had a break on Dunk Island while the leader of the opposition, Gough Whitlam, holidayed in Cairns. Busst intruded on their holidays and convinced both of them of the need to protect the reef.[28]

This strategy of personal representations to politicians and senior bureaucrats and use of personal networks, including old-school-tie networks, had been a feature of the first-wave movement. But it was clear that in the new economic climate rational argument and personal suasion would be inadequate. In August 1968 Johannes Bjelke-Petersen became premier of Queensland and he and a number of his ministers had personal interests in some of the oil-exploration companies.[29] The intransigence of the Queensland Government presented legal and administrative obstruction to federal intervention. With political block-age at this level, the campaigners had no choice but to take their cause to the public.

In the south of the state a second strategy based on the media and public education was already under way. There was public interest in Judith Wright's role as a poet involved in conservation, on which she managed to capitalise. A new national newspaper, the *Australian*, had discovered during the Ellison Reef case that conservation stories sold well, and Wright always kept them informed. The young members of the Littoral Society came up with more direct methods of public education. By August 1968 they printed thousands of 'Save the Barrier Reef' bumper-stickers which soon dispersed across the country. According to Wright, it was the first use of stickers in Australian campaigning and the strategy was soon taken up by various causes in the 1970s.[30] At the same time they were collecting a petition against further oil and gas drilling on the reef, and WPSQ branches were working away in their local regions. The Gold Coast branch set up a stall and exhibit at the local show and polled visitors about their attitudes to the reef. An astonishing 976 to 2 people opposed any drilling of the reef. The results sent WPSQ on a state-wide project to poll 5000 Queenslanders on their views on mining or drilling the reef. It was an enormous task for a voluntary organisation and took many months, but proved that in 1969, 95 per cent of Queenslanders supported WPSQ's stance.[31]

The events that raised public awareness about the dangers to the reef were several environmental tragedies that had nothing to do with WPSQ. In January 1968, the oil tanker *Torrey Canyon* was wrecked off the coast of Cornwall, England; then there was a gas blowout from one of Esso–BHP's oil wells in Bass Strait, the second since 1967. These disasters were followed by the spectacular leak of the Santa Barbara oil well off the coast of California in January 1969 and a series of horrific oil incidents in Australia and around the world which continued into 1970. Here was evidence that conservationists' predictions were not mere doom and exaggeration. WPSQ no longer had to convince the media of the dangers of oil leakages and spills; Santa Barbara was a front-page story, and photographs of dying wildlife and polluted beaches were powerful images.[32]

By January 1970 WPSQ had branches around the state, and it was beginning to mobilise large numbers of Queenslanders. New groups such as fishing and skin-diving clubs and trade unions began to join the campaign. In 1969 a new group was formed; the Save the Reef Committee was chaired by Labor Senator George Georges, but its members included supporters of conservative parties.[33]

The campaign had secured some powerful reinforcements but the fight had taken its toll on leading WPSQ members. While working on the reef campaign, they had also maintained their national magazine, fought for the preservation of the Cooloola Sands region and a number of rainforest areas, and undertaken short-term projects like a week-long conservation school at Binna Burra Lodge in the Lamington National Park. John Busst was seriously ill and Arthur Fenton, WPSQ honorary secretary, who was working in the equivalent of two full-time jobs and had most of his house taken over by WPSQ paperwork, was also unwell. To add to their troubles, the pro-development forces were fighting back with a number of pro-mining geologists and scientists, including Rhodes Fairbridge, professor of geology from Columbia University. He told the Royal Society of Queensland that the reef should be exploited 'immediately and to the hilt'. Conservationists were mere 'sentimentalists who want to put a barbed-wire fence around everything', he claimed. This was only slightly more sophisticated than the attacks on environmentalists that emanated from unnamed sources inside the Queensland Mines Department. WPSQ members were accused of being communists determined to prevent the United States 'from getting needed minerals for the space programme' because of their opposition to sand-mining at Cooloola; but on another occasion WPSQ's opposition to a Japex oil rig was said to be proof they were tools of American oil companies who were trying to exclude Japanese business from the lucrative reef oilfields. The scientific lobby contributed to this attempt at marginalisation. When in 1968 the Australian Academy of Science finally published its survey of national parks and reserves that had been in progress for a decade, it came out in favour of exploitation of the reef's minerals and oil provided a full and thorough scientific survey had been made. Although both the Australian Littoral Society and the GBRC finally agreed to oppose oil drilling in reef waters in early 1969, the GBRC still tended to characterise WPSQ as 'unprofessional stirrers'.[34]

The third strategy adopted by the movement was initiated by members of the ACF. Early in the campaign, Sir Garfield Barwick, president of the ACF, pointed out the legal anomalies about who actually owned the reef. Historically it was not even certain that the United Kingdom had ceded legal rights over the waters to the colony of Queensland, nor was there certainty about the division of powers between state and federal government over continental waters.[35] As a former attorney-general and minister for external affairs in Menzies governments and now chief justice of the High Court of Australia, Barwick was sensitive to such legal questions, which could be used as a lever to assert federal government rights over those of the state of Queensland. This was one of the themes that came to the fore at the ACF's major contribution to the Barrier Reef campaign, a symposium held in Sydney in May 1969, just five months before the first of the newly leased areas, a reef off Mackay, was due to be drilled.[36]

In the end it was the second strategy, the overwhelming public hostility to drilling, that won the first reprieve for conservation. After a public boycott campaign and disastrous corporate publicity, Ampol, joint venture partner in the Japex oil rig, decided at the last minute to postpone drilling and offered the state government $5000 towards the staging of a public inquiry into drilling on the reef. The Queensland government was not interested in supporting an inquiry, but Ampol had given the federal government a chance to step in, and the Gorton government finally persuaded Premier Bjelke-Petersen to agree to a joint Commonwealth–state inquiry. There were obstructions as one of the oil companies declined to suspend its operations for the inquiry and WPSQ was unhappy with the stacking of the inquiry against conservationists—international oil companies would be employing their own Queen's Counsels against the three unfunded voluntary conservation organisations, WPSQ, the Australian Littoral Society and the Save the Reef Committee. Furthermore, there was still no guarantee of a moratorium on mining or drilling or of a biological survey, which had always been the movement's key demands. Finally, in March and June 1970 the prime minister upgraded the inquiry to a royal commission and promised legal aid for conservation representation. WPSQ at last had an institutional means to reach its objective—official acknowledgment of the ecological values of the reef and full legal protection of it. They now had the vehicle to make authority heed these points, but there was no guarantee that the royal commissioners would decide in their favour.[37]

As a process for resolving environmental disputes, legal inquiries can have debilitating effects on community organisations. Regular attendance at hearings is not usually possible for voluntary societies, and the written, often technical, evidence is too massive to be examined closely. The media, too, tend to tire of the legal proceedings and the issue loses its newsworthiness. Fortunately, by this stage scientific members of the GBRC were assisting the conservation organisations in interpreting the evidence. The royal commission hearings ran for two years and the commissioners took another two years to write and present their report. John Busst did not live to read it, and Arthur Fenton died soon after. The commissioners divided over solutions for managing the reef but the

Whitlam Labor government used the report to legislate for a marine national park and established the Great Barrier Reef Marine Park Authority to manage it. The intention and role of the authority were affirmed by the Fraser Liberal government when it persuaded the Queensland government to sign the Emerald Agreement to co-ordinate policy between the two levels of government in 1979. The fate of the reef was finally out of the hands of commercial interests and under the protection of an independent statutory authority.[38]

### Diverging Strategies: The Role of ACF

The view of the ACF that comes through in Judith Wright's account of the Great Barrier Reef campaign contrasts with interpretations by scholars and by the ACF's own official assessment of its role. James Bowen argues that the ACF symposium on the reef held in May 1969 was 'a conservation event of great national significance, and one of the most important contributions to conservation of the Reef'. Geoff Mosley is more reserved in his assessment, limiting his comments to noting that the ACF was 'solidly involved with the future of the Great Barrier Reef'. For those working on the ground, perhaps unappreciative of the number of other 'national' demands that pulled at the ACF, its efforts were worse than pathetic, they were counterproductive. With oil spills and gas blow-outs in the news, revelations of Bjelke-Petersen's personal interests in oil-exploration companies, and the first rig due to start drilling in a matter of months, WPSQ was desperate for some moral and public support from the ACF against drilling of the reef in early 1969. Instead, the ACF cautiously refused to make public comment and put its efforts into organising a symposium on the future of the reef. Initially WPSQ welcomed this contribution, only to find that the symposium was stacked against the interests of conservationists. The ACF had invited a number of geologists to speak, including the exploration manager of Conzinc Riotinto and Esso's manager of government relations. The only biologist on the platform was an older member of the Great Barrier Reef Committee who was known to be in favour of exploitation of the reef; there was no marine ecologist, no speaker from north Queensland, no active conservationist. With only a few months left to prevent the first oil rig going in near Mackay, Queensland activists had to take time to respond to the ACF's inappropriate attempt at mediation and even-handedness. To make matters worse, there was no plenary session and only brief time was set aside for questions; the draft resolution proposed by the ACF was weaker than one that Judith Wright and John Busst had sponsored at the ACF's previous annual general meeting.[39]

In protest, Judith Wright decided not to attend, while John Busst worked out tactics on moving an amendment with the young members of the Australian Littoral Society. In the event, no amendments were allowed and no one was given time to speak from the floor against exploitation of the reef. As Busst described it, the meeting was 'a bloody shambles'. Queensland members wrote to the ACF objecting to the process and requesting that their concerns be published in the newsletter, but this was refused. Even the federal coalition government, which wanted to respond to the great public feeling over the reef, was frustrated by the ACF's position. The ACF was not only more backward than public opinion: it was actually shielding mining interests.[40]

The ACF was founded in 1965 by mostly Canberra-based scientists, and it is not surprising that in the political conservatism of the 1960s the body reflected their professional caution. It was founded on the initiative of Francis Ratcliffe, a CSIRO entomologist, who had been approached to help set up a branch of the World Wildlife Fund; he convinced his fellow scientists that there was a more urgent need for a 'body that could speak for the country as a whole on conservation matters'. Following his scientific forays into the fruit-eating habits of flying foxes and the problems of South Australia's arid pastures in the interwar period, Ratcliffe had eventually moved to Australia to take a position in CSIR's division of economic entomology in Canberra in 1937. When Ratcliffe spoke on the plan to establish the foundation at a wildlife conservation seminar held at the University of New England in January 1965, it was warmly welcomed by conservationists. Judith Wright recalled the enthusiasm she, Len Webb, and others in Queensland felt about the plan. 'We were full of the euphoria that comes to small embattled groups when the idea they are working for begins to break through; … the conservation movement began to feel itself a happy few, a band of brothers and sisters, but with achievements ahead.'[41]

Ratcliffe's vision was for a scientific and professional organisation. In his paper at the University of New England he argued that the foundation's secretary 'ought to be a man of some status in scientific circles, as he will have to command the respect of departmental heads with whom he will have to negotiate and university professors and the like whom he will have to coopt for special tasks'. But he also saw it as 'an organization in which the amateur and the professional can collaborate with maximum benefit'. In a paper he prepared for the ACF council meeting of September 1965, he was already calling for the foundation to come up with a process that could accommodate the demands of amateur conservationists seeking political outcomes and the needs of governments, to which he argued the foundation has 'even greater obligations'.[42] Although a number of prominent active conservationists such as Judith Wright and Milo Dunphy were approached to join, most of the ACF's early members came from business, government or scientific circles. Some of its early officers included S. Baillieu Myer, Sir Maurice Mawby (of Conzinc Riotinto and chairman of the Australian Mining Industry Council) and senior public servants such as R. G. Downes from Victoria, who inevitably took the ACF down a more conservative path. These contacts helped the ACF to raise funds from some of Australia's biggest companies, including mining and paper-manufacturing corporations, and obtain an annual federal government grant of $50,000; the ACF was the wealthiest environmental organisation in the country, but it was also among the most conservative.[43] A young Milo Dunphy was drafted onto the executive in 1969 and he recalled the frustrations of working in this atmosphere. 'I ... thought, good grief, this thing is pretending to be a national conservation organisation and it isn't. It's just an old boy brigade.'[44] Three years after its inaugural meeting, while students were putting up the barricades in Paris and the Australian anti-war movement was mobilising for the moratorium, Francis Ratcliffe was still calling on the ACF council to clarify its identity; was it 'primarily a pressure group, or primarily a body which works ... behind the scenes, for long-term improvement and progress in the conservation field?' By the start of 1970, WPSQ's activism on the reef had attracted a state membership of 1600; yet the ACF, with a national profile and significant funding, had managed to attract only 2284 members Australia-wide.[45]

Francis Ratcliffe took early retirement so that he could devote more time to the work of the foundation, but in September 1970 he had to withdraw from the executive because of ill-health. With his usual dedication, he had hoped to return to the committee in the new year, but he died at the age of sixty-six in December 1970. His successors at the foundation favoured a cautious approach. In his report as retiring president in October 1971, Sir Garfield Barwick argued that the 'Foundation must continue to eschew spectacular protest and undue emotional involvement'. In 1972, following an internal reorganisation of the ACF, the *Bulletin* magazine criticised its conservatism and attacked the foundation as 'an organisation which looks, on paper, only slightly less elaborate than the management of BHP'. The tensions that had emerged in the reef campaign were also surfacing in other national conflicts as frustrated grassroots conservationists felt undermined by the ACF's gentlemanly style.[46]

### Little Desert

Development pressures of the 1950s and 1960s not only threatened new areas of the continent but also undermined past environment movement gains. In South Australia, almost 17,000 hectares of wildlife reserves on the Eyre Peninsula were revoked by government for farming between 1954 and 1960. The Flora and Fauna Advisory Committee headed by Professor John Cleland objected, to no avail; but when plans for the sale of Hallett Cove became publicly known in 1957, the newly formed National Trust waged a campaign to save the unique glaciated pavements of the area. The battle for Hallett Cove was the first step towards the reinvigoration of community environmentalism in South Australia. In 1962 the Nature Conservation Council of South Australia was formed and, with the Town and Country Planning Association and the South Australian Ornithological Association, it led objections to plans to open up Crown lands along the South Australian–Victorian border.[47] Declining wool and wheat prices lowered the scheme's viability, but the developer, the AMP Society, then approached the Victorian government with a similar scheme for the Victorian lands. When an old-style rural politician keen to prove his development credentials was made Victorian minister for lands, the scene was set for the remobilisation of Victoria's environment movement to save the Little Desert region from alienation.

In many respects, the Little Desert campaign was the last mobilisation of the first-wave movement, but the success of the campaign attracted younger people into the Victorian organisations who transformed the movement's identity and profile. The Little Desert campaign was a protest against political interference in rational bureaucratic decision-making by Victorian resource management departments and agencies. Public servants who were not normally movement actors were forced to defend their positions and won support from the community organisation, the Natural Resources Conservation League, which suddenly had a significance that resource conservation had not had since the forest and soil conservation battles of the interwar era. The league did not win the battle on its own, however. The success of the campaign rested on the expansion of the opposition to include other traditional conservation groups and their arguments concerning national parks and fauna and flora protection. The environment movement provided the moral framework for the media and bureaucracy to wage a campaign against a recalcitrant minister.

The AMP Society approached the Victorian government in 1963 with plans for development of 40,000 hectares of Little Desert in western Victoria as farmland. This prompted a number of public meetings of community organisations, government representatives, apiarists, ornithologists and town interests, including a local conference hosted by the Wimmera Regional Committee at Nhill, which were held in the Mallee and Wimmera regions in 1964. Regional committees had been sanctioned by the government as a means of providing community views on land decisions. Some local feeling was expressed in favour of a large national park for the area, which would encourage local tourism; but when the government informed AMP of the need for road infrastructure and reserve provision, the society reconsidered its proposal, formally withdrawing in March 1967.[48] Soon after, a new minister for lands, Sir William McDonald, was appointed. McDonald held traditional rural views about the obligation to develop land and Little Desert adjoined his electorate of Dundas. His desire to facilitate a Little Desert farming scheme was perhaps based on a belief that it would present him as an active minister and a keen supporter of regional development, particularly in the face of advice from his own Lands Department which had reported in 1963 that the land was 'marginal farming country'.[49] Keen to promote the scheme, McDonald began the bureaucratic process by requesting a report from the Land Utilisation Advisory Council which he as lands minister chaired. The agricultural economists on the council condemned the scheme, insisting that farms would not be viable in the current economic climate, but McDonald ignored the reports. In October 1968 and April 1969 he introduced a special Land Act to allow the subdivision of the western Little Desert into fifty farms of between 1200 and 2100 hectares and a national park of 32,000 hectares.[50] In doing so, he was alienating his own public servants—particularly the economists from the Agriculture Department, who apparently began to leak information about the failings of the scheme to the Melbourne media. The Agriculture Department also had close working links with university-based agricultural scientists, who also began to publicly disapprove of the scheme.[51] At the same time the Victorian conservation movement began to mobilise. The area that McDonald offered as national park was not biologically representative and they would not agree to land settlement until a biological survey had been carried out.[52] By the end of May 1969, the government was faced with opposition from economists, conservationists, and one of its own departments. Feeling besieged, the minister made a statement to cabinet that drew on traditional views of development, free enterprise and individual opportunity, implying that the pessimistic calculations of the agricultural economists were unpatriotic. Public debate over Little Desert had become much more sophisticated about land use questions, but it was the lower price of wool quoted by the Australian Wool Board two weeks later that finally convinced the government to amend its earlier decision. A revised scheme of twelve farms of 1600 hectares and an additional wooded section of 500–600 hectares ceded to the national park system was announced in late July. Having modified the scheme, the government then moved quickly to implement it, sending in bulldozers to clear roads and fence lines.[53]

The tactics employed in the Little Desert protest were borrowed from traditional conservation campaigning. Despite McDonald's intransigence, there was not the level of institutional blockage that environmental campaigners were to experience in Queensland, New South Wales and Tasmania, as this chapter will discuss shortly. Compared with campaigns in other eastern states, there were a number of chinks in the armour of political power—the government did not have the support of the upper house, leading members of the bureaucracy were against the project, the government lost a by-election in the course of the campaign, and a federal election was due in the next few months. The most successful movement events were traditional—two mass public meetings held at the height of the crisis, which confirmed the extent of public feeling against the scheme.

Since April 1969 several organisations including the Royal Australasian Ornithologists Union, the Victorian National Parks Association, the Field Naturalists Club, the Natural Resources Conservation League, apiarists, and the Country Women's Association had all joined the campaign. The presence of the bulldozers on site inflamed feeling against the government, irrespective of its revised plan, and triggered the formation of a new group, the Save Our Bushlands Action Committee in early August 1969. In just over two weeks the action committee organised a public protest meeting that attracted more than 1000 people, including Dr Jim Cairns, the leader of Melbourne's Vietnam Moratorium Campaign. As the government remained intransigent, the action committee drew up a Bushlands Magna Carta to protect remaining Crown lands from any further alienation, and presented it to an even larger protest meeting in October. Community outrage had been further aroused by allegations that one of the new roads in the area was to serve the property of the minister's brother-in-law. Although McDonald successfully took legal action against the *Age* for the story, the damage was done. It was no longer a matter of protecting fragile bushland, or objecting to public subsidisation of inappropriate land development, or protesting against the government's failure to listen to its own specialist public servants—it was now also a moral protest against political corruption. The allegation confirmed the high moral ground of the environment movement and the moral failings of the Little Desert scheme. By this stage, various political strategies had been initiated: the Labor and Country Parties who controlled the upper house formed a committee of inquiry into the Little Desert scheme, and in the last weeks of the federal election campaign Gough Whitlam, the leader of the opposition, promised that the Labor Party would make Little Desert a sanctuary if it won office. In December, funding for roadworks in Little Desert was blocked by the opposition parties in the upper house and the state government lost a by-election in the seat of

Dandenong. Within a week of this loss, the government decided to shelve the development of Little Desert.

One of the legacies of the campaign was a new institutional arrangement. The Land Utilisation Advisory Council was replaced by a Land Conservation Council which had public representation, including two members from the environment movement.[54] Although the campaign had started at least partly as a defence of bureaucratic processes, it had ended with a commitment to accountability. The mood of the new environment movement was wariness of bureaucratic and political control, and the expansion of democratic space was one of the new demands.

Accountability and democracy were two values that new movement activists demanded both internally and externally. The groups which had fought this campaign had been the traditional prewar social base of the movement; only one group, the Monash University Biological Students Society, had young members, and they were still in the tradition of the field naturalists.[55] The ACF had followed events; it had participated in one deputation and contributed one press release supporting the Australian Academy of Science's recommendation that all public lands should be withheld until park assessments had been undertaken. In the director's words, its role in this campaign 'was not that of a public pressure group'.[56] The second legacy of the campaign, however, was the raising of environmental consciousness in Victoria and the discovery of the broad appeal that environmental issues could have. The movement grew rapidly after the Little Desert campaign, and the demand for a body that would represent environmental issues generally resulted in the establishment of the Conservation Council of Victoria in October 1969. Within a few years of the council's formation, some of the participants in the Little Desert protests found themselves on the outside of a now more confrontational movement. This was not merely a matter of age; the defining characteristic was the commitment to the moral protest of social movement activity versus the comfortable incorporation that had been a feature of the postwar movement. As in the other states, there were individuals, such as Ros Garnet and Gwynnyth Taylor, who had joined the first-wave movement but embraced the new mobilisation and radicalisation of the movement with enthusiasm.[57]

### Myall Lakes

The tensions in Victoria between older and younger members were reflected in other Australian environmental campaigns in this era. In New South Wales a number of older groups that had been traditional public pressure groups were discovering that their customary methods of operating were impotent in the face of new aggressive economic development. Their testing ground was to be the Myall Lakes. 'Most of us have a region we regard as home,' Milo Dunphy noted in relation to the lakes in 1981.

> Mine is eastern NSW. The inventory of its estuaries and coastal lagoons is the inventory of my life. At two I was in a canoe on the Myall Lakes; at 10 watching the mullet jump at Durras lake; at 12 rowing quietly up to the best fishing spots in the Shoalhaven estuary. ... The highlight of each year of my youth was a 4 or 6 weeks holiday at an estuary or lagoon as my father combined his domestic responsibilities with his absorbing task of mapping new park proposals.

Not every inhabitant of New South Wales had had Milo's intimate contact with its beauty spots, but coastal holidays had come to be taken for granted as part of popular culture. In 1968 when the Sim Committee's report into sand-mining, conservation and scientific use of New South Wales's north coast was finally made public, it recommended that, of 640 kilometres of coastline, only 96 kilometres be set apart for national parks, and of these, only 19 kilometres should exclude sand-mining. For a committee that had been formed to deal with conservationists' objections to sand-mining and representations to ministers for national parks, it was a disaster.[58]

Conservationists' representations on protecting the Myall Lakes, about 200 kilometres north of Sydney, began in the early 1950s. The Caloola Club, a conservation education and field naturalist group, was one of the earliest to request a faunal reserve at Myall Lakes. Between 1955 and 1962 it was followed by other local and state-wide groups, such as Hunter Manning National Parks Association, the state National Parks Association and the Fauna Protection Panel, who drew up park plans, made representations for fauna reserves, and called for planning for the region. Rutile mining was under way by the early 1960s, however, and the Departments of Lands and of Mines vetoed such proposals. As beach mining developed in the early 1960s, the National Trust began writing to the government protesting against the devastation. It was in response to these community complaints that the newly elected Liberal–Country Party government set up the Sim Committee in 1965 to investigate park requirements and the conflict between sand-mining and park proposals. Park proposals were placed on hold while the committee carried out its investigations, but mining leases continued to be granted by the minister, Tom Lewis. Furthermore, there was only one environmentalist on a committee made up of government and mining industry representatives, and after two years the minister changed the committee's terms of reference, removing their objective to examine park requirements.[59]

The real campaign for Myall Lakes thus began in 1968 when conservation groups discovered the extent of their betrayal. Disparate
groups such as the National Trust, the National Parks Association, the
Australian Planning Institute of NSW and the Royal Zoological Society
came together to form the Myall Lakes Committee. The Sim Committee
had recommended only small areas of the Myall Lakes be declared
national park, and so the Myall Lakes Committee commissioned planning consultants to produce an extensive park proposal covering 40,000
hectares. It began an intensive public education campaign with media
releases, tours to the region, leaflets and car stickers, as well as standard
lobbying of politicians over the proposal. Conservationists were disappointed when in 1970 state cabinet approved a national park of only
15,000 hectares. However, awareness of the ecological and scenic values
of the region had been raised and in September 1971 the State Planning
Authority refused an application by Mineral Deposits Limited to mine
the high dunes on the north shore of Myall Lake. Six months later the
mining company lodged an appeal against the decision; a Sydney
architect, Walter Bunning, was appointed to conduct an inquiry into the
appeal and began hearings in March 1973. Once again the environment
movement had to fight a rearguard action with the mining company
and the industry front group, the Rutile and Zircon Development
Association Limited, and the New South Wales branch of the Australian
Workers Union on one side and the Myall Lakes Committee, the Total
Environment Centre, the National Trust and the ACF making submissions against the appeal. Political pressure on the inquiry seems
likely, given that Premier Askin announced the government's decision
to allow mining on the Smith Lake side of the dunes five days before the
recommendations of the inquiry were handed down. The environment
movement was disappointed yet again at the extent of the concessions to
the US-owned company, whose royalty payments, according to the Total
Environment Centre's calculations, 'would only pay for half a mile of
highway per annum'. The campaign had half-failed, Milo Dunphy
concluded some years later. 'The northern half was mined but we saved
the southern half. ... perhaps they were a bit too gentlemanly, and the
people who were elected to [environmental] offices were more conservative than you can afford to be as a conservationist.'[60]

### The Colong Caves

By the late 1960s, New South Wales environmentalists were discovering
that gentlemanly behaviour was getting them nowhere. Myles Dunphy,
now a septuagenarian, found not only that his old tactics no longer
worked, but also that battles he had already won had to be refought by

a new generation. The Colong Caves in the southern Blue Mountains had first been reserved from sale by the New South Wales government in 1899. In 1913, Myles Dunphy and Bert Gallop had bushwalked through the area when it was still a wilderness, its paths and depths known only to the locals. Myles incorporated the region into his plans for the Greater Blue Mountains National Park, which the National Parks and Primitive Areas Council began to promote in 1932. In 1939 the Department of Mines considered a mining lease in the area, but after protests from the National Parks and Primitive Areas Council the region was again dedicated as reserve. In 1956 new mining applications were lodged; this time the Mountain Trails Club objected, and most of them were refused. Three small leases, however, were allowed within the reserve in 1957 and in the 1960s were acquired by Commonwealth Portland Cement Ltd, a subsidiary of Associated Portland Cement Manufacturers (Australia) Ltd. In 1967, the minister for lands, Tom Lewis, whose electorate included the Colong Caves, allowed another lease in an adjacent area. 'Dad was beside himself,' Milo Dunphy recalled, 'because his system of talking people around in the bureaucracies was failing on Boyd Plateau, at Colong Caves, at Myall Lakes. And here were all these marvellous park proposals of his that were starting to be torn apart by the ... miners.' Myles Dunphy was not the only old-style conservationist who had become used to polite personal representations to senior bureaucrats and politicians. Milo was secretary to the National Parks Association, whose president had been taken into the confidence of Tom Lewis and informed of the limestone mining plans and had accepted the minister's word that there was nothing anyone could do about it. Some tempestuous meetings followed and a new president was elected. A new generation of activists was not prepared to take such reversals lightly, and one of the country's most imaginative and tenacious environment campaigns to date was launched.[61]

In May 1968 at the University of Sydney, a meeting of a number of groups interested in fighting for the Colong was held. It was an interesting gathering of the old and new of the New South Wales environment movement. David Stead's widow, Thistle Stead, was there representing the old Wild Life Preservation Society, and Milo Dunphy and members of the Sydney University Conservation Society represented the new activists. The meeting decided to form a special committee to fight for this issue and so the Colong Committee, initially representing fifty organisations which would later grow to 150, was born. Conservationists' outrage over the Colong stemmed not just from the horror of a 50-million-tonne quarry and crushing operations which would destroy spectacular scenery and cause siltation and pollution of the Kowmung River for the production of cement; it was also fuelled by the ease with which the government had excised a section of a national park for a quarry. 'If we cannot preserve ... the focal point of our best national park, together with the hub and catchment of that park—we cannot preserve anything,' the *Save Colong Bulletin* declared. A multi-layered campaign was launched that would exploit every available opening to government and political parties, out-research and outwit the company, and keep the issue before the public for many years until it was finally won.[62]

The new committee brought together an array of skills and talents into an effective alliance. Members used their professional associations to educate the public and the government on the project. Father James Tierney, a Catholic priest who chaired the committee from 1969 to early 1972, gathered a petition by 150 Catholic priests asking for the revocation of the lease, which was presented to the New South Wales parliament in October 1969. A week later a second petition from 192 medical doctors, including Sir Lorimer Dods and Sir Charles McDonald, was presented. A number of original committee members— Milo Dunphy, Professor R. N. Johnson, Bruce Vote—who were architects convinced the New South Wales chapter of the Royal Australian Institute of Architects to endorse the campaign; subsequently a number of architects began to advise their clients against using the company's cement. Cavers and bushwalkers were also involved from the start; when the minister for mines, Wal Fife, declared there were no caves at nearby Church Creek, about eighty speleologists and conservationists held a week-long 'cave-in' in August 1969 at 'Fife Cave', occupying the 360-metre cave they had named in the minister's honour.[63]

These simple variations on traditional community politics succeeded in arousing public interest and convinced the state Labor Party opposition to support revocation of the leases. It raised the matter in parliamentary debates, and pledged protection of the Colong Caves and incorporation into the Kanangra Boyd National Park. The problem, however, was to convince the coalition parties who were in government, and the committee mounted pressure both from within the Liberal Party and at the ballot box in the state election in the early months of 1971. Three members of the Colong Committee stood as Australia Party candidates to gain publicity for the caves; one was Brian Walker, who had publicly resigned from the Liberal Party in protest over the issue and stood in the seat of Collaroy in Premier Askin's own electorate. Supporters who were Liberal Party members had already succeeded in passing resolutions condemning the limestone quarry at the Liberals' state council meetings in 1968 and 1969 and at their annual convention. The Young Liberals had also called on the government to reincorporate the caves into the national park, and by 1970 a number of Liberal members of parliament openly supported the committee. In June 1970 two Colong supporters who were Liberal Party members persuaded the Liberals' state council to appoint a committee to investigate the issue. The following September the party committee agreed to a site inspection, which Colong supporters regarded as a turning-point in their campaign. Having experienced the natural beauty of the site for themselves, committee members were prepared to argue with Minister Tom Lewis about *how* to save the area, not *whether*. Lewis was reportedly overheard leaving the gathering declaring it had been 'worse than a cabinet meeting!'[64]

That left Colong supporters in the position of having to convince both the government and the company that there were alternative sites available for limestone mining. New South Wales cement production was being undercut by a cheaper Tasmanian product and Commonwealth Portland Cement needed cheap and easy access to limestone near its Maldon works. The company and the government insisted that this limestone could be obtained only from the caves region. One of the Colong Committee's earliest decisions had been to commission a geological report into alternative limestone deposits, which estimated that a nearby site contained 50 million tonnes of limestone not the 600,000 tonnes of the Mines Department's survey. The difficulty was in convincing the company that its information was wrong.[65] On two occasions the authority of the minister was publicly undermined by Colong supporters' superior information. Now it was the company's turn to lose public confidence as the environment movement used the company's own practices.

The Colong champions were taking on not just a cement company but the world's largest cement company. Commonwealth Portland Cement was a subsidiary of Associated Portland Cement Manufacturers, which was 74 per cent owned by Blue Circle Cement, a London-based transnational corporation. The committee had meetings with company representatives in Australia and the United Kingdom but the greatest pressure was applied at the company's annual general meetings of shareholders. Sam McMahon (brother of Sir William McMahon who was soon to be appointed prime minister) was a supporter of the Colong campaign and a shareholder of Associated Portland Cement Manufacturers. In 1969 he bought parcels of shares and transferred more than 1200 single shares to Colong Committee members, enabling them to attend and vote at the company's annual general meetings. Over 100 conservationists showed up at the annual general meeting in April 1969, outnumbering company representatives two to one. Outside, a street demonstration with witty placards such as 'We keep on askin Askin and playing on Fife' greeted shareholders. Inside, conservationists attempted to amend the financial accounts to include a commitment to reconsider mining the Colong Caves, but the motion was lost, 18,808,741 votes to 88, on going to proxies. The meeting lasted more than three hours but, despite conservationists' impassioned arguments, the company committed itself to nothing more than reviewing the need for operations in the Colong; the whole operation had to be repeated again the following year. The 1970 annual general meeting attracted even more conservationists and was just as uproarious, with the chair repeatedly disallowing motions put from the floor. The company tried to circumvent environmentalist shareholders in 1971 by holding the annual general meeting in Melbourne, but the company succeeded only in making the Colong Caves a national issue as Victorian conservationists armed with proxies converged on the meeting. David Eden abseiled down a Melbourne building to deliver his proxies, the fourth spectacular abseil protest of the campaign, previewing the theatricality of the annual general meeting that was to follow. Soon after the 1971 annual general meeting, and following a confused phone call between a Colong member and Sir John Reiss, chair of Blue Circle in London, Associated Portland Cement Manufacturers surrendered its lease.[66]

The Colong was a landmark campaign of the Australian environment movement. It marked a clear break between old and new protest forms in New South Wales and was the first time Australian environmentalists had used shareholder rights to confront a corporation. Its imaginative protest forms and its confrontation of the government and the company at every level became a model for other campaigns. Because of the Colong Committee's successful pre-emptive interventions, the campaign did not progress to a blockade stage; but it did indicate to later environmentalists the lengths to which they now had to go to confront inappropriate development—even having to pay for research that the company and government should have undertaken.

Early in 1967, before the Colong Committee had been formed, Dr Geoff Mosley, then assistant director of the ACF, had worked with the National Parks Association to raise the Colong issue. The ACF's input was limited to supporting the conservation cause at a mining warden's hearing, but it was not missed in a vibrant and successful campaign. Instead, it was an environmental defeat in the south of the country that would have dire repercussions on the ACF and on the whole movement.

### Lake Pedder

In May 1967 a proposal by the Hydro-Electric Commission (HEC) for a power scheme on the Gordon River which would flood Lake Pedder was submitted to the Tasmanian parliament. Four years earlier, representatives from bushwalking and other outdoor clubs and conservation groups had formed the South-West Committee to press for a preservation policy and national park plan for the region. The beautiful Lake Pedder, with its unusual sandy beaches, was a hub for outdoor recreation. Plans to dam the lake and submerge it under 15 metres of water, which the HEC euphemistically described as 'enlarging', split the committee. As Geoff Mosley recalled, the South-West Committee 'agonised over the proposed dam but ... concentrated on their park proposal'. For those bushwalkers who had already developed a wilderness philosophy, there was no indecision: the lake had to be saved as a national park and for its own sake. Led by Peter Sims of Devonport, they set up the Save Lake Pedder National Park Committee; within weeks they had collected 10,000 signatures on their petition in a state with a population of less than 400,000. Sims went to the mainland and alerted environmentalists to the issue, addressed the annual general meeting of the ACF, and organised public protest meetings in Tasmania. In response to the public uproar, the Legislative Council formed a select committee of inquiry to investigate the proposal. It took submissions from mainland and Tasmanian conservationists and heard evidence on alternatives to flooding Lake Pedder. But the select committee, like the Sim Committee on sand-mining in New South Wales, was stacked against the conservationists. Although the HEC was a statutory authority, it did not give the committee full support; evidence that the HEC had in fact investigated alternative proposals came to the committee's notice only at the last minute. Rather than take on the power of the HEC, the select committee criticised its lack of disclosure, recommended a stronger national parks and wildlife policy and administration for the state, and argued for the creation of an enlarged national park for the region, but ultimately found in favour of the HEC's scheme. It was typical of the HEC's lack of accountability that both houses of the Tasmanian parliament voted in favour of the Middle Gordon scheme without full evidence of alternatives in October 1967.[67] A brief political opening for the movement had closed shut.

The campaign to save the lake seemed over, but disenchantment with the decision contributed to the defeat of the Reece Labor government in May 1969. The Liberals and Independent Lyons had made sympathetic statements in favour of the lake, but it soon became apparent that they would take no action. In early 1971 record numbers of bushwalkers, including 1000 in one weekend alone, visited the lake before it disappeared. Some bushwalkers had never given up the fight, and one of those outstanding campaigners was Brenda Hean. Kevin Kiernan's memory of her was in the John Watt Beattie tradition of Tasmanian environmental politics—'Brenda's vision of Pedder was as an expression of the divine.' Dick Jones agreed: 'Brenda Hean found [Pedder] her spiritual centre.' As the political mood around the country changed in response to domestic and international events and the McMahon government stumbled in the federal sphere, there were hopes of new political openings to review the decision. In Tasmania, a member of the Legislative Council, Louis Shoobridge, went to see the lake for himself and was converted to its cause. In March 1971 he and Hean called a public meeting, which overflowed the Hobart Town Hall. The meeting called for a referendum on the lake's protection. The movement was remobilising, and the following week a small group of people formed the Lake Pedder Action Committee (LPAC). The parliament refused to consider Shoobridge's referendum proposal, despite the record crowd watching from the public gallery. The LPAC was already organising a campaign that, like the Colong movement before it, would press its cause at every level of Tasmania's political and economic structures.[68]

The LPAC adopted many of the tactics already tried and tested by conservationists in the Great Barrier Reef and Colong campaigns, but they also set up mainland branches in the eastern states to rally national support. The rigid conventionalism of Cold War political culture still hung over Tasmanian politics. At the first stage of the campaign to save the lake, Premier Reece had complained that the South-West Committee was 'interfering in public affairs'; even in this second phase Reece attacked a young Kevin Kiernan's involvement in the campaign because he had not turned twenty-one years of age (then the age of majority) and the Tasmanian attorney-general refused to receive the petition of a quarter of a million Australians because it was 'in conflict with government policy'. Circumventing and showing the rigidity of state political structures became an important part of the campaign. The Victorian branch held protests outside the Tasmanian Tourist Bureau in Melbourne and civil disobedience resulted in eighty people being arrested there in April 1972. The LPAC also brought national activists to Tasmania. Jack Mundey, leader of the New South Wales Builders Labourers Federation, was flown to Hobart to build links with the trade union movement. At a large protest meeting Jack Mundey called for a 'blue ban', but the factionally aligned and conservative Tasmanian Trades and Labour Council was unmoved. Another New South Wales activist brought in to assist the campaign was Milo Dunphy. 'The opposition had been run on too nice a level' was Milo's view. 'I asked myself what's the best thing I can do. I decided that was to tear into the Hydro-Electric Authority and the Tasmanian politicians as the locals feel they are unable to tear into them. ... So I tore strips off them and ... it galvanised' the audience. For his efforts Milo was described by the *Mercury* as a 'crazed left-wing conservationist', but his attack on the HEC became an important facet of the campaign as the LPAC took on the unquestioned power of the commission which had maintained a hold on the Tasmanian political imagination for more than four decades. Other supporters like Keith McKenry were already developing a critique of the HEC's suspect energy projections and costs and lack of public disclosure. With ecologists like Dick Jones active in the leadership of the LPAC, scientific support was also belatedly rallied; UNESCO, along with a group of 184 scientists who petitioned the Tasmanian government, appealed for the flooding to be halted.[69]

At the state political level both major parties had closed their doors to the environmentalists. When elections were called in April 1972, the Lake Pedder supporters found that they had no choice but to set up their own party, the United Tasmania Group, which became the world's first Green Party. Labor under Reece's leadership won the elections. The group's candidates came within a hundred or so votes of getting elected. The shores of Lake Pedder were already being inundated; the only hope was for the federal government to intervene, and that was where the LPAC turned next.[70]

Campaigners and supporters from across the country had already swamped the office of the Prime Minister, Sir William McMahon, with protest letters. A protest caravan was set up across the road from Parliament House in Canberra. In the lead-up to the federal elections of December 1972, numerous Labor members of parliament had come across the road and promised their support to retain the lake. To maintain the momentum, on 8 September 1972, Brenda Hean and Max Price set off from Hobart in a light aircraft to skywrite over the Canberra skies. They never made it. The plane presumably crashed, possibly at sea since no wreckage has ever been located. There was evidence of a break-in at the plane's hangar and Hean had received threatening calls in the previous few days. A report from the minister for police refused to acknowledge any evidence of tampering, and the case was closed in November 1972. The fight went on.[71]

Labor won the historic election of 1972, but Whitlam's instructions to his new minister for the environment, Dr Moss Cass, were to 'stay out of Tassie'. The Whitlam government's relations with the environment movement are further explored in Part III. As for Lake Pedder, it stayed drowned.

In 1972 to early 1973, Pedder supporters maintained a vigil at the lake, checking the rising waters and rescuing what wildlife they could. The LPAC had mobilised too late for a blockade of the dam construction and now all its members could do was watch its unique marine forms and geographical features drown. To understand the emotion behind the campaign, one has to read descriptions of the beauty that was being desecrated. Dick Jones was not a bushwalker and he had not seen the lake when he joined the LPAC. 'I was surprised at my reaction to Lake Pedder,' he recalled in 1981.

> Really was surprised at the impact that had on me as a physical place ... the swirling mists around me, the mountains and the water and the vegetation ... the moods were so ephemeral, they came and they went so that you could get enormously different experiences in the one place. You could go back to it again and again.[72]

Feelings were bitter in late 1972 and early 1973. But members of the LPAC committed themselves to one last action. They could not save Lake Pedder now, but they could try to ensure that an environmental defeat on this scale would never happen again. Their target this time was not a government or an industry; it was the movement's leading national organisation, the ACF.

### Division and Expansion

Like the Great Barrier Reef campaigners, the Pedder activists had looked to the ACF to give public and moral support to their campaign. Instead they too won little more than a symposium held in November 1971 and the publication of the *Pedder Papers* in late 1972. But even these, as Dick Jones pointed out at the ACF's stormy annual general meeting of 1972, were 'still only concerned with the decision-making process—not the saving of Lake Pedder'. The ACF's failure went back to the Tasmanian Select Committee of 1967 when the foundation was still only two years old. Francis Ratcliffe was a worrier, and a controversial political issue at this stage made him very uncomfortable. His mode of operating was to make approaches at senior bureaucratic and political levels, using the contacts of executives from the foundation, but any political or bureaucratic advice obtained from Tasmania in this period was bad from an environmental point of view. Despite Peter Sims's appeal to the foundation, it took no stand in 1967; although Geoff Mosley gave evidence to the Legislative Council's Select Committee, he did it in his personal capacity not as representative of the ACF. That caution was still being articulated by the director, Dick Piesse, when he spoke at a meeting of the Tasmanian Conservation Trust in May 1970. 'The work of the ACF is not always readily apparent since it is often considered not expedient to divulge certain activities either to members or the public. This is because much information is supplied confidentially, or approaches are best made to government leaders outside the glare of public controversy.' With Pedder's beaches drowning, activists like Dick Jones were no longer prepared to heed such a defence of inaction. 'If the Foundation was not to do better than it had done over Lake Pedder, the grass-roots conservationists would be better off without the ACF,' he declared at the annual general meeting in 1972, which had a record attendance, thanks to Tasmanian and Victorian Pedder supporters. Sir Garfield Barwick as president kept control of the meeting, disallowing a number of motions from the floor. As Dick Jones recalled events some years later, 'some of the young people who came from Hobart were in tears of frustration and emotion at the terrible situation, and one councillor from Queensland was pouring scorn upon us as a rabble—unwashed and unclean'. Not all the critics were young. The veteran conservationist Thistle Stead was there, adding her voice to concerns about the foundation's failings on Pedder.[73]

Of course these were not the only campaigns galvanising environmental sympathisers around the country. Urban pollution had also been gaining international and national prominence, and small groups had sprung up around a number of causes in every state. In 1971 the Associated Chambers of Manufactures of Australia agreed to introduce biodegradable detergents in response to pollution concerns.[74] By the end of the 1960s the need for co-ordinating councils to communicate between groups, and for environment centres to provide an organisational base to wage campaigns, was apparent everywhere. The strategic differences in the movement in Tasmania resulted in two generalist organisations there, the Tasmanian Conservation Trust (1968) and the Tasmanian Environment Centre (1973). Thirteen South Australian conservation groups affiliated to form the Conservation Council of South Australia in February 1971. Western Australia had formed a Nature Conservation Council in April 1967 but, stimulated by the offer of administrative grants from the federal government, the council broadened its goals and dropped 'Nature' from its title to become the Conservation Council of Western Australia in 1973. The Total Environment Centre was established in Sydney in 1972 'to be a cutting edge for the environment movement'.[75] The Conservation Council of Victoria, now Environment Victoria Inc., was formed in the aftermath of Little Desert in late 1969, and the Queensland Conservation Council followed soon after in 1970. In 1973, the federal government provided funding for the first time to environment centres around the country, a total of $100,000 in grants; it was less than the ACF's annual grant of $150,000, but it was a good base for the new state umbrella organisations.[76] With the ACF operating at the national level there were now environmental organisations capable of responding to each level of government. But it was not the arrangement of its organisational base that had hindered the movement in the 1960s, it was differences of opinion about how to move forward.

In the early 1970s, the battle between developers and environmentalists was still a David and Goliath struggle. 'Even in the conservation camp,' Judith Wright noted, 'there was caution, temporising, playing for advantage, and attempts to come to terms with, rather than face, opponents whose enormous power discouraged many.'[77] The lesson of Lake Pedder was that industrial development would not wait for gentlemanly agreements to be reached. Environmentalists had to learn how to fight and to fight with commitment.

# PART III

# The Campaigning Movement: 1973–1983

The demonstrators are shivering on a cold, windy dockside waiting for a uranium shipment, or soaked to the skin in a forest blockade. They have been there with their small group for hours, not knowing when things might start happening, or even if things will start happening. They think that this is what it must be like in a war—endless hours of discomfort and boredom punctuated by brief moments of intense conflict. The television crews and the police are there as well, talking amongst themselves and occasionally passing a comment to the protesters about the weather or a forthcoming cricket match. Then the police begin to look more purposeful and tension fills the air. The young activists feel their stomachs knotting a little as they realise that this is what they have come here for. They take up their positions and the police move in.

Anyone who has been involved in non-violent direct action knows this feeling. Such action is only a small part of the repertoire of green groups, but it often highlights the preparedness of the movement to use militant methods to defend the environment. It was not, however, recognised widely as a valid tactic by the movement until the advent of the green bans in Sydney in the early 1970s. By then the failure of traditional campaigning modes in the face of industrialism backed by new, aggressive, more intrusive technologies had become apparent to many younger activists who had witnessed the sufferings of the people and countryside of Vietnam under carpet bombing, napalm and 'pacification' programs.

Apocalyptic scenarios, emanating from overseas sources such as the Club of Rome and US scientists Paul and Ann Ehrlich in the early 1970s, also had a profound effect on the thinking of many people in Australia. The Club of Rome's *Limits to Growth*[1] raised concerns about resource depletion and pollution on a global scale, while Paul Ehrlich evoked the Malthusian nightmare of human population growth outstripping the ability of the environment to sustain it. These publications had some impact on the types of environmental activism that occurred in Australia in the 1970s, but their main influence was to promote a stronger sense of urgency about environmental issues, a crisis that would not be solved by restrained behaviour by environmentalists.

The reverses of the late 1960s and early 1970s would, on their own, undoubtedly have pushed nature conservationists into more militant campaigning modes, but the urban environmental campaigns of the early 1970s, drawing on traditions of left-wing and working-class struggle, helped establish the picket, the blockade, the rally, and other confrontational activities as integral parts of green movement tradition and mythology. They also established the possibility of a link between the ideological and organisational forms of the Australian Left, including a number of trade unions, and the newly emerging environment movement.

Comparisons can be drawn here between the Australian and European movements. In West Germany, in particular, the green movement recruited heavily from amongst urban Leftists who were disenchanted by the centrism of the social democrats and the dogmatism of the communists.[2] The increasing importance of wilderness issues in Australia, however, compared with the dominance of nuclear and pollution issues in Europe, ensured considerable philosophical differences between the European and Australian movements, with the former maintaining a clearer left orientation. However, neither the leftism of the Europeans nor the wilderness focus of the Australians should be overstated.

Even though there were some differences between the movements in Germany and Australia, Jan Pakulski argues that they followed similar processes in their formation and consolidation. These were:

> a proliferation of groups and bodies involved in protest activities; a thematic extension of protests on a broad range of issues; a globalisation of concerns from local-specific to general and universal; a coalescence of protest actions into multi-issues events that involved many different associations and groups; growing contacts, co-operation and co-ordination between various movement bodies; and the emergence of leading personalities and exemplary figures at the extra-local, national level.[3]

Such processes characterised the development of the Australian environment movement from the early 1970s to the early 1980s. This was a time when a sense of urgency drove a new generation of environmental activists to adopt different methods of campaigning and to develop organisations based on a tougher approach to campaigning for the environment. Along the way, new leaders arose out of the new forms of activism.

The new campaigning approach was being adopted by the movement at a time when Australians had elected their most reformist federal government. The Whitlam government came to power in 1972 on a wave of optimism that had been created to a large extent by the extensive social movement activity of the time. The flip side of the anti-war, anti-imperialist, anti-authoritarian sentiment of the movement demands during the late 1960s and early 1970s was the call for such things as educational, health and environmental reform, an increasingly independent role on the world stage, and the greater empowerment of local communities. The Whitlam government responded to the radical demands of Australian social movements, including the emerging environment movement; before it disintegrated as a result of conservative manoeuvrings and its own incompetence, it changed the country forever.

The two chapters in Part III examine the rapid growth of the movement during the 1970s and early 1980s. Chapter 4, 'Taking to the Streets', looks at two issues that mobilised tens of thousands of young activists in very militant campaigns. These were the green bans in Sydney and other Australian cities between 1971 and 1975, and the anti-uranium campaigns conducted between 1975 and 1984. The environmental issues associated with them were different, but they shared a strong, grassroots campaigning orientation and a link with both the political Left and sections of the organised trade union movement. This chapter also analyses the impact of the failure of the campaign to stop the damming of Lake Pedder on the country's major national conservation organisation, the Australian Conservation Foundation, and how the ensuing conflict inside the ACF epitomised the changing nature of the movement around Australia.

Chapter 5, 'Taking to the Bush', analyses the major national conservation campaigns during the period. These include the campaigns to stop sand-mining on Fraser Island, to protect the New South Wales rainforests from logging, to prevent the damming of the Franklin River, and to protect the whole of the south-west Tasmanian wilderness. These conservation campaigns have been selected because they exemplified the bitter struggle, still being conducted, between the environment movement and the politically powerful resource industries. Conflicts over forestry, mining and energy went to the heart of the debate that is now called sustainable development.

# CHAPTER 4

# *Taking to the Streets*

While an aggressive industrialism, based on resource-extraction industries and aided by powerful politicians and compliant bureaucracies, was destroying whole areas of rural Australia in the 1960s, the forces of finance and entrepreneurial capital were tearing the heart out of Australian cities, especially Sydney. The skyline of Sydney's central business district was changing rapidly as old, often historic, buildings were demolished to make way for concrete and glass towers. Many of the people being displaced by these developments were traditional working-class residents of Sydney's inner suburbs. Paradoxically, the people who were doing the demolition and construction work on the ground—riggers, scaffolders and so on—were members of the New South Wales Builders Labourers Federation (BLF) whose actions, in collaboration with local residents' groups, would form the main resistance to these developments and would challenge the whole system of making decisions about Australian cities. Their actions would also profoundly influence the way in which decisions on the environment as a whole were made and the environmental consciousness of Australians.

## Green Bans

The Green Bans movement was part of a world-wide phenomenon of the 1970s and early 1980s in which urban social movements, from Mexico City to Madrid, battled with dominant interests to define what Castells calls 'urban meaning'.[1] It was, he says, important for the dominant class to remove a sense of place and history from the city. Such attitudes were regarded as anachronistic in an era when cities like Sydney needed to be linked to the ever-changing flows of an increasingly global economy. The new power in the city belonged to those who

128

controlled the flows—of capital and of information. However, their interests and the meaning they attempted to give to the city did not go unchallenged and, as communities fought back, they contested the future direction of the city.

This was what happened in Sydney during the early 1970s. As a result, new priorities in urban planning were established; new actors like the Commonwealth government were added to the forces directing urban development; and demands for public participation in decision-making were heeded. What emerged, however, was not a historic compromise but a stand-off. The conflict over urban meaning is written into the fabric of life in Australian cities.

The story of the Green Bans has been told often.[2] They were so successful because they combined three important factors: widespread community mobilisations; supportive trade unions that could exert economic power to counter the developers; and ideological coherence that was contributed especially by the Communist leadership of the BLF. When a reform ticket won the 1968 union election, the new leadership of Bob Pringle, Joe Owens and Jack Mundey (all members of the Communist Party of Australia) dropped their salary to that of workers on the job. The union headquarters also became an important after-work meeting place for builders' labourers instead of the abode for aloof union officials it had previously been. Most importantly, the new leadership had come to power with the promise of limited tenure, that is, any official would serve only two terms or six years before retiring. This was a challenge to established trade union officials, many of whom had held their positions for most of their working lives. However, it was popular among the rank and file, who mistrusted officials who were attracted to the positions because of the career prospects they offered.[3]

After Mundey, Owens and Pringle were installed as leaders, the BLF developed a reputation for supporting radical causes and for militancy. The union was active in the campaign against the Vietnam War; it strongly supported Aboriginal land rights, gay rights and affirmative action for women (including in the union); and it made more efforts than most to ensure the inclusion of migrants in the union's decisions. BLF president, Bob Pringle, achieved notoriety in 1970 by sawing down the goal posts at the Sydney Cricket Ground the night before the Rugby Union test against the apartheid-based South African Springboks.[4] The most significant step in the union's development, however, came with the 1970 wage claim and strike. After a campaign marked by workers' determination against the employment of scab labour and Mundey's skill in using the media, the union won its demands. The increased confidence among union members is reflected in an anecdote, often quoted by union activists: before the strike, workers would say 'I'm only a BL'; after the strike they would say 'I'm a bloody BL!'[5]

The BLF entered environmental issues in 1971, when Bob Pringle approached a group called the Battlers for Kelly's Bush, which was attempting to save the last remaining bushland on the Parramatta River from development.[6] Under normal circumstances, women like Betty James, Kath Lehany and Chris Dawson, the leaders of the Battlers, would not have dealt with a trade union, especially one led by Communists. However, they were desperate. The local community had all but lost the fight to save the bushland from a housing development by A. V. Jennings. Some members of the BLF were as reluctant to aid people from an elite suburb like Hunters Hill as the women had been to approach the union; but Mundey's view was that the union would be doing this for all people and that working-class people needed open space too. Mundey's view prevailed and a black ban was placed on any work by builders' labourers. At the BLF's request, the Battlers called a public meeting to officially request the union to put a ban on the site; 450 people voted in favour.[7] When a Jennings spokesperson stated that the company would use non-union labour, a lunchtime meeting at another site passed a motion saying, 'If one blade of grass or one tree is touched in Kelly's Bush, this half-completed building will remain for ever half-completed as a monument to Kelly's Bush.'[8] The ban held and Kelly's Bush is still bushland.

Requests to the BLF for help soon poured in from all parts of Sydney. Along the way black bans became Green Bans.[9] The bans covered demolition work on various sites: a network of freeways in the western suburbs, a residential development at Eastlakes, at the historic Rocks, on the Playfair buildings, the Pitt Street Congregational Church, the Theatre Royal, Centennial Park, in Woolloomooloo, Darlinghurst, and the famous Victoria Street. Green Bans were placed on the Theatre Royal and Centennial Park because of their value as cultural heritage; and on areas like Woolloomooloo not only because they illustrated working-class cultural heritage but also because they were the homes of low-income people. The union agreed with the local community that these areas should retain their existing residential character against developers' plans to intrude commercial high-rise buildings.

The residents' action groups and BLF members were involved in many confrontations with police during the period 1971 to 1974, especially at The Rocks, Woolloomooloo and Darlinghurst. These conflicts unearthed some personalities among the residents who have passed into legend along with Mundey, Pringle and Owens: the redoubtable Nita McRae from The Rocks, Father Edmund Campion from Woolloomooloo, Margaret Grafton and Colin James from Darlinghurst, and Mick Fowler from Victoria Street. Another resident of Victoria Street, the heiress and publisher of the local newspaper *Now*, Juanita Nielsen, disappeared in 1975; she was undoubtedly murdered, although her body was never found. She had been active in the Victoria Street campaign and had been campaigning against the increasing numbers of sex shops in Kings Cross just before her disappearance. Mick Fowler became famous for his six-month battle against eviction from his home in Victoria Street.

The Sydney Green Bans ignited enthusiasm for environmental issues all over the country. Bans were placed on sites in Port Macquarie, Newcastle, Perth, Fremantle, on residential development in the Adelaide Hills, and at Battery Point in Hobart. A company involved in a forest dispute in Queensland faced a ban in Sydney,[10] and Mundey tried unsuccessfully to persuade the union movement to oppose the flooding of Lake Pedder.[11] Some links had been established between the BLF and nature conservation organisations. Milo Dunphy from the Total Environment Centre, Geoff Mosley from the Australian Conservation Foundation (ACF) and Vincent Serventy from the NSW Nature Conservation Council all developed good relations with Mundey and the BLF.[12] Nevertheless, there was no time for a more productive relationship to develop before the anti-Green Ban forces mobilised to destroy the BLF.

Support for the Green Bans was widespread and crossed class lines. Builders' labourers rubbed shoulders with the elite during the campaigns to save the Theatre Royal and Centennial Park. The Nobel Prize–winning novelist Patrick White enthusiastically supported the Green Bans and the BLF; he said in 1973, 'How much longer can the citizens of Sydney ask these men to endure the responsibility for protecting a citizen's right to live comfortably and without anxiety, a responsibility that should be taken by the government, if the government were in good faith.'[13] It is the sole example in recent Australian history of a movement led by Communist trade unionists that captured the imagination of a broad cross-section of the public.

Despite this cross-class support, developers and right-wing politicians verbally abused the BLF. Some of the bitterest criticism came from inside the union movement. The BLF's social and environmental policies did not sit well with many right-wing union leaders, but they particularly disliked the BLF's policy of limited tenure for union officials. This was a major challenge to union bureaucrats everywhere which, if it caught on, would end many careers.

In September 1973 Jack Mundey stepped down as secretary of the New South Wales BLF in line with the limited tenure policy. This was the signal for a number of attacks on the union. The first came from the

Master Builders Association, who persuaded the Arbitration Commission to de-register the federal union, led by Norm Gallagher. This was probably part of a ruse by Gallagher, who belonged to a rival, Maoist, Communist Party. By not contesting the de-registration, Gallagher was able to attack the New South Wales branch leadership and win back federal registration.[14] Because Mundey, the branch's best strategist, did not hold an official position, the branch was vulnerable; after a struggle that lasted until March 1975, Gallagher's team took control. Former leaders like Mundey, Pringle and Owens were expelled, and Gallagher made his peace with the developers. In the early 1980s Gallagher was convicted in a Victorian court of taking bribes from developers.

While the Liberal state government under Robert Askin remained a staunch defender of the developers and a bitter enemy of the Green Bans movement, the newly elected federal Labor government under Gough Whitlam took on a number of policy challenges raised by the campaigns. The two ministers who were in the best positions to do this were Tom Uren, who headed the Department of Urban and Regional Development, and Moss Cass, the new environment minister.

One of the first moves of the Whitlam government was to address some of the weaknesses in local government revealed by the Green Bans movement. Activists like Jack Mundey (and many since) advocated replacing local and state governments with regional governments,[15] but the power of the states was entrenched. Uren attempted to go round the states and give directly to local authorities the resources they needed. Consequently, the Commonwealth directed area improvement programs to needy local authorities such as those in the western suburbs of Sydney, and extended the equalisation principle in the Grants Commission to include local government.[16]

A direct outcome of the Green Bans was the intervention by the Commonwealth into the Woolloomooloo campaign which, by 1973, had reached a stalemate. Making use of the Commonwealth's ownership of a significant parcel of land in the area, Uren appointed activist and architect Colin James to lead a consultation process with the local community and then represent them in negotiations with developers and government. This led to an agreement on the future of the district; it included retaining and renovating 90 per cent of the historic houses and provision of low- and middle-income housing, including a sizeable proportion of public housing.[17] The same thing happened in the inner Sydney suburb of Glebe, where the Commonwealth purchased existing housing stock from the Church of England and refurbished it for public housing. This was an attempt to show the State Housing Commission that the public housing scheme could be used to preserve historic houses.[18] Previously, state governments had provided new public housing in outer suburbs and had attempted to preserve historic areas like The Rocks with gentrification and tourism.

In 1973 the Whitlam government, urged by various conservationists, decided to identify important areas of the natural and built environment as part of what was called the National Estate, an idea that had come from the United States.[19] The program was overseen by ministers Uren and Cass. Uren asked Mundey to be one of the seven members of a Committee of Inquiry into the National Estate in May 1973. Premier Askin threatened to withdraw cooperation with the inquiry while Mundey was a member. Uren then replaced Mundey with that equally 'difficult' environmentalist Milo Dunphy, whose father Myles had also been an Askin target.

Even Robert Askin had to respond to the Green Bans agenda. In 1973 his government commissioned a report on the state's planning policies. This report acknowledged the need for better public participation, a new system of regional planning authorities, greater emphasis on environmental considerations, and greater attention to the social and economic consequences of planning.[20] Some of these recommendations were weakened, however, before it got to the parliament as the Environmental Planning Bill. When Labor defeated the Liberals in the 1976 state elections, the new premier, Neville Wran, promised to review this legislation. The act that finally passed through the state parliament in 1979 was good legislation for its time, acknowledging a number of the Green Bans movement's demands: it provided for environmental impact assessments, third-party appeal rights, and the right to seek an injunction to enforce the legislation.[21] The Wran government also introduced heritage legislation in 1978. This legislation implicitly recognised what is undoubtedly the most important legacy of the Green Bans—the right of people to be involved in making the decisions that affect their lives. From then on, almost every popular environmental campaign carried with it the demand for public participation measures to be respected by government.

The Green Bans were unique, and they fascinated people around the world. Urban citizens' movements, like that in Madrid at the end of the Franco era, provoked considerable changes in urban policy but they lacked that link with a strong, well-organised union that created such dramatic moments in Sydney and other Australian cities in the 1970s.

## The Whitlam Government

The Whitlam government, with its strong reform agenda, held out most promise in the first half of the 1970s that environmental protection would be pulled into the mainstream of the Australian Settlement, a goal long sought by conservationists. In many ways the Whitlam government can be seen as a re-emergence of 'left Deakinism' after so many years of the 'right Deakinism' of Menzies and McEwen. Its emphasis on government intervention to secure social justice, especially wage justice, and to promote economic development, exemplified by Rex Connor's efforts in the minerals and energy sector, are in the tradition of social democratic governments like that of Chifley. However, this period also saw the beginnings of the break-up of the Deakinite consensus as white racism made way for a non-racial immigration policy and Aboriginal land rights. As well, Left nationalists like Jim Cairns (and even Whitlam) challenged great power allegiances; tariffs were reduced; and previously marginalised groups like women began to enter the political mainstream.

The year 1972 was significant, not only for green politics but also for Australians' sense of nationhood. The re-emergence of radical nationalism, the Aboriginal Tent Embassy set up outside Parliament House, the outpouring of grief around the country at the death of a mountain lake in the south-west Tasmanian wilderness—all showed that many Australians were beginning to think of their country, and the land itself, in a new light. The Whitlam government, elected in December 1972, was both a result of this new sense of nationhood and a formulator of new visions. The social movement activity of the 1960s and early 1970s, of which the conservation movement was one part, helped to shape the context in which the Whitlam government emerged as the most radical reform government in Australian federal politics.

The environment portfolio, given by Whitlam to Moss Cass at Tom Uren's behest,[22] was generally regarded as the one with the lowest prestige. Advisers like Pat Troy and Peter Ellyard and Uren himself had been among the few people developing environmental policy prior to 1972; it was overshadowed by high-profile reform agendas like health, education and social services. Nevertheless, with Cass as minister and reform in the air, environmentalists were optimistic. The increasingly desperate Tasmanian activists began haunting the corridors of power in Canberra, seeking to persuade Labor caucus members to prevent the final blow leading to the death of Lake Pedder. The irrepressible Leigh Holloway was at the forefront of these efforts,[23] trying to convince the new government to honour Uren's promise of an inquiry into Lake Pedder. Cass usually did not have the numbers in cabinet and the media soon began calling him 'the minister for lost causes'. Nevertheless, he usually had the backing of powerful ministers like Uren, and he attempted in early 1973 to get cabinet to set up an inquiry into the damming of Lake Pedder. This was finally approved, in spite of many delays and opposition from Whitlam, who was worried about fallout for his Labor colleague and Tasmanian premier, Eric Reece. The findings of this inquiry, calling for a moratorium on work on the lake and investigating ways of restoring it, were rejected by cabinet but supported by caucus. Whitlam did not follow through on the caucus vote, and Lake Pedder was drowned.

The Environmental Protection (Impact of Proposals) Act was passed in 1974, after seemingly interminable delays that had some environmentalists, such as the Western Australian forest campaigners, gnashing their teeth. The act gave the Department of Environment power to intervene in disputes concerning development proposals. Many of the media reports at the time put Cass at loggerheads with the minister for minerals and energy, Rex Connor, over such issues as sand-mining on Fraser Island and uranium mining. Interestingly, Cass acknowledges Connor's crucial support on several key environmental issues.[24]

### Trouble at ACF

Jack Mundey was invited to stand for election to the council of the ACF in 1973 and was duly elected. This seemed astounding, given the establishment nature of the ACF. The organisation had Sir Garfield Barwick as its founding president and the Duke of Edinburgh as its current president; its council included high-ranking public servants like Alfred Dunbavin Butcher and Dr Geoff Downes, and several mining company executives who, according to Milo Dunphy, were there 'on a brief to keep this emerging conservation movement under control'.[25] However, as detailed in Chapter 3, there was a great deal of disenchantment with the ACF among grassroots conservationists and Mundey was part of a revolution in the affairs of the ACF that exemplified what was beginning to happen in other parts of the environment movement around the country. Conservationists with a more activist, campaigning orientation began moving into prominent positions within many organisations, and several of these 'troublemakers' put themselves forward for the 1973 election of the ACF council. Mundey joined Milo Dunphy (who had joined some time before at the request of the 'old guard'), Dr Dick Jones and Dr Ian Bayly, fresh from the Lake Pedder campaign, and other activists who formed a majority of the council. Mundey might have been unusual in his militancy, even by the standards of people like Jones and Dunphy, but there was nothing like the difference there would have been if he had been in the previous council. In Jones's words, the ACF was run by 'executives from ICI and top public servants from Victoria and university professors ... people who were upper middle class, who had feet in other camps, who were very unlikely ever to have an activist view of conservation, which in my book is a euphemism for doing nothing'.[26]

Even the newly elected federal government under Gough Whitlam had thought the old council was too conservative. Launching the first edition of the ACF's new magazine *Habitat* in June 1973, Whitlam warned that it could not perform its agenda-setting role properly if it was too conservative and 'an established body, all the best people belong to it'.[27] Moss Cass, the new environment minister, encouraged the reformers by threatening to cut the ACF's grant by $100,000 if the organisation did not become more active.[28] If the 1972 annual general meeting of the ACF had seen the masses registering their discontent, then the 1973 meeting was the revolution. It began with strong criticism of the failure of the executive committee to carry out the decisions of the previous annual general meeting. Then council set about electing the vice-presidents, the treasurer and the executive committee, and co-opting additional members. In what Milo Dunphy described as 'the worst defeat the Melbourne Club had ever seen', the eighteen activists on council voted en bloc to ensure that reformists got these positions. The council then went further and promoted Geoff Mosley to the position of director over the heads of people like Dick Piesse and the newly appointed John Blanch.[29] The meeting dissolved into turmoil and seven 'old guard' members of the council, including Butcher, Warren Bonython from South Australia and Graham Chittleborough from Western Australia, immediately announced their resignations.[30] In April 1974 these seven people published a document entitled 'How the ACF Was Taken Over', which criticised the process by which the 'takeover' occurred. The fact remained that the process had been both democratic and constitutional, and the ACF probably lost little, if anything, out of it in terms of its credibility with the public or the movement.[31] The Duke of Edinburgh took the events well, given his obvious sympathies with the conservatives, and stayed on as president. His only stipulation was that those staff members who were going should be treated generously.[32]

The loss of people like Warren Bonython and Graham Chittle-borough was sad. They were dedicated conservationists of the old school who have remained committed to the environment and active in causes up to the present. Nevertheless, what had happened in the ACF was one dramatic episode in the evolution of the movement in Australia and worldwide. Young activists, influenced by the student and anti-war movements of the 1960s and responding to the increasing intrusiveness and destructive capacity of industrialism, demanded more militant action from the conservation organisations. In doing so they turned a polite old boys' network into a mass social movement that was prepared to challenge the most powerful interests in society to achieve its goals.

## The Anti-Uranium Movement

David Allworth was working late one evening in July 1977 in the office of Movement Against Uranium Mining in Melbourne. He received a call from someone in the Seamen's Union saying that a uranium shipment was coming in on the *Columbus Australia*. David had been organising one protest after another, and the thought of having to gear up for one more was too much. He decided to go home; he walked out and closed the office door, but then his conscience got the better of him. He went back into the office and rang fellow anti-uranium activist, Jim Falk, to organise a protest against the ship's arrival.

The resulting demonstration on the Melbourne docks, happening only a few days before the Labor Party's national conference, was a crucial moment in the campaign against the mining and export of uranium. It ensured that anti-nuclear sentiments took hold among conservationists and in the Australian population generally. It provided another opportunity for the development of a clear left–ecology orientation, along the lines established by the Green Bans movement. This left–ecology axis had been given further momentum by the 1975 Radical Ecology Conference in Melbourne, one outcome of which was the early anti-uranium movement. It also enabled the environment movement to form close working relationships with both anti-nuclear trade unions and Aborigines. The alliance with the unions would be badly shaken by the forthcoming wilderness campaigns, but the link with Aboriginal groups, although occasionally stormy, has remained strong to the present.

A small nuclear disarmament movement had existed in Australia during the late 1950s and early 1960s along the same lines as the Campaign for Nuclear Disarmament in Britain. Nevertheless, there was little controversy in Australia about the nuclear weapons testing being done by the British at Maralinga and Monte Bello between 1952 and 1963,[33] probably because of the combination of official secrecy and lack of media scrutiny. Uranium mining also took place at Mary Kathleen in Queensland and Rum Jungle in the Northern Territory between 1944 and 1963, and Mary Kathleen reopened quietly in 1974. Rum Jungle, especially, left a serious pollution legacy.[34] Enthusiasm about the benefits to be gained by exploiting Australia's large uranium reserves increased during the years of the Whitlam government, but there were words of caution as well. In 1975 various Labor Party members began voicing their opposition to the mining and export of uranium; one of these was the environment minister, Dr Moss Cass.[35] He insisted on an inquiry into uranium mining under the *Environmental Protection (Impact of Proposals) Act 1974*. The test case for this inquiry would be the proposed Ranger uranium mine, which, along with the deposits at Jabiluka and Koongarra, were in the Kakadu area which the conservation movement was urging the government to set aside as a national park. On 19 January 1976 the prestigious International Union for the Conservation of Nature and Natural Resources sent a telegram to the ACF affirming the international significance of Kakadu. It read:

> It [Kakadu] will provide protection to a unique area of special interest to science and world conservation combining wildlife, scenic and Aboriginal cultural values ...
>
> IUCN is disturbed to learn that the area is threatened by mining and is making representations to the Australian Government asking that no mining or other development take place in the area.[36]

The inquiry, which was appointed on 16 July 1975, became generally known as the Ranger Inquiry. In the chair was Mr Justice Fox, senior judge of the Supreme Court in Canberra, and the other members were Graeme Kelleher and Professor Charles Kerr. The terms of reference were widened to include most aspects of uranium mining and the worldwide nuclear industry.[37]

This inquiry gave a jolt to the environment movement. Some groups had been keeping an eye on the issue since the early 1970s and Friends of the Earth (FOE) swung into action even before the inquiry began. In May 1975 they organised an anti-nuclear bike ride to Canberra and a demonstration outside Parliament House (where, in street theatre, Minerals and Energy Minister Rex Connor struggled with his conscience). They were joined by other conservation groups, sections of the women's movement, student organisations, Aboriginal groups, the Australia Party and the Communist Party.[38] By 1976 umbrella groups were formed—Campaign Against Nuclear Power, Movement Against Uranium Mining, and Campaign Against Nuclear Energy. In early July 1975 fourteen interstate environmental representatives (ten of whom were from FOE) conducted a fact-finding tour of the Northern Territory, visiting the Ranger mine site with members of the territory's Environment Council and meeting with the local Oenpelli people.[39]

While groups like the ACF made submissions, most of the work in the inquiry for the environment movement was carried out by FOE.[40] Its representatives followed the inquiry around the country, although, in the absence of adequate funding, they were forced to go by train or hitch-hike.[41] However, FOE was not prepared to wait for the inquiry to produce its report before it began campaigning, as the Australian Council of Trade Unions (ACTU) had decided to do. FOE in Sydney set up a mobile 'uranium ban wagon' on the back of a flatbed farm trailer to take the issue to the public. The display showed the nuclear fuel cycle and its dangers, and a mural about Kakadu. It also featured information about alternative energy because, even at this early stage in the campaign, activists realised the importance of environmentally acceptable alternatives to nuclear power.[42] The potential dangers of nuclear energy were not the only reason for many people's interest in energy conservation and renewable energy. The oil price rises in the early 1970s had alerted many, including governments around the world, to their vulnerability in the face of the instability of oil politics; energy efficiency could reduce this vulnerability. Unfortunately for the cause of energy conservation, Western governments found other ways in the 1980s to stabilise oil prices.

The anti-uranium campaign began heating up in May 1976. Early in the month bike riders from Melbourne, Sydney and Brisbane headed for Canberra in a well-organised action that involved street theatre, public meetings, and media interviews along the way; it culminated in a brief occupation of Mining Industry House and a friendly meeting with the Aboriginal Embassy outside Parliament House.[43] Then uranium mining at Mary Kathleen caused industrial action by Australian railway unions that brought all mining to a halt. On 19 May a shunting supervisor at the Townsville railway yards and Australian Railways Union member, Jim Assenbruck, acted on his union's anti-uranium policy and refused to load sulphur for the mine at Mary Kathleen. He was immediately stood down, and all other workers in the yard went out in support of him. The strike soon spread throughout north Queensland and, on 24 May, the union called a nationwide 24-hour strike.[44] The strike resulted in the reinstatement of Assenbruck, and the sulphur was shipped to Mary Kathleen. However, at the ACTU conference called in Sydney on 4 June to discuss the handling of uranium, the strong anti-uranium position of the Australian Railways Union and supporting unions was matched by an equally strong pro-mining position by the Australian Workers Union that covered workers in uranium mines. The resulting compromise supported a moratorium on the mining and export of uranium until after the publication of the Ranger report.

The powerful Australian Workers Union and the right-wing leadership of the Queensland Trades and Labour Council under Jack (later Sir John) Egerton were strongly pro-uranium; but many others (including a number of right-wing unions) adopted a policy opposed to the whole nuclear fuel cycle and have maintained this to the present day. It was the left-wing unions—the Seamen's Union of Australia, the Waterside Workers Federation, the Australian Railways Union, the Amalgamated Metals, Foundry and Shipwrights Union, the Electrical Trades Union—that led the charge against uranium mining inside the union movement. In some cases the links between left union activists and officials went back to the post-war peace organisations such as the Australian Peace Council, with their opposition to Western imperialism and to the Cold War.[45] Besides the Australian Railways Union, the main unions to use strike action against uranium shipments were the strategically placed Seamen's Union and Waterside Workers Federation, but these often did not have the backing of their own federal officials.[46]

The publication of the first Ranger Report in October 1976 gave official support to the arguments of the emerging anti-uranium movement. Although the report did not recommend against mining, it did not, as some business and media interests wanted to believe, give the green light for the mining and export of uranium. In fact, the report concludes by saying: 'Policy respecting Australian uranium exports, for the time being at least, should be based on a full recognition of the hazards, dangers and problems of and associated with the production of nuclear energy, and should therefore seek to limit or restrict expansion of that product.'[47]

The report went on to discuss risks in the mining and milling of uranium and the operation of nuclear reactors; it said that, while these exist and provide a need for 'close regulation and constant surveillance',[48] they do not, in themselves, constitute a compelling reason for banning uranium mining. However, the report also listed a number of other problems with the nuclear fuel cycle that made a dependence on the nuclear industry of doubtful benefit to any country. These were the difficulties of disposing of the low- and medium-level wastes associated with the mining; the possibility of nuclear theft and sabotage; and, most importantly, the connection between mining uranium and the increased possibility of the proliferation of nuclear weapons.[49] In fact, the report made the blunt assertion, 'The nuclear power industry is unintentionally contributing to an increased risk of nuclear war.'[50] One of the unexpected aspects of the report was its emphasis on the need for energy conservation as a feasible and desirable energy option.[51]

Although the first Ranger Report did not recommend a ban on the mining and export of uranium, it did provide the movement with backing for many of the arguments that activists were using against the whole nuclear industry, including the desirability of energy conservation.[52] The report also called for public debate on the issue, suggesting that many of the questions are ultimately social and ethical and that 'final decisions should rest with the ordinary man'.[53] The Fraser government, however, used the release of the report to authorise, two weeks later, the export of uranium for existing contracts, and the fight was on. In November and December 1976, 7000 people marched through the streets of Australian cities, with the largest number in Melbourne. This led to the formation of the national coalition called Uranium Moratorium,[54] building on the popularity of the Vietnam Moratorium movement of the early 1970s. A demonstration organised by the Movement Against Uranium Mining brought together between 10,000 and 15,000 people in Melbourne. The movement in other states put less energy into the April mobilisation and more into the National Signature Drive,[55] which collected over 250,000 signatures calling for a five-year moratorium on uranium mining.[56] More demonstrations occurred around the country in August 1977, with 10,000 people marching in Sydney and 20,000 in Melbourne.[57] At a rally in Brisbane on 22 October 1977 more than 400 people were arrested; this style became typical of events in Queensland under conservative premier Bjelke-Petersen, as the anti-nuclear campaign overlapped civil liberties issues.[58]

The anti-uranium movement was made up of a variety of political, church, union and other groups, and environmental issues were not necessarily at the top of the agenda for many of them. FOE members remained the most committed conservation activists doing grassroots anti-nuclear work. In late 1977 FOE set up a tent marking the Atom-Free Embassy 200 metres from the front entrance of the nuclear research establishment of the Australian Atomic Energy Commission at Lucas Heights near Sydney. Despite some harassment by the police, the embassy stayed put and, in true FOE style, a 'leak was sprung' from within Lucas Heights. This leak showed that the commission had placed an indefinite embargo on aspects of its research on solar energy 'which it considered desirable to omit for policy reasons'.[59] FOE's 'leak bureau', which advertised in editions of *Chain Reaction*, had another coup in late 1976 when a 'suitcase full' of documents turned up at the office revealing evidence of price-fixing within the uranium industry.[60] In May 1977 FOE also continued its bicycle rides against uranium to Canberra with the theme of alternative technology.

Confrontation between anti-uranium demonstrators and police now began, especially around blockades and pickets of uranium shipments. Between 20 and 23 June 1977 demonstrators in Sydney attempted to prevent the ship *ACT 6* from taking 200 tonnes of yellowcake from Lucas Heights. When the truck convoy got into the Glebe Island container terminal through a back entrance, the demonstrators scaled fences or slid down a bridge embankment to reach the site and disrupt the loading of the yellowcake. About forty were arrested.[61]

The confrontation with Victoria Police at Swanston Dock in Melbourne on 2 July, described at the beginning of this part, was the defining moment of the direct action campaign against the export of uranium. The demonstration was called to protest against the arrival of the *Columbus Australia*, carrying yellowcake from Mary Kathleen and bound for the United States. The demonstration began at 10.30 on a Saturday morning with about 300 people, and a delegation attempted to persuade the ship's captain to unload his cargo. The Waterside Workers Union held a meeting and decided that, if the police moved against the demonstrators, it would black-ban the ship. With the presence of demonstrators on the wharf preventing the loading of the ship for safety reasons, and the wharfies declaring that any attempt to move them would result in a black ban on the ship, the authorities were in a difficult position. They resolved this in a heavy-handed manner: mounted police led a charge against the protesters, resulting in many injuries and thirty arrests, including the state secretary of the wharfies' union, Ted Bull. The wharf was cleared, but at a cost. A meeting of Melbourne wharfies decided on a 24-hour strike in protest at the police action and the *Columbus Australia* was black-banned.

This incident increased the opposition to uranium mining within the union movement, and also strengthened the anti-uranium feeling at the Labor Party conference that was meeting in Perth at the time. The conference passed a motion which, while allowing exports to fulfil existing contracts, declared a moratorium on uranium mining and treatment and declared a Labor government would repudiate any commitments by a Coalition government to mine, process or export uranium.[62]

However, pro-uranium forces inside the union movement, led by ACTU president Bob Hawke, were moving to counter opposition to mining inside the union movement. At the ACTU congress two months later, Hawke and the pro-uranium forces pushed through a motion that was significantly weaker than the one passed by the Labor Party. It called on the government to hold a referendum on the uranium issue, but it also required unions to consult their rank and file before any action was taken against uranium mining or shipments.[63] Further meetings decided that existing contracts would be met, and that no labour would be available for new mines until there had been satisfactory progress on solving the hazards associated with the storage of nuclear waste and the possibilities of nuclear proliferation. The unions also demanded that the 'legitimate demands' of the Aboriginal people be met. This was certainly not a victory for the government, which was hoping for bipartisan support in the parliament for uranium mining, but neither was it a declaration of implacable opposition from the union movement. The battle would continue in the community, in the union movement and in the Labor Party but, from the government's decision to mine in August 1977 until November 1978, the main focus was the opposition to mining maintained by the Aboriginal people of the Northern Territory.

Some movement activists pinned their hopes on the ability of the Northern Land Council to stop mining at Ranger. Northern Territory

Aborigines had repeatedly stated their total opposition to uranium mining and the second Fox Report had been sympathetic to their feelings on the issue. However, a realistic assessment of the strategic position of the Northern Land Council showed that it was in a position to negotiate but not to block. Firstly, Fox had indicated: 'There can be no compromise with the Aboriginal position; either it is treated as conclusive or it is set aside ... In the end we form the conclusion that their opposition should not be allowed to prevail.'[64] Under the federal government's Aboriginal Land Rights Act which applied to the Northern Territory, a Land Council veto over mining at Ranger could be overridden by the government under a national interest provision.

Government pressure was now applied to the Aborigines to accept an agreement on uranium mining at Ranger. After negotiations which were criticised by several Aborigines as involving too little consultation, the chair of the Northern Land Council, Galarrwuy Yunipingu, announced that the council would sign the agreement. Yunipingu's role was criticised at the time by a number of Northern Territory Aborigines (and subsequently by white conservationists).[65] An injunction restraining the council from signing was taken out in the Northern Territory Supreme Court by two of its executive members, Dick Malwagu and Johnny Marali No. 1. This delayed, but could not prevent, the final signing on 1 November 1978.

The anti-uranium campaign, as a significant component of the environment movement, reflected all the characteristics of a successful social movement. It had expanded horizontally to form umbrella groups, and these in turn had linked with other movements, such as the trade unions and indigenous groups. It had challenged principal institutional norms and sociopolitical patterns by its prediction of the authoritarianism implicit in a state dependent on nuclear industry, its critique of centralised technology, and its espousal of renewable energy. It had also connected with political power by directing its message to significant sections of the trade union movement and the Labor Party. This strategy, of course, depended on Labor winning power and, once in power, implementing a policy of no uranium mining. In all ways, this would be a difficult task.

Nevertheless, opposition to uranium mining continued and to a certain extent was consolidated by the re-emergence of the nuclear arms race between the United States and the Soviet Union, especially after the election of Ronald Reagan to the US Presidency in 1980. Opposition to uranium mining in Australia became part of the international campaign against the nuclear fuel cycle, its connections with nuclear weapons, and aggressive posturing by nations on the international stage. Large anti-nuclear rallies continued to occur in the larger cities, opinion polls continued to show large sections of the Australian public opposed to uranium mining,[66] and the alliance between anti-nuclear trade unions and the movement held firm. However, uranium mining had begun at Ranger, and any hopes that a Labor government might reverse this course were dashed when the pro-mining Fraser government was returned at the 1980 election. Inside the trade union movement the pro-mining forces did not have the numbers to win pro-uranium policy positions at ACTU conferences, but they held enough strategic positions, including members of the leadership, to ensure that union action against uranium mining was not effective. Bob Hawke's resignation as ACTU president and his replacement by the anti-uranium Cliff Dolan did not alter this situation. The latest act in this campaign will be discussed in Chapter 6, but uranium mining will continue to be an issue for the movement for many years to come.

# CHAPTER 5

# *Taking to the Bush*

The early 1970s had seen the emergence of a militant environment movement that launched vigorous campaigns against poor urban planning and Australia's involvement in the nuclear fuel cycle. It also linked up with some of the more radical sections of the older social movements—the Left and the trade unions—and all this at a time of massive social change and the presence of the most reform-minded national government in the country's history, led by Gough Whitlam.

However, another dynamic was emerging during this period. The upsurge of interest in the environment during the 1960s coincided with an increased vigour by the forestry industry and government forestry commissions to knock down native forests for the more productive pine plantations, to introduce woodchipping to native forests and to expand logging in rainforests, especially in New South Wales. Sand-mining was also providing a serious threat to sensitive coastal areas, especially in New South Wales and Queensland, and the Tasmanian Hydro-Electric Commission had virtually completed its preparations for the damming of Lake Pedder by 1973 and was looking to further projects in the state's south-west wilderness. Many of the well-educated younger generation, politicised by the Vietnam War and the emergence of new ideas and new social movements, looked at the aggressive intent of the Australian resource industries in the 1960s and 1970s and decided that those forces were just as destructive as the ones that had caused such damage to the people and countryside of Vietnam. These campaigns to defend Australia's native forests and wilderness areas embodied the same enthusiasm and militancy that was seen in the green bans and anti-uranium struggles, but they also helped drive a wedge between the greens and the trade union movement. Curiously, however, wilderness campaigns achieved a level of political success that neither the anti-uranium nor the green bans campaigns did. The ecocentrism of these wilderness campaigns also presented a challenge to the radical humanism that had always been the main ethical framework for Australian reformists.[1]

### Fraser Island

One of the most bitter battles fought by a militant, campaigning, nature conservation group against a large corporation using intrusive resource extraction technology was over sand-mining on Fraser Island. The corporations were the American company Dillingham, which held mining leases over 12,000 hectares of the island in partnership with the Australian company Murphyores. Another American company, Queensland Titanium, held 1000 hectares. Fraser Island Defence Organisation (FIDO) was formed in February 1971 to challenge sand-mining as an appropriate land use for such a unique island.[2]

Fraser Island is the largest of the remarkable sand islands off the coast of southern Queensland, formed by the northward movement of sand from the New South Wales coastline. Its sands, which go down as far as 60 metres before hitting bedrock, its high dunes, its varied vegetation—from heath to rainforest—its perched lakes, its complex hydrology and its archaeological remains make it an area of high conservation and cultural significance as well as extraordinarily beautiful. Fraser Island is also part of the Great Sandy region which includes the coloured sands of Cooloola. The plan to mine much of the island for rutile, zircon and ilmenite was seen by conservationists as potentially even more destructive than the logging that had taken place for many years.

FIDO decided, quite early on, to use the outflanking strategy adopted by the Great Barrier Reef campaigners. In other words they attempted to avoid the bloody-minded opposition of dominant interests in the local Maryborough–Hervey Bay community and the fierce pro-development attitudes of the Queensland government led by Joh Bjelke-Petersen, by using the beauty and environmental significance of Fraser Island to generate support in the rest of the country and to win the backing of the federal government to prevent the issue of export licences for the minerals which had to be sold overseas. Any link with political power achieved by Fraser Island campaigners would have to be outside the unfriendly territory of Queensland. Direct action, in the form of protests, civil disobedience and even rallies, was almost completely absent from the campaign.[3] In this, it differed from many of the other big campaigns of the period. FIDO's main campaign tools were public education, including safaris to the island, lobbying of governments and political parties, and legal challenges.

The campaign to prevent sand-mining on Fraser Island began in early 1971 with the formation of FIDO under the leadership of its president and spokesperson, John Sinclair. It was preceded the previous year by a campaign led by Noosa doctor, Arthur Harrold, and WPSQ's Kathleen McArthur to stop sand-mining at Cooloola. That campaign was successful but its very success made it more difficult for Sinclair and his group to get anywhere with the Queensland government when the miners' attention focused on Fraser Island. Harrold had been able to get support from within the Queensland coalition government, and Premier Bjelke-Petersen was determined that he would never again be out-manoeuvred by environmentalists.

Sinclair had been the founding secretary of the Queensland Naturalists Club in 1967 and, in line with Sinclair's more activist leanings and after meeting Judith Wright, this became a branch of the Wild Life Preservation Society.[4] Members from this group as well as others from Hervey Bay, Maryborough and even Brisbane formed a 'protection committee' for Fraser Island. This grew into the Fraser Island Defence Organisation.[5] Well-known barrister and civil libertarian Lew Wyvill was one of the founding members, as was Eileen Beswick, who was the secretary of both the Cooloola Committee and the Queensland Conservation Council. Other long-term members of FIDO were Mary Hansen, Freda Goodsell, Rhonda Cook and Billie Watts.[6]

### FIDO and the Whitlam Government

As with all environmental issues, the campaigners needed to focus their energies so that the 'right levers were pulled' in order to get the desired outcome. FIDO considered a number of these. Given that the campaign was being conducted in the early 1970s, the most obvious strategy was to link up with the union movement and get green bans imposed on sand-mining on Fraser Island. In contrast to the later hostility to nature conservation issues from much of the labour movement, there was considerable support for FIDO from several unions. This culminated in 1975 in an attempt by the Queensland Trades and Labour Council to impose a ban on mining but, by this time, the New South Wales Builders Labourers Federation was on the defensive and right-wing unions like the Australian Workers Union would have no part of a ban.[7]

The second option was to appeal to the federal government to use its constitutional power to reject export licences for the products of sand-mining on Fraser Island. The Labor Party under Gough Whitlam had come to power in Canberra in 1972 and conservationists held out great hope for it. In Moss Cass they had an environment minister who seemed ready to fight in cabinet for the right causes. The Whitlam government also passed the *Environment Protection (Impact of Proposals) Act* in 1974, giving the environment minister power to call for environmental impact assessments or to hold inquiries into environmental issues. However, on 13 December 1974, four days before the act became law, Whitlam and Minerals and Energy Minister Rex Connor secretly approved $43 million worth of mineral sands export.[8] This action caused John Sinclair to say of Connor that his 'duplicity and hypocrisy was only equalled in my experience by that of Johannes Bjelke-Petersen'.[9] Sinclair was only slightly more enamoured of Whitlam. Although caucus gave a surprisingly narrow margin of support to Connor and Whitlam, Cass was able to use his powers under the Impact of Proposals Act to get an inquiry into Fraser Island, undoubtedly the single most important move by government for obtaining environmental protection of the island. The inquiry's recommendations against sand-mining were released on 26 October 1976. FIDO's tactic of inviting Labor politicians to Fraser Island to see the place first-hand was undoubtedly significant in gaining crucial support from members of the Labor caucus for the inquiry.[10]

## Sinclair and the Courts

FIDO's third and most costly tactic was to issue legal challenges to the sand-miners. The organisation objected in the Mining Warden's Court in February–March 1971 to the granting of over 5000 hectares of mining leases to Murphyores and Dillingham, including high dunes near Lake Boemingen.[11] The Queensland Mining Warden's Court was (and still is) biased in favour of miners and against good environmental outcomes. It has always been under-resourced, lacking in expertise, appointed by the mines minister and capable only of making recommendations to that minister. In the Bjelke-Petersen era, such a process could have only one outcome—victory for the miners. Nevertheless, FIDO went back to the court in September 1971 to object to Murphyores' application to exempt six 'cold storage' leases and did the same again in 1973. In June 1974 Sinclair again failed to have the court recommend against the granting of leases against Queensland Titanium, but this time the court made the mistake of publishing its reasons. This gave Sinclair a basis to appeal the decision, which he took finally to the High Court. In a landmark case which, among other things, helped to define 'the public interest', Sir Ninian Stephen upheld the appeal.

Although this was the only legal victory FIDO had against the miners and Sinclair was to suffer greatly in defamation suits, especially when Premier Bjelke-Petersen was awarded large costs in an action brought against him by Sinclair, these court cases kept Fraser Island in the spotlight and helped create a legend around FIDO and Sinclair. The Fraser government agreed to the banning of mineral exports from Fraser Island on 11 November 1976, an action that environmental lawyer and historian, Tim Bonyhady, believes could have been a sop to the environment movement, given the government's support for uranium mining or, more mundanely, a response to the collapse in the 1970s of mineral sands prices.[12] Nevertheless, the Fraser government can take the credit for stopping the destruction of large areas of a precious part of Australia. Final protection of the island came with the ending of logging in December 1991 and the inscription of Fraser Island on the World Heritage List in early 1992.[13] Sinclair's achievements in getting this level of protection for the island were recognised when he was named as Australian of the Year for 1976. The main threat to the island now comes from the 300,000 tourists a year who can 'love the island to death'.

### New South Wales Forests

The main contribution of the Fraser Island campaign to Australian social movement practice was to demonstrate the viability of using federal government powers to circumvent a hostile or unhelpful state government. On the other hand the northern New South Wales rainforest struggles in the late 1970s and early 1980s demonstrated that local campaigning and imaginative direct action could be effective when allied with adept lobbying of government.

In the era after World War II, long after conservation-foresters like Swain had been sidelined and forestry commissions had been captured by the industry they were supposed to be regulating,[14] rapid changes in technology, industry organisation and forestry policy were ensuring that vast changes were occurring in Australia's native forests. Improved transport moved logs more easily to the mills, and loggers could gain easier access to forest areas that were previously out of reach. The introduction of chainsaws also meant greater mobility and higher productivity by the loggers. From the 1950s native forests began to be cleared to make way for more productive pine plantations, and in 1967 the New South Wales government reached an agreement with the Japanese-Australian company, Harris–Daishowa, to woodchip in the state's south-eastern forests, a decision that sent shock waves through the conservation community.[15] At the same time the timber companies began to modernise and small firms were taken over by larger ones, a process that resulted in most mills on the state's north coast being owned by either Boral or Adelaide Steamship.[16] These changes, of course, meant significant job losses, a problem for which the conservationists were (often wrongly) blamed.

## Conservationists and the Forestry Commission

Crucial to all these developments was the role of the Forestry Commission. In 1973 two young environmentalists—Richard and Val Routley—published their influential critique of the commission's ideology and practices in *The Fight for the Forests*. Although conservationists had been conducting native forest campaigns for some years, this was the first clear articulation of the battle lines between conservationists and the forestry industry. The Routleys' description of the Forestry Commission's 'wood production ideology'—derived from its elevation of wood production as the dominant value of native forests and its denigration of their aesthetic, amenity and conservation values— was reinforced many times during the next two decades as conservationists fought to defend native forests from destruction and found the Forestry Commission in the front line against them. The Routleys' analysis of the phenomenon of 'regulatory capture' is an appropriate starting-point for similar analysis of any government body that has regulatory authority over a resource industry.

As we saw in Chapter 3, Myles Dunphy's vision of a Greater Blue Mountains park came under threat in the 1960s from mining of the Colong Caves and from plans to add 7000 hectares of the Boyd Plateau in the Kanangra–Boyd wilderness in the Blue Mountains for the purpose of a pine plantation.[17] This was the first major conservation campaign to stop the clearing of native forests for pines;[18] it signalled the beginning of the big New South Wales forest campaigns that would continue until the early 1980s. Its success in 1975 would also be followed by many others.

The New South Wales Forestry Commission released its 'Indigenous Forest Policy' in October 1976. This publication stated that general-purpose timber harvesting in most rainforest areas would be phased out because of their 'biological and scenic significance'. However, just as the Routleys had savaged the underlying assumptions of the commission's much-trumpeted FORWOOD conference in 1974,[19] so the mainstream conservation movement quickly concluded that this was another example of Forestry Commission duplicity and that 'phasing out the logging really meant phasing out all the accessible rainforest not included in the very small FC Fauna Reserves'.[20] The Colong Committee, along with other major state-wide conservation organisations like the Nature Conservation Council and the National Parks Association, had committed itself in the early 1970s to supporting the campaign to preserve the extensive rainforest on the southern side of the Queensland–New South Wales border. These forests, contained in the Wiangarie, Roseberry and Mount Lindsay State Forests, were contiguous with the long-established Lamington National Park in Queensland and their protection in a national park would have been a major achievement for rainforest conservation.

## The Terania Creek Campaign

In January 1973 Jim Gasteen, Russ Maslen, John Brown and Jack Meek and others formed the Border Ranges Preservation Society and began campaigning for a Border Ranges National Park. This campaign lasted several years and, while the local media black-banned the issue after a while, *Sydney Morning Herald* journalist Joseph Glascott wrote many well-researched articles on it. Henry Gold contributed to the campaign with his stunning wilderness photographs, and the Sydney conservation groups lobbied heavily on behalf of the society. Unfortunately, the intransigence of the conservative state government up to 1976 was matched by that of Lin Gordon, the Labor minister for forests in the cabinet of Neville Wran. Gordon was supported by other ministers like Don Day and Pat Hills, who endorsed his dismissal of the Border Ranges National Park proposal at the 1976 state Labor conference with the statement 'the State needs the timber and the local people need the jobs'.[21] In October 1977 the Wiangarie and Roseberry State Forests were listed on the Interim National Estate Register, and Wran tried to remove the issue from 1978 elections by promising to buy up sawmillers' quotas and create a small national park on the border as well as some pine plantations. Although the pro-conservationists in cabinet felt this was the best they could do at the time, Wran later described it as 'one of our slip-ups'.[22] At the same time a seemingly much less important rainforest campaign had been going on at a little place near the northern New South Wales town of Nimbin called Terania Creek.

Hugh and Nan Nicholson, like many other young idealistic people, had moved to the Nimbin area in the early 1970s. Although they had not been to the Aquarius festival in early 1973 they were imbued with the same spirit that drew people into communities at Tuntable Falls, Darmananda and The Channon. Many had come to this region because they could live near the remnant Big Scrub rainforest and so feel closer to nature. Therefore, when Hugh and Nan found out in 1974 that the Forestry Commission intended to clearfell the Goonimbar and Whian Whian State Forests at the northern end of Terania Creek for eucalypt plantations, they were horrified. The 770 hectares threatened at Terania was small compared with the 33,000 hectares that the Border Ranges Protection Society was attempting to have set aside as national park, but it was on the doorstep of numerous young, idealistic, well-educated new settlers, many of whom had participated in, or been strongly influenced by, the anti-war activities on university campuses in the late 1960s and early 1970s. For the first four years the Terania campaign, begun in 1975 by the Channon Residents Action Group (renamed in 1976 the Terania Native Forest Action Group, TNFAG, as its agenda broadened),[23] was not regarded as a serious threat by the forestry industry or the state Labor government. Although people like Peter Prineas from the National Parks Association had been involved early, the Sydney-based conservation organisations felt that this issue was less worthy of their time than the Border Ranges campaign.

During these years TNFAG's work was conventional enough. Its members researched rainforest ecology and the policies of the Forestry Commission, and made submissions to government to prevent the logging. Part of the Forestry Commission's argument about Terania was that it was not really rainforest and instead was a 'moist hardwood' brush box forest.[24] The Forestry Commission especially pursued this line of argument in the Isaacs inquiry, set up by Premier Wran later in the campaign, but it was rejected by forest ecologists like Len Webb who had been providing TNFAG with scientific information for some time. After the Labor Party came to office in the state in 1976, TNFAG concentrated on the demand for an Environmental Impact Statement before logging went ahead; this was in line with Labor Party policy and the government's draft Environmental Planning and Assessment Act, introduced by Planning and Environment Minister Paul Landa after Labor's victory at the 1978 election. This finally went through the parliament in November 1979. In February 1977 Wran and Landa indicated to TNFAG that they were not willing to intervene on Terania[25] although Lin Gordon announced in late 1977 that, as the result of further scientific assessment, Terania rainforest would not be logged and that the brush box stands would be logged selectively. This might have satisfied TNFAG some years earlier, but the group's understanding of rainforest ecology had increased enormously since then, as had its distrust of the Forestry Commission.[26]

This nature conservation campaign ceased to be conventional on 16 August 1979, when construction began on the road into the Terania forest. A protesters' camp had been established on the Nicholsons' property near the entrance to the forest on 11 and 12 August, and the Forestry Commission's action on 16 August coincided with the Channon market. The protesters turned the market into a rally and organising meeting for a blockade. Five years of research, meetings, submissions and lobbying by such stalwarts as the Nicholsons, Bren Claridge, Victoria and Michael Murphy, Kerry Selwyn and Les Doroughty turned in the space of twenty-four hours into a frenetic, pitched battle in the Terania forest. On Friday, 17 August, the police escorted a bulldozer down the road.

The twenty-two protesters responded by blocking the road with their cars, which were soon removed. Then they put themselves in the bulldozer's path. There were seventeen arrests on the first day.[27] One day Hugh Nicholson asked the police to move their vehicles from his property and showed his title deeds to prove ownership. Still the police did not move, so Nicholson took a petrol can and began outlining the position of the cars on the grass with the petrol; the police quickly moved their cars.[28] As the confrontation moved to the forest, new tactics were tried. Protesters climbed trees and attempted, tree by tree, to slow the process down. The loggers, on the other hand, were trying to get the trees down as quickly as possible, often regardless of risk to the conservationists in the forest. Terania achieved national prominence, and conservationists soon appreciated its symbolic and strategic importance in spite of its limited forest area. The National Trust had given strong moral support since March 1979. Conservationists began moving to Terania from all over northern New South Wales and southern Queensland. Friends of the Earth sent a busload of supporters from Melbourne, and the Newcastle Trades and Labour Council expressed its support. There was support also from such Aboriginal activists as Burnam Burnam, who hailed the protesters as the new Aboriginals. A rally held at Terania Creek on the first weekend in September attracted 1500–2000 people.[29]

The four weeks of the blockade radically changed the nature of campaigning for nature conservation. Direct action in a forest dispute was novel, and the Terania protest showed the effectiveness of theatre in getting the conservation message to the public. The protesters staged set-piece actions, using non-violent methods, to convey their moral opposition to the logging. As well, they had Benny Zable, a well-known artist and resident of Nimbin, whose doleful presence would also grace demonstrations at the Franklin, the Wet Tropics, Roxby Downs, and many other places. With his black costume, gas-masked face and sign saying 'Consume, Be Silent, Die,' he often infuriated police to the extent where he would be arrested merely for standing silently in a protest. The action at the Terania blockade was captured by ABC journalists Jeni Kendall and Paul Tait, whose television news stories brought the issue into the homes of people all over the country. Their documentary 'Give Trees A Chance', an excellent coverage of the events, has never been shown on television. John Seed, the founder of the Rainforest Information Centre in Lismore and a key environmentalist who started at Terania Creek, used the video in talks he gave on rainforest protection around the world. As Ian Cohen, one of the greatest exponents of environmental theatre, says:

> With the backdrop of river and ocean, police blue and forest green, gaudy boat and technicolour bulldozer, one has an exceptional setting for theatre. Theatre of the environment uses the vulture of the media (usually a tool of the establishment) to present the story; we dangle and perform, often in precarious circumstances, making ourselves and our act irresistible to the press. It is a play, an irreverent game, yet at the same time it provides a vital conduit for messages otherwise unable to be transmitted into a monopolistic realm. Lacking financial resources, we penetrate this powerful field as if by magic and in doing so create an alchemy for change.[30]

Popular art forms were never far away: musicians and poets were part of camp life and of the direct action.[31]

In the meantime Neville Wran, who was initially reluctant to act on Terania, was being rapidly convinced otherwise. He told ABC radio journalist Robin Williams that his 'Science Show' based on 'Give Trees A Chance' had convinced him he had to act. Wran declared a moratorium on logging and announced an inquiry into the issue under retired Supreme Court judge Simon Isaacs. A judicial inquiry can be the worst way to settle a forest dispute (as conservationists would find out in the late 1980s) and Judge Isaacs was not the right man for the job. Conservationists were convinced he did not know what he was doing and, in spite of the effort put into it by many conservationists, most of them left it before the judge delivered his verdict eighteen months after it started.

Terania raised other issues for the environment movement. The most significant were the organisational and tactical aspects of non-violent direct action. Although the protesters had always emphasised the importance of resisting violence and sabotage, there were several examples of the latter, not least the chainsawing and spiking of trees. The loggers presented the conservationists with a tactical problem. Because they were being held up by the protesters and because they could fell only as much brush box as could be taken out each day, the loggers decided to cut as many trees as possible, leave them on the ground and transport them out when they could. The protest camp discussed this situation but decided against sabotage, Nevertheless, two protesters, acting unilaterally, went into the forest, spiked some trees with nails and chainsawed logs lying on the ground so that they were useless for milling. The police, the forestry companies, the local press and the protesters' spokespersons condemned the act, but it actually stopped the logging. As many of the protesters conceded, the most questionable tactic had achieved the breakthrough.[32] While sabotage has generally been discouraged in most direct action organised by environmentalists in the years since Terania (and most claims otherwise have been made by industry groups or their supporters with little evidence to back them), there has often been a tension between those who want a greater degree of central control and tighter discipline over direct actions and those, like the Nomadic Action Group, who have been prepared to go their own way. Disagreements about tactics for non-violent struggle are most likely to arise where there are no institutionalised outlets for expressing grievances, although Australia has yet to witness the damage to property that has been a feature of the Earth First! movement in the United States.

The organisation of the protest action at Terania was a model for many other direct action campaigns by environmentalists. Although many people at the protest found the alternative methods of organisation anywhere from 'quaint' to 'downright frustrating', and the activity tended to attract some strange people,[33] the whole thing worked. The food was good, child care was available, accommodation was adequate; thousands of leaflets and press releases were written, printed and distributed, and evening meetings tended to come up with reasonable decisions.[34] In fact, consensus decision-making, meeting facilitation and conflict resolution have become part of the everyday workings of many protest actions and green organisations. The New South Wales rainforest campaigns certainly saw a tension between the mainstream conservation organisations, such as the Australian Conservation Foundation (ACF), The Wilderness Society, the Nature Conservation Council, and the smaller, cutting-edge groups that staked out new arenas and methods of operation. However, as direct actionist Ian Cohen says, this tension can be productive because, when it works as it should, the large groups provide public credibility and follow-through, and the small ones provide the innovation that gives new life to the movement.[35]

### The Northern NSW Rainforests Campaigns

The prominence of the Terania campaign and the lead-up work done on the Border Ranges National Park project built up momentum for the preservation of all the state's rainforests. Time and again conservationists demanded that the Forestry Commission carry out an environmental impact statement (EIS), as set out in the Wran government's Environmental Planning and Assessment Act, before the go-ahead could be given to any logging project in an area of high conservation value, a move that would have made it difficult for the commission to justify any of its activities in rainforests. Conservationists also began studying threatened areas like Washpool, between Grafton and Glen Innes, and Hastings, near the Comboyne Plateau in northern New South Wales, to determine their worth for protected status.[36] Local conservationists at Dorrigo argued that logging should be stopped in the Bellingen State Forest in an area of 6000 hectares known as the Black Scrub, and that it should become part of a corridor joining New England and Dorrigo National Parks. The Forestry Commission, not anxious to take on the 'alternatives' again, conceded the area to the state's National Parks and Wildlife Service even though it had previously promised it to the millers.[37]

In mid-1982, three years after Terania, a group of about a hundred people from the local alternative community and further afield decided to cut through the malaise that had descended on the whole rainforest issue with the handing down of Justice Isaacs' pro-logging decision on Terania and the shilly-shallying of the Wran government. They formed the Nightcap Action Group and determined to complete the process begun by the Terania campaign and to work for a Nightcap National Park, a proposal that would connect Terania Creek with the Goonimbar State Forest. The resulting confrontations between police and protesters and loggers and protesters, first at Griers Scrub and then at Mount Nadi, were more desperate than those at Terania.[38] The conservationists' strategy of calling for an EIS before logging in environmentally sensitive areas was shown to be successful when, at the height of the action at Mount Nadi, the well-known environmental lawyer, Murray Wilcox QC, obtained an injunction to stop the logging from Mr Justice Cripps in the Land and Environment Court. On 22 October Justice Cripps ruled that an EIS was necessary where logging could have an adverse impact on areas of conservation value.[39] Facing opinion polls showing a large majority in New South Wales favouring rainforest preservation, and being lobbied from all quarters (not least, according to Milo Dunphy, by his wife Jill Hickson) to save the rainforests, Wran acted. At a meeting which lasted all day and discussed only the rainforest issue, cabinet decided to protect 93 per cent of the list of seven non-negotiable areas given to Wran by conservationists several months earlier. Although the numbers in cabinet were said to be 12–6 in favour of the rainforests, it was obvious that it was Wran's determined leadership on the issue that had secured the vote. At the 1983 state Labor Conference Wran stated: 'When we're all dead and buried and our children's children are reflecting upon what was the best thing the Labor government did in the 20th century, they'll all come up with the answer that we saved the rainforest.'[40]

Wran showed vision and commitment on the rainforest issue but he also acted with commendable pragmatism. His party was torn between the demands of rival constituencies—the timber workers and all those in the labour movement who were concerned about unemployment resulting from environmental protection on the one hand, and the conservationists on the other. The former were traditional Labor supporters, well-represented in the caucus and the party as a whole. The latter were a new force on the political scene and, while they were unlikely to look too hopefully to the coalition given its anti-environmental leanings, they still had many reservations about Labor's ability to deliver. By taking up the cause of nature conservation with such enthusiasm Wran set the pattern for Labor—both state and federal—to secure at least the preference votes of the green constituency and keep Labor in office at many elections. Wran was from the Labor Right, not the Left that had given such strong support to campaigns like the green bans and the anti-uranium movement; while the hearts of many in the environmental movement might have been with the Left, the Right had the numbers in the party and could deliver the policies in government.

Although a strategic alliance was created with sections of the New South Wales Labor Right, conservationists were not popular with many trade unionists, who saw them as middle-class, unsympathetic to the problems of ordinary workers, and ever-ready to pursue campaigns that would result in job losses. There is, of course, a degree of truth in this, and a seeming inevitability about the course of action that led to the fracturing of the close relationship between the labour and green movements. Watson criticises the inadequacies of the conservationists' alternative employment proposals at Terania and says that they were little more than 'theoretical and programmatic', designed to ward off criticisms about job losses more than providing real ideas for jobs outside forestry.[41] According to Watson, conservationists and timber workers needed to find common ground. This could have been achieved with a strong union (like the New South Wales Builders Labourers Federation), a secure value-added niche for the hardwood timber industry, and greater exposure by workers to ecological arguments.[42] Watson omits to point out that, by 1979, the Mundeyites inside the union movement had been thoroughly defeated; significant sections of the native forest timber industry were just as reluctant to seek compromise as the greens; and, in the absence of a sympathetic union, there were few ways of educating timber workers on forest ecology. It is difficult to see what other action New South Wales nature conservationists could have taken in the late 1970s to avoid the damaging split with the unions.

The northern rainforest campaigns and the maintenance of a strong alternative community in the region created a strong and continuing green movement in northern New South Wales. The North-East Forest Alliance continued the struggle to protect those forest areas that did not make it into Wran's rainforest package; the anti-nuclear campaigner, Helen Caldicott, was almost elected to the House of Representatives as an independent Green for the seat of Richmond in 1990; and conservationists have opposed numerous developments they considered to be destructive of the environment, including the Club Med proposal at Byron Bay in the mid-1990s. In 1986 the New South Wales rainforests were listed on the World Heritage register.

The northern New South Wales activists were winning their campaign in 1982 just as another group of rainforest campaigners farther south was poised for a showdown that would be seen across the world. The Franklin campaign achieved wilderness protection for most of the Tasmanian south-west; it helped bring the Labor Party to power federally; and it changed the way federal powers are interpreted in the Constitution. It also did more than any other campaign (with the possible exception of Greenpeace's harp seal and whale campaigns) to instil in the country the widespread view that nature had rights beyond its use value to humans; it consolidated an internal culture in the movement that was reflected in anti-hierarchical organisational practices, consensus decision-making and various other 'countercultural' attitudes; and it created a new national conservation organisation—The Wilderness Society.

### South-West Tasmania

In June 1981, 23-year-old Peter Robertson rode his bicycle from Perth, across the Nullarbor Plain and ultimately to Hobart, raising money for the Tasmanian Wilderness Society along the way. Like many other passionate young people around the country, Robertson was drawn to the intensifying conflict over the attempt by the Tasmanian state government to dam the Gordon River below its confluence with the Franklin in the South-West Tasmanian wilderness.

The Franklin campaign is often spoken of as though it was the first great wilderness campaign of the modern environment movement. Of course, as we have demonstrated, it was not. It was occurring at the same time as hard-fought campaigns in the south-west forests of Western Australia and, as we have seen, the northern rainforests of New South Wales. It was preceded, as we saw in Chapter 3, by the dramatic and unsuccessful campaign to stop the damming of Lake Pedder, also in the Tasmanian south-west. In fact, most commentators acknowledge that, without the Lake Pedder failure, the Franklin success would have been impossible.

Out of the ashes of the Lake Pedder campaign came a new energy and a new determination among Tasmanian environmental campaigners. Most of them knew that it would not be long before they faced new challenges and these were most likely to come in the state's south-west.

This new militant attitude, which communicated itself to mainland activists, was captured by Dick Jones when he stated, 'You've got to be tactically unfettered. You have to be reasonable when it's necessary to be reasonable. You have to persist when it's necessary to persist. There are times when I wouldn't have persisted and other people who seemed to be fanatical, dragged me along ... these people proved to be correct.'[43]

Of all the difficult times in Tasmania in the decade after 1973, the worst time for conservationists was in the years after the flooding of Lake Pedder and before the formation of The Wilderness Society in order to counter the rumoured building of the Franklin Dam. The tension that had existed in the Pedder campaign between the 'respectable' conservationists such as those in the Tasmanian Conservation Trust and the 'hotheads' in the Lake Pedder Action Committee (LPAC) continued after 1973 with disputes between the LPAC and the South-West Committee over whether the movement should push for a large or a smaller national park for the south-west,[44] the sort of dispute that had dogged campaigning groups in the past and would continue to do so.

### Formation of the Tasmanian Wilderness Society

In the summer of 1976 Bob Brown and Paul Smith did what few had ever done—rafted down the Franklin. According to Smith, Brown was not enthusiastic about the trip because he was more intent on the threat of nuclear weapons.[45] However, conservationists were convinced that the Franklin River was the target for the Hydro-Electric Commission's next damming venture, especially after bushwalkers found some plans in a hut belonging to the commission.[46] Brown took some time to consider his options but, by mid-1976, buoyed by his trip down the Franklin and the sense of urgency communicated by fellow conservationists, he committed himself to the campaign. In 1974 Kevin Kiernan and others had set up the South-West Action Committee. In July 1976 the committee formed itself into the Tasmanian Wilderness Society at a meeting of sixteen people squeezed into Bob Brown's house in Liffey near Launceston. Kevin Kiernan was its first director; in early 1979 Bob Brown took over that position and held it for the rest of the campaign.

The campaign to save the Franklin became so big because thousands of activists worked hard and their efforts caused tens of thousands of ordinary Australians to mobilise; but Bob Brown was the individual at the apex of the campaign. This occurred partly because that the media looked for a marketable leader, but the reasons for Brown's enduring role in the conservation movement and green politics go deeper. He is a mass of intriguing contradictions. He is modest, even self-effacing, and yet understands his ability to move and inspire thousands of people. He often seems artless and absent-minded, but has a sharp strategic mind and can focus with ruthless determination on a problem. He is hated by his enemies—he has been shot at and bashed during campaigns—but he is deeply loved by those who know him and admired by many who do not. His generosity and integrity made him a central, unifying figure throughout the Franklin campaign and, although his role changed after he became a Tasmanian and then a federal politician, he maintains a special place in the environment movement, especially with nature conservationists.

Just as LPAC had developed a truly national campaign largely by setting up supporting groups in mainland cities, so the South-West Action Committee and TWS also had supporting groups in other states. A South-West Tasmania Action Committee had been set up in Sydney in November 1974 by Geoff and Judy Lambert and it continued after the establishment of the Tasmanian Wilderness Society in 1976. A branch of TWS was also set up in Melbourne in 1979, largely through the efforts of Karen Alexander. These groups helped to publicise the issue around the country. During the campaign about thirty regional TWS offices were set up at such centres as Armidale, Newcastle, Wollongong and Cairns. After the 1983 elections some folded, but a number stayed on to become branches in the new Australia-wide organisation, The Wilderness Society. The process of horizontal expansion of the campaign was well under way by 1979, and TWS also had solid support from other groups such as the ACF.

The national nature of the Franklin campaign is underlined by an analysis of the origins of the key campaigners. In contrast to campaigns like Terania Creek and Nightcap, where the key activists were locals, the Franklin campaign had a large number of outsiders.[47] As the profile of the Franklin rose and detailed knowledge of the issue became available, many mainland activists made their way to Hobart and took important roles in the campaign: Peter Thompson, Judy Richter, Vince Mahon, Bob Burton, Cathy Plowman and Pam Waud were from New South Wales; Peter and Margaret Robertson from Western Australia; Rob Blakers from Canberra; Geoff Law and Karen Alexander from Melbourne. International input was provided by Chris Harris from South Africa and Norm Sanders, originally from the United States. Bob Brown, born in central New South Wales, had moved to Liffey, near Launceston, in 1972. The fact that so many activists were outsiders did nothing, of course, to endear them or their cause to many long-term Tasmanians.

It was, however, a Tasmanian, Kevin Kiernan, who made the single most important discovery in the campaign—Kutakina Cave. Kiernan had been active in the Lake Pedder campaign and was with Olegas Truchanas when the famous nature photographer was drowned in the Gordon River in 1972. In 1976 he became the first director of the Tasmanian Wilderness Society. In that year he summed up in a news-letter the strategic direction conservationists would take to save the Franklin and the philosophical orientation that the movement would adopt in wilderness campaigns throughout the 1980s: 'We have to try to sell not the wilderness experience—that is, wilderness as a recreational resource—but the right of wilderness to exist ... an emphasis on the philosophical and the eternal—that is, wilderness for its own.'[48]

This approach, taken up by TWS and most other groups over the next decade, was a breakthrough in wilderness campaigning. While not rejecting utilitarian arguments for protecting wilderness, it placed a new emphasis on non-utilitarian reasons for doing so. It not only articulated a 'post-materialist' sentiment on the part of the campaigners, but also recognised that many other Australians were ready to accept such messages. Kiernan, who was always happier going caving than attending interminable meetings and dealing with the conflicts of environmental politics, went to the Franklin looking for caves in the south-west after 1976. On one trip he found a cave full of old bones and, on his third trip to the cave in 1981 with Bob Brown and Bob Burton, he realised its full significance. Further work with anthropologist Dr Rhys Jones estab-lished that these were Aboriginal relics dating back nearly 20,000 years. This crucial site would have been inundated by 75 metres of water if the Gordon-below-Franklin project had gone ahead.

### The State Government, the HEC and The Wilderness Society

The Hydro-Electric Commission unveiled its options for a new dam in the south-west. It proposed a dam on the Gordon River above the junction of the Olga (Gordon-above-Olga) or, its preferred option, one on the Gordon below the junction with the Franklin River (Gordon-below-Franklin). The Labor premier, Doug Lowe, favoured the former, but the Hydro-Electric Commission and many of his ministers wanted the Gordon-below-Franklin. The issue split the cabinet but, fortunately for conservationists, before Lowe was ousted from the leadership of the parliamentary Labor Party in November 1981, he nominated South-West Tasmania for World Heritage nomination.[49] Lowe had intended to hold a referendum on the dam issue in which Tasmanians would have a 'no dam' option. The new Labor administration, however, under Harry Holgate, gave voters only two choices—Gordon-above-Olga or Gordon-below-Franklin. TWS campaigned for people to write 'No Dams' on their ballot paper. This suggestion was followed by 45 per cent of voters, while 47 per cent favoured the Gordon-below-Franklin.[50] TWS and the ACF spent $100,000 on this campaign; according to Peter Thompson, they doorknocked 85–90 per cent of the state's inhabitants and staffed virtually every polling booth.[51] The 'No Dams' campaign was continued in a number of by-elections during 1982. In the Lowe by-election of march 1982, 12 per cent wrote 'No Dams' on their ballot papers, while 40 per cent did so in the Flinders by-election later in the year.

In the Tasmanian state elections of May 1982, the greens performed poorly. This emphasised the necessity of focusing on federal politics as the only arena where the conflict could be won, a strategy that had worked in both the Great Barrier Reef and Fraser Island campaigns. The election had been won by the Liberals under Robin Gray, whose support for the Gordon-below-Franklin was even more emphatic than that of Labor. In Gray's words, 'For eleven months of the year the Franklin is nothing but a brown ditch, leech-ridden, unattractive to the majority of people.' He authorised work to begin on the dam immediately, and was deaf to the pleas of the Fraser government in Canberra to accept compensation for not building the dam. Fraser had to choose between taking on his Liberal colleague and forcing an anti-dam position on Tasmania using federal powers, or maintaining the traditional Liberal policy of respecting states' rights. In effect, Fraser did a little of both. On 14 December 1982 South-West Tasmania was placed on the World Heritage List at the request of the federal government, but at the same time Fraser refused to intervene in Tasmania's affairs. Several Liberals made public their opposition to the dam. Peter Reith, later to achieve prominence as a pragmatic conservative in the federal parliamentary Liberal Party, won a by-election in 1982 on an anti-dam platform (although he took no stand on the issue once in parliament), and Tom Spender and two other prominent Liberal politicians marched arm-in-arm with Tom Uren in an anti-dam rally in Sydney.[52] Nevertheless, no amount of lobbying was able to persuade the federal coalition to adopt an interventionist policy.[53]

*The Blockade and the 1983 Federal Election*

On 14 December, the same day as the South-West was placed on the World Heritage List, TWS began its long-awaited blockade of the dam site. Preparations for it had begun as early as mid-1981, when Cathy Plowman made a round-Australia trip canvassing support for the action among TWS branches. Despite the widespread knowledge of TWS's plans, word did not get out until July 1982.[54] During this time the ACF and TWS had maintained a working relationship in the campaign.

Tensions were aroused by the fact that much of the finance came from the ACF, while TWS contributed almost all the activists and most of the publicity. The role of people like Bob Burton and Karen Alexander was vital in maintaining this working relationship.

The ACF president, Murray Wilcox, convened a meeting of representatives of conservation groups from around the country at Tullamarine Airport in Melbourne on 19 December 1982. This meeting decided in principle to campaign against the Liberals at the forthcoming federal election.[55] A further meeting was held at Tullamarine on 6 February 1983 to set up the National South-West Coalition. Only a few days earlier Malcolm Fraser had called the election for 6 March and Bob Hawke had replaced Bill Hayden as leader of the Labor Party. The stage was set for a dramatic election in which the Franklin Dam was one of the main issues. The conservation movement threw its support behind the Labor Party in the House of Representatives and the Democrats in the Senate. The blockade had been announced on 26 July 1982; a vigil had begun on Butler Island in the Franklin River in September, culminating four months later in G-Day when 228 people were arrested in various actions. Scenes of the blockade ensured that all voters took with them to the polls the impression of environmentalists fighting to preserve a beautiful wilderness river; their most lasting image was the breathtaking photograph of Rock Island Bend taken by Peter Dombrovskis and reproduced on hundreds of thousands of election posters by TWS.

With the Labor Party's election success, the environment movement had achieved an outstanding victory. It had mobilised thousands of Australians in a major campaign; it had won the support of the Labor Party for federal action against a recalcitrant state government intent on ignoring its responsibilities for proper management of a World Heritage area; and, with the passing of the World Heritage (Properties Conservation) Act, introduced into the Senate by the Democrats in the previous parliament, federal legislative protection was accorded the South-West and any other listed areas. Just as significantly, it introduced young activists to the movement and many of these would go on to become key environmental campaigners around the country. The Franklin campaign represented the coming of age of the environment movement. It had mobilised large numbers of activists and supporters around the issue and developed the skills and resources to force its way into the mainstream of Australian political life. It was also able to pressure the federal government into seeing the environment as an issue that, in many ways, had to be dealt with at a national level; in the next chapter we shall look at the constitutional significance of the federal government's decision to override the powers of the Tasmanian government on this issue. Those

early conservationists who tried unsuccessfully to persuade Alfred
Deakin to adopt this approach would have been pleased. However, the
successes of a rapidly professionalising movement in pushing environmental protection into the 'Deakinite consensus' was coming at a time
when that consensus was falling apart.

The constitutional and political basis might have been laid for
environmental protection to become part of mainstream Australian
society, but the country was also experiencing the impacts of a global-
ising economy, the push for deregulation and micro-economic reform,
the emergence of strong regional economies, and the weakening of
White Australia and patriarchal structures. If care for the environment
was going to become part of a new, national consensus (and this was
still a big 'if'), then it was difficult to know what other values it could
co-exist with.

# PART IV

# The Professional Movement: 1983–1990

If the second phase of the environment movement's development ended in the early 1970s in a traumatic defeat—the flooding of Lake Pedder—the third ended in 1983 with a resounding victory. The Franklin blockade, the Labor electoral victory and the High Court decision upholding the Hawke government's action all signalled the movement's ability to mobilise tens of thousands of people right around the nation, to influence the outcomes of elections, and even to act as a catalyst for constitutional change. The decision by the Labor Party under Hawke to support federal government intervention against a recalcitrant state to enforce an international conservation agreement had a strong influence on the movement's strategy. Since it came after the Wran Labor government in New South Wales had acted to save the state's northern rainforests, movement strategists began to feel that, by influencing Labor governments, radical new environmental policy outcomes were possible in the next few years.

If one of the goals of a social movement is to link up with political power, the Franklin campaign had shown how effectively that could be done. The failure of the anti-uranium movement to convince the Labor Party to ban uranium mining dampened this optimism. Nevertheless, there was the belief among many that, if the movement could continue to organise mass campaigns around Australian environmental icons, professionalise its operations and hone its political skills, then major gains were possible.

The new Hawke government, however, had more urgent priorities than saving the environment. The Prices and Incomes Accord with the Australian Council of Trade Unions, the floating of the dollar, the deregulation of the financial system, a more effective industry policy—these were all planks of the Labor platform. Neither Hawke nor Keating, its two outstanding personalities, were interested in pushing beyond the Franklin decision to forge a closer alliance with the environment movement. As well, Barry Cohen, the environment minister after 1983, while not incompetent, was no shining light in the ministry and not regarded by the movement as a close ally.

These priorities indicated the primary objective of the Hawke–Keating era. This period effectively saw the end of what Bob Leach calls the Deakinite consensus[1] and Paul Kelly calls the Australian Settlement.[2] The elements of Australia's traditional political culture had begun to crumble in the 1960s with the retreat of Britain from east of Aden (and its less than satisfactory replacement by the United States) and the increasing rejection of a discriminatory migration policy. Malcolm Fraser, Australia's prime minister in the late 1970s and early 1980s, fought a last-ditch battle to hang on to the Right Deakinism of Menzies (as opposed to the Left Deakinism of Chifley), but the intellectual coherence of the forces of economic rationalism and the overwhelming logic of the globalisation of the economy persuaded the hard-headed pragmatists of the Hawke government that they needed to throw off sentimental attachments and to embrace the reality of a competitive Australian economy in a fast-growing region.

Such a direction sat uneasily with the objectives of the environment movement. At one level, if Australia were to become 'the clever country', then Australian entrepreneurs could have taken new opportunities opening in the areas of environmental management, renewable energy, information technology, clean production and cutting-edge technology. Unfortunately, Australian capitalism was historically linked with the powerful resource extraction sectors of the economy and these were hostile to many of the demands of the environment movement. When the call came for economic growth, it was partly answered by the opening of new areas of the manufacturing sector and tourism, but there was still a great reliance on those traditional sources of economic growth— mining, forestry and agriculture. In the meantime many government regulatory agencies, born largely of the predominantly social liberal rhetoric of Australian Deakinism and whose task was supposedly to restrain the more anti-social and destructive side of capitalist economic development, continued to act largely as captured agencies for the industries they were supposedly regulating. This was the case whether one looked at forestry, mining, damming or pollution concerns. Consequently, the threats presented to the goals of maintaining biodiversity and ecological sustainability ensured that the 1980s would be a decade of environmental conflict, just as the previous decade had been.

The environment movement during the 1970s had begun to challenge principal institutional norms and the main sociocultural patterns, a process that Alain Touraine argues is a key characteristic of social movements. Both Touraine and Castells emphasise the fundamental conflict between social movements and ruling elites and the liberatory potential of these movements. Both argue that, when these movements fail to achieve their liberatory potential, they degenerate into utopian marginality or are incorporated into the liberal state.[3] The environment movement in the 1980s, however, manifested both liberatory and corporatist tendencies, something the action-identity approach has difficulty explaining. From 1983 to 1990 key conservation organisations like the Australian Conservation Foundation (ACF), The Wilderness Society, Greenpeace and World Wide Fund for Nature developed almost conventional organisational structures, employed skilled researchers, lobbyists and public advocates, and impacted on governmental policy-making processes in ways that only industrial or trade union groups had previously been able to do. At the same time they developed approaches to environmental management and economic development that were—implicitly at least—a major challenge not only to sociocultural norms but to socioeconomic ones as well. The mainstream of the environment movement was desperate for the sort of partial institutionalisation that would see its policy program implemented by government and, if a growing rapport with the Labor Party was a way of achieving that, then most key environmental activists accepted its necessity. In keeping with its increasingly professional approach, the movement adopted, by the end of the decade, ecologically sustainable development (ESD) as the main framework for such incorporation. ESD, however, at least for environmentalists, was not a so-called 'balance' or compromise between the demands of rampant developmentalism and those of conservation. It was a set of principles that included the maintenance of biodiversity, the precautionary principle and inter-generational equity that are not easy for even the most liberal form of capitalist economy—let alone one dependent on resource-extraction, like Australia's—to accommodate.

In this era of deregulation, the environment movement urged strong government intervention; in a profane age where 'greed was good', it promoted the sacred nature of wild places. In the face of the technocrat's suspicion of the public, the environment movement supported demands for community consultation and participation. Given these contradictions in Australian political life, it is a testimony to the professionalism and commitment of the movement that, by the end of the 1980s, it had achieved so much, especially in terms of nature conservation. Moves were under way to achieve the sort of historic compromise between the forces of capitalism and technocracy on the one hand and environmentalism on the other that had been achieved at the turn of the century between capital and labour with the Deakinite consensus.

However, such a compromise could be achieved only by fundamental changes to the nature of Australian economic development. By the beginning of the 1990s the forces opposed to such changes were regrouping; the next phase of the movement's development would be much more problematic than that of the period 1983 to 1990.

Part IV is divided into three chapters. The first, 'Forest and Wilderness Campaigns', examines a number of the prominent wilderness struggles that maintained the strong campaigning focus from the 1970s but added to this a highly professional, well-organised approach by the conservation groups involved. These groups became increasingly skilful at impacting on public policy as the 1980s progressed. Chapter 6 focuses on urban issues and pollution, and tries to give an idea of the enormous variety of issues dealt with by groups in these areas. We show that these issues tended to be taken up by smaller, local organisations, but that the questions raised—energy, pollution, urban planning—all added new dimensions to the environmental challenge to technocratic dominance. Chapter 7, 'Green Politics', examines the two main political streams of the movement. The dominant one was that exemplified by the ACF's executive director, Phillip Toyne, who was able to persuade the federal Labor government of the day to implement key policies dear to the heart of the environment movement. The minor stream, that of independent green politics, was exemplified by the Tasmanian wilderness campaigner, Dr Bob Brown. After leading the Franklin campaign, he became an independent green member of the state parliament, and was joined there by four other greens by 1989. These two streams acted, for the most part, in a complementary way with separate existences, one as a partial 'insider' with government and the other largely an outsider with one foot in the parliamentary arena. Much had been achieved by the end of the decade, but there was still an unresolved question about the extent to which the liberal state could achieve a strategic partnership with the environment movement. While a growing number of Labor politicians was becoming concerned about the greens having too much influence, many movement activists were equally concerned that the partnership with the Labor government could come at too high a price.

# CHAPTER 6

# *Fighting for Wilderness*

The period from 1983 to 1990 saw the environment movement maintaining its ability to mobilise in large numbers, often on a national basis,
and displaying a higher level of professionalism among its key
campaigners to achieve important wilderness protection outcomes. The
campaigns of national significance tended to be of three types. The first
centred on areas like the Wet Tropics of north Queensland and Kakadu
in the Northern Territory, for which the movement had been able to
gain wide public recognition of the World Heritage values. The second
was attempts to stop woodchipping in old-growth forests in such areas as
south-east New South Wales, East Gippsland in Victoria and the south-
west of Western Australia. Here the conflict was bitter because the
political influence of the forest industries at least equalled that of
the greens, and the outcomes were (and still are in the late 1990s)
indeterminate and not at all satisfactory to the movement. The third was
those campaigns that involved intensive work by a few activists but did
not necessitate mass mobilisations. The most important of these was the
creation of a World Park for Antarctica. First, however, it is necessary to
understand the political and constitutional fall-out from the conservationists' victory in the Franklin campaign.

Tasmania played a surprisingly important role in the history of
Australia's modern environment movement up to 1983. A tiny state with
a population smaller than that of Brisbane had seen the Lake Pedder
and Franklin campaigns and the establishment of the world's first Green
Party. The period from 1983 to 1990, the period in which green politics
became an integral part of the national political scene, would also see
the island state as a focus of environmental activity.

The campaign to save the Franklin, culminating in the Hawke Labor
victory in the 1983 federal election, had two big impacts on Australian

politics. The first of these was constitutional. Writs were issued in the High Court by both the Tasmanian and Commonwealth governments under the National Parks and Wildlife Conservation Act 1975. The Tasmanian government argued that the Commonwealth decision to halt work on the dam invalidly interfered with the state government's constitutional power in relation to lands.[1] The Commonwealth argued that it had the sole power to enter into agreements with other countries on any topic and that this enabled it to frame legislation to implement these agreements. The High Court ruled on 1 July 1983 in favour of the Commonwealth and the external affairs power, which had been clearly established in 1982 in the High Court case *Koowarta v. Bjelke-Petersen*, could now be used by the federal government to intervene in the affairs of a state government in order to protect conservation values in areas that were World Heritage listed. Nevertheless, such a clear-cut legal decision did not necessarily translate immediately into action by the federal government. The Hawke government would pursue a timid path on federal intervention on the environment until the appointment of Graham Richardson to the environment portfolio after the 1987 election.

The second major impact was on the environment movement itself. The movement had thrown its weight behind Labor in the 1983 election and that result had cemented a great victory. Clearly, if the peak conservation groups could campaign effectively, move public opinion and have a possibly decisive impact on election outcomes, they could expect to exercise considerable political influence. Hawke's powerful support for stopping the damming of the Franklin, allied with the work done by Wran in New South Wales on the northern rainforests, persuaded many in the movement that the Labor Party was their best bet for getting good outcomes for the environment.

Meanwhile, at the coalface of the environment movement, campaigns were building. Various factors were at work: the need to protect wilderness from logging, dams and other threats; a growing 'wilderness ethic'; increasing understanding of the vital ecological role of rainforests; and the lessons learned from the militant struggles of Terania Creek and the Franklin. All these combined to ensure that some of the country's biggest environmental campaigns during the 1980s would be over wilderness. Nevertheless, it would have been difficult at the start of the decade to believe that one of the most bitter conflicts would be in and around the sleepy far north Queensland town of Cairns. The area in contention, the tropical forest area extending from just north of Townsville to north of Cairns, would become known as the Wet Tropics World Heritage Area.

## Queensland

In June 1980 Cairns played host to the World Wilderness Congress. At the congress, in words that would come back to haunt him, that well-known bulldozer driver and Queensland Premier Joh Bjelke-Petersen said that the Wet Tropics 'provides a living museum of plant and animal species in what is one of the few remaining examples of undisturbed coastal rainforest in the world'.[2]

The congress had an enormous impact on many environmentalists in the Queensland far north who had, for some time, attempted to set up their own environment centre. With this increased motivation they set up the Cairns and Far North Environment Centre in March 1981.[3] Campaigns sprang up like that to stop rainforest logging at Mount Windsor[4] and discussions began on a possible World Heritage listing for the area's tropical rainforests. It was not until July 1983, however, when the Douglas Shire Council decided to bulldoze a road 37 kilometres through a national park from Cape Tribulation to the Aboriginal settlement of Bloomfield, that a major campaign took place.

Dr Aila Keto and Dr Keith Scott, from the Rainforest Conservation Society, were commissioned by the Australian Heritage Commission in 1984 to compile a report on World Heritage listing for the Wet Tropics. They said: 'The Wet Tropics ... is one of the most significant regional ecosystems in the world. It is of outstanding scientific importance and natural beauty and adequately fulfils all four criteria for the inclusion of natural properties in the World Heritage list.'[5]

The scientific expertise of Keto and Scott laid the basis for much of the strength of the local campaigning, as did the fieldwork of local National Parks and Wildlife officer, Peter Stanton, and the research of former director of the CSIRO's rainforest ecology section, Dr Len Webb. In an interview with Gregg Borschmann for the Melbourne *Age*, Webb said:

> If we have an unlimited future for mankind on this planet, we have to retain this [i.e. Wet Tropics] because it won't evolve again in any reasonable time scale. Could you imagine a rhinoceros, or an elephant or a kangaroo if you'd never even seen one? Well it's the same with a chemist and a chemical compound ... he has got to have the key from nature.[6]

The importance of good research to back up grassroots campaigns was also illustrated by the work done by Geoff Tracey and Len Webb in mapping the vegetation profile of the Wet Tropics area. These maps were then converted by Mike Graham of Cairns and Far North Environment Centre to a single map that was used for the campaign from then on.[7]

However, the wholehearted support given to the Cape Tribulation–
Bloomfield road by the Douglas Shire Council and the Queensland
government made it impossible for the conservation movement to use
conventional lobbying backed by sound research to defeat this dire
threat to the Wet Tropics. These methods should have been enough,
because proposals for such a road had been refused by the Department
of Main Roads on a number of occasions because they were neither
technically nor economically feasible. The road had been originally
built in 1968 by a local landowner-developer, George Quaid, without any
authorisation. Two years later the Queensland government gazetted the
by-now overgrown track with the intention of making it a 20-metre-wide
road reserve. The Cape Tribulation National Park was created in 1980
and, when the Douglas Shire Council began work on turning this
beautiful walking track into a major road in 1983, the state government
allowed it to go well outside that 20-metre limit—effectively, into the
national park.[8]

Conservationists were also concerned that erosion from the roadworks would cause siltation of the fringing inshore reefs of the Great
Barrier Reef; this fear was well founded, as was seen during the first
major downpour after the road was built, when tonnes of silt poured
down over these reefs. The state government advanced a number of
reasons for building the road, including Environment Minister Martin
Tenni's famous statement that it was there to stop heroin traffickers and
white slavers.[9] The environment movement, however, was in no doubt
that it was there to assist real estate developers.

Once the council had announced in August 1983 that the road would
go through, conservationists began mobilising. Public meetings were
held in places like Port Douglas and Mossman, followed by impassioned
pleas for people to join the opposition.[10] In Port Douglas the Wilderness
Action Group was set up out of one of these meetings in September. It
was to become the core of the blockade.

Attempts to stop the road by injunction failed and, by mid-November,
the activists were discussing a possible blockade. Last-minute negotiations began between council chair Tony Mijo and the federal environment minister, Barry Cohen, in late November but, before they could
be re-convened, the bulldozers had crossed the Daintree and work on
the road began.

The blockade started on the first day of work on the road. Rupert
Russell, a writer and naturalist, was the first arrested. At the same time a
small group of blockaders had travelled by boat to the Bloomfield end
of the road, where council contractors had just begun work. With no
police around, battle was joined.

[The] driver, Doug Roots, on the leading dozer, did not stop when he reached the campaigners. Three jumped on the blade. They were driven into a lantana thicket. One girl was sandwiched between the blade and the bushes, and could not be seen by the driver. Thinking this was a sure way to get herself killed, she climbed up onto the blade with the other three. The driver continued to clear lantana.

At this stage there were no police or photographers present. The dozer eventually called a halt and told the protesters to get off his machine ... They hopped down off the blade; he started working again, they jumped back on the blade. This time the driver raised the blade high and charged up a hill, shaking the blade from side to side.[11]

This sort of conflict continued until the police arrived at 11 a.m. the next day. The main action, however, would continue at the Cape Tribulation end.

On day four of the blockade, police and council workers were confronted by protesters high in the trees in the path of the bulldozers. The most sensational action, however, occurred on Monday, 12 December: police and council workers were confronted on their arrival at the site with protester John Nolan, tied to a wooden cross symbolising the crucifixion of the ancient life force, with a human barricade in front of him—of protesters buried up to their necks in the red clay! The police wasted many hours digging protesters out of their 'tombs'.

All the while, the conservationists were hoping for intervention by the federal minister, Cohen, using the Great Barrier Reef Marine Park Act, since siltation from the road construction could cause great damage to the reef. However, Cohen made it clear to the media on 9 December that he did not intend to intervene; again in February 1984, at a rainforest conference in Cairns, he stated, 'It is no use petitioning Barry Cohen to invoke the Act to save every bit of bushland in the country.'[12] By the end of the month, the rainy weather had set in and work on the road stopped. On that last day the exhausted protesters formed a circle around the bulldozer. In Mike Graham's words:

It was raining about every quarter of an hour and the NAGs were all over the top of the bulldozer doing rain dances and making rain happen regularly— it was working—it was magic ... [then] conservationists and the police had an all out pitched physical battle. People were picked up and hurled and thrown ... and after about half an hour it all came to a standstill. There were a couple of people that nearly got buried by the dozer and the dozer driver freaked out and stopped operating it and then there was a lengthy confab on the police radios for about an hour, during which time the senior constable came out and instructed two lady policemen there not to fraternise and at the end of the time, the police made an announcement that all the equipment and everything would be removed from the national park and they were all going home.[13]

At various times more mainstream conservationists like Aila Keto voiced concerns that the direct action would lose popular support for the issue, but that certainly did not seem to be the case. The media interest generated by the conflict ensured that spokespersons like Mike Berwick and Rosemary Hill were able to get their message about the Wet Tropics to audiences around the world; activists arrived in Cairns from all over Australia (and even from other parts of the world); and money poured in to the campaign.

In 1984 the Australian Heritage Commission asked Aila Keto and Keith Scott from the Rainforest Conservation Society to produce a report on the possible World Heritage values of the Wet Tropics. Their report stated unequivocally that most of this area had these values in abundance, and their judgment was backed by rainforest experts around the world. Also in 1984, the Truloves, a couple who had a tourist business at the end of the road, took the Queensland government to court because, they argued, construction of the road had breached a number of sections of the state's Nature Conservation Act. This action failed and, although their legal advice was that they could well win on appeal, there was no money to pursue it further.

With expert opinion, direct action and legal judgment all failing to stop the road and protect the Wet Tropics, the movement turned its attention to lobbying the federal Labor government. Barry Cohen's political judgment told him that taking on the government of Joh Bjelke-Petersen was political suicide and that nominating the area for World Heritage listing, as the Australian Heritage Commission had requested, would have lost Labor the 1984 election. In a frank assessment of the situation as he saw it, he said:

> I do not believe there is a big pro-environment vote in this country ... there are a lot of people who are concerned about the environment and might make it their number one issue, but most of these people politically vote for us anyway ...
>
> Now where do they go? To the Liberals? The Liberals would be 100 times worse than us. And believe me under Howard they are going to be 1000 times worse.[14]

The government was running scared of a conservative agenda (especially one that people in southern states often found repulsive), and saying to a social movement, 'Where else are you going to go?' This combination of strategies had been seen from Labor as far back as the Vietnam War. Jo Vallentine, elected as an anti-nuclear senator in 1984, reported Hawke snarling the question at her over uranium mining.[15] However, the newly appointed director of the Australian Conservation Foundation (ACF), Phillip Toyne, was gaining access to significant people in the party beyond Cohen. This was largely made possible by the contacts in the Labor Right of Jonathan West, the former director of The Wilderness Society (TWS). Through West, Toyne made contact with Graham Richardson, who was still a backbencher, and through him with other powerful figures in the party.[16] Toyne was able to supply research showing that 88 per cent of people polled in Melbourne, 84 per cent in Sydney and 74 per cent in Brisbane favoured 'urgent action' by the federal government to save the tropical forests.[17] With the sort of information the movement was funnelling to party strategists, it was obvious to Labor that unilateral action by the federal government to list the Wet Tropics would not even necessarily lose it the local Cairns seat of Leichhardt. Hawke told Cohen to nominate unilaterally the Wet Tropics for World Heritage listing (and to try to settle the boundaries for Stage III of Kakadu) and the environment movement had been, in the Labor Party's parlance, 'brought into the tent'.[18] Hawke's promises persuaded the ACF and TWS to support Labor in the 1987 election. While it is difficult to find a Labor figure (including Richardson) who will admit that the green vote ever won Labor an election, the environment movement has never been so tardy and it was anxious not to let Labor forget it.

Labor always found it easier to meet green demands when these were for highly scenic areas where the resource industries were poorly organised, or where there was disunity among industry groups such as loggers and tourism operators. This applied to South-West Tasmania and the Wet Tropics, although Kakadu would present the federal government with a major problem because of the large reserves of uranium and other metals in the area.

### Kakadu

One of the longest-running campaigns also illustrated the particular affinities and tensions that exist between conservationists and Aborigines—the battle for Kakadu.

Kakadu includes the entire catchments of both the South Alligator and East Alligator Rivers, and protection of both these catchments made good environmental sense. The history of the area's protection, however, has occurred in stages. Stage I was proclaimed a national park in 1979, though with the Ranger uranium mine site excised from it, and it was nominated for World Heritage listing in 1981. Stage II was proclaimed in 1984 and announced for World Heritage listing in 1986. At the same time the possible uranium mining sites of Koongarra and Jabiluka were excised from Stage II and the borders of Stages I and II respectively. Stage III, consisting of the old pastoral leases of Gimbat and

Goodparla, was announced in 1987. The fact that the Commonwealth, and not the Northern Territory, government had the power over these decisions was crucial because, while the Fraser and Hawke governments were often not as sympathetic as conservationists would have liked, they were nowhere near as hostile to the environmental or Aboriginal causes as the government in Darwin.

The most famous parts of this area, the whole of which is now on the World Heritage List, consist of the magnificent wetlands and the escarpments. Other parts of the park may not have the same aesthetic qualities but, in terms of their biological diversity, are of even greater significance. For example, the tidal flats contain twenty-one of Australia's twenty-nine mangrove species, and the open woodland and tall forest areas have a very high diversity of species. This became an important issue during the campaign because, while few people were prepared to cavil about the quality of the wetlands, many in government and industry were critical of the quality of the other areas. At one point, for example, the minister for resources and energy, Gareth Evans, described the largely woodland area of Kakadu Stage III as 'clapped-out buffalo country';[19] and naturalist Harry Butler, then acting as an adviser to the Northern Territory government, called Stage II a 'clapped-out Holden' and said it did not merit World Heritage listing.[20]

The area is important to two other groups of people besides conservationists. For the Gagadju and Jawoyn—the traditional owners—it was their country. Their complex and profound relationship with this land was powerfully expressed in rock art throughout the area. For miners, the area was enormously rich in minerals—gold, platinum, palladium and uranium. Kakadu therefore became a battleground for groups that had diametrically opposing interests and views of the world.

Although there was a small amount of uranium mining in the 1950s and early 1960s, Kakadu became a significant site of environmental conflict only after the setting up of the Ranger Inquiry under Justice Fox by the Whitlam government. Fox delivered his report in 1977, on the basis of which the Liberal Fraser government decided to allow uranium mining at Ranger under stringent environmental conditions. In an attempt to find 'an elusive compromise between development and conservation', Justice Fox also recommended that the South Alligator River catchment be protected by the establishment of Kakadu National Park and that Aboriginal land rights legislation was needed.[21]

The conservation groups that were most active on Kakadu were the ACF, TWS, and the very active Northern Territory Environment Centre. Geoff Mosley and Milo Dunphy from the ACF had both maintained a distant involvement from the late 1970s, and the ACF had tried unsuccessfully to purchase the Gimbat pastoral lease in the late 1970s to maintain the ecological integrity of the South Alligator catchment. TWS was vigorous in campaigning on the issue, especially in the period 1986–88, and the Northern Territory Environment Centre, which has had a line of capable coordinators up to the present, provided a constant, if under-resourced, presence in the territory for the issue. People working on the Kakadu campaign from TWS included Chris Harris, Katherine Fitzpatrick and Michael Rae (Harris was also a consultant to the Northern Land Council) and from the Northern Territory Environment Centre Lyn Allen and, from 1988, Michael Krockenberger. Phillip Toyne's role was vital from early in his tenure at the ACF in liaising with the Hawke government. Toyne was helped by the contacts he had developed during his work with Aboriginal people prior to moving to the ACF.

The agreement reached on Kakadu between Toyne and Richardson in December 1986 not only laid a basis for the environment movement to recommend a vote to Labor in 1987: it also laid the basis for the direction of the campaign that culminated with the final decision on Coronation Hill in 1991. The Hawke government had agreed in September to exclude all further exploration and mining from Stages I and II and to nominate Stage II for World Heritage listing. Now it also agreed to include the Gimbat and Goodparla properties as Stage III except for about one-third of the area (euphemistically called a 'Conservation Zone') which was available for mining and exploration. The federal government also tentatively approved the proposal by BHP to mine gold, platinum and palladium at Coronation Hill, which was in this Conservation Zone. The stage was then set for the main campaign, which was to conclude the Kakadu project by incorporating Stage III into the park. This would maintain the integrity of the South Alligator catchment, include this stage with the other two in World Heritage listing, and stop mining from going ahead at Coronation Hill, a mine that could have impacted adversely on both the conservation and cultural values of the region.

In 1988 Mike Krockenberger went up to Darwin to take over from Lyn Allen as the coordinator of the Environment Centre. Soon after arriving, he was involved in the first direct action that began to make Kakadu a household name. Three members of TWS—Chris Harris, Richard Ledger and Scott Wootten—occupied the Coronation Hill site and prevented work there for a number of weeks. TWS had obtained advice that there was some doubt about the validity of the lease, and so BHP was not keen to have the occupiers arrested and bring attention to the lease issue. Nevertheless, the action received enormous media coverage.[22]

The conservationists' environmental arguments received much-needed support from the CSIRO, which had been doing studies in

Kakadu since the 1970s. These showed that Stage III was an important transitional zone between the monsoonal ecosystems and those farther south, and was crucial for mammalian species in particular. This information was used to counter arguments by the Northern Territory government, the mining interests or resource ministers in the Hawke government that Stage III was severely degraded.

The key decision came in late 1989. In September a lobby team with representatives from the three concerned groups met with Richardson to discuss the future of Stage III. According to Richardson, the idea that emerged came from the Left's Stewart West, at that time minister for administrative services. He suggested reducing the Conservation Zone in Stage III from 2200 square kilometres to under 50.[23] This would not prevent the mine from going ahead but it would prevent the establishment of any other mines in the zone and it would put the issue into a holding pattern until the movement could get enough support to stop Coronation Hill.[24] Hawke gave full support to the deal in cabinet and Keating put up only mild opposition; but there was real anger from economic ministers such as Cook, Button, Dawkins and Walsh, as well as Bob Collins, then a backbench senator from the Northern Territory. This did not bode well for future arrangements on the environment in a post-election Labor cabinet. Nevertheless, the decision hammered home green support for Labor over the coalition for the 1990 federal election.

Conservationists found that they were having to fight rearguard actions in 1989–90 as well as pushing the agenda forward. There were many in the Labor government who wanted to widen the three-mine uranium policy, and much effort had to go into lobbying the Labor Party not to give the go-ahead for mining at Koongarra and Jabiluka.

However, it was the working relationship with the Aboriginal people of the region, especially the Jawoyn Association and the Northern Land Council, that provided the key strategic element for the campaign. Although some of the Jawoyn supported mining at Guratba (Coronation Hill), most, including the three custodians of the area, did not. The Jawoyn people opposed mining at Coronation Hill because they believed that it would bring catastrophe to the land. The area was home to the Dreamtime spirit Bula, and the precious minerals were his blood. If Bula was disturbed, devastation would be unleashed upon the Earth.[25] The problem was that much of this was secret knowledge, and the Jawoyn were reluctant to talk to whites about it. This prompted miners to assert that the Jawoyn did not know much about it or that they made it up.

Around 1988 there was a shift in strategic thinking by the Northern Land Council, which, up until then, had been reluctant to intervene in the Coronation Hill dispute. Possibly because of the influence of some environmentalists and, even more importantly, because they sensed that

Aboriginal people could win a significant victory with a strategic link with conservationists, the council entered the campaign against mining with vigour. An important meeting was held in late September 1989 at the Eva Valley cattle station owned by the Jawoyn: the ACF, TWS, Greenpeace and the Northern Territory Environment Centre met with the traditional owners to lock in a decision about Coronation Hill. With this achieved, conservationists could lobby more confidently with the federal government; a week later the government took the significant step of drastically reducing the size of the Conservation Zone. There had been tensions between conservationists and Aborigines during this period, largely because Aboriginal people felt that they were being harassed from all sides—miners from one side and conservationists from the other and that the latter did not necessarily support the cultural reasons for stopping mining as much as the environmental ones. However, the conservationists felt they had no alternative but to put their case forward and, fortunately for them, people like Chris Harris and Phillip Toyne had many years' experience and the tensions were managed with sensitivity.

The other decision made by the Hawke government at this time was to ask the Resource Assessment Commission to assess the economic, environmental and cultural issues surrounding mining in Kakadu. The environment movement, through the ACF, was represented at the inquiry. The commission did not recommend against mining on environmental grounds because it felt that the impacts of the mine could be effectively minimised. However, it did find that mining would adversely impact on important cultural values.[26] The mining industry, much of the business community, all of the coalition, and the majority of cabinet members were hostile to the findings, and Keating was breathing down Hawke's neck for the Labor Party leadership. Hawke went into the cabinet room on 21 June 1991 to oppose mining at Coronation Hill with much riding on the outcome. Because he was the prime minister, Hawke won the day and the mine was stopped; but it was at an enormous cost. Hawke's support in the caucus was seriously undermined by this unpopular decision, and the position of those in the party who felt that the greens had become too influential was strengthened. Nevertheless, the environment movement had won a significant victory, even though the creation of a national park or a World Heritage area in a heavily mineralised part of the country can never be taken as permanent.

### Forests

One set of issues around the country has never had a satisfactory resolution: those where conservationists and resource industries have confronted each other over the industry's access to native forests. Wood-chipping companies joined forces with forestry unions, sympathetic politicians and forestry bureaucrats in the 1980s to limit the effectiveness of forest conservation campaigners.

## Tasmania

TWS in Tasmania emerged from the Franklin campaign with a full head of steam and a national organisation. However, it was concerned that the great majority of Tasmania's forests were still vulnerable, especially to the threat presented by the woodchippers.[27] The woodchipping industry in Tasmania was controlled by three companies, Associated Pulp and Paper Mills and Tasmanian Pulp and Forest Holdings, both owned by North Broken Hill Pty Ltd; and Forest Resources, which was wholly owned by Petersville–Sleigh, which in turn was 49 per cent owned by the Adelaide Steamship Company.[28] Tasmania also produced a large proportion of Australia's woodchips.

Anticipating an early renewal of Tasmania's woodchip licences, TWS began to campaign for a Western Tasmania National Park to protect the remaining wilderness of this area. It included the Gordon Splits, the Southern and Lemonthyme forests and the Spires, each of which had little or no national park or World Heritage status to protect it.[29] At around the same time, the ACF, TWS, the Tasmanian Conservation Trust, and other local groups set up the Forest Action Network to research these park proposals, forest management practices, and the economics of the woodchip industry.[30] This campaign was accompanied by a TWS campaign for the preservation of the undisturbed, forested Douglas–Apsley area of the central east coast of Tasmania, and one for separate wilderness legislation for Australia at both state and federal levels, the latter identified with TWS campaigner, Margaret Robertson. TWS called on the federal government to set up a joint Commonwealth–state authority to manage the whole park area and to assist the Tasmanian government to find alternatives to continued logging in the area.[31]

At this point it is worth pointing out the potentially vital role to be played by the Commonwealth government in this unfolding drama. It obviously had responsibilities under the *World Heritage Properties (Conservation) Act 1983* for the newly created South-West Tasmania World Heritage area, but it was also committed under the *Australian Heritage Commission Act 1975* to compile a list of places that qualified to be on the National Estate. Although it had no power to restrain state or local government or private owners, its own actions in National Estate areas had to comply with the act; and it could ensure that the owners gave adequate protection to such a place if they sought Commonwealth approval for a grant or a licence, such as one for export. The Common-wealth was also empowered by another act to reject approvals if the proposed actions in National Estate areas would cause destruction and there were 'feasible or prudent' alternatives available. In the case of woodchipping in National Estate forests in Tasmania, this meant that the Commonwealth could make export licences contingent on the preparation of environmental impact assessments and on whether or not adequate attempts had been made to seek out 'feasible or prudent' alternatives.

The conservation groups, especially TWS, lobbied hard to prevent the federal government from caving in to the Tasmanian government under Liberal Premier Robin Gray and the three woodchip companies. The companies wanted an extension of their licences to a common expiry date in 1988 and to avoid further restrictions such as providing an environmental impact statement (EIS). TWS was able to extract an awkward compromise: it allowed the extension to 1988, but made the licences dependent on the companies' provision of an EIS into the effects of export woodchipping up to and beyond 1988.

While anti-uranium activists were picketing the July 1984 Labor Party national conference on the outside, wilderness activists were inside lobbying delegates. The TWS team of Chris Harris, Bob Burton, Michael Rae, Karen Alexander and Jonathan West lobbied on the Daintree, western Tasmania and wilderness generally. At one point the party's draft environment platform contained the sensational statement that a Labor Party government would 'stop all programs of woodchipping of native forests except those planted for exploitation'. The draft was quickly changed when its import became clear to the party hierarchy.[32] Despite some other gains, the Labor Party after the conference had still not committed itself strongly to wilderness protection or to stopping the advance of the woodchip companies through National Estate forests. The adoption of the three-mine uranium policy, the failure to stand up to Bjelke-Petersen over Daintree, and the equivocal stand on wood-chipping meant that the Labor Party was still a long way from providing the sort of political power the environment movement needed to connect with. Nevertheless, there was little alternative. The Liberal Party had begun to go looking for the ghost of eighteenth-century British liberalism and late-nineteenth-century Australian states rights-ism, and the Democrats had no chance of winning lower house seats. Anyway, the Labor Party had shown that it would listen to the movement's arguments; and speaking with Labor was not a total waste of time, as it was with the conservatives.

On 19 April 1985, 2000 people took to the streets of Hobart under the banner 'Stand up for the forests' to announce the opening of the forests campaign. It should be realised that, from the start, the activists had only one potential ally that could make decisions on the Tasmanian forests, and that was the federal Labor Party. The Labor Party in Tasmania supported logging and woodchipping as it had supported the Hydro-Electric Commission, and the Liberal state government was prepared to adopt almost any measures to ensure the continuation of forestry industries and to thwart the aims of the conservation movement. Premier Robin Gray adopted a 'hairy-chested' approach to issues of wilderness and forests. At one point he stated in parliament: 'I think all members will realise that prior to the advent of the woodchip industry the east coast forest areas were covered largely with decadent and rotting forests. As a result of the introduction of woodchipping to that area an extensive area has been regenerated and is now carrying very productive young forests.'[33]

Compare this statement with the lyrical ecocentrism of Bob Brown's 'Our place is between the forests and the machines',[34] and it becomes clear that this is not an argument where much common ground exists. Given the tenacity of TWS and the deep-seated belief among many in the community that forestry jobs could be protected only by maintaining existing forestry practices, it is clear that confrontations would take place whether Liberal or Labor was in power. However, it is also clear that the particular personality of Robin Gray made that conflict more likely and more severe.

In response to the federal government's call for an EIS from the companies into Tasmania's woodchip industry, a draft statement was publicly released in February 1995. The conservation groups called on people to make submissions to the EIS with a well-organised information program through the Forest Action Network. Bill Hare from the ACF described what his organisation considered the failings of the EIS as

> a failure to consider alternatives to the woodchip industry's proposed plans, inadequate provision of basic resources, environmental and economic data and the virtual discounting of major National Estate values such as wilderness. Significant information was withheld ... A wilderness study by the Forestry Commission, an archaeological report and management plans for the Douglas–Apsley and South-West conservation area were also suppressed or withheld.[35]

TWS condemned the draft even more summarily. 'The failings of the draft EIS are so severe that we do not believe they will be rectified by the preparation of a final EIS by the proponents. We therefore recommend that the draft EIS be rejected and a public inquiry be instigated under the Environment Protection (Impact of Proposals) Act.'[36]

During this period Possums Against Woodchips Society (PAWS), consisting of TWS members dressed as eagles, pygmy possums, owls and cockatoos, was set up. They demonstrated outside the empty Tasmanian parliament, demanding an alternative home to replace their forest homes that were about to be destroyed, and then carried their message to Canberra. Many public meetings were also held all around Tasmania. When the companies released the final draft of the EIS in late September, TWS contemptuously referred to it as 'a lemon', little different from the draft statement and 'the most transparent piece of industry propaganda ever prepared'.[37]

In October 1985 the federal minister for the environment, Barry Cohen, recommended to the minister for primary industries (as was his responsibility under the Australian Heritage Commission Act) that logging be excluded from twenty-two key areas on the National Estate. This was rejected by primary industries minister John Kerin, who maintained that the federal government had few, if any, powers with respect to protecting the National Estate.[38] Relations between the Tasmanian Wilderness Society and Cohen had never been altogether cordial and they deteriorated when TWS members expressed their views on Cohen's handling of his portfolio by handing him thirty pieces of silver on a visit to Hobart. Cohen is Jewish and the insult, though unintended, was not lost on the minister.[39]

Tasmanian Premier Robin Gray called a state election for 7 February 1986, and fought it largely on the pro-development line that he had always espoused. Although he won comfortably, a second green independent, Dr Gerry Bates, joined Bob Brown in the parliament. The Greens had begun to displace Labor as the main beneficiary of pro-gressive voters in Tasmania. A week after the election, Gray sent the bulldozers into Farmhouse Creek, confirming Brown's prediction that Gray 'wants your vote on Saturday and the forests on Monday'.[40] For ten years this creek had been the boundary between the clearfelled areas of the Picton Valley and the South-West wilderness. Now a road was to be constructed that crossed the creek and pushed toward the World Heritage area. The same activities also began in the other sig-nificant area for conservationists, the Lemonthyme Valley near Cradle Mountain. Conservationists moved quickly. They set up a blockade in the Lemonthyme forest and began a vigil at Farmhouse Creek, where a pugnacious Hobart bricklayer, Alec Marr, perched 20 metres up a gum tree directly in the path of the bulldozers.

On 7 March the Battle of Farmhouse Creek began. At 10.30 that morning a group of sixty timber workers, under the direction of Tony Risby of Risby Forest Industries, alighted from buses and utilities; they poured down into the creek, where about forty protesters had positioned themselves on and under machinery and around the trees. Bob Brown was dragged by the timber workers from under an excavator and manhandled across the creek. Once released, he bounded back to the excavator but was again seized and roughed up.[41] Other protesters were also treated roughly by the workers, some worse than Brown away from the cameras. One worker started up his chainsaw and began to cut into the tree that Alec Marr had been camped in for the past eleven days. Two young women embracing a small rainforest tree had the tree chain-sawed between their legs by the vigilantes. All the while the police looked on and did not intervene, although Gerry Bates insisted they do so. One young policeman told Brown that they were under orders not to intervene.[42] The whole exercise, of course, was captured by the media and the Battle of Farmhouse Creek was the major news story across the nation the next day. Brown asserted, 'The battle of Farmhouse Creek will ring down through the generations as a watershed in the campaign to save the forests, not only in Tasmania but throughout Australia.'[43] Farther north, blockaders at the Lemonthyme were being treated just as harshly without the consolation of having the media on hand to publicise their plight. Two days after the Farmhouse Creek events shots were fired at Bob Brown as he and another conservationist, Judy Richter, and a journalist, Hugh Maclean, were walking along a road. Maclean, with his Vietnam training, dropped straight into the mud but the other two were left standing in shock.[44] The shooter was later arrested and received a fine of $200.

Soon after, the new federal environment minister, Senator Graham Richardson, took his famous helicopter ride over clearfelled as well as pristine Tasmanian forests, and was converted to the conservationists' cause. The most important battle was now fought inside the federal Labor cabinet. Writing in April 1986, Bill Hare claimed that these events and the history of Tasmanian woodchipping went to the heart of a number of major unresolved environmental issues in Australia:

1. federal–state politics and the degree to which party political considerations affect the outcome of major issues
2. the perceived importance of the environment politically and electorally
3. the role of the Australian Labor Party in environmental reform
4. the administration of environmental law and access in the courts
5. the ongoing role of forestry bureaucracies and the relationship between these and the industries they service and the forestry profession.[45]

At least the first four of these would be severely tested over the next two years as the Commonwealth, under a Labor government, attempted to come to terms with the limits and possibilities of its power, especially with respect to difficult environmental decisions that went together with important land use considerations. The Commonwealth also had to come to terms with the increasing importance of the environment movement and the ready acceptance of its message in the population at large.

The Commonwealth government effectively signed off the woodchip licences in June although, as Geoff Law says, Hawke attempted to mollify an angry Bob Brown by saying that no logging in National Estate forests would take place unless the Commonwealth was satisfied that National Estate values would be protected.[46] It is possible that Richardson's influence with the prime minister was being felt at this stage as well. Richardson had promised the ACF that he would fight hard for environmental outcomes, that the environment ministry would be as influential in cabinet as any other and that he would fight to save old-growth forests, although he could give no guarantee that forests in the National Estate would not be logged.[47] This approach was quite different to that taken by Richardson's predecessor Cohen; it was also unexpected, given the senator's well-earned reputation as a hard-nosed right-wing Labor numbers man.

Confrontations between conservationists and the forestry industry continued in the Tasmanian forests during the second half of 1986, in spite of a Memorandum of Understanding between the Commonwealth and Tasmania that logging in National Estate areas would proceed only after consultation between the two governments. The final straw was Gray's approval for logging in the Jackey's Marsh–Quamby Bluff area, a move that would make ugly logging scars on pristine areas of the Great Western Tiers.[48] Hawke was furious. On 19 December he established a review of Tasmania's National Estate forests to determine if there were 'feasible and prudent' alternatives to logging, as well as the suitability of these areas for World Heritage listing. He called on the Tasmanian government to stop all logging operations in National Estate forests until the inquiry was complete, and indicated that he would use his powers under the Constitution to override the Tasmanian government if necessary. Gray refused to cooperate. In February 1987 Hawke introduced into the parliament the Lemonthyme and Southern Forests (Commission of Inquiry) Bill 1987, which passed through the Senate in April. TWS activists maintained their blockades and vigils in the forests throughout this period, including tree-sitting (with protesters carrying enough food and water to last them for weeks).

The subsequent inquiry was set up under Mr Justice Helsham, a retired Equity Court judge from New South Wales; Robert Wallace, an economist from Flinders University; and Peter Hitchcock, a former forester who had done substantial environmental assessment work for the NSW National Parks and Wildlife Service.[49] Only Hitchcock had any background in environmental science. The environment movement was grateful to Hawke for taking on Gray; but many were worried that the inquiry had been given the job of making recommendations on World Heritage listing, one they believed should have been carried out by a suitably qualified body like the Australian Heritage Commission.

While the conservation movement was pondering whether or not the Labor Party was worth the effort and cost of mounting a major election campaign, the coalition was making sure that support for the conservatives would not be an option in the 1987 elections. The coalition environment policy was more concerned with protecting states' rights than the environment; under it the Franklin River would have been dammed by Robin Gray and the Wet Tropics, left to development pressures under the Bjelke-Petersen government, would have been largely destroyed within a short time. The conservation movement launched a Vote for the Forests campaign for the 11 July election, which saw Hawke win a third term. Fortunately for Labor (and the environment) Joh Bjelke-Petersen's 'Joh for Canberra' push sank the coalition. The ACF and TWS both campaigned for the Labor Party in the House of Representatives and the Democrats in the Senate; they claimed that their campaign had delivered the Labor Party 2.2 per cent of the vote, a claim only partly denied by the coalition.[50] This was reinforced by Malcolm Mackerras, who estimated that the Labor Party won by 50.8 per cent to 49.2 per cent on a two-party preferred basis,[51] an outcome in which green votes were crucial. During the 1987 campaign the coalition had pledged to eliminate all grants to the ACF and to abolish the Department of Arts, Heritage and the Environment, neither of which endeared them to the conservation movement.[52] The coalition realised after the election the mistake it had made in not listening to the environment movement; Alexander Downer, who had been a staunch advocate of states' rights before the election, stated that this approach had left the party 'high and dry' (although he also called environmentalists 'uncompromising zealots').[53] The new shadow environment minister, Chris Puplick, immediately set to work to mend fences. He challenged the Holy Writ of states' rights within the coalition, and announced support for the World Heritage listing of the Wet Tropics. Nevertheless, the New Right agenda in the Liberal Party was too strong for social liberals like Puplick and he was ultimately defeated by the economic fundamentalists, the 'dries'.

Meanwhile, the conservation movement was becoming increasingly disturbed by the direction being taken by the inquiry headed by Justice Helsham. Many felt that Commissioners Wallace and Helsham showed little understanding of the information being provided to them by the eleven environmental consultants hired by the commission.[54] Their fears were confirmed by the commission's report when it was released in May 1988. In a split decision, Helsham and Wallace concluded that only 10 per cent of the area under investigation was worthy of World Heritage nomination. The third commissioner, Hitchcock, dissented, recommending that the whole area, plus some others, should be nominated. The situation was made more controversial when nine of the eleven consultants hired by the commission dissociated themselves from the majority decision, saying that they agreed with Hitchcock's conclusions. The Australian Heritage Commission also wrote to Richardson rejecting the majority conclusions and supporting Hitchcock. The conservation movement was enraged. As 600 people rallied in Hobart's biggest demonstration since the Franklin, Richardson was left to ponder the political truism that you never set up an inquiry unless you know its results in advance;[55] the resolution of the problem was now left to a divided cabinet.

Richardson encouraged the environment movement to make a 'deafening roar' about the decision (they needed little encouragement) and he went into battle in cabinet with economic ministers like Button, Kerin, Dawkins and Walsh. For fourteen hours over three separate meetings the cabinet debated competing submissions from Resources Minister Peter Cook and Environment Minister Richardson. Cook's submission supported the Helsham recommendations, while Richardson attempted to overturn Helsham and have 70 per cent of the area nominated for World Heritage. According to Richardson, the decisive intervention on the argument came from Keating, a man not generally recognised as being pro-environment.[56] The environment movement, however, was not as overjoyed as Richardson, the master of compromise, had expected. People like Bob Brown and Geoff Law were grateful for his strong support but could not help thinking about those areas that had been left out—the spectacular tall eucalypt forests in the lower Weld valley and the east bank of the Picton, the forests of the Douglas–Apsley catchment, and a number of other places of undoubted World Heritage value.[57] It was also incorrect to argue that 70 per cent of the forests had been protected by the cabinet decision. In fact, 70 per cent of the entire area was protected, but this represented only 30 per cent of the forests.[58] There was also a sting in the tail of the cabinet decision as a subsequent agreement between Hawke and Gray on 30 November 1988 included no more unilateral Commonwealth proposals for World Heritage listing by the Commonwealth, no more forest inquiries, and continued logging in National Estate forests in Tasmania subject to a new agreement.[59] The protection of these areas would have to await the signing of the Green–Labor Accord in Tasmania after that state's 1989 election.

The environment groups involved in the Tasmanian forests issue—TWS, the ACF, the Tasmanian Conservation Trust, and a number of

local groups—constantly stated that their struggle was integrally linked
with the future of forests all around Australia. The battle to preserve
wilderness and National Estate values against development pressures,
state governments hostile to conservation, and a federal government
usually too cautious to intervene were themes in mainland states, from
the south-east and north-east forests of New South Wales, to East
Gippsland in Victoria, to the karri and jarrah forests of south-west
Western Australia.

### New South Wales

In both New South Wales and Victoria similar campaigns took place to
stop the woodchipping of native, especially National Estate, forests and
to set up reserve systems that would protect biodiversity. In New South
Wales the main campaigns were in the south-east of the state, while the
struggle in Victoria took place over the forests of East Gippsland, which
were contiguous with those of south-east New South Wales. Both states
had Labor governments for most or all of the period from 1983 to 1990,
and these governments claimed to be sympathetic to environmental
reform. Nevertheless, the timber industry, and increasingly woodchipping, had made substantial inroads into both areas by 1983. The
conservation movement faced a hard struggle to combat the political
influence of the timber industry, local communities dependent on the
timber industry, and the timber unions.

The large nature conservation groups in New South Wales had
diverted enormous resources into the big campaigns in the north of the
state for a number of years; with those campaigns won and World
Heritage listing for the rainforests under way, desperate cries could be
heard from the south-east, where woodchippers had been established
since the late 1960s. The large Japanese woodchip company, Harris–
Daishowa, had released an EIS supporting its claim for the renewal of its
woodchip licences in June 1986, with the most urgent threat to the
Coolangubra and Tantawangalo wilderness areas near the south coast
town of Eden. These areas, like those of East Gippsland, contain rare
plant alliances, moving from north to south from warm temperate to
cool temperate rainforest, and are also home to some rare and
endangered species of flora and fauna. The most famous of these is the
Long-footed Potoroo, which is found in both the south-east and East
Gippsland forests but few other places. The regeneration from areas
that had been clearfelled for woodchipping had created major fire
hazards since there was no canopy to reduce winds and moisture loss.[60]
Both Coolangubra and Tantawangalo had been nominated for National
Estate listing with the Australian Heritage Commission.

National and local conservation groups established the South-East Forest Alliance in 1985 to fight against the extension of the Eden woodchip licence and for the establishment of Coolangubra and Tantawangalo national parks. These objective were opposed by the Labour Council and the timber industry on the grounds that they would cause job losses. This claim was refuted by the conservation movement, whose representative pointed to the declining yield of hardwood quotas as the result of overcutting, indicating severe problems for employment in the area's logging industry in the coming years.[61] Some local activists were Debra McIlroy, Tony Fleming, Ian Fraser, Roland Brechwoldt and Sid Walker; the highly professional Jeff Angel, operating out of the Total Environment Centre, led the Sydney end of the campaign. As is often the case, several of these local activists went on to become skilled co-ordinators and lobbyists for large conservation organisations. In the first couple of years the South-East Forest Alliance did not emphasise actions like blockades, unlike the Tasmanian campaign. Peak groups like the ACF and TWS were more interested at this stage in the Lemonthyme and southern forests campaign in Tasmania than in the south-east forests of New South Wales.

Nature conservation groups had been impressed by the Wran government's actions over the rainforests in the state's north and by its support for developing the country's first wilderness act. However, when Wran surprisingly retired in June 1986, they were quick to point out to the new premier, Barry Unsworth, that he could not stand on the achievements of the Wran period and they expected support on the south-east forests. Meanwhile, Liberal leader Nick Greiner, aware that his party's anti-rainforest policies in the 1985 election had cost them 2–3 per cent of the vote,[62] attempted to win back the support of conservation-minded Liberal voters. The shadow environment spokesperson, Tim Moore, said his party would not condone the logging of rainforests, the reduction of present national park boundaries or logging or mining in national parks. He was, however, undermined by his coalition partner, the Nationals, whose leader, Wal Murray, stated, 'There is no way the National Party would agree to the locking up of essential timber resources inside national park boundaries.'[63] In spite of Liberal attempts to maintain a 'light green' image, the National Party ensured that in the lead-up to the election, there would be few promises made on the environment that would be welcomed by the nature conservation movement.

With the federal government indicating that it wanted the state government to take a hard stand, the conservation groups decided to put pressure on the Unsworth Labor government in the lead-up to the 1988 state election. In the Heathcote by-election of November 1986 the Labor Party candidate won on the preferences of a local environmental independent, Jim Powell. The tactic succeeded. Environment Minister Bob Carr indicated that the Labor Party would look favourably on the creation of the two national parks. Soon after, he also committed the Unsworth government to wilderness legislation. Labor continued to be the movement's best chance at both state and federal levels. In the lead-up to the 1987 federal election, Liberal leader John Howard said that he would maintain the Eden woodchip licence. Showing that he had learned little from public discussion about forests (or about the credibility of conservation groups with the voting public) he also stated, 'Eucalypt forests are very hardy. They can be knocked around by fires, logging and disease and they still recover.' He also attacked conservationists by saying, 'anyone who wants to stop this industry [logging] or slow it down has got rocks in their heads'.[64]

Conservationists also took to the courts to try to protect the south-east forests. The Australian Heritage Commission had placed Coolangubra and Tantawangalo on the interim register of the National Estate and the NSW National Parks and Wildlife Service had recommended them as national parks, but clearfelling began in mid-1987. Wendy Jarasius, an individual conservationist, took out an injunction in the Land and Environment Court on behalf of the Towamba Valley Protection Society to stop the logging. Her injunction was upheld, largely on the grounds that the court decided that the logging activities were on such a scale as to require an EIS.[65]

Unfortunately for the forests of New South Wales, the coalition under Nick Greiner won the March 1988 state election and the national parks were not established. The new Liberal minister for natural resources, Ian Causley, refused to accept the National Estate listing of Coolangubra and Tantawangalo; he approved a secret twenty-year agreement to supply Harris–Daishowa with 530,000 tonnes of woodchip annually from state forests.[66] The federal government, this time with Senator Peter Cook as resources minister, approved a further fifteen years of woodchipping, and allowed logging in 9 per cent of National Estate forests while biological and resource surveys were carried out in the rest. The decision was criticised by conservationists on the grounds that he did not make sufficient inquiries about the ability to find suitable alternatives outside National Estate forests. The suspicion remains that Richardson 'played dead' on the south-east forests, in contrast with his active approach to the Tasmanian forests the same year, because he was angry that New South Wales conservation groups did not give stronger support to the Labor Party under Richardson's factional colleague, Barry Unsworth, in the 1988 state election.

As the result of a continuing high level of protests in the south-east in 1988–89, Greiner agreed to preserve more than 40,000 hectares of old-growth forest, but most conservationists were unhappy at the result. A more concerted attempt at direct action at an earlier stage in the campaign, like that of the Tasmanians at Farmhouse Creek and Lemonthyme, might have achieved a better outcome, but this would need to have happened before the Unsworth government lost power in March 1988.

## Victoria

A more successful campaign was waged by the conservation movement in neighbouring East Gippsland. There had been disputes over East Gippsland forests since the mid-1970s, made worse by plans to introduce woodchipping. This was ameliorated somewhat by the establishment of some national parks along the coast and in the drier inland; but large areas of spectacular forests, especially on the Errinundra Plateau and in the Rodger River area, remained vulnerable. These forests are very diverse, containing one-third of Victoria's plant species, forty-four of the state's ninety-four eucalypts, half the vertebrate animals, and twenty-one distinct plant communities.[67]

Conservationists hailed the victory of the Cain government in the 1982 state election because Labor's policy opposed export wood-chipping and promised an inquiry into the timber industry. The new government also agreed to a two-year moratorium on logging in the Rodger River basin, but then things started turning sour. The Nomadic Action Group set up a blockade against the clearfelling for logging that was occurring on the Errinundra Plateau, a move that was criticised by the mainstream groups because, they felt, it lessened the possibility for 'making short-term gains similar to Rodger River'.[68] Also, the inquiry into the timber industry was a disappointment: its terms of reference emphasised employment and economic issues ahead of environmental ones, and it was given a ridiculously short time to do its work. The groups felt that Professor Ian Ferguson would present a report that would not be favourable to conservation, and they were right.[69] In December 1985 the Victorian government released a draft Timber Industry Strategy based on Ferguson's report that recommended woodchipping take place in forests currently being logged. The federal government gave the export licence, apparently without an EIS, after the Victorian environment minister, Evan Walker, informed it that there would be no environmental damage from the industry.

The setting up of the East Gippsland Coalition in early 1985 was a step forward for the campaign in Victoria. The coalition was composed of the ACF, the Conservation Council of Victoria, TWS, the Native Forests Action Council and the National Parks Association; it was coordinated by such capable people as Linda Parlane and Janet Rice. Margaret

Blakers and Peter Durkin also played key roles in the coalition. As often happened, this campaign was backed by excellent research. The East Gippsland Coalition spelt out its proposals for proposed parks in the area in the report *A Greenprint for the Forests*, released in September 1985, a project identified with Marg Blakers. A grant from the ACF in late 1983 made it possible to develop an impressive study entitled *Jobs in East Gippsland*. The latter, in fact, showed how 450 extra jobs could be created by the year 2000 by restructuring the timber industry and developing local tourism and agriculture.[70] Such good material made lobbying of government much more effective. Conservationists believed this lobbying was successful not only in persuading the government's Land Conservation Council to support their national park proposals (with some omissions) but also in persuading it not to depoliticise unpopular anti-environment decisions by making supposedly 'independent' recommendations. In other words, the council took a neutral rather than a positive stand on woodchipping, forcing the state government to make a political decision.

The East Gippsland Coalition did more than research and lobby, however. It campaigned in marginal seats in Melbourne for the 1985 state elections, supporting the Labor Party on the grounds that 'they have conservation policies on East Gippsland but their record of implementation leaves much to be desired'.[71] The election of a Liberal government, on the other hand, would be 'catastrophic for conservationists in Victoria' because the Liberals were bowing to the timber industry in the state.

By late 1986 the East Gippsland campaign had developed momentum, reflected by the turnout of over 6000 people at a Keep Gippsland Green rally in Melbourne. Those attending heard Bob Brown give a message of hope about the chances of victory and Linda Parlane describe the majesty of the East Gippsland forests.[72] Conservationists also began building up campaigning teams in marginal seats and a Spectrum poll taken in the first half of 1987 in the marginal seat of Warrandyte showed that 60 per cent of voters were opposed to logging in East Gippsland and that 21 per cent of Labor voters would consider changing their vote on the issue.[73] It was hardly surprising that, in December 1987, the Victorian government proclaimed national parks for the Errinundra Plateau and Rodger River.[74]

### Western Australia

A similar situation existed in the south-west forests of Western Australia. Woodchipping had begun at Manjimup in 1976, despite the protests of conservationists. Bauxite mining had also occurred in the northern jarrah forests of the south-west since the early 1960s and, by the mid-1980s, Western Australia had five bauxite mines, four aluminium refineries, and advanced plans for an aluminium smelter. The mining had caused extensive damage to the jarrah forests, and conservationists were highly critical of the rehabilitation efforts at the sites.[75] The Liberal government of the time led by Charles Court was hostile to conservationists and, like most Western Australian governments of any political colour, supportive of resource-based development projects. The conservation movement had worked closely with the Labor Party when it was in opposition and was pleased with the extensive and ambitious platform that the party took into the 1983 election.[76] The Western Australian conservation movement also had a number of energetic and articulate leaders who were active Labor Party members;[77] many in the movement felt that they would see long-cherished goals achieved under the Burke Labor government. One of the first tests of this relationship was when the Burke government decided to dismantle the old National Parks Authority and set up a new amalgamated department known as the Department of Conservation and Land Management (CALM). This move split the conservation movement with Labor supporters arguing in favour of the new super-department. The opponents were to be proved correct as the department, under its chief executive officer, Sid Sheay, became one of the biggest hurdles to effective conservation in the state government.

Few Western Australian conservationists would wax lyrical about any of the Labor governments that existed between 1983 and 1993, and many disillusioned Labor Party supporters defected to the Greens and the Democrats during this period; but the Liberals had made too little effort to deal with environmental issues to be considered an acceptable alternative. So Labor maintained conservationists' support largely on the basis that the movement had nowhere else to go.

The campaign to save Western Australian forests has been divided between two organisations—the South-West Forests Defence Foundation, which addressed logging and woodchipping issues in karri forests, and the Campaign to Save Native Forests, which addressed the damage caused to jarrah forests largely by bauxite mining. Neil Batholomauus was one of the key figures in the latter organisation at this time; with such people as Alan Tingay, Beth Schultz and Barbara Churchward, he also played a vital role in the wider conservation movement. This campaign had already seen blockades organised by the Campaign to Save Native Forests and a well-publicised class action taken in the District Court in Pennsylvania, the United States in 1981 by the Conservation Council of Western Australia with the ACF as a co-plaintiff. The case was lost, but it aroused enormous public interest not only in

Western Australia but in the rest of Australia and the United States. The council raised $50,000 in donations for the case, ten times more than they had raised for any other campaign.[78]

The campaign to protect the karri forests fared little better. The groups followed a strategy, similar to the other states, of trying to get the state government to establish an expanded national park system to protect forest areas of high conservation value; to refrain from allocating native forests to wood production until they had been fully assessed for their biological, recreational and heritage values; to improve forest management practices; and to stop woodchipping in native forests. Heavy lobbying finally persuaded the state government to establish the Shannon and D'Entrecasteaux national parks, but CALM's draft regional management plans and timber strategy revealed an old story. Timber uses were given higher value than non-wood uses such as tourism and conservation; there was little ecological basis to recommendations for either conservation reserve or timber uses; and a clear run was given to the woodchippers. The ever-present threat of mining in national parks did nothing to allay conservationists' concern for the forests.

Much space has been devoted here to the forest campaigns because they tied up the energies of a great many activists during the 1980s, and because they reflect the difficulties faced by conservationists when faced by a determined, politically influential resource industry. However, conservation groups were active during the 1980s on many issues. They campaigned strongly on places as diverse as Shark Bay, various arid lands, and Antarctica. Only rarely did one organisation control a major wilderness campaign. Often many groups would be active together on the same campaign: the ACF, TWS, perhaps Greenpeace or Friends of the Earth, state-based conservation councils or environment centres, and any number of local groups. In such circumstances it was essential for the groups to agree on both objectives and strategy, or the campaign would dissolve into bitter internal feuding. We have already seen that there was often tension between direct actionists like the Nomadic Action Group and the mainstream organisations over strategy. The campaign to protect Antarctica illustrated the potential for conflict when one group sets an objective that is, as some would say, 'blue-sky stuff' while others take a more limited, pragmatic approach that they believe is more likely to win. The Antarctic campaign was significant also in that, apart from some educative work by the ACF's Antarctic Action Group, there was little public mobilisation.

### Antarctica

Much of the effort of the Antarctic campaigners, both nationally and internationally, went into lobbying decision-makers. As such, it constitutes a case study of a wilderness campaign contrasting with others like the Wet Tropics, South-West Tasmania or Kakadu. As a potential source of minerals, Antarctica might have aroused the same sort of fierce dispute as the National Estate forests. The possibility of mineral wealth was of great interest to a number of governments, including the Australian, but because there had been little mineral exploration and no exploitation at all, there were no existing vested interests to mount an effective effort against a World Park.

The Antarctic campaign had begun in the late 1970s with the form-ation of the Antarctic and Southern Ocean Coalition as an international lobbying body, with Jim Barnes as the coordinator and the ACF as a founding member. It was not until the early 1980s that the vital Australian end of the campaign began in earnest.[79] From the start there was a science orientation to the campaign; for example, Paul Broady, a University of Melbourne botanist and Antarctic researcher, was the first convenor of the ACF's Antarctic Action Group. Conservationists used traditional arguments for the importance of the Antarctic for scientific research, and at the same time pointed out the Australian government's use of science as a cloak for its economic interests, especially in Antarctica's possible mineral wealth.[80] Conservationists were united on the need for working within the Antarctic Treaty that had been signed by twelve nations in 1959 because it stated that Antarctica was to be used for peaceful purposes and it promoted the protection of wilderness. According to Geoff Mosley, 'The least risky option would be to confirm and consolidate the existing Conservation-Scientific regime by estab-lishing Antarctica as a World Park within the Antarctic Treaty System.'[81]

In 1984 the ACF convened an Antarctic Strategy Meeting of all interested environment organisations. The issue to be decided was what attitude the movement should take to the proposed Antarctic Minerals Convention. At this meeting there was a clear division. On the one hand, the ACF, led by Geoff Mosley, rejected the convention altogether and supported the creation of a world park; on the other, Annette Horsler from Fund for Animals (supported, somewhat surprisingly, by Greenpeace) argued that Australia should sign the proposed con-vention and support a system of smaller 'national parks'.[82]

This was a hard-fought argument. It was not resolved until Green-peace changed its position to support the world park idea after sending one of its ships to the Antarctic in a publicity exercise in 1986, and Lyn Goldsworthy replaced Annette Horsler as the project officer of Fund for Animals.

The Australian Foreign Affairs Department was strongly in favour of the Minerals Convention and worked hard behind the scenes to counter the world park proposal. This was despite some expression of support for the conservation option by the minister, Bill Hayden. The Australian conservation movement also struck trouble in obtaining support from the international conservation body, the International Union for the Conservation of Nature (which has both government and non-government member bodies). Although Mosley received support from the floor at IUCN general assemblies, this was usually undercut by the organisation's secretariat. This did not prevent the IUCN from claiming credit when the world park proposal was finally accepted.

The Convention for the Regulation of Antarctic Mineral Resource Activity was agreed to mid-1988 and was then open for signing by Antarctic treaty members until 25 November 1989. The announcement of the convention had been a victory for the pro-mining nations, especially the United States.[83] However, if one member nation refused to sign, it would lapse. The conservation movement was encouraged when France indicated that it was considering not ratifying the convention (no doubt as a result of lobbying by Jacques Cousteau). The coalition also announced its opposition to the convention early in 1989, easing the way for Hawke to announce on 22 May 1989 that Australia would not sign and instead recommended the establishment of a wilderness park.

The Minerals Convention was, therefore, replaced by the Madrid Protocol on Environmental Protection which placed an indefinite ban on all activities relating to mining (with a review after fifty years). The United States, however, has never signed the protocol.

### Conclusion

The term 'biodiversity' became a key concept for the environment movement arising out of the campaigns of the 1970s and 1980s and the scientific understandings that informed them. This word became overlaid with emotional and value-laden meanings for conservationists— it became, for many, almost an absolute value in itself. Economic development should not occur, it was felt, at the expense of the multiplicity of life forms that might be threatened by human activity. The challenge for conservationists, then, was to support a concept that produced principles and even models of development that did not endanger the stability of ecosystems. As with biodiversity, the concept of ecologically sustainable development was refined in the context of struggle and here the many campaigns fought over urban and pollution issues, especially those based on sound scholarship, helped the movement counter the technocratic optimism and, at times, profoundly anti-ecological approaches of economic planners.

# CHAPTER 7

# *Urban Issues and Pollution*

Wilderness and forestry issues tended to dominate the Australian environment movement throughout the 1980s, in contrast with Europe, where anti-nuclear and urban issues tended to define the movement. Consequently, the energies of activists and grassroots campaigners alike tended to be taken up with campaigns over ill-advised development projects like woodchipping, mining and dams in wilderness areas, leaving such issues as renewable energy, freeways, pollution and urban planning to a few stalwarts. Jonathan West says that this was a deliberate decision by the 'leading core' of Australian environmental activists who adopted a *preservationist* rather than a *conservationist* ideological stance.[1] This orientation among key activists towards nature conservation and, more especially, towards a wilderness ethic was certainly a major influence on this strategic direction. However, the defeat of the Mundey forces inside the union movement and the failure of the anti-uranium movement (see Chapter 6) to gain sufficient political leverage through alliance with sympathetic unions also helped to convince environmentalists that they needed to be able to mobilise public opinion on key issues. They decided to focus their energies on opposition to various resource extraction projects that endangered areas of high conservation value and campaign for effective and complete protection for these areas.

Increasingly, then, resource usage and pollution issues were taken up by local community groups that would form to oppose particular developments, often with little contact with the larger environmental organisations and far from comprehensive views of what the environmentally sustainable alternatives might be. Any analysis of the environment movement, however, would be incomplete without including the efforts of these local groups, often derogatively described as having a 'NIMBY'

(Not In My Back Yard) attitude. Such a group might be created as the result of concern within the community about a particular development proposal or an existing development. It might have a narrow, self-interested perspective; or its members might be unable to campaign effectively or call upon sufficient resources to achieve their goals, and so they would drop from sight, usually never to be heard from again. However, sometimes a group would have a core of activists who were able to bring a spark to the campaign; they would develop beyond self-interest to adopt an ethically sound perspective, and they would win some or all of their objectives. Even where these campaigns were not successful in stopping a particular project, they mobilised many people whose attitudes to the environment were changed forever and who, in some cases, went on to become activists themselves. Even more importantly, their attempts to come to grips with issues like energy use, industrial pollution, waste management strategies, agricultural pesticide use, and reduction of car dependence in cities all helped to develop a more comprehensive approach to sustainable development, both in the movement and in the wider community.

Although many of these issues were taken up at the local level, considerable campaign energies were expended by the larger con-servation organisations, key activists and well-known personalities aligned with the movement. Friends of the Earth maintained strong campaigns on energy and recycling concerns; Greenpeace ran some big anti-pollution campaigns; and state conservation councils in most states, notably the Total Environment Centre in Sydney, provided strong support in a number of urban and planning issues. The Australian Conservation Foundation (ACF) began to play a stronger role in these issues as the decade progressed. Academics like Peter Newman, Ian Lowe and Mark Diesendorf, who were closely aligned with the move-ment, provided valuable research for activists, as well as skilfully popularising cutting-edge ideas in such areas as sustainable transport and energy policies.

Campaigns on urban environmental and pollution issues during the 1980s were too numerous to discuss comprehensively, so this chapter will look at only a few of the significant campaigns, especially those that helped movement activists develop a more sophisticated view of ecologically sustainable development. These campaigns will be dealt with (perhaps a little arbitrarily) under thematic headings of energy, uranium and greenhouse; industrial pollution; and sustainable cities.

### Energy, Uranium and Greenhouse

By 1983 the anti-uranium movement was on its last legs. It had attempted to persuade the Labor Party to adopt a strong stand against uranium mining but had failed. The movement prepared to make its last stand at the Labor Party conference in July 1984 and at Roxby Downs.

Like the Green Bans movement of the early 1970s, the anti-uranium movement was associated with the Left rather than the Right of the Labor Party. As we have seen, the efforts of Labor Right leaders like Hawke, and others from the centre like Bill Hayden, John Dawkins and Peter Walsh, had moved the Labor Party from an anti- to a pro-uranium position. In 1982 the Victorian state secretary, Bob Hogg, proposed to the Labor Party's national conference an amendment to party policy: that there should be 'no new mines', but that Roxby Downs could go ahead provided purchasing countries met certain conditions relating to non-proliferation. Conference also insisted that certain standards on health and waste disposal be met. In June 1984 the Labor Party ended a two-year ban on uranium exports, a decision which led to the adoption of the three-mine policy. Nabarlek, Ranger and Roxby Downs mines were given the go-ahead, although sales to France were banned because of that country's nuclear testing. The roles played by such South Australian Labor figures as John Bannon and Peter Duncan were crucial in these debates. They were especially keen to see Roxby Downs approved because of its importance to the South Australian economy. Duncan managed to combine opposition to the Northern Territory mines consistent with his membership of the Left, but contradicted this by supporting Roxby Downs.

Like the Labor Party, the union movement was also going soft on the issue. Some unions, especially those where the Left was strong, maintained their energetic opposition but the support for mining from key unions with members in the industry was enough to keep the ACTU's opposition within strict limits. By 1984 union concerns tended to be confined to such issues as proliferation, waste and health.

### Roxby Downs

The campaign against uranium mining focused on the Roxby Downs project during the period from mid-1983 to the end of 1984. The strategy of winning inside the Labor Party and the union movement was rapidly losing ground, and so the last throw of the dice by the movement was to try to show the mine owners that the economic feasibility of uranium mining was questionable at best. Movement researchers believed that the mine would have only marginal economic viability and by mounting a blockade at this remote site, they would let mine owners BP know the extent of the popular opposition to be expected if the project went ahead.

The first major direct action of the Roxby campaign was in mid-1983. The Coalition for a Nuclear Free Australia (CNFA) organised a blockade and part-occupation of the site for one week, during which more than 200 protesters were arrested. Solidarity protests were held in London and Germany.[2] Then, after the July 1984 Labor Party conference decision, the CNFA decided to organise a rolling blockade, with contingents from different states taking turns. A wide variety of groups and individuals took part in the blockade. These included the Nomadic Action Group, fresh from their actions on the Franklin, other environmental activists, anarchists, and radical Christians.

The blockade was set up outside the mine entrance; some actions were coordinated by general meetings and others were carried out separately by affinity groups. There was even more civil disobedience at the second blockade than at the first. Actions included dismantling sections of the boundary fence, women plugging a shaft with a 3-metre 'tampon' (adorned with such messages as 'Womyn know about hidden blood—plug the shaft—stop the cycle').[3] Superglue also came into its own at Roxby, with locks being filled and some demonstrators gluing themselves to objects. At one stage a small group chained themselves to a cattle grid to prevent water trucks from entering the site, an action that closed down the mine for a day.[4] At the same time protesters in Adelaide were carrying out such actions as blockading two truckloads of ore from Roxby at the port, an action that resulted in eighteen arrests.

There was some tension between demonstrators and the local police, although the Queensland contingent (being used to rough treatment from the law in the Deep North) thought there was nothing unusual in this. It was reported that one young woman who stayed on with some others after the end of the blockade had her arm broken when they were finally evicted by the police.[5] The local white population in the town of Andamooka was also hostile, and a number of incidents occurred; protesters who were chased out of town sought sanctuary with the local Aboriginal community.[6]

There was also tension between the organisers and the activists on the ground; some of the latter felt that CNFA was actually opposed to the protest continuing. One protester from Queensland who reached South Australia in the blockade's last week stated that he had heard CNFA on the radio claiming that the blockade had been called off.[7] Ian Cohen also reported tension between organisers and some protesters in the 1983 blockade, but felt there were faults on both sides.

The anti-uranium movement continued to argue, as it had in the 1970s, that Australia needed to improve energy efficiency rather than move towards dangerous high-tech alternatives like nuclear power. However, despite the strong influence of energy gurus like Amory

Lovins, there had not been adequate technological development in such areas as wind and solar energy and photovoltaic cells for the arguments in favour of renewable energy to be particularly strong. Nevertheless, the 1980s saw this technology make progress around the world; scientists and engineers seemed to drive the argument in the popular arena almost as much as they drove the research process.

### Renewable Energy

While most media attention in the early to mid-1980s was on the mass mobilisations for nuclear disarmament, for wilderness protection in south-west Tasmania and against uranium mining, renewable energy proponents were operating at an important but less prominent level. Alan Langworthy, Mark Diesendorf and Hugh Outhred of the Australasian Wind Energy Association made considerable efforts to expand the organisation's connections beyond the boffin network to take in many grassroots people who supported wind energy. The Australia and New Zealand Solar Energy Society was also set up around this time and was dominated by CSIRO scientists. During the late 1980s this organisation began to gather into its fold some politically skilful young members, such as Andrew Blakers, Trevor Lee and David Mills, and its publication *Solar Progress* had a solid readership, as did the more populist *Soft Technology*, now *ReNew*, put out by the Alternative Technology Association.

The increasing scientific concern during the 1980s with possible global climate change resulting from enhanced greenhouse emissions provided extra popular acceptance for calls to reduce dependence on fossil fuels. A historic international conference in Villach, Austria in 1985 warned of the strong possibility of increased global mean temperatures in response to enhanced greenhouse emissions. This was followed by the 1990 report by the Intergovernmental Panel on Climate Change, which forecast 'a rate of increase of global mean temperature during the next century of about 0.3°C per decade ... this is greater than that seen over the past 10,000 years'.[8] Such pronouncements from the most respected atmospheric scientists in the world produced an even greater effect on the way Australians thought about energy than the uranium and nuclear power debates. The difference from the situation of the 1970s was that there had been many important breakthroughs in renewable energy technology by the late 1980s. In Australia, by the late 1980s, 'Australian scientists could boast the development of a world-class solar power station design, the world's best material for solar energy collectors, the world's highest-performing silicon solar cell and the design and manufacture of world-class electronics essential for the control of renewable energy systems.'[9] In contrast, by 1994, Australian research and development had been reduced to what Gilchrist calls 'banana republic levels'.

In the late 1980s Australia still had a government (and an opposition) whose main priority was maintaining economic growth and a bureaucracy that had been captured by the industries it was supposed to regulate. The fossil-fuel industries and many other industry groups were also powerful and alarmed at any moves by Australian governments to act in a determined way to reduce greenhouse emissions. Consequently, when the federal government signed the interim planning targets for greenhouse emissions in 1990, promising to stabilise emissions by 2000 and reduce them to 1988 levels by 2005, state governments continued to plan for more coal-fired power stations, refused to look seriously at demand management in the electricity industry, and closed down renewable energy projects. By the early 1990s the stage was set for a showdown between some of the major industry organisations and their allies in government, and those sections of the environment movement for whom energy efficiency was essential to ecologically sustainable development.

## Industrial Pollution

Although most Australian governments had responded to increased awareness of pollution problems by passing environmental protection legislation during the 1970s, the attitude that the Australian environment could, in most instances, effectively absorb most pollutants remained. Governments continued to see their main role as one of industry facilitation, and so regulation, especially of industry's environmental performance, remained a secondary consideration. Just as wilderness campaigners had to fight not only the timber industry but also a captured forestry commission as the regulatory agency, so anti-pollution campaigners found that departments of mining, primary industry and even the environment were often reluctant to enforce basic standards.[10]

The environment movement, often operating alone as local action groups, sometimes working in co-operation with state or national conservation organisations, tended to fight two types of battles against pollution. The first was against existing forms of pollution—poorly treated sewage, hazardous industrial waste, harmful pesticides. The second was against the siting of potentially polluting industry in inappropriate places with inadequate safeguards or using unacceptable technology.

Examples of the latter were common throughout the country during the 1980s. Sometimes opposition was aroused when fear of the unknown among a local community coincided with poor public communication by government and industry. Every now and then, however, local opposition was joined by wider groups because the movement perceived that public policy issues were at stake. This was certainly the case in the two case studies selected—the siting of hazardous industrial plants at Kurnell in Sydney and at Wesley Vale in Tasmania.

### Kurnell

The Kurnell Action Committee formed in 1985 to oppose the application by Bayer Australia to build a chemical formulation and storage facility on the historic peninsula, a few kilometres from the last remaining wetlands in the Sydney metropolitan area. The area had been placed on the interim listing for the National Estate and is one of the most important refuges along Australia's east coast for birds migrating from the northern hemisphere. It was also the first landing place of Captain Cook in Australia in 1770 and has archaeological significance. The residents' action was part of a larger concern by Kurnell residents and the local council about the state government's intention to rezone the area for noxious and hazardous industry. On the committee were Garry Smith, Byron Hurst, Val Bush, Pam Aldridge and Marg Boalch. Kate Short from the Total Environment Centre also played a significant role, especially during the public inquiry. Bayer wanted to formulate such compounds as insecticides, herbicides, cattle dips and sprays and sheep drench, and reserved the right to manufacture other chemical compounds in the future.[11] The proposed plant also included a waste incinerator, which residents feared would become a disposal unit for most of Sydney's toxic wastes.

The committee organised an impressive campaign. Members arranged leafleting, rallies, public meetings, pickets and, of course, they lobbied heavily and won the strong support of the local council, state politicians, and some unions. The Total Environment Centre and the ACF also weighed in on the side of the residents, although there was some suspicion by the locals concerning the links of the Total Environment Centre with the Labor government.[12] A commission of inquiry set up by the Unsworth government to look into the Bayer proposal received more than 300 submissions; when the commission gave its report in January 1987, it rejected the company's application. The state government then rejected the project, but the question of the noxious and hazardous zoning for the peninsula remained. This was addressed by the government in a draft Sydney regional plan for Kurnell, which reduced the toxic industry zone to about 20 per cent of its original size and placed it within the boundaries of the already existing Australian

Oil Refinery. The government also came up with a definition of toxic chemical industry, something that had not happened before.

The Kurnell campaign was a good example of the different attitudes to the Labor government of the New South Wales urban environment movement and the nature conservation movement. The Kurnell Action Committee was angry that a Labor government had decided to put a noxious and hazardous industry zone in the area, and did not have the same incentive as the nature conservationists to work for Unsworth's return in the 1988 state election. The same division occurred in relation to the Harbour Tunnel, Darling Harbour, the Parramatta Stadium and the Sydney Monorail.[13] Nature conservationists had generally been pleased with the Labor governments of Wran and Unsworth, especially for their achievements on national parks. They were also unenthusiastic about the policy positions of the Liberal opposition under Nick Greiner. Local groups in Sydney, however, had been fighting various developments being pushed by Labor; they wanted to punish government or, at least, for the environment movement to take a neutral stance. The Total Environment Centre was in a particularly invidious position. People like Milo Dunphy wanted the return of the Labor government and liked Environment Minister Bob Carr; but, because the centre supported the total environment (both urban and rural), it had to take a critical approach to Labor on issues such as Kurnell. Consequently, the movement as a whole went soft on supporting Labor in 1988 and, when the Liberals under Nick Greiner were elected to office, conservationists found themselves faced with a government that was possibly even less sympathetic with the environment.

*Wesley Vale*

Another campaign that brought together local, state and national environment organisations and forced governments to address the question of setting strong environmental standards was the building of a paper pulp mill at Wesley Vale on the north coast of Tasmania in the latter part of the 1980s. The project was owned by North Broken Hill and the Canadian company Noranda and the proposed mill would process 1.8 million tonnes of woodchips a year into 440,000 tonnes of bleached paper. It was a project that, at least in its early days, had the enthusiastic backing of the state and federal governments because it seemingly met the objection that was often raised about woodchipping, that it was a product with no value added. Even groups like the ACF had some initial qualms about opposing the mill, especially since most Australian paper was imported. However, it soon became obvious that Wesley Vale offered no respite for Tasmania's forests, because a mill of such enormous size would require extra woodchips to be viable. Since the conflict over Wesley Vale was occurring at much the same time as the Helsham Inquiry, the two issues became strongly linked as far as the environment movement was concerned, even though the major concern about the mill was always its potential for polluting Bass Strait.

Tasmanians had few grounds for believing that a potentially polluting facility would not become an actually polluting one, given Tasmania's record on pollution control. The state government's quaint habit of giving ministerial exemptions from the Environment Protection Act (often to the most polluting sites); the extremely high levels of zinc, mercury and other heavy metals, as well as organic wastes, in Hobart's Derwent River during the 1970s, all from industrial sources; and the scandalous pollution of Macquarie Harbour on the west coast of Tasmania from the nearby mines—all pointed to a government that was not likely to enforce strict environmental guidelines on industry.

In March 1988 a local group known as Concerned Residents Opposing Pulp Mill Siting (CROPS) was formed to oppose the mill. The local campaign brought together a coalition of the Tasmanian Farmers and Graziers Association, the Tasmanian Fishing Industry Council, some trade unions, state environment groups, the ACF, The Wilderness Society (TWS) and Greenpeace. Spokesperson for CROPS was Christine Milne, a local teacher who had been arrested at the Franklin blockade and had led a successful campaign to prevent the demolition of low-cost walking huts at Cradle Mountain. Milne was an unassuming but articulate leader of the campaign, with a sharp intellect and a fierce determination; Graham Richardson described her as 'one tough lady'. These qualities served her well as the leader of the Greens in the Tasmanian parliament. CROPS argued that the site was inappropriate, and other groups joined in the criticism, especially when the company released its environmental impact statement (EIS) on 27 October 1988. This was such an inadequate document that it drew fire from many quarters. United Scientists for Environmental Responsibility and Protection, which had formed in Tasmania in June 1988 as a result of the Helsham Inquiry, weighed in on the Wesley Vale EIS, as did overseas experts, other conservation groups, and even ten different departments and authorities of the Tasmanian state government. One of these stated: 'The lack of detail, obfuscation and generous use of motherhood statements is characteristic of the whole document, and quite frankly, it is an insult to the intelligence of professionals employed by the government who are required to comment on it.'[14]

The company's addendum to the EIS, which was intended to give the company a chance to reply to criticisms and comment that had come forward during the month given to public scrutiny, was an arrogant response which, in Graham Richardson's words, might as well have said 'up yours'.[15] The company stated that the oceanographic work that was being called for by the Tasmanian government 'will cost the company hundreds of thousands of dollars and cannot be justified until the project approval is secured'.[16] One of the main concerns expressed by community groups and government departments was the high level of organochlorine emissions going into the sea; since the plant's bleaching process depended on chlorine, the production of these persistent and dangerous chemical compounds was inevitable. The Tasmanian government attempted to stand firm and oblige the company to meet its standards but, when the company applied pressure and threatened to withdraw the project, Gray caved in. His announcement on 3 February 1989 that parliament would be recalled to weaken environmental controls on the mill (in the delightfully named Doubts Removal Bill) was actually written on North Broken Hill letterhead. Soon after, graffiti began appearing on Hobart walls saying 'Vote 1 North Broken Hill and cut out the middleman'.[17]

With Christine Milne launching last-ditch stands to convince the Commonwealth to stop the project, the federal cabinet finally gave its approval for foreign investment to the application from Noranda but insisted on stricter environmental standards and monitoring. However, ministers were shocked when Noranda decided to pull out of the project because it did not want to provide an unfortunate precedent for stricter standards to be applied to its mills in Canada. This surprising withdrawal left the ACF director Phillip Toyne describing the result as 'a lucky escape, not a win'.

The Wesley Vale dispute had several significant spin-offs. Firstly, as Christine Milne pointed out, it boosted green consumerism: the massive media coverage given to the campaign as a whole, and especially to the question of chlorine bleaching of paper, led to a greatly increased demand for unbleached and recycled paper products.[18]

Secondly, recurring land-use disputes like the forests and Wesley Vale highlighted the difficulties for the Commonwealth government in resolving these conflicts. Wesley Vale demonstrated the need for more rigorous procedures for assessing the competing demands of the environment and development, and for de-politicising the process. The Hawke government's answer was to set up the Resource Assessment Commission (RAC). According to Economou: 'The RAC's role would conform to the essence of "accordism"—that is, it would seek to depoliticise information and scientific data by filtering the wide range of inputs at the evaluative stage while attempting to reconcile hitherto irreconcilable interest groups from the development and environment sides of the land-use debate.'[19]

Thirdly, Wesley Vale was a landmark in the struggle of resource ministers inside the Hawke Cabinet to win control of the debate over environment versus development. From then on, ministers like Kerin, Alan Griffiths and Button, with help from the ACTU, pressed for a pro-development stance. While the environmental record of the Hawke government was a big winner for it in the 1990 election, there would be few wins on the scale of Wesley Vale in the future.

Anti-pollution campaigners often found they had more to worry about than recalcitrant industries and captive bureaucracies. As the Tasmanian Wilderness Society found, a public utility like the Hydro-Electric Commission could be just as hostile to environmental arguments as the most intransigent private corporation. They also found that many 'experts', especially those whose training was in the applied sciences, would defend their anti-environment, pro-development positions with vigour. Engineers figured prominently among these professional groupings. Whether they were building roads, dams or power stations, engineers all too often saw bigger as necessarily better, technology as value-free, public participation as an obstruction to effective decision-making, and supply rather than demand management as the most effective planning tool. Nowhere was this better illustrated than in the conflict over ocean outfall of Sydney's sewage effluent.

### Sydney Ocean Outfall

For years the Sydney Water Board had given cursory treatment to its sewage and then released this effluent into the ocean at outfalls at Malabar, Bondi and North Head, assuming that it would be dispersed by the ocean and not pollute the waters surrounding Sydney. Sewage effluent is a problem, of course, in many parts of the country in large cities and high-growth areas, especially where treatment plants are outdated. The situation is worse in those centres where local authorities have attempted to solve the problem of disposing of industrial liquid waste by permitting companies that produce such waste up to a certain level of hazard to dispose of it via the sewers. Thus the normal sewage treatment plant that has to deal with human waste and waste water also had to deal with large amounts of animal fats, oils, solvents, acids, and many other potentially damaging industrial materials. A Criminal Justice Commission inquiry in Queensland in the early 1990s found that large volumes of liquid industrial waste had been illegally dumped into sewers in the Brisbane region for many years,[20] and anecdotal evidence suggests that the same practices have occurred in most other places.

In 1985 a group known as Stop The Ocean Pollution (STOP) began operation. Its chief researcher, Richard Gosden, was determined to put an end to ocean outfalls, believing they were an inadequate means of sewage treatment and presented environmental and health hazards. Other groups, like People Opposed to Ocean Outfalls (POOO) and Campaign to End Sewage Smells (CESS), a small group based at Malabar, joined the campaign at much the same time. However, all the work of unpaid activists like Gosden and Kirk Willcox of STOP, Ben Brown and Mark Toal of POOO, and Sue and Alan Cass and Brett Newboldt of CESS could not compete with the slick public relations of the Water Board, which used its enormous resources to convince the people of Sydney and the media that nothing smelt in Sydney's sewerage system. STOP tried to get the media to take up the issue and POOO organised an annual march at Manly against ocean outfalls but, in the absence of proof that the outfalls were causing problems and in the face of the board's publicity asserting that there were no problems, the campaign had little momentum.

However, in 1986 a local newspaper began publishing STOP's research into the problems of ocean outfall; the resulting publicity forced the Water Board to set up a service called Surfline to report on surf pollution. This service was often criticised by local groups and sections of the media as just more of the board's public relations. Nevertheless, at least some Surfline reports were serious enough to embarrass the Water Board.[21] In 1988 research by a PhD student, Sharon Beder, showed that there were critical voices from within the bureaucracy, especially the State Pollution Control Commission. Among other things, she uncovered critical reports and memos from a commission engineer Robert Brain, and the results of the 1987 Malabar Bioaccumulation Study, which revealed that pollutant levels in fish caught in the study area were many times greater than the limits set by the National Health and Medical Research Council.[22]

As soon as this information hit the press, there was uproar. The wall of secrecy and bureaucratic obfuscation that had surrounded the operations of the board and the effectiveness of ocean outfalls began to crumble. The board was pressured into releasing the results of the second Malabar Bioaccumulation Study that showed levels of organo-chlorines in fish well over the limits. The local groups that had been marginalised for so long were now regarded as credible by the media and, by the beginning of 1988, many thousands of people had joined to lend support to STOP and POOO. The annual march and rally at Manly in March 1989 was huge, and 240,000 people attended the Turn Back the Tide concert on 24 March 1989.

Meanwhile, the Liberal government of Nick Greiner had established an independent review of the Water Board's proposals and this recommended that the system be upgraded at a cost of $6 billion over twenty years. However, it did not recommend secondary treatment of the sewage,[23] and the state government was remarkably slow in deciding how the upgrades would be done. In December 1989 Greiner announced a $7 billion program over twenty years to clean up Sydney's beaches and surrounding waters. The Water Board also moved in the late 1980s against the massive illegal dumping into the sewerage system of hazardous liquid material such as grease-trap waste, although this continues to be a considerable problem.

This issue illustrates that a public utility can be just as much an opponent of environmentalists as private industry, and that a professional group that has its hands on the reins of power can act in imperious and undemocratic ways. Once again it demonstrates that a regulatory agency, in this case the State Pollution Control Commission, acted to cover up information on the outfall system and prevent public knowledge. It also shows how important it is for action groups to have good research capacity.

### Toxic Waste

Environmentalists reacted to the problems of hazardous waste pollution in the 1980s by developing a commitment to a waste management hierarchy that placed waste avoidance and minimisation at the top and then promoted recycling and reuse, treatment, and disposal, in that order. The movement in South Australia was able to persuade the state government to introduce container deposit legislation in the early 1980s, although the packaging industry thwarted similar moves in other states. Other recycling and reuse schemes were promoted by conservationists, notably the Victorian Waste Exchange overseen by the well-known environmentalist, Ian Pausacker.

Although there was little controversy in the movement about these priorities, there was some disagreement about what should happen at the lower end of the hierarchy: integrated waste treatment facilities, high temperature incineration of intractable wastes, and landfills. The movement is united on the need to emphasise dealing with waste at the source rather than end-of-pipe solutions, but there has been conflict over what should be done with the hazardous waste that seemingly cannot be minimised or prevented, at least in the short term.

A series of pollution scares around the world during the 1980s alerted authorities and the environment movement to the need for coherent waste management strategies, but they also created a fear in the community about toxic waste. This fear was compounded by the resentment in lower socio-economic areas, where people felt that they were more likely to get such facilities than the more affluent. Plans to establish an integrated waste treatment plant often ran into organised community resistance. This was nowhere more evident than in attempts to build a high-temperature incinerator to destroy the considerable amounts of intractable waste such as PCBs, organochlorine pesticides like DDT and dieldrin, and CFCs. The problem with these compounds is not so much their toxicity. Rather, many are very persistent and accumulate in the food chain. About 8000 tonnes of hexachlorobenzene (HCB) was stored at ICI's plant at Botany Bay, but most intractables like PCBs and CFCs were spread all around the community.[24]

Incinerators got bad press all around the world in the 1980s, much of it deserved. Operators tried to save money by working the incinerators at temperatures that were too low and did not use their expensive scrubbers; regulatory authorities were reluctant to enforce standards. As a result of this damaging combination, local communities were subjected to smothering by smoke, acid gases, and other pollutants potentially harmful to health. The realisation that Australia had somewhere between 60,000 and 90,000 tonnes of such materials made it essential to think about disposal options. The ACF decided to give in-principle support to a high temperature incinerator 'as part of a comprehensive system for the minimisation, management and disposal of intractable waste'.[25] Organisations like the Toxic and Hazardous Chemicals Committee of the Total Environment Centre, represented by Kate Short and Arnold Ewald, and the Conservation Council of Victoria, represented by Peter Christoff, were appointed to the advisory committee to the Joint Task Force on Intractable Waste; they gave cautious approval to the incinerator option but emphasised the need for full environmental safeguards.[26]

One serious concern among environmentalists was the large number of fires occurring in chemical warehouses. The first big one was at Butler's warehouse in Melbourne in 1986, when smoke drifted over inner western suburbs. One result of this was the formation of the group Hazardous Materials Action Group (HAZMAG), based in the western suburbs, led by Colleen Hartland and Matt Ruchel. Ruchel was later to become Greenpeace's toxics campaigner. Earlier fires had prompted the Victorian Environmental Protection Authority to draft some of Australia's first cradle-to-grave industrial waste strategies, but it was the huge chemical fire at the inner-city Coode Island installation that brought home to many the need for the Victorian government to confront issues of the location of dangerous industries in Melbourne. Unfortunately, by then the Victorian Labor government under Joan Kirner was in such a shambles it lacked the political ability to manage such a process.

Early representatives from conservation-oriented zoological and ornithological groups, including the nature writer, Charles Barrett (far right), at a meeting which attempted to persuade state governments to put a national conservation strategy in place (Birds Australia)

*Left* John Beattie, the Tasmanian wildlife photographer with his heavy camera equipment, the first in the environment movement's great tradition of Australian wilderness photographers (Archives Office of Tasmania) *Right* A young Myles Dunphy from his Mountain Trails Club days (Dexter Dunphy)

An outing of the Melbourne Women's Walking Club in the 1920s (Ella Nott, reproduced with permission from Uphill After Lunch, copyright Melbourne Women's Walking Club Inc., 1987)

*Left* National Park Campaigners, Romeo Lahey and Arthur Groom at a bush camp in 1938 (A. Clelland, National Parks Association of Queensland)
*Right* Judith Wright, probably in November 1967, during a trip to Sydney and Canberra to campaign for the protection of the Great Barrier Reef (News Ltd)

Milo Dunphy leads Prince Phillip, Geoff Mosely and other conservationists on a well-dressed walk in the bush in the early days of the Australian Conservation Foundation (Australian Conservation Foundation)

*Left* Jack Mundey, leader of the Green Bans movement in Sydney in the early seventies, standing in front of a restored building in The Rocks (Australian Conservation Foundation) *Right* Milo Dunphy, director of Sydney's Total Environment Centre and ACF Councillor, out bushwalking (Australian Conservation Foundation)

Anti-uranium mining protest at Roxby Downs, 1984 (Angela Jones)

Protesters dig themselves into the Cape Tribulation-Bloomfield road during
Wet Tropics campaign, early 1980s (Cairns and Far North Environment
Centre)

Bob Brown in the Lemonthyme forest, 1986 (Bill Hare, Australian
Conservation Foundation)

*Left* Christine Milne, leader of the campaign against the Wesley Vale pulp mill
and later a Tasmanian Green politician (Kevin Murphy) *Right* Anti-nuclear
activist and senator, Jo Vallentine (West Australian)

Greenpeace in an anti-chlorine bleaching action, Millicent, South Australia, 1992 (Greenpeace)

Performance artist, Benny Zable, outside federal Parliament. His presence has added drama to many environmental and peace campaigns over two decades. (Franklin Scarf)

Protest against the loss of old fig trees in Brisbane anti-road protest, 1995
(Courier-Mail)

Protestor on the occupation platform high up a giant karri tree, WA forests
protest (Carole Perry)

Protest against genetic engineering of food outside Monsanto's Melbourne office, 1998 (Marsha Phelps)

Rock star and ACF President, Peter Garrett, with former ALP federal minister, Tom Uren in the centre foreground. To their left is Jacqui Katona of the Gundjehmi Aboriginal Corporation and on the right is the senior traditional owner of the Jabiluka land, Yvonne Margarula leading a march against the Jabiluka uranium mine, Northern Territory, July 1998 (Clive Hyde, courtesy, Northern Territory News)

If storage of intractables was to be an option, the possibility of a fire at such a facility would have to be unthinkable. Long-time ACF member Peter Brotherton was placed on the Joint Taskforce on Intractable Waste which advised the Commonwealth, New South Wales and Victorian governments on the issue. The taskforce supported the incinerator option, with the town of Corowa on the border between New South Wales and Victoria as its preferred site. Corowa residents were incensed when they found out, and the chances of setting up a high-temperature incinerator anywhere else in the country diminished rapidly.

While some organisations like the Total Environment Centre had also given their support to the concept of a high temperature incinerator, others like Greenpeace and Friends of the Earth did not. Sharon Beder, whose experience with the Sydney Water Board had not given her a high regard for regulatory agencies, distrusted such technology and believed that not having an incinerator would provide greater incentive for companies to explore recycling and minimisation strategies for these wastes. It would also give greater opportunity for the development of alternative, and less dangerous, methods of destroying the compounds.[27]

### Pesticides

One of the most difficult struggles waged by anti-pollution activists was the campaign to ban organochlorine pesticides, especially the residual ones like DDT, dieldrin, aldrin, heptachlor and chlordane. These chemicals were used in agriculture and in the urban pest-control industry. They are long-lasting and are stored in the bodies of many animals, including human beings. They are toxic, and some are strongly suspected of causing cancer and many other health problems. The reason for the long duration of this campaign, despite the many serious doubts about safety, was the strength of the opposition—the powerful pesticide industry and those sections of the farming lobby that felt dependent on such chemicals. In fact, the list of those opposing the ban on organochlorines, for one reason or another, is impressive. It included the National Health and Medical Research Council, agricultural authorities, health professionals, environmental regulators, and politicians.

In spite of the pivotal role of Rachel Carson's *Silent Spring* in the development of a global environmental consciousness, the power of the pesticides industry continued to grow during the decades after 1960. In fact, according to Greenpeace, pesticide sales world-wide increased from $US850 million in 1960 to over $US26 billion in 1991.[28] The industry has exerted enormous influence on Australian governments, largely exercised through agriculture departments at state and federal levels. If anything, the pesticide industry has actually become more influential, given the increased importance of pesticide-dependent crops like cotton and herbicide-reliant practices in land care and forestry. It has fought hard to prevent the banning of any pesticide on the basis that 'if one goes, they could all go'. The closeness between the pesticide industry and regulators has been enhanced by the industry's practice of paying conference fees and travel expenses for bureaucrats, and a career path often leads from government departments to good jobs in the industry.[29] It comes as no surprise, then, that government officers have seen their role with regard to pesticides predominantly as making sure farmers have access to necessary pesticides and supporting industry self-regulation, rather than the heavy regulatory hand of government. One department head in New South Wales described his state's new Pesticides Act as 'ushering in a new era of pesticide use and management. The department will administer the Act as a cooperative venture with manufacturers, retailers and users of pesticides in the interests of all consumers.'[30]

The role of the National Health and Medical Research Council, the Commonwealth body that evaluated the public health impact of pesticides, has also often been criticised by environmentalists. According to Kate Short:

> It takes a curiously narrow view of scientific research and appears unwilling to investigate the final experiment in pesticide assessment, the real-life human experience. Council routinely dismisses evidence of harm because they judge it as 'anecdotal' and thus without scientific validity. They refuse to take the community's experience seriously or to defend their approach to regulatory science in open debate.[31]

Many environmental activists who investigate claims of pesticide poisoning are also alarmed by the attitudes of health professionals in state health departments and in the community. The difficulty of furnishing proof of harm is often cited by bureaucrats and this attitude also seems to be part of the culture of the medical profession generally; thus a local doctor who becomes concerned about the possibility of pesticide poisoning in the local community is often too cowed by concerns about professional standing to take a stand. When the pro-pesticide attitudes of the building industry and local governments are added to those of the industry, the regulatory agencies, and the health professionals, it is little wonder that the campaign to ban the organo-chlorine pesticides was so difficult.

The earliest advocates in Australia against organochlorines were Dr John Pollak and Herbert Beauchamp from the Toxic Chemicals Committee of Sydney's Total Environment Centre. John Pollak, a biochemist at the University of Sydney, first came to attention for organising a petition from among some of the country's best-known scientists against the use of such weapons as napalm and Agent Orange in the Vietnam War. He started the group Social Responsibility in Science with the famous environmental philosopher Charles Birch in 1969. As the result of one of his studies, he managed to draw attention to the serious pollution levels in Sydney Harbour, especially around the current Olympic Games venue at Homebush Bay. Pollack's friendship with Milo Dunphy and his meeting with Herbert Beauchamp led to the formation of the Toxic Chemicals Committee as part of the Total Environment Centre in 1980.

The Toxic Chemicals Committee took up several issues in the early 1980s, including the effects of Agent Orange, but made its most significant move against organochlorines when it organised a conference called Hazardous Chemicals in the Australian Environment in August 1983. Several others joined the committee around this time, including Arnold Ewald, Kate Short and Robert Verkerk. Short, a political science major with a lively intelligence and a defiant spirit, soon became the best-known public advocate on chemical issues in the country. Verkerk, who had a background in the pest-control industry (and coincidentally had chemical sensitivity)[32] set up the first non-chemical pest-control company in the country as a positive alternative to chemical spraying for termites.

Nevertheless, the campaign to ban organochlorines dragged; it was hampered not only by the resolute opposition, but also by the difficulties of getting complex information across to the public in order to get support. The Toxic Chemicals Committee had put out many publications pointing out the dangers inherent in pesticide use, but there was little movement by government and, of course, the committee was involved in many other campaigns, such as suspected pesticide poisoning in Coffs Harbour and in various cotton-growing districts. John Pollack complained in 1986 to New South Wales agriculture minister Hallam that it had taken six years to persuade the government to take organochlorines off supermarket shelves, only to be told, 'Well, that's not so long.'[33] The turning-point came in 1987, when shipments of Australian beef were rejected by US authorities because they contained residues of organochlorines, especially dieldrin, that exceeded the permitted limit. This had probably resulted from spraying for agricultural purposes and termite control. The dispute resulted in much more rigorous monitoring procedures and greater public awareness of the issue, and withdrawal of the chemicals from all agricultural uses (except for limited use in Queensland). The fear of vanishing beef export markets engendered action in the regulatory authorities that years of advocacy had been unable to achieve.

The focus of the campaign then shifted to Western Australia. A former forest activist, Naomi Segal, set up the group Householders for Safe Pesticide Use in 1986, in response to her perception of a widespread pesticide problem from use of organochlorines to control termites. She put a small classified advertisement in the newspaper telling people that, if they were treating their houses for termites on an annual basis, they might be doing something not permitted by legislation. She immediately received fifty-five responses. There had been a number of serious incidents, including organochlorine-contaminated eggs from a backyard coop that were well over acceptable limits. In the worst example, a potter had his studio sprayed with heptachlor by a man who had been a licensed operator for twenty years. The application was so overdone that pools of heptachlor were left on the floor; people had to be evacuated from the building, and many became ill. The owner reported this to Segal and the case was one of several examined by an ABC 'Four Corners' team soon afterwards, along with numerous other incidents, such as deaths at a pheasant farm and a horse farm, and the high levels of organochlorines measured in mothers' breast milk.

Public opposition persuaded the WA Environmental Protection Authority in 1988 to review the spraying program against Argentine ants. This concluded that the organochlorine sprays were having more environmental impact than the ants, and the program was cancelled. In the same year, Greenpeace and Householders organised a joint occupation of the WA Health Department to demand better public information on heptachlor and chlordane. The protesters wrote 'poison' with hard-boiled eggs, Householders produced women who had discovered high organochlorine levels in their breast milk (one of whom was prepared to feed her baby on camera), some women came with hens, and one had a basket of contaminated eggs that she wanted to present to the Health Department. The department was not amused, but it soon began enforcing and tightening the legislation. It prosecuted a number of pest controllers who were in breach, and placed newspaper advertisements alerting people to the health implications of these chemicals.[34]

In 1989 both the state Labor government and the Liberal opposition gave commitments to banning organochlorines. In that year Housing Minister McGinty banned the spraying of heptachlor in existing buildings, and in 1990 he banned them from new buildings in the state housing sector. Such action persuaded Termi-Mesh, a company that manufactured a physical termite barrier, to set up in Western Australia, and many others followed. This made it more difficult for supporters of organochlorines to argue that there was no viable alternative to their usage in termite control. Over the next five years Segal pursued her campaign tirelessly. She co-operated with the Duggin Committee of the National Health and Medical Research Council, which was investigating the use of organochlorines; she was influential in that committee's final report, published in 1992, which stated (somewhat ambiguously) that the chemicals should be banned immediately for existing buildings and later for new ones. This led to a further investigation by the federal government's National Registrations Authority; its report judged that the alternatives to organochlorines were viable and that therefore the chemicals should be banned. This was finally achieved in 1995 everywhere except in the Northern Territory.

It is remarkable that such a campaign took so long, given that organochlorines are only one type of pesticide that represents a danger to human health and the environment. Many others such as organophosphates, carbamates and the synthetic pyrethrins, as well as many other non-pesticide chemicals, have been criticised by environmentalists. There are also more complex problems: the effects of combinations of chemicals that are individually relatively harmless, and the effects of supposedly inert additives like solvents and surfactants. Fortunately, capable people like Mariann Grinter and Kate Short and Matt Ruchel of Greenpeace continue public advocacy in this area. However, they are a small minority of those who are active in the environment movement.

Another toxic chemical problem confronted the residents of Mount Taylor in the suburb of Kingston near Brisbane. Their houses, mostly bought during the early to mid-1980s, stood on rezoned land that had previously been a goldmine and a toxic waste dump. In April 1987 a nasty-looking substance began rising to the surface in people's back yards; test drilling begun by the local council a week later confirmed the presence of acid sludge. Dissatisfaction with the lack of determined action by the council and a seeming lack of sympathy by the state government led local residents to set up Residents Against Toxic Substances (RATS), with Thelma Towers as its spokesperson. Subsequent investigation revealed that the site had been used as an illegal industrial waste dump and that contaminated fill had been used in sub-divisional work.[35]

In a bitter three-year campaign RATS fought the state government's attempts to deal with the problem in what the residents regarded as an unsatisfactory and patronising manner. Once again, a seemingly ordinary person, Thelma Towers, emerged to lead one of the most effective community actions of the period of National Party government in Queensland.[36] The Kingston Task Force, set up by the state government under Dr Sally Leivesley, never had the confidence of the residents. When Labor was elected in 1989, RATS indicated to the new government that a former conservationist who had become an environmental chemist, Greg Miller, was the only expert who had their confidence. His company, Envirotest, and a Griffith University consultancy were employed to review all the scientific and medical evidence on the issue. As a result, much of the area was closed, capped, landscaped and turned into a park; the homes of affected residents were purchased and demolished, and the people relocated.

Kingston achieved the same kind of status in Australia as Love Canal in the United States, a notorious residential development built over a toxic waste dump. The Kingston incident persuaded state governments to look seriously at the issue of contaminated sites. Where legislation was not adequate to deal with the problem, it was introduced, as with the Queensland Contaminated Land Act 1990. Nevertheless, the lack of environmental regulation or enforcement that characterised all governments' policies toward industry through the 1960s, 1970s and 1980s left a legacy of contamination that will continue to challenge the environment movement and governments for a long time.

*Clean Waters*

The most successful campaign by any environment organisation to pressure industry to take their environmental responsibilities more seriously and the regulatory authorities to enforce environmental compliance was Greenpeace's Clean Waters campaign in the first half of 1990.[37] The campaign, under the direction of Paul Gilding, targeted five companies around Australia—Caltex in Sydney, BHP in Port Kembla, Nufarm in Melbourne, Pasminco–EZ in Hobart, and BHAS–Pasminco in Port Pirie. After background research had been done by campaigners or supporters in the various centres, the Greenpeace ships *Redbill* and on occasions *Rainbow Warrior II* visited and conducted direct action to highlight the failure of these companies to adhere to their requirements under environmental law, and of the various state authorities to monitor their performance, enforce compliance and prosecute serious breaches.

At each place Greenpeace either took samples from effluent discharges and compared them with the companies' licence conditions, or obtained data from the government under freedom of information. At Sydney, Port Kembla and Melbourne, the group blocked discharge pipes in direct actions of questionable legality but with great media impact. Their test sampling revealed that Caltex was well over its licence conditions for phenols. At Port Kembla they highlighted the fact that the BHP subsidiary, Australian Iron and Steel, not only breached its licence conditions on ammonia and chromium but had also obtained permission to dump into the harbour 1.6 billion litres of effluent a day, containing 180 tonnes of phenols, 16.5 tonnes of oil and grease, 3.9 tonnes of ammonia, 62 kilograms of cyanide, and 45 kilograms of chromium.[38] No wonder fishing was banned in the Port Kembla Harbour! In Melbourne, Greenpeace revealed that, although there were no standards laid down for dioxin emissions, these toxic substances were being discharged from the Nufarm plant that was producing the herbicide 2,4-D.

As a result of the widespread publicity surrounding Greenpeace's campaign, the New South Wales State Pollution Control Commission was forced to prosecute both Caltex and BHP under the Environmental Offences and Penalties Act, which provided for up to $1 million in fines. This was a step forward for regulatory enforcement in that state; it also demonstrated the ludicrous situation where the commission depended on the data from a company's own monitoring to get a conviction against that company. Actually, it was ironic that the commission in New South Wales and the Environment Protection Authority in Victoria came under such scrutiny as a result of Greenpeace's campaign because they ran a stricter environmental protection regime than the other states. In Queensland, for example, there was only one successful prosecution under the Clean Waters Act up to 1991.[39] The campaign raised vital issues of non-compliance by industry and non-enforcement by government; but it also showed that such campaigns can cause a disproportionate focus on one industry or one pollutant, such as dioxin, to the exclusion of other sites and pollutants that might be causing even greater problems.

The campaign also had positive spin-offs in terms of new environmental protection legislation. The New South Wales government amended the Environmental Offences and Penalties Act to remove from the environment minister the gatekeeper role that vetted civil prosecutions under the act. Henceforth, the Land and Environment Court would determine whether or not a proposed civil action was reasonable or vexatious. The South Australian government introduced the Marine Environment Protection Act in 1990. This act, though not properly in force until 1993, introduced the important provision for making licences and monitoring data public. The Goss government, elected in Queensland in 1989, came to power on a promise of environmental protection legislation to replace the outdated Clean Waters and Clean Air Acts; but it was 1994 before it introduced the legislation and then only after a Criminal Justice Commission inquiry had revealed instances of massive non-compliance and non-enforcement in that state.

Unfortunately, while the act is a good piece of legislation, those sections which provide for public consultation and appeals over licences have not as yet been proclaimed. The campaign also, no doubt, prompted many people in industry to read the writing on the wall and begin to work on achieving improved standards of environmental performance. It also possibly gave an impetus to manufacturing industry's involvement in the federal government's Ecologically Sustainable Development process that began soon after the 1990 federal election.

A significant result from the campaign in Melbourne was the renewed interest in an old site at Fawkner, where Nufarm had manufactured DDT, 2,4-D, and other pesticides in the late 1950s. Several minor but irritating prosecutions by the local council in the late 1960s and early 1970s had prompted the company to leave the site, which it then sold. The local council approved the rezoning of the site to residential on the same day that Greenpeace raided Nufarm. Tests of the plant revealed levels of chlorphenols, furans and dioxins that were unacceptably high, and the rezoning was rescinded.

### Sustainable Cities?

The directions taken by urban planners for Australian cities continued to present major challenges to environmentalists during the 1980s, despite the urban planning legacy of the Green Bans, the ground-breaking work done by Melbourne activists associated with the *Seeds for Change* project, and the anti-freeways campaigns of the 1970s. Clearly, the major problem was the urban sprawl that afflicted all Australian capital cities. Urban sprawl reinforced car dependency, which worsened air pollution (in spite of improved emission standards) and caused the degeneration of suburbs affected by the development of major roads. As urban environmentalist Peter Newman says, 'when individuals seek to optimise their private environmental quality through either seeking lower densities at the urban fringe or through the prevention of higher densities in the present urban fabric, then the increased dispersion of the city will almost certainly mean an overall decline in urban environmental quality'.[40] Urban sprawl is also linked with higher per capita energy consumption, waste generation, and costs of providing infrastructure such as water, sewerage, power, roads and public transport;[41] thus it presents problems not only for local authorities but also for local communities in terms of maintaining amenity and social justice.

Environmental conflicts in cities focused on numerous issues during the 1980s—bushland clearing, industry location, pollution, rezonings and, of course, freeways. Probably the key issue for planning a city according to principles of sustainability is that of transport. The system a city devises for moving its citizens around determines, to a large extent, such outcomes as air quality and neighbourhood vitality. Therefore, when residents' groups decided to oppose freeway or major road developments and, in the course of their campaigns, urged traffic restraint and public transport options, they were contributing to the debate on ecologically sustainable development. Whether they were called privately funded toll roads, ring roads, arterial bypasses or freeways, major road constructions were still fought by local groups, and sometimes by the wider movement. Two examples will show how the environment movement reacted to such developments—the campaigns against Route 20 in Brisbane and against the Harbour Tunnel in Sydney.

### Brisbane's Route 20

With high population growth in south-east Queensland during the 1980s, there was increasing pressure for major infrastructure projects in the region. One of the main problems was the large volumes of traffic that converged on the Brisbane city centre from outlying areas every day. To remove some of this pressure, the National Party government of Queensland in the late 1980s planned a Western Arterial Bypass (as it was known officially) as an upgrade of an already busy, but winding, Route 20, which many cars used in order to bypass the city centre when travelling from the north to the south of Brisbane. The upgrade would turn a largely two-lane road into a four-lane highway with a median strip along much of its course, and require several resumptions of residential property. It would also straighten many of the road's curves and level a steep incline which, until then, had prevented big trucks from using Route 20. Vastly greater usage of the road was predicted, much of the expected increase coming from industrial traffic.[42]

Opposition to the upgrade came initially from a non-militant group called the Bardon Protection League, whose main concern up until the announcement of the project had been the protection of local bushland from encroaching residential development. Route 20 affected many people along its course, however, drawing in people from suburbs outside Bardon who brought with them a sense of urgency and an organised approach to gathering information and to mobilising the community. The new organisation became known as Citizens Against Route 20 (CART). The group organised well-attended public meetings and its placards appeared everywhere. Its talented spokesperson, David Engwicht, seemed to have something to say on the issue in every newspaper or television news edition, all backed up with impeccable information and a flair for the dramatic.

Although there was some suggestion early in the campaign that CART preferred the Main Roads Department to build an alternative route some way to the west, the committee dismissed this option in early 1988. Instead, they demanded a public inquiry into Brisbane's transport system, taking full account of public transport, cycling and alternative land-use policies. This broader demand was more difficult to explain to people, but it avoided the political pitfalls associated with alienating supporters from other areas.

During the Brisbane City Council elections, CART put pressure on the Liberal administration of the lord mayor, Sallyanne Atkinson, and persuaded her to withdraw her support from the project. The state government, however, remained adamant that the road would be built. At this stage a division appeared in CART: one section advocated a primary focus on gathering information and lobbying influential people; the other, consisting of Engwicht and activists like Nathalie Haymann, emphasised community mobilisation and direct action if need be. The main strength of the latter group was the prominence of young married women who, up to that point, had not taken leading or militant roles in the organisation.

CART was always efficient in distributing thousands of copies of community newspapers to keep people up to date, not only with latest events but also with cutting-edge ideas on traffic management and alternative solutions. In mid-1988 the group produced hundreds of copies of a small book entitled *Traffic Calming: A Solution to Route 20 and a Vision for Brisbane*. Largely the work of David Engwicht, the book brought together research from all over the world and was trail-blazing in the Australian scene. It subjected road planners' logic to a rigorous critique and outlined viable traffic restraint alternatives, many of which operated in other cities around the world. Engwicht, who had not completed senior high school, went on to become a consultant with an international reputation on alternative methods of traffic management and community conflict resolution.

No EIS had been planned for Route 20 but, mid-way through 1988, the state government promised one, with a degree of community consultation in the process (a rare event in Queensland at that time). Somewhat naively (as it turned out) CART held off its plans for direct action and presented its argument for city-wide traffic demand management to the consultants doing the EIS. The final report reflected, however, the narrow engineering perspective of the consultants and their reluctance to hand in a report that their employers would not want to read.

A change of government in Queensland in 1989 shelved plans for the bypass. Although the Goss Labor government undertook several minor upgrades to facilitate its use by much heavier traffic, the planned four-lane freeway was never built. The 'victory' was important for inserting demand management into the world-views of Queensland urban environmental activists. However, it did little to break the stranglehold of road engineers on transport planning, and it did not stop the Goss government from attempting to build the ill-fated South Coast Motorway in the 1990s, a decision that mobilised thousands of angry residents and was a significant factor in Labor's loss at the 1995 state election.

### Sydney Harbour Tunnel

The Sydney Harbour tunnel project also demonstrated the weaknesses of the EIS process and official reluctance to take a sustainable development approach to transport planning. In 1985 a consortium composed of the construction company Transfield and the large Japanese company Kumagai Gumi approached the New South Wales state government with an idea for a toll-financed tunnel under Sydney Harbour. The Harbour Bridge was suffering congestion at peak hours, and the Wran government jumped at the opportunity. The EIS, carried out for the consortium by consultants Cameron McNamara, was bitterly criticised by the North Sydney Municipal Council under mayor Ted Mack and by the Society for Social Responsibility in Engineering. These groups even publicly accused the consultants of breaching the Engineering Code of Ethics.[43] Several community groups also weighed in but the combination of political and bureaucratic commitment was too strong for North Shore groups like Save Our Sydney or even the formidable Ted Mack to overcome. Mack summed up the urban environmental response to traditional road engineers and urban planners:

> Congestion is actually an excellent thing because it is the main means of control, in fact it is the only means of control. It is an interesting thing throughout the world that when people do anything to increase the average speed of cars which interestingly enough is about 16 km/hr in most cities in peak hours. If you do anything to increase that speed, right, then simply more cars come till the level falls again to 16 km/hr. It all seems to work on a public acceptance level which is pretty common the world over. I know it's not a very publicly acceptable argument, but you really don't have to do anything about the road problem. You just leave it the same and let congestion determine the shape of the city.[44]

### Transport Alternatives

Opposition to freeways often preceded or went hand-in-hand with campaigns for better public transport and other alternatives. In 1988 the Conservation Council of Victoria supported a campaign against state government plans to extend Melbourne's Eastern Freeway, and the following year it joined with the Public Transport Users Association and other groups in a wider campaign for a better public transport system for the city.[45] In Western Australia the work of various urban environmental groups prompted the Fremantle City Council to conduct a pilot energy conservation project, beginning in 1984 and finishing in 1987. This project poured resources into improving bicycling facilities and promoting fuel conservation measures and energy-efficient urban planning, including the use of vacant or under-utilised land for urban infill residential development. The council also supported energy-efficient housing developments.[46]

In Queensland CART converted itself into Citizens Advocating Responsible Transport and worked with other groups to promote its vision of a more sustainable urban environment. Groups like the Bicycle Institute and Friends of the Earth in the various states regularly organised bicycle rallies and public transport days to promote alternatives to the motor car; heightened consciousness of the twin dangers of ozone depletion and greenhouse effect gave added weight to their arguments. Nevertheless, at the end of the decade car dependency was as entrenched as ever and the major determinant of directions in regional planning. Mayors or state transport ministers who flirted with ideas of scrapping major road projects and replacing them with more environmentally acceptable alternatives were either pulled into line by their bureaucrats or reminded of the dire consequences at the ballot box of allowing the traffic to block up. Confrontations between community groups and transport planners over major road projects in Australian cities would extend well into the next decade.

# CHAPTER 8

# *Greenies and Numbers Men*

The period from 1983 to 1990 saw activism from a large section of the organised conservation movement which attempted to achieve protection for Australia's native forests and wilderness areas and from many and varied community-based groups, sometimes but not necessarily associated with official conservation organisations. By the end of the eighties conservationists could point to many significant victories but it was also obvious that, at both national and global levels, ecological crises loomed. Adoption of the goal of ecologically sustainable development gave the movement a more intellectually credible framework for policy formation and campaigning but key strategists in the movement believed that a more coherent political strategy was also necessary. These people tended to divide into two camps. The major stream wanted a professionalised movement combining mass mobilisations and campaigning with skilful lobbying so that they could become partially institutionalised, as most social movements attempt to do. The minor stream tended to make a more radical analysis of the social changes necessary for an ecologically sustainable society and was sceptical of the ability of parties like the ALP to make difficult decisions on the environment. Its adherents wanted an independent Green party.

It was the Franklin campaign that gave impetus to both these streams, although their origins went back to the early seventies. Independent green politics was given a major boost in Tasmania when Bob Brown took over from environmental activist Norm Sanders as the independent member for Denison in the Tasmanian Parliament in 1982. Then, soon after the High Court decision on the Franklin, a small group within the Wilderness Society, consisting of such experienced activists as Pam Waud, Chris Harries and Bob Brown himself, began making contact with like-minded people around the country to consider a unified, green political strategy. Before that could happen, however, a very incoherent but dramatic political alternative appeared on the scene.

## The Nuclear Disarmament Party

By 1984 the anti-nuclear agenda had widened to include opposition to nuclear weapons and the re-heating of the Cold War. In some states organisations that had focused on uranium mining and export were wound down and many members joined groups whose primary focus was nuclear disarmament. Opposition to uranium mining was, of course, also an important concern of these groups. In other areas organisations like Movement Against Uranium Mining and Campaign Against Nuclear Energy began to work more closely with peace groups like People for Nuclear Disarmament. In June 1984 an energetic but eccentric Canberra doctor, Michael Denborough, helped to set up a new political party, the Nuclear Disarmament Party (NDP). This new party had only three policy planks—no foreign bases, no nuclear ships or planes on Australian territory, and an end to uranium mining. A number of delegates to the Labor Party national conference walked out after the decision on uranium mining and joined the fledgling party; many others joined over the next few months as public meetings were set up in towns and cities all over Australia. Labor Party stalwarts inside the mainstream peace movement spoke against the new party, arguing that only the Labor Party could form government and deliver an anti-nuclear program. Likewise, the Democrats were dismayed by the NDP's emergence, believing that they were the only truly anti-nuclear party and that activists should support and join them.

The NDP had some well-known members and supporters. For the federal elections held in late 1984 the party's Senate ticket was headed by a high-profile former Labor Party member, Jean Melzer, in Victoria; by popular peace activist Jo Vallentine in Western Australia; by Michael Denborough in the ACT; and, most notably, by the charismatic lead singer of the rock band Midnight Oil, Peter Garrett, in New South Wales. The NDP attracted more than a million votes around Australia; Peter Garrett received a high primary vote for the Senate in New South Wales but failed to receive enough preferences from the other parties to win. However, lesser-known Jo Vallentine was elected to the Senate for Western Australia; she represented her state as an anti-nuclear independent and then as a Green until the early 1990s.

The combined Democrat and NDP vote in the 1984 election (which reached as high as 16.9 per cent in New South Wales) reflected more than a high vote for distinctly anti-nuclear parties. It was this election that first revealed a break-up of the two-party system. A politically progressive, pro-environment third force was emerging, and although much of this would be captured by the Australian Democrats over the next decade, parties like the NDP and later the Greens would capture a section of it as well. An interesting question in green politics during this period is why the Democrats were not able to capture the vast majority of disaffected votes and members from the major parties. A superficial reason given by some is that it was because the Democrats had their origin with Don Chipp and his disaffection with the Liberal Party in the late 1970s, and were therefore less attractive to this largely left-leaning constituency. However, a constant theme among social movement activists, who should have provided the Democrats with ideal recruits, was that the party did not have its social and ideological origins in the movements. The Democrats' predominant theme that they were there to 'keep the bastards honest' (in Don Chipp's words) might have been popular with many people who were cynical about major parties, but it did not resonate with many social movement activists and supporters who thought that an alternative political party should work for social change.

This desire among many for a political party that contained the same view of the world as social movements was echoed in much of the confusion and controversy that surrounded the short history of the NDP. Former Liberal parliamentarian Edward St John, who played a key role in the election campaign, was critical of the 'cult of amateurism' in the NDP that offended his strong professionalism. A year later he said:

> I believe in effective democratic leadership; 'they' distrusted leadership, and believed in 'grassroots' democracy. I believe in orderly meetings with majority votes where necessary, chaired by persons experienced in such things; 'they' preferred 'consensus' and rotating 'facilitators'. I believe there must be minutes, and while I chaired the meetings, minutes were duly kept and confirmed. This was not always the case later ... They believed that anyone should be free to attend any meeting and to speak, even though not elected to the body concerned ... I believed in a pyramidal structure for the NDP throughout Australia ... But they believed in 'non-hierarchical structures' ...[2]

Poor Edward St John. Those who have struggled through the 'tyranny of structurelessness' which is so typical of social change groups know how frustrating long, meandering meetings can be. Nevertheless, there is also a strong commitment, especially among grassroots activists, to such practices; any alternative party with its roots in the social movements has to find a balance between such processes on the one hand, and efficiency and accountability on the other.

The issue that destroyed the NDP, however, was the dispute over the role being played by the Socialist Workers Party (SWP). The SWP was a revolutionary socialist organisation whose pro-Soviet position offended many, like Garrett and Vallentine, who wanted a more even-handed treatment of the superpowers. The SWP's strong caucusing and party discipline also caused distrust among many who feared that this relatively small party with its well-trained cadres could take over the NDP. The issue emerged forcefully at the party's first national conference in 1985 where the purported sinister role of the SWP was raised, to which the SWP replied with accusations of 'McCarthyism' and 'red-baiting'; many of the party leaders, including Garrett, Vallentine and St John, walked out.

Ordinary members were left confused and despairing after the walkout. Michael Denborough, the SWP, and other non-aligned activists remained in the party, 'owning' the name (and the party's considerable mystique) while the others attempted to set up various anti-nuclear organisations such as Peace and Nuclear Disarmament Action (PANDA) and the Nuclear Free Australia Party. Jo Vallentine remained alone in the Senate as an anti-nuclear independent, and the rump NDP succeeded in getting Robert Wood elected to the Senate for New South Wales in the 1987 election. He was removed from the parliament because he did not meet constitutional citizenship requirements and his place was taken by the second on the NDP ticket, Irina Dunn.

Although the NDP's founders made little attempt to consult with the mainstream nuclear disarmament or environment movements before setting up (and it is doubtful if the leadership of either would have given them much joy if they had) there is no doubt that the popularity of the NDP depended on the enormous amount of work done by the peace and environment movements, especially the goodwill generated by the Franklin campaign.[3] Christoff argues that this was a manifestation of 'guerrilla electoralism' in much the same way that direct action groups like the Nomadic Action Group had, from time to time, pushed the mainstream movement into more militant stands. As a matter of course, most social movements have to link up with political power if their social change agenda is to be met, at least in terms of action by the state. The anti-uranium and nuclear disarmament movements had, since the mid-1970s, developed a strategy that focused almost exclusively on the Labor Party. When that party in government adopted a pro-mining policy (limited to three mines) and was equivocal at best on issues of nuclear disarmament, it left the way open for a new kind of politics. The Democrats were still seen as too mainstream; the debate had only just begun on whether or not a Green Party should be established. Into this political vacuum lurched the NDP—naive, chaotic and irreverent, but also creative and vibrant.

## Getting Together

The vexed question of how to organise politically on the basis of social movement activism brought together activists from the Franklin and anti-nuclear movements, as well as many others, on the Easter weekend of 1986. The Liffey Group, consisting of Franklin veterans,[4] contacted others around the country who were interested in green issues, and a conference was organised for that weekend at the University of Sydney.[5] Approximately 500 participants represented environment and peace groups, alternative communities, economic co-operatives and many other organisations at the Getting Together Conference; they were asked to discuss a range of strategies for social change, including setting up ethical investment projects, a coalition, a congress or a Green Party. Looking back, the prospect of a coherent strategy coming out of a conference of such diverse groups was even more remote than for those attending the Broad Left Conference down the road on that same weekend. The Getting Together Conference overwhelmingly rejected supporting a Green Party, and the coalition proposal that was accepted struggled on for perhaps twelve months before folding. A number of Liffey Group members, as well as activists like Drew Hutton from Brisbane, wanted a Green Party to be created from the conference but they 'didn't want trouble'. The Getting Together Conference provided the opportunity for a mass social movement to feel a stronger sense of identity and gave participants an insight into the movement's diversity, but it could not reconcile different philosophical and strategic directions. Its main contribution to green strategy was to demonstrate to people like Brown and Hutton how not to set up a Green Party.

The main outcome of the conference in terms of outlining a view of green politics as incorporating the social change perspectives of all the progressive social movements was the book *Green Politics in Australia*, edited by Hutton and containing chapters by Bob Brown, Jo Vallentine, Aboriginal activist Burnam Burnam, eco-feminist Ariel Kay Salleh and others. While radical ecocentrism tended to dominate the views of groups like TWS, green politics, on the other hand, was also influenced by the radical humanism of the New Left as well as the particular insights of the peace movement. Social Justice and Grassroots Democracy were concepts drawn from the New Left while Non-Violence came from the peace movement and these went together with Biological Diversity as the West German Greens' four pillars—the most influential summary of green politics in the 1980s.[6] This combination of ecocentrism and New Leftism was reflected in the work of such green politicians as Bob Brown and later Christine Milne who often pursued human rights and social justice issues as strongly in the Tasmanian parliament as they did environmental issues.

In 1987, an initiative proposed by Melbourne anti-nuclear activist, former Left Labor Party member and academic, Joe Camilleri, attempted to bring together left and green forces around Australia into 'a new political movement'.[7] Many on the Left could not live with 'green' in the organisation's name because that would irretrievably narrow the group's public profile and greens, especially from New South Wales and Tasmania, would not join if the word was left out. Finally, the organisation was called the Rainbow Alliance. Given this division and the coolness of mainstream environment and social justice groups towards the new organisation, the Rainbow Alliance never really became a strong, national, alternative voice.

### Tasmanian Green Independents

The Tasmanian elections of 1989, held in the immediate aftermath of the Wesley Vale campaign, marked a major step forward for green politics in that state. The election of 13 May saw Bob Brown and Gerry Bates joined by three more green independents—Christine Milne who had led the campaign against Wesley Vale, Lance Armstrong, a Uniting Church minister active in the peace movement, and Di Hollister, a teacher who had also been active in the Wesley Vale campaign. The lack of any green political organisation in Tasmania meant that the selection of running mates for the two sitting Greens was basically left to Bob Brown with help from Joan Staples, not the most democratic of preselection systems but one that came up with some excellent green politicians. The green independents had received enormous media coverage during the election campaign and emerged with five members of the Tasmanian House of Assembly and the balance of power in that house. In fact, the greens had averaged 17.1 per cent across the state and Bob Brown, with a personal 23.5 per cent vote, polled second to Liberal Premier Robin Gray in state-wide primary votes.[8]

The election provided the first major test of the ability of Greens and Labor to work together to achieve reformist outcomes. Premier Gray had decided to tough it out by refusing to resign his commission and to recall parliament early and by forming a ministry. The situation was placing enormous pressure on the green independents which was relieved by two events. The first was a big public meeting in the Hobart City Hall attended by 1700 supporters that reminded the independents that they still had a great deal of community support.[9] The second was the announcement of charges being laid against Edmund Rouse, one of the state's most prominent businessmen, for attempting to bribe a Labor parliamentarian, Jim Cox, to cross the floor and support the Liberals. Rouse was the chairman of Examiner Northern Television and the subsequent trial placed some doubts over the role played in the affair by Robin Gray. The recall of parliament several days later on 28 June finally saw the Gray government defeated on the floor of the house and Labor prepared to govern with the support of the Greens.

The Greens were not prepared to accept ministries in the Labor government led by Michael Field as they felt this would have locked them into support for policies they could not in all conscience support. Therefore, they agreed to an Accord under which they would support the minority Labor government in return for major policy commitments. Bob Brown's attitude was 'What we get at the outset is all we're going to get', and so he drove a hard bargain with Premier Field, culminating in the signing of the Green–Labor Accord on 29 May.[10] In the end the Greens achieved large gains. These included massive expansions to the national park and World Heritage Area regimes, the cessation of logging in National Estate areas not already approved under the federal–state forestry agreement, a total ban on mining in national parks, deposit legislation on bottles and cans, limiting the state's export woodchip quota to 2.2889 million tonnes per annum as well as public disclosure of electoral gifts and donations and freedom of information legislation.[11] Bob Brown promised that the Greens would 'keep a hand on the shoulder of government' and, although there was much euphoria about the arrangement, there were still some in the movement who had misgivings about the ability of these two political forces to co-operate for any length of time, especially given Tasmanian Labor's traditionally strong pro-growth stances.[12]

Even before the 1989 state election informal discussions on resolving land-use conflicts had taken place between the Tasmanian Farmers and Graziers Association and the conservation movement. After the signing of the Accord and the coming to power of the Field government this process was formalised with participants being the Forest Industries Association of Tasmania, the Tasmanian Trades and Labour Council, the Tasmanian Farmers and Graziers Association, the Forestry Commission, TWS, the Australian Conservation Foundation (ACF) and the state government. The Salamanca Agreement, signed on 31 August 1989, committed the parties to work toward a long-term forest management strategy which would be set out in a final agreement by 1 September 1990.[13] The process was institutionalised by the setting up of a ministerial council, the Forests and Forest Industries Council.

Negotiations between conservationists and the other groups in the Salamanca process broke down in mid-September over such issues as resource security and protection of biodiversity. Veteran TWS activist, Bob Burton, felt that conservationists should be wary about entering into such a process again without such things in their favour as a majority of environmentalists on the committee, an independent chairperson, no bureaucrats involved and the maintenance of a strong extra-parliamentary campaign while the negotiations are continuing.[14] This provided the last straw for the Accord which had already been put under strain because of other conflicts between the Greens and the Labor government. The Accord formally came to an end in October 1990. The immediate issue was the Field government's decision to increase woodchip exports beyond the level agreed to in the Accord but the Greens had objected strenuously to other government policies such as cutbacks to education and were frustrated by lack of access to government.

## Greens and Labor

The breakdown of the Accord raised serious questions about the direction of reformist politics in Tasmania and even the rest of Australia. It is often argued that Tasmania's unusual Hare–Clark electoral system allows smaller parties and independents like the Greens to obtain representation in a lower house of parliament and this situation cannot be duplicated in other states or the federal parliament. However, it is also feasible to suggest that the days of the single umbrella party with a large mass base and a multiple constituency representing the aspirations of the many people who are passionately committed to values-based stances are numbered if, in fact, they have not already passed. Mass-based social movements have thrown up issues such as biodiversity protection, gender equality and indigenous land rights in such an uncompromising way that it is very difficult for a party such as the Labor Party to fit them under the Labor umbrella with such existing constituencies as the more conservative unions.

Nevertheless, at this point in time, it is only the major parties—Labor and Coalition—that can form government and have the potential to implement the programs of social movements. Consequently, while the environment movement might supply much of the membership and support base for the Greens and the Democrats, the peak groups will always be most concerned about which party or parties will form government. Therefore, in Queensland, which has no proportional representation and no upper house, the conservation movement had no hesitation in supporting the Labor Party in the state elections of 1989. The movement had been locked in a do-or-die struggle with the National Party government of Sir Joh Bjelke-Petersen and the revelations of widespread corruption surrounding his government gave the Labor Party the first real opportunity since 1957 of taking government from the conservatives. The key groups (later to become known, not always affectionately, as the six-pack) developed a log of claims that they served on all parties contesting the 1989 election. As expected Labor came out well ahead and, consequently, earned the strong support of the conservation groups, organised collectively as Green Challenge.

Unfortunately, Labor Premier Wayne Goss's advice on election night that everyone should take a 'cold shower' about the election victory applied to the area of environmental reform just as much as it did to social justice. Goss moved reasonably quickly in such areas as building up the national park regime from a pitifully small 2 per cent of the state but was very cautious and slow-moving in such other areas as stopping rainforest logging, coastal protection and pollution control. However, painful memories of the Bjelke-Petersen era prevented for several years environmentalists' frustration from boiling over into overt criticism.

The high point of green political influence with the federal Labor government undoubtedly came with the 1990 federal election. On the basis largely of responses to a questionnaire the ACF and TWS recommended that their members give their first preferences to the Australian Democrats and Greens in Western Australia and Tasmania and their all-important second preferences to the Labor Party. The responses of Labor and Coalition were almost the same on many issues but the two conservation groups justified their preference for Labor because of 'the continuing Commonwealth management of Kakadu and Uluru, enrichment of uranium, land use planning of Cape York, protection and listing of the National Estate, integrity of national parks and the federal government's willingness to protect Australia's environment even in the face of state opposition'.[15] Undoubtedly, the conservation groups' main concern about the Coalition was the influence of the Liberals' coalition partner, the Nationals, who supported uranium enrichment and who were clearly opposed to challenging the states over environmental policy.[16] They had also seen the good record of Labor in office that had delivered World Heritage listings for South-West Tasmania, the Wet Tropics and Kakadu and the saving of 80 per cent of the Lemonthyme and southern forests after the farce of the Helsham inquiry.

Even more spectacular than the fact that Labor won the election on what many observers regarded as the recommendation of the environment movement was the powerful showing of the Democrats and, to a lesser extent, the Greens. In the absence of a national Green party the Democrats averaged 11.3 per cent in the House of Representatives and increased their Senate representation from seven to eight. Jo Vallentine was re-elected as a Greens candidate from Western Australia while a progressive independent, Ted Mack, was elected to the House of Representatives and Democrat leader, Janine Haines, and green independent, Helen Caldicott, made strong showings in the lower house seats of

Kingston in South Australia and Richmond in northern New South Wales respectively. Democrat and Green preferences went approximately two-thirds to Labor. Writers such as Papadakis pointed to what he saw as a dealignment of voters from traditional parties (as distinct from a realignment of voters with new parties).[17] While this trend was undoubtedly real, Paul Keating showed in 1993 that Labor could win back, even if only temporarily, at least some of the vote they had lost to third-force parties in 1990.

For the year leading up to 24 March 1990 opinion polls had predicted that the environment would be a major factor in the election. Methodological problems made questionable some of the assertions made about the importance of various issues to electors but most pollsters were willing to assert that the environment was of great importance if not 'second only to the economy' as the most important issue. Other polls registered high levels of voter support for banning logging in National Estate forests and preparedness to pay extra taxes to prevent environmental destruction.[18] Clearly, two decades of campaigning and consciousness-raising had effected an impressive victory for the environment in the 1990 election but it had a down side. Anti-green parliamentarians and cabinet ministers in the Labor Party began questioning the importance of the green vote for Labor victories and, even more importantly, for the future of the Labor Party itself. The most extreme exponent of this view who regarded Labor's concern for the environment as distracting the party from its primary responsibility of ensuring economic growth was Finance Minister, Peter Walsh. He also felt that the strategy of 'courting the green vote ... legitimised a move away from the Labor Party by traditional Labor voters'.[19] With a recession hovering, increasing community concern about unemployment and increased militancy from resource industries and resource ministers in cabinet the stage was set for some reverses for the movement and a subsequent election where environmental issues would be swamped.

### More Trouble at ACF

Australia has a number of national conservation groups but none that can truly claim to be the national voice of the grassroots environment movement. Greenpeace addresses important nuclear and pollution issues but has a lesser involvement in such areas as nature conservation and urban planning. Greenpeace is also more of a permanent campaigning group than a conservation body organised on a nationwide basis. TWS certainly has a strong presence in many parts of the country but concentrates only on wilderness and forest issues. The ACF comes closest to being the movement's national voice. Although it has had branches (or chapters) in various states and its council consists of five members from each state, there has never been any attempt to make these councillors representative of the grassroots movement. Candidates simply put up for election and are voted on by individual members and there is certainly no guarantee that, for example, the state conservation councils will have representation. Nevertheless, there is an obvious need for an organisation to coordinate national campaigns and to liaise with the federal government and the ACF is usually seen as the organisation best placed to do this. It would also seem that the major changes in strategic direction taken by the ACF paralleled those that were also occurring in much of the rest of the voluntary conservation movement.

Just as 1973 had marked the end of the first phase of the ACF's development so 1983 marked the end of its second and the beginning of a new era both for it and for much of the rest of the movement. Some of those like John Sinclair, who had been part of the more militant, campaign-oriented new guard in 1973 were now part of the old guard. While the key concern of the 1973 militants had been to make the ACF (and the conservation movement as a whole) more effective at campaigning, the goal of the post-1983 generation was to make more effective connection with political power on the basis of a proven ability to mobilise many thousands of people and to have a profound effect on public opinion on a range of issues. To do this the ACF would need not only the proven campaigners like Milo Dunphy, Bob Burton, Jack Mundey and John Sinclair on its council but they would also need what could be called 'political carriers'. These were environmental activists who possessed the skills to make good connections with those who exercised political power.

The ACF emerged from the Franklin campaign riding a wave of optimism after such an impressive victory (although not a little resentful that, although they had footed as much as $250 000 of the campaign's expenses, they received what they considered to be too little credit). The next ten years, however, would see the ACF emerge as one of the best-known non-government organisations in the country whose public advocates were some of the most recognised faces on the media and whose representatives enjoyed unprecedented access to government. The fight for the forests would not end in a clear victory but the Wet Tropics, Kakadu, the establishment of the new rurally-based scheme, Landcare, Shark Bay and Antarctica were all successful campaigns in which the ACF played a significant, if not pre-eminent, role.

Even though the ACF covered a broad range of issues—from nature conservation to land-use planning and pollution—policy issues rarely divided the council. Some members occasionally were frustrated by what they saw as an inappropriate amount of time taken up with issues like kangaroo shooting, some were annoyed that a lot of time was spent on the national conservation strategy for no real outcome, some thought the ACF devoted far too little time to the population issue and Jack Mundey constantly bemoaned the lack of attention by the ACF to urban issues.[20] However, the issues that did divide the organisation were more to do with strategic and administrative concerns.

A key problem that had surfaced even before the Franklin campaign but became an obsession with ACF activists in the years following 1983 was how the organisation could better get its concerns addressed by government. Some urged stronger support for the Australian Democrats, others like Alan Tingay from Western Australia felt that the ACF should put more effort into 'greening up' the Labor Party while others, perhaps the largest single group, felt that the ACF should be wary of advocating a vote for any one party and concentrate on getting its message across more effectively to all parties that showed any willingness to listen. There was one thing that almost all could agree on and that was that the ACF was not lobbying the bureaucracy or politicians anywhere near as effectively as it should. Support for Labor in the 1983 election had not been controversial inside the organisation because of the importance of South-West Tasmania and the disaster that would ensue from a Liberal victory. However, Labor had shown no similar urge to move on such other important issues as ending uranium mining, protecting National Estate forests and unilaterally nominating the Wet Tropics for World Heritage listing.

For a number of influential members, much of the problem lay with those who had control of the relationship with the government, especially Dr Geoff Mosley, the man who had been the organisation's director since the 1973 changing of the guard. Mosley's dedication to the cause was unusual even in a voluntarist movement like that for conservation. His knowledge was encyclopaedic, his research extremely thorough and his policy development work outstanding. Nevertheless, his penchant for long, lecturing sessions with politicians and others was felt to be counter-productive by many in the ACF and some resented what they saw as his tendency to impute base motives to people who opposed him. Penny Figgis, a councillor for the Northern Territory and, at one time, the national liaison officer for the ACF in Canberra, was a trenchant critic of the organisation's lack of professionalism in the area of lobbying. She gave instances of the ACF representatives taking up the valuable time of government ministers urging them to 'do something' on soil conservation, or whatever, rather than going in to the meeting with a submission that contained clear, well thought-out suggestions for action.[21] Her prescriptions for successful lobbying are now an integral part of the armoury of environmental lobbyists but they did not appear to be so in the early 1980s.

It is hardly surprising, then, that Figgis became part of the group of independents on the Council who became increasingly opposed to Mosley and they became more and more convinced that, in spite of his obvious abilities in many areas, he was not the right person to be director at this stage of the organisation's history. There was, of course, also a hard-line group who were totally opposed to Mosley and were part of the regular 'Friday-night caucus' before council meetings (although this did not include the 'independents').[22] However, when old allies like Milo Dunphy turned against Mosley, it was then just a matter of time before a crisis occurred. With the atmosphere becoming increasingly poisoned, the ACF president, Hal Wootten, stepped in and proposed to Dr Mosley that he move from the position of Director to that of Projects Director with no loss of salary or entitlements, a proposal that Mosley indicated he would not accept voluntarily. The decision therefore was left to council which, on a straw vote of 20 to 8, indicated support for Wootten's proposal.[23]

Geoff Mosley felt hurt by the Council's action and some of his supporters were bitter.[24] John Sinclair was clearly upset not only by Mosley's treatment but also by the caucusing of the 'young Turks'. He complained that the situation had degenerated to the point where 'Council meetings do little more than rubber stamp decisions previously adopted at these private meetings which excludes most, but not all, of the staff'.[25] Penny Figgis, in the same newsletter, rejected such assertions and, while she admitted that 'a group of Councillors who advocate a more politically effective, activist ACF meet informally before Council', she insisted that 'Council decision making is very firmly determined by a large group of independently-minded Councillors who do assess issues on their merits' and that, 'on a few very vital occasions this middle group has voted with the activist group but I contend this occurred because of conviction and not conspiracy'.

Earlier in the year Wootten had been forced to refute publicly an article which had appeared in the *Age* on 17 December 1985 and which had quoted anonymous 'Foundation sources'. Wootten acknowledged that, since he had become president eighteen months previously, council proceedings had been dominated by conflict between two factions (presumably the 'old guard' around John Sinclair and the new guard who wanted a more activist and politically skilful organisation). However, Wootten denied the report that the two groups were divided on policy issues and insisted that, 'Their differences, aggravated by personality clashes, were largely over internal management issues. One group tended to be impatient to make changes which they believed would greatly increase the ACF's effectiveness; the other group tended to support the status quo.'[26] The suggestions of a Wilderness Society takeover were denied by Wootten who pointed to the presence of only

5 out of 36 councillors with a close TWS connection. A former Councillor, Peter Springell from Queensland, attempted to put the issue into
historical perspective:

> While not wishing to belittle the monumental efforts of Geoff Mosley,
> John Sinclair, and many others in any way, I must point out that their
> disappointment with regards to the winds of change are simply part of the
> process of growing old. If they were to accept their inevitable fate gracefully,
> perhaps they would see the up-and-coming young turks within the ACF in a
> much more favourable light.
>      After all, they have had their day in the '70s, when they in turn put the
> noses of their elders out of joint too.[27]

There were other divisions among the ACF council and staff. There
was a division between progressives and conservatives that roughly
corresponded to those who supported and those who opposed Mosley.
The Left consisted of people like Dick Jones, Jack Mundey and Leigh
Holloway while Milo Dunphy, John Sinclair and Geoff Mosley were part
of the Right. Another division was between committed nature conservationists like Dunphy and George Heinsohn and those like Mundey
who wanted more emphasis on the urban environment and Peter
Brotherton who led the way for the ACF on pollution issues.
     Beside all the personal conflicts, disappointments, frustration and
tragedies there emerged one very clear direction that a significant
number of key environmental activists wanted the ACF and the rest of
the conservation movement to take. There were plenty of grassroots
activists and many visionaries but the one element that was not a strong
enough part of the movement's resources was the 'political carriers'—
people who had the skills and personal qualities to persuade governments or potential governments to adopt the movement's key demands.
A number of talented people had occupied the role of national liaison
officer for the ACF—Penny Figgis, Joan Staples, Jane Elix—and
Jonathan West was learning his way around the federal Labor government for TWS, but the ACF still needed someone who could give it the
strong direction and credibility that was needed to open doors in
Canberra. If Geoff Mosley was not thought to be that person, then they
had to find someone else. That person turned out to be Phillip Toyne,
a lawyer from Alice Springs. Toyne had worked for Aboriginal groups in
the Northern Territory since 1975 as legal counsel, adviser, negotiator
and public advocate. He had played a large part in the passage of the
Pitjantjatjara Land Rights Act and the transfer of Uluru to its traditional
owners. He was encouraged to apply for the director's job by people like
Wootten and Figgis and was unanimously accepted for it in September
1986.

## 'Political Carriers'

While sometimes criticised for his lack of administrative skills, Phillip
Toyne was generally acknowledged to be a superb negotiator and public
advocate with enormous energy and political acumen, in fact the
perfect 'political carrier' who rode the wave of environment movement
successes in the late 1980s to perfection. Nevertheless, it should be
remembered that his success was also the result of the presence of two
other politically astute people. Toyne was quite happy to acknowledge
the importance of Jonathan West in showing him how the Labor Party
worked and introducing him to key people in the government.[28]
However, it was that masterly politician, Graham Richardson, whose
promotion to Environment Minister after the 1987 election provided
Toyne with the right 'ear' in government and the access to Hawke when
it was necessary.[29]

'Richo' was a Labor Party Right machine man *par excellence* and a man
who obviously loved the game of politics. The title of his book, *Whatever
It Takes*, sums up not only the way the man operated but also the way he
liked to display his political persona. Nevertheless, he seemed to have a
genuine belief in the environment that went beyond its potential as a
vote winner for Labor. His account of this 'conversion', walking through
Tasmanian forests, is pure Richo.

> We walked around some of the area, sat by the lake and talked. Bob Brown
> wanted chunks of forest, or preferably the whole area, put into World
> Heritage classification and protected forever. So utterly convinced of his
> cause, Bob can be utterly convincing; his passion and sincerity are very
> difficult to overcome and by the time we arrived back in Hobart I was a
> convert. Having been shown the awesome forests and streams he wanted
> protected, I wanted to become a warrior for his cause. This was a bad day
> for the logging industry in Australia but a very good one for me, the
> environmental movement and the Labor Party. It didn't take too long to work
> out that we had a perfect convergence: what was right was also popular.[30]

Once again, the Milo Dunphy strategy of taking a politician for a walk in
the bush worked—this time with a vengeance.

Richardson inherited from Cohen more than that minister's reluctance to tackle Queensland Premier Bjelke-Petersen over the Wet Tropics.
It is fair to say that, since the Franklin decision in 1983, the Hawke
government had been decidedly reluctant to tackle hard environmental
issues.

In the lead-up to the 1987 federal election Toyne negotiated with
Richardson for the Hawke government to list the Wet Tropics and
Kakadu Stage III for World Heritage. For many environmentalists this
made up for the disappointments surrounding the Tasmanian and

south-east forests of New South Wales, especially when it looked likely that the Coalition led by John Howard would be a disaster for the environment. Interestingly, Toyne recommended that the ACF should not endorse Labor or any other party at that election but should confine itself to a vigorous and well-publicised critique of the policies of the various parties. This position was supported by Hal Wootten and six other Councillors but the other twenty-nine all voted for endorsement of Labor in the House of Representatives and Democrats in the Senate.[31]

This provoked soul-searching among some in the ACF, including Hal Wootten who pointed out that, if the ACF were to endorse a particular party at elections, 'It should not happen regularly, or as a matter of course, but only when there are great and significant differences between the parties competing for government.'[32] Of course, it was easy enough for conservationists to make out a case that every election was vital for the environment and decide to take a partisan stand accordingly. Also, given that the Liberals were driven by the ideological goals of states' rights and an extreme form of economic rationalism, both inimical to environmental outcomes, it was easy enough for Labor to say, 'Well, you might not like our policies but at least with us you'll get something. With the Coalition, all you'll get is a fight.' The same dynamic occurred at the state level. Great things were promised for the environment—in New South Wales by Wran and Unsworth, in Victoria by Cain, in South Australia by Bannon, in Western Australia by Burke and Dowding, and in Queensland in 1989 by Goss. In some cases they made good on those promises, but all too often they disappointed the movement. Nevertheless, the idea of Coalition governments was usually unthinkable and so conservationists became used to dealing with Labor governments, warts and all, and learned to take the good with the bad.

The 1987 federal election also gave rise to a critique of the conservation movement that pointed to the 'elitism' of the decision-making process that led to the decision to allocate preferences to the Labor Party and the Democrats.[33] Doyle is undoubtedly correct to point to the absence of accountability in many environment movement decisions. Much of this is due to the fact that, especially during elections or at crisis moments in campaigns, governments or political players present fleeting opportunities for the movement to make big gains. With no time for wide consultation a decision needs to be made, preferably by people who have been living and breathing the issues for a long time and these are usually staff members or officers in the larger or key groups. As Doyle points out, these key people are often self-selected on the basis of inter-personal relationships.[34] Canvassing the issues, even among relatively small circles, would lose time and require much explanation. It is often easier to confine the final crucial decision to a few people in the expectation that it will be accepted by the movement afterwards as providing the best possible outcome. Unfortunately, such practices can become ingrained and the possibility increased that decisions taken are out of step with the thinking of most people in the movement.

It is an irony that such a tendency exists when there is another common practice which is at the other end of the ideological spectrum and which is capable of creating just as much controversy inside the movement. This is the practice of consensus decision-making. At its best it empowers all people involved in a campaign and makes for more thoughtful decisions that everyone can live with. At its worst it is a time-consuming exercise that empowers those who most want to hear themselves talk and frustrates those who actually want to do something. Consensus was the main form of decision-making in direct action campaigns like Roxby Downs, the Franklin, Daintree and the south-east forests and it has been used by the Green parties since their formation in the early 1990s but it tends to be replaced by more formal meeting procedure and decision making in larger conservation organisations like the ACF. Often the two forms coexist uneasily, sometimes in the one organisation.

Such concerns, however, were to remain secondary in the years after 1991 as resource industries regrouped to assert their economic influence and governments became increasingly concerned about the impact that environmental protection measures could have on economic growth. In taking a step forward in the 1990s, the movement also went two steps back.

# PART V

# Dancing in the Dark:
# The Movement in the 1990s

The environment movement after 1990, buoyed by its achievements during the 1980s, attempted to push a strong environmental agenda into the Australian mainstream by challenging the dominant development paradigm. It did this by taking part in the federal government's Ecologically Sustainable Development (ESD) process after the 1990 election. The business community responded to this challenge in two ways. One was to contest the definition of ESD, arguing for purely technological solutions to environmental problems and the need for 'balance' or 'compromise' between economic and environmental objectives. The other, more militant, approach was to insist that free-market, deregulatory approaches would solve the country's economic woes. Governments responded by insisting on the need to maintain limited, incremental approaches to environmental reform. This incrementalism, in reality, has meant little more than finding new ways for the rich and powerful to stay that way while the pace of reform goes nowhere near matching the rate of environmental degradation.

While the Australian green movement influenced many reforms in the period up to 1990, it also caused headaches for many in the political and economic elites because, in spite of the movement's credibility in the eyes of much of the electorate, sooner or later it would be difficult to meet the movement's continuing demands within existing institutional arrangements. The environment movement might not have coined the term 'ecologically sustainable development', but in the 1990s it emphasised such aspects as maintaining biodiversity, intergenerational equity, the precautionary principle and demand management, which are clearly incompatible with much of the culture and practice of contemporary Australian industrial capitalism. Melucci resurrects the term 'contradiction', stripped of the deterministic connotations given to it by traditional Marxism, to explain the incompatibility among the elements or parts of a system.[1] Australian elites have attempted to resolve these contradictions that threaten to cause structural change, usually by accommodation and partial institutionalisation of the movement. This was what happened in Australia, especially during the 1980s, when incrementally reformist Labor governments acceded to many of the green movement's policy positions. However, the limited extent to which this accommodation was able to occur was seen in the federal government's failed ESD process after 1990, when the combined efforts of government bureaucrats and industry effectively prevented the implementation of the recommendations of the ESD working groups.

The movement has presented a major problem for Australian elites, especially those involved in the resource sectors and their supporters. This is not because of the methods the movement uses or the heightened consciousness of the activists, but because it challenges a fundamental dynamic that is essential to the maintenance of elite power. That challenge, if it were to fail or if power-wielders were able to mitigate the problem sufficiently, would decline or die. However, if the problem defies piecemeal solutions and half-hearted measures, and this is certainly the case with current environmental crises, reversals suffered by the movement will be temporary and new generations of activists will continue the struggle well into the next century.

We finish with a sombre assessment of the movement's fortunes in the 1990s, facing hostile governments whose agendas were dominated by economic fundamentalism, the political influence of the resource-based sector of the economy (reflected particularly in the federal government's decision to argue for increased greenhouse emissions at the 1997 International Climate Change Conference at Kyoto), and the desire for rapid economic growth. This downturn in the movement's influence reflects the dialectical nature of social movement activity, especially that of the green movement. Ruling elites in the industrialised world have determined that global economic problems can be solved only by such measures as the deregulation of national economies, privatisation, and an increasingly productive workforce in societies that favour openness and competition ahead of co-operation and community. Such policies, however, can unleash the most environmentally destructive forces, especially in a country like Australia where those industry sectors with an advantage over international competitors tend to be in the area of resource exploitation. At the same time, and in spite of government efforts to commercialise all aspects of social life, some of the highly educated, politically aware, mobile young people who might otherwise earn high salaries in large corporations are drawn to the environment movement, thus ensuring the continuation of conflict.

# CHAPTER 9

# Counter-Moves

The mood of optimism generated by the strong green influence on the 1990 federal election persuaded many in the conservation movement that this was the time to push environmental responsibility to the centre stage of national political life. A small group of environmentalists had tried unsuccessfully to persuade Alfred Deakin in 1908 that federal government intervention to ensure protection of the environment was as necessary as intervention to ensure wage justice or industrial protection. Now, however, the movement could claim widespread support for environmental protection to appear as a key consensus value in Australian political life.

### The ESD Process

The federal government responded to scientific and lay concern over global warming and ozone layer depletion and the Bruntland Report's 1987 call for sustainable development. It began facilitating national debate on ecologically sustainable development (ESD) in 1990 at the same time as the United Nations Conference on Environment and Development was having its first preparatory meetings for the Earth Summit to be held in Rio de Janeiro in 1992. This course of action was fully supported by the environment movement because it held the potential for bringing together economic development and environmental concerns in order to prevent big conflicts over land and resource use like those of the 1970s and 1980s.

From the start, however, there were signs that the ESD process might not go as well as the environment movement hoped. Hawke moved Graham Richardson out of the environment portfolio and into social services. This might not have been much of a loss to the movement:

Richardson understood the sort of wins-and-losses approach that went with making a World Heritage nomination, but might have floundered in the greater complexities of ESD. Unfortunately, his successor, Ros Kelly, never had as much clout in cabinet as Richardson. Clout was needed at this time; there were numerous pitfalls, and the 'ecological' side of ESD had many enemies, including quite a few in the Labor cabinet. After the upheaval in cabinet over Coronation Hill, and especially after Hawke's replacement as prime minister by Keating, the tide inside the Labor government turned against ESD, and probably ebbed in relation to the environment as a whole. Although opinion polls showed the environment as a major concern among many, there can be little doubt that the case for governments seeing it as a lower priority was boosted by high unemployment and economic insecurity in this period.

After the federal government's ESD discussion paper was released in 1990 and both industry and the environment movement had responded,[1] the government set up nine working groups: agriculture, fishing, forest use, energy use, energy production, transport, tourism, mining, and manufacturing. Membership of the groups was drawn from state and federal governments, the Business Council of Australia, the Australian Council of Trade Unions (ACTU), and the CSIRO, as well as conservation, consumer and social justice movements.[2] Conservation interests were represented by the Australian Conservation Foundation (ACF), The Wilderness Society (TWS), Greenpeace, and the Worldwide Fund for Nature (WWF); TWS, sceptical about the Forest Use Working Group, refused to participate, and Greenpeace withdrew during the process. Despite their reservations about the integrity of the process, the ACF and the WWF remained in it to the end. In an attempt to fill the gaps left by dealing only with industry sectors, the federal government set up groups to address 'intersectoral' issues such as women's, Aboriginal, migrants', health, waste minimisation, reuse and recycling, and population. Greenhouse issues were examined by a special co-ordinating group as well as from the perspectives of several working groups.

After the working groups had finished their deliberations in early 1992, their submissions went to committees of state and federal public servants; these committees weakened or even omitted many of the original recommendations and no action plans or timelines were determined. By this stage, conservation groups were so outraged at the gutting of the working groups' recommendations that they boycotted the process. Even non-conservation groups were angered by the public servants' actions. These bureaucrats were so attacked by industry, farmers, engineers and unions at a two-day conference in late 1992 that

the second day was called off.[3] Several of the conservation representatives on the working groups later related that they often found
industry representatives, despite their vested interests, easier to work
with than the bureaucrats. In a phenomenon seen many times in
environmental disputes, bureaucrats in industry facilitation departments were even more committed to cutting corners on the environment to ensure short-term industry profitability than were the industries
themselves. This was often the case even where the industry facilitators
were also environmental regulators of these industries.[4]

There were positive spin-offs from the process, such as the ACF's
Green Jobs campaign and Green Fridge Quest, but lack of political and
bureaucratic support at both federal and state levels undermined the
*National Strategy for Ecologically Sustainable Development* and the *National
Greenhouse Response Strategy*. The complexity of the issues, the movement's lack of experience in mobilising support around them, and
industry's increasing sophistication in countering a conservation
message all made it difficult to get public support for the environment
movement's position.

### Greenhouse Response

Conflict over the National Greenhouse Response Strategy illustrates the
difficulties faced by the movement. Australia holds the shameful record
as the highest per capita emitter of greenhouse gases in the world, with
energy-related carbon dioxide emissions increasing by 13 per cent
between 1987 and 1992, compared with 5 per cent for the OECD
countries as a whole.[5] The strategy, published in 1992, was, in Peter
Kinrade's words, 'vague and non-specific, lacking targets, timetables and
systematic prioritisation [and] does not provide processes for assessing
the impacts of projects with major greenhouse implications, such as new
power stations and freeways'. The strategy was framed as a no-regrets
one, in that measures would be implemented if they had net economic
as well as social and environmental benefits. If the original strategy was
weak, its implementation has been even worse. A score-card issued by
the ACF in June 1995 for greenhouse responses by federal and state
governments gave only New South Wales a pass mark of six out of ten.
(It was the only state to have legislated obligation to cut greenhouse
emissions.)

If anything, the Coalition government of John Howard was even more
reluctant about meeting greenhouse targets than the Keating government. With a United Nations Convention on Climate Change coming
up in Kyoto, Japan, in December 1997, the Howard government
presented a case for less stringent restrictions on emission targets than

other countries, or none at all, given Australia's position as a net energy exporter. This prompted several overseas governments to criticise the Australian position. The environment movement charged that the federal government was receiving advice from the Australian Bureau of Agricultural and Resource Economics, whose research was being partly funded by a consortium of resource organisations, including the coal industry.[6] In the context of the United Nations Intergovernmental Panel on Climate Change advancing ever more persuasive views on the likelihood of global warming as the result of anthropogenic emissions, Australian governments continued to sanction inefficient energy policies that were embarrassing on the international stage. This embarrassment continued at the climate change convention at Kyoto, where Australia demanded an 18 per cent increase in greenhouse emissions and, after much haggling, was allowed 8 per cent.

Greens Senator Bob Brown pointed out that the Howard government's pleas for special consideration on greenhouse were deceptive and hypocritical. Far from doing all it could to reduce emissions, Brown said, Howard's government had taken such measures as abolishing the Energy Research and Development Corporation in the 1997 Budget, thereby depriving energy efficiency and renewable energy programs of much-needed funding; it had cut spending to energy-efficiency programs by 50 per cent; it refused to make retention of native bushland a condition of grants from the Natural Heritage Trust;[7] and it continued to massively subsidise the cost of diesel fuel to mining companies.[8]

The worst area of performance by any government, according to the ACF greenhouse score-card, was transport and urban planning, in spite of the prevalence of anti-freeway activism in all capital cities around the country during the 1970s and 1980s. In Perth activists were fighting the Northern City Bypass—a seven-kilometre, high-capacity road bisecting the most intensive urban area in the state. In Brisbane the group VETO fought the Goss government's South Coast Motorway, trying to per-suade Labor and, after 1995, the Coalition government to develop more sustainable transport systems for the fast-growing south-east of Queensland. In Melbourne groups like Alternatives to Freeways Now and Campaign Against Freeway Extensions opposed the Linking Melbourne freeway project, and in Sydney about 300 community groups came together in a coalition called LinkUp to fight several major freeway proposals.[9] All these groups proposed the usual mixture of demand management, urban planning linked to more efficient transport options, and much-increased public transport and cycling alternatives. Even relatively progressive administrations, like those of Bob Carr in New South Wales and the Brisbane City Council under Jim Soorley, lacked the confidence to implement a full-scale demand management program of denying people road space for their single-occupancy vehicles.

## Mining

A sectoral report on mining was produced by the ESD working group; it said little new. Any gains made in terms of consensus on improving environmental management systems in the industry were outweighed by the desire for retribution felt by many pro-mining interests after Coronation Hill.[10] The conservation movement did not have an abiding interest in mining as it had, for example, in forestry, and this is reflected in the meagre treatment given to industry-wide issues in conservation publications over the years. Environmental campaigns tended to focus on particular sections of the industry, especially mineral sand and uranium mining. These campaigns were particularly bitter when they involved wilderness areas like Kakadu and Fraser Island. This piecemeal approach to mining issues began to change with the publication of a major report by the ACF entitled *Mining and Ecologically Sustainable Development* in 1994. The report conceded some improvement in such areas as pollution control and mine site rehabilitation, but its list of recommendations included splitting the industry facilitation function in government departments from that of environmental regulation, conducting a national audit of rehabilitated mines, banning mining in coastal dune areas of high conservation value, and establishing protection for Aboriginal sacred sites. Environment organisations, along with other non-government organisations, worked to highlight the destructive activities of Australian companies abroad, like BHP at Ok Tedi in Papua New Guinea. The ACF also worked with the Mining Council of Australia during 1997 to develop an industry code of practice which, although it represented a step forward in terms of an environmental management ethic for the industry, contained several obvious weaknesses. Also, among the member companies were several whose practices would need to change considerably to comply with the code.

The pro-mining forces in the post-Coronation Hill era focused on the need to fast-track big developments, or in the jargon that developed in government circles, 'facilitate major projects'. Politicians as different from each other as Keating, Hewson and Goss began talking publicly about the need to 'cut red, black and green tape'. Keating's *One Nation* economic statement in 1992 was remarkably free of any mention of ESD and full of the urgency of 'facilitating major projects'. Consequently, the conservation movement found itself having to deal with mining projects such as MIM's lead-zinc mine at McArthur River in the Northern Territory and its Ernest Henry zinc project near Cloncurry,

Queensland, both of which were allowed abbreviated and inadequate environmental impact assessments.[11] While mining companies and governments were concerned about 'green tape', they became agitated about the possible delays to projects emanating from the High Court's Mabo and Wik decisions. Statements by the conservative Queensland Premier, Rob Borbidge, in 1996 about the problems confronting the proposed Century zinc project in the state's north-west were intemperate and hasty, to say the least.

The conservation movement's victories were hard-won; they should not have required the effort put into the campaigns, given the nature of the proposals. The fight by conservationists on central Queensland's Capricorn Coast, near Rockhampton, to prevent sand-mining at Shoalwater Bay was especially difficult. Sand-mining was proposed in an area whose near-pristine values had been preserved because it was an army training area, and more destructive land uses had therefore been kept out. The area's environmental significance, indicated by its 1980 National Estate listing; its importance for providing water for local communities; the environmental impact statement (EIS) provided by the company Pivot that was almost universally condemned; and the minimal economic benefits to be derived from the project—these should all have been enough to bring this proposal to a halt. Local environmentalists, many of whom had been part of the Mount Etna Caves campaign of the 1980s, conducted a lively campaign, helped by state and national groups; Peter Garrett had a high profile throughout. Nevertheless, environmentalists had to work extremely hard to present a convincing case to the inquiry set up under the Commonwealth's Impact of Proposals Act.[12] The inquiry recommended against mining, and federal cabinet accepted the recommendation in September 1994. The mining industry, however, fought the issue just as hard as the conservationists. The Australian Mining Industry Council was less worried by the economic loss caused by the project's demise than by a decision which denied a section of the industry access to available minerals.

Mining companies continued to press during the 1990s for access to national parks and other areas of high conservation value. Yet pollution control and site rehabilitation practices were often abysmal. The 1993–94 inquiry by the Queensland Criminal Justice Commission into liquid waste, for example, heard of many mine sites around the state where companies had simply walked away at the end of the mine's life, leaving the rehabilitation of the site to be paid for out of the public purse. Newspaper reports in 1997 revealed that the inquiry did little more than touch the surface of this problem, with some of the biggest names in Australian mining being responsible for massive non-

compliance with environmental regulations. Queensland environmentalists have called for a wide-ranging inquiry into mining.[13] Such an
inquiry was unlikely, however, given the power of the industry in that
state and the support given to it by both major parties.

Despite the mining companies' poor record, Environment Minister
Robert Hill and Resources and Energy Minister Warwick Parer issued a
joint statement after the Coalition's victory at the 1996 federal elections,
announcing the government's decision to allow mining and exploration
within old-growth and wilderness forests proposed for protection under
the Regional Forests Agreements process. This decision was in line
with the mining industry's view that it had the technology and the
experience to be trusted in environmentally sensitive areas; the industry
went to great lengths to convince the public, through advertising, that
this was so. The Western Australian Liberal government of Richard
Court levelled the most direct challenge to the environment movement
by excising 368 hectares from the D'Entrecasteaux National Park for
a sand-mining operation—no doubt a sign of things to come.[14] The
Howard government also relinquished its powers over export licences
for all minerals, with the exception of uranium. This power had been
the lever to prevent sand-mining on Fraser Island and was immediately
challenged by environmentalists. Minor advances included an ESD
working group report on mining, improvements in pollution control
and rehabilitation technology by the mining industry, some legislative
improvements, and an industry code of practice; but it was obvious by
1997 that there would be many more conflicts between conservationists,
governments and miners.

The biggest conflict was over that perennial problem, uranium
mining. Labor's three-mine policy, in operation since 1983, had angered
both the proponents and opponents of uranium mining. Conservationists wanted a no-mine policy; the uranium industry wanted its
activities treated the same as all other types of mining. The Liberals had
always been unambiguously pro-uranium. During the 1996 federal
election campaign John Howard said, 'You either allow uranium mining
from any source in Australia, subject to environmental safeguards,
proper regard for Aboriginal interests and subject to nuclear safeguard
provisions ... or you don't allow any.'[15] In July 1996 the federal
government allowed Western Mining Corporation to conduct a $1.2
billion expansion at Roxby Downs, effectively allowing for a doubling
of the mine's capacity, without presenting an EIS. Uranium miners
began gearing up to take advantage of the opportunity offered by the
expansion of nuclear power projects in Asia. By mid-1997 eighteen
sites were being explored, four of which showed promise: the Energy
Resources of Australia (ERA) mine at Jabiluka, surrounded by the

Kakadu National Park; the CRA Kintyre mine, excised from the Ruddall River National Park in Western Australia by the Labor government of Carmen Lawrence; and the two South Australian proposals at Beverley and Honeymoon, the former owned by Heathgate Pty Ltd and the latter by MIM Holdings.[16] The environment movement prepared for another gut-wrenching struggle. Friends of the Earth and the ACF began informing the public on the issues surrounding the nuclear industry, especially the disposal of nuclear waste. TWS sent its campaign co-ordinator, Kevin Parker, on a national tour during the first half of 1997 to mobilise public opinion against the forthcoming expansion.

### Genetic Engineering

Nowhere can the inherent conflict between the principles of ESD and the logic of liberal technocratic society be better seen than over the issue of genetic engineering. As Bob Phelps, the co-ordinator of the Gen-Ethics Network, points out, 'The assumption that all of nature's limits should be overcome by technology underpins the use of genetic engineering.'[17] The issue is not simply one of science or ethics. It is also a question of power. Who controls the technology? Who benefits and who loses? What sort of society do we want to live in? A social movement with a core belief in placing limits on human intrusion into nature is immediately at odds with a technocratic approach that believes that, if it can be done, and some benefit can be derived, then do it.

In 1988 Leigh Holloway persuaded the ACF director, Phillip Toyne, that the foundation should be addressing the issue of genetic engineering. When Midnight Oil came up with $20,000 a year over three years to fund such a program, Toyne decided to appoint the veteran environmental campaigner, Phelps.[18] Although Peter Garrett wanted to push the issues into the public arena, it was difficult to get the media interested in anything that was not an already-existing disaster. Even more frustrating was the attitude of the federal government. After the 1990 election, an inquiry into genetic engineering by the House of Representatives Standing Committee on Industry, Technology and Commerce included in its recommendations that a national legal framework replace the existing voluntary guidelines. However, the federal government did not accept the recommendation for community participation in the exercise. It also decided to set up a Genetic Manipulation Authority but, instead of giving this regulatory role to the Commonwealth Environment Protection Agency, it put it in the hands of John Button's Department of Industry, Technology and Regional Development—the department that was also in charge of facilitating genetic engineering developments.[19] Phelps's work and that of the

Gen-Ethics Network have not had a high public profile, however; the media seems more interested in the clever things the industry can do, rather than the disturbing implications for the future.

### Biodiversity Campaigns

World Heritage areas—the best-known achievements of the movement during the 1980s—came under threat in the 1990s. Not only were no new areas assessed or put forward for listing,[20] but even existing World Heritage areas came under threat from various forms of development, and conservationists often had to fight vigorous campaigns simply to maintain the status quo. Just as importantly, areas with values that could easily gain them protected status, even World Heritage nomination, were in danger of potentially destructive developments.

Campaigns by environmentalists for World Heritage protection to various areas during the early 1990s stalled under the Keating Labor government and came to an almost complete halt under the conservative Howard government after 1996. These included campaigns in New South Wales for listing the Blue Mountains, in South Australia for the Lake Eyre Basin, in Western Australia for the Kimberleys, in Tasmania for the Tarkine, and in Queensland for Cape York. Most of these areas were also sites for developments that threatened to undermine the values that potentially qualified them for World Heritage. Nomination of the Lake Eyre Basin was blocked by pastoral and mining interests but was also, at one stage, seriously threatened by a surprisingly large proposal for a 3550-hectare cotton plantation on the Cooper River requiring 42 billion litres a year to irrigate it.[21] The 300,000-hectare Tarkine wilderness in north-west Tasmania, regarded by the Tasmanian and national conservation movements as worthy of World Heritage listing, did not contain one national park. The Tarkine was also threatened by logging and mining. Tasmanian conservationists launched a major campaign for its protection, including direct action against a link road right through the middle of it. The conservation values of the Kimberleys were threatened by the proposal for a dam on the Fitzroy River for cotton farming, while mining represented the biggest threat to the values of Cape York.

Close relations between conservation and indigenous groups over particular issues of common concern in the 1970s and 1980s had laid the groundwork for continuing co-operation in the 1990s. For example, the ACF and TWS worked closely with indigenous groups on Cape York to establish a common approach to issues. At a meeting at Yarrabah in November 1991 representatives from twelve Aboriginal and Islander groups met with nine state and national conservation groups to thrash out an accord that covered such areas as land rights, consultation, mining, watershed management, fishing rights and ranger training.[22] According to Mark Horstman:

> If we are serious about social justice and about remaining a progressive force for change, then we will have to resist the temptation to support unilateral declarations of large areas of Aboriginal land as National Park or World Heritage at the expense of the legitimate claims of traditional custodians. Only if we negotiate management of significant areas with indigenous communities will we be able to protect both the ecological and cultural values of the Peninsula.[23]

In September 1993 the ACF, TWS, Greenpeace Australia, together with the Australian Greens and the Australian Democrats, launched a common position on ownership of land, the impact of dislocation on Aboriginal people, compensation, and claims under native title legislation.[24]

The defeats of the Goss government in Queensland and then the Keating government federally interrupted developments that would have led to agreement among the major stakeholders on Cape York, with Aboriginal and conservation interests protected and World Heritage nomination a distinct possibility. The Queensland Coalition government's refusal to recognise the subsequent Cape York Land Use Agreement between conservation, Aboriginal and pastoral groups ended this promising process; the actions of Premier Borbidge were described as 'one of the most mean-spirited acts in recent Australian politics' by the ACF's executive director, Jim Downey.[25]

Not all parts of the environment movement, however, were happy with the concept of 'indigenous wilderness', fearing that Aboriginal hunting in claimed national parks could undermine the protection many had fought to get for these areas. Mark Horstman quotes one veteran of the Daintree campaign as saying, 'No longer will they be National Parks but government-sanctioned killing fields of our once protected ecology. Almost 100 years of protection ripped up, shot up, burnt up, stuffed up.'[26] The Colong Foundation argued in a calmer manner, in response to the New South Wales government's policy of granting 7.5 per cent of the state's land tax to Aboriginal communities for land purchases, saying, 'plans of management of Aboriginally owned and controlled areas granted under the National Parks and Wildlife (Aboriginal Ownership) Amendment Act 1996 should prohibit all commercial exploitation, except guided tours, visitors centres and similar non-developmental operations.'[27] Clearly, there is still some way to go before a 'green–black alliance' is free from serious tension. However, a great deal of groundwork for developing such an alliance has been done, and environmental and indigenous movements undoubtedly have a closer relationship than most other social movements.

Even existing World Heritage areas came under threat during this period. A decision by the Goss government to allow developer Keith Williams to go ahead with his proposed Port Hinchinbrook development without a proper EIS created a threat to the integrity of the Hinchinbrook Channel and the Great Barrier Reef World Heritage area. Direct action was taken by local conservationists to prevent the developer removing mangroves from the beach against the express direction of the federal environment minister, John Faulkner. The conflict that developed between state and federal Labor governments was resolved when the Coalition was elected at both state and federal levels. Then the Queensland government simply put its support completely behind the developer, and the new federal environment minister, Robert Hill, refused to intervene. The Wet Tropics of north Queensland were also endangered by state Coalition government plans to resurrect the stalled proposal for the Tully Millstream dam and to extend mains power north of the Daintree River, a scheme that would replace the solar power systems currently there. The former scheme was scrapped, but the latter is still a possibility, and threatens to set off an explosion of residential and resort development that could damage the area's World Heritage values.

Business groups and government resource agencies usually defined ESD in a way that implied it was all about trade-offs. What, they asked, is an acceptable trade-off between environmental destruction and economic growth? Do we have to pass on to future generations everything that we inherited in terms of environmental quality or can some of that be converted into inter-generational *capital* resources? Environmentalists, on the other hand, insisted that the one thing that could not be traded away was biodiversity. They pointed to the 5 per cent of our mammals that have become extinct in the 200 years of European settlement, representing two-thirds of the world's total mammal extinctions over that period. They also pointed to the 123 mammals, 150 reptile species, 41 frogs and 100 bird species that were threatened, saying that such threats to biodiversity were unacceptable under any reasonable definition of ESD. State and federal governments responded to demands in this area with strategies to protect threatened species but attempts to protect biodiversity by maintaining habitats were much more difficult, especially when that involved the competing demands of rural industries. The federal government signed the Biodiversity Convention at the Rio Summit, passed the 1992 Endangered Species Act, and developed the National Strategy for the Conservation of Biodiversity. New South Wales passed ground-breaking legislation, its

1995 Threatened Species Conservation Act, and a new group, the
Threatened Species Network, became an addition to the conservation
movement in the early 1990s. However, serious conflicts pitted conservationists against farmers and forest industries over farming in arid and
semi-arid lands, tree clearing, logging and woodchipping.

The Arid Lands Coalition of conservation organisations was set up to
counter the threats to biodiversity from unsustainable practices, mostly
pastoral, across Australia's rangelands. The Coalition focused on such
problems as soil erosion, weed invasion, feral animals and salting; it
pointed out that these impacts, resulting predominantly from cattle and
sheep grazing, resulted in a heavy loss to native plants and animals, with
disappearance of nearly half the original mammal species. Conservationists represented on the National Strategy for Rangeland Management argued that rangelands pastoralism was not economically viable,
and that it compounded this by being ecologically destructive. They
argued for major structural change in the rangelands:

- ensuring that pastoral land use is based on land capability assessment
  and ecological criteria
- the immediate removal of non-native grazing animals from known
  marginal areas
- the removal of massive subsidies which still characterise Australian
  agriculture ...
- ensuring that Aboriginal people are able to resume their role as land
  managers
- ensuring that the views of the Australian community are taken into
  account when assessing priorities for land use allocation and the
  protection of biodiversity.[28]

It also became clear to conservationists in the 1990s that the clearing
of native vegetation was one of the most serious environmental problems the country faced. It was estimated that 550,000 hectares a year was
cleared[29] and that this clearing was linked with soil degradation,
greenhouse emissions, and loss of biodiversity. Conservationists argued
for regulatory control, with Queensland as the crisis state. Attempts by
the Goss government to develop guidelines for broadacre clearing on
leasehold land staggered on until Labor lost office in 1996. In May
1997 the Borbidge government, in an attempt to extinguish native title
on leasehold land, brought in legislation to change existing land tenure.
Such a move would make sensible land management practices, advocated in the National Rangelands Management Strategy, ineffectual: the
strategy assumed that regulatory mechanisms like tree-clearing guidelines could be exercised over leasehold land but would be difficult to
apply to some other forms of land tenure.[30] Such a policy would also

make it difficult to meet Australia's agreement at Kyoto to limit green-house emissions to an 8 per cent increase, generous as that figure was, since reduced tree-clearing in Queensland would have to be a major part of a national greenhouse strategy.

## National Forest Policy

The Resource Assessment Commission inquiry into forests, set up by the Hawke government in 1990 to establish a rational, considered approach to the conflicts over the future of Australia's native forests, released its conclusions in March 1992. Although they were somewhat watered down from original drafts, these conclusions vindicated much of what the conservation movement had been saying in its forest campaigns throughout the 1980s. The RAC's conclusions included the need for a significantly larger reserve system; the cessation of logging in old-growth and wilderness forests; and strict controls on all native forest logging, with monitoring of long-term effects.[31] Commonwealth and state governments then met to draw up a National Forest Policy to implement these recommendations under the Inter-Governmental Agreement on the Environment. The conservation movement was disappointed with the final statement of that policy, issued in December 1992, feeling that it had too many loopholes and left too much to interpretation.[32] Nevertheless, the statement did include a moratorium clause that said, 'until the assessments are completed, forest management agencies will avoid activities that may significantly affect those areas of old-growth forest or wilderness that are likely to have high conservation value', and outlined a process for protecting old growth and wilderness forests. That was too much for the Coalition government in Tasmania and it refused to sign.

When the prospect of a hostile Coalition government under Hewson vanished after Keating's victory at the 1993 federal election, the conservation groups mobilised to pressure Labor. They wanted, finally, a worthwhile national forest policy that brought an end to logging in old-growth and wilderness forests, gave protection to forest areas of high conservation value, and promoted a rapid transition to a plantation-based industry. At a meeting in Canberra on 16 and 17 July 1994, forest activists from around the country developed a campaign to expose the issue to the public and to pressure the Keating government to imple-ment the *National Forest Policy Statement*.[33] A National Day of Action took place on 11 September 1994, with rallies around the country, and a Forest Embassy was set up on the lawns of Parliament House on 4–8 November. TWS also organised blockades at threatened forest areas in Western Australia, New South Wales, Victoria and Queensland. Support

for the campaign's aims came from a broad cross-section of the community, including artists, scientists, and the churches. A Newspoll in
December of that year found that 80.3 per cent of Australians supported an end to woodchipping in wilderness and high-conservation-
value forests.[34]

The Keating government seemed to respond positively to this
campaigning. The environment minister, Senator John Faulkner,
recommended to the resources minister, David Beddall, that 1311 high-
conservation-value forests be excluded, under the moratorium clause in
the *National Forest Policy Statement*, from that year's round of export
woodchip licences. Despite optimism among conservationists, Beddall
renewed all existing licences on 19 December and added three new
ones, issuing licences for most of the 1311 areas recommended for
exclusion. There was a public outcry. Tasmanian Labor senator and
strong supporter of the movement, John Deveraux, resigned from the
party and, although Keating made a speech announcing a timetable for
phasing out woodchipping, the furore continued. Rallies took place in
capital cities and thousands of letters poured in to the government from
movement supporters. The best news came when the Tasmanian Conservation Trust won a legal challenge against the granting of a licence to
the company Gunns, on the grounds that proper processes had not
been followed in the issuing of the licence. Pressure on Keating by
conservationists was matched, however, by the Forest Protection Society.
Members unleashed a blockade of Parliament House in January 1995
with about $100 million worth of trucks in an exercise that, conser-
vationists charged, was undoubtedly subsidised by the forest companies.[35] Keating announced on 27 January that 509 of these areas
would have interim protection, but dropped this to 452 at the end of
February.

The federal government decided it had to take the heat out of the
annual debacle of woodchip licence renewal and in March 1995 signed
an agreement with the states (including Tasmania this time) to manage
forests 'so as to conserve biological diversity, heritage and cultural values
for current and future generations and at the same time develop a
dynamic, internationally competitive forest products industry that can
operate on a sustained yield basis and develop value added industry'.[36]
Implementation of this agreement would be achieved through Regional
Forest Agreements, which would provide for comprehensive, adequate
and representative reserve systems. The operating principle for the
reserve system was that protection would be given to 15 per cent of
each forest community existing before 1788, together with biological
diversity, wilderness, heritage and water quality. The state governments
assessed the forests in collaboration with the Commonwealth.

Forest campaigners threw themselves into the public consultation in the belief that this was their last chance to reach a reasonable resolution of the forest issue. Conservationists were disappointed with the Regional Forest Agreement that was developed for East Gippsland[37] in 1997 and the one for Central Highlands was likely to be just as disappointing. Conservationists in New South Wales were initially happy with the process in that state, with new national parks and wilderness areas being announced by the Carr government,[38] but problems began emerging there in 1996. Some of the regional groups were satisfied with the outcome, but other groups like TWS were less so. The Western Australian process was disastrous from the start and conservationists were pessimistic about the outcome there. In Tasmania, although the Greens held the balance of power in the state parliament, the outcome was extremely disappointing for conservationists. Curiously, the one state where the process seemed to work well was Queensland. Under the unsympathetic Borbidge government, an unlikely working relationship between conservationists and the Timber Board created a good participatory process and an effective scientific framework for assessment. Through all this the role of the Commonwealth, first under Keating and then under Howard, was to extract the Commonwealth as much as possible from the whole native forests issue.

The point that the native forests issue had reached in mid-1997 reflected a massive weakness in public policy development and a breakdown in political responsiveness on the part of the major parties. Despite many polls showing overwhelming community support for strong action to protect native forests, governments—state and federal, Liberal and Labor—constantly sought solutions that did not meet people's expectations and maintained industrial practices that had little credibility in the eyes of the public.[39]

## The Industry Counter-Attack

The difficulties encountered by the environment movement in the 1990s cannot be put down entirely to the vagaries of 'protest cycles' or the effects of recession and unemployment. Significant sections of business and industry developed strategies to head off the 'green challenge'. Some of these strategies were crude and obvious, but others reflected careful thought. There were attempts, sometimes effective, to paint conservationists' actions as eco-terrorism or to accuse greens of violence and sabotage when there was no evidence to suggest this. The most serious of these was a hoax bomb on a railway line in Tasmania with a banner saying 'Save the Tarkine: Earth First' two days before the 1993 federal election. Gullible newspaper editors featured headlines linking the action with environmentalists and the Greens' Judy Henderson missed winning a Senate seat by 1 per cent.

Industry has also backed a number of support groups based on the assumption that community groups, especially those professing concern for the environment, have more credibility than those from industry. Some of these groups had a genuine grassroots base but others were obvious fronts. Mothers Opposing Pollution was undoubtedly a front for the cardboard milk packaging industry,[40] while the Forest Protection Society, though its name suggested that it was attempting to portray itself as a conservation group, was openly pro-logging. It did receive funding from the forest industry,[41] but it also had a strong base among forest workers, especially female members of logging families.

Nevertheless, Roberta Garner's description of environmental 'countermovements' in the United States, with their mass-based protests against environmental reform, evokes little resonance in the Australian context.[42] In this country most of the pro-industry, anti-green message has come from industry sources or closely aligned right-wing think-tanks. Industry certainly became much more sophisticated during the 1990s in its dealings with environmental concerns and with the environment movement. Doug McEachern divides industry responses to the environment into 'rejectionists', 'accommodationists' and 'environmentalists'.[43] Only a tiny section of industry is in the 'environmentalist' group; operations usually combine 'rejection' and 'accommodation'. Business groups and right-wing think-tanks brought 'experts' to Australia to throw doubt on environmentalists' claims, such as global warming and the hole in the ozone layer, and Hugh Morgan of Western Mining railed against environmentalists, calling them the new enemy of capitalism, replacing the old enemy, socialism.

On a more sophisticated level, organisations like the Business Council of Australia and the Australian Mining Industry Council (since 1996 the Mining Council of Australia) promoted ESD in the business community, representing it as a concept that could be used by industry to promote its agenda of technological innovation, free-market mechanisms, and industry self-regulation.[44] With unemployment rates close to 10 per cent, governments were desperate for new investment and major projects; they were readily convinced that environmental protection could be assured by voluntary codes of practice and that the mining industry, for example, was technologically advanced and responsible enough to explore for minerals and mine in environmentally sensitive areas.

The environment movement faced other problems in dealing with the determined and sophisticated strategies by industry to avoid environmental regulation. Mention has already been made of the weaknesses of regulatory regimes in a climate where both major parties espoused deregulatory, economic rationalist philosophies and where government agencies have been captured by the industries they are supposed to regulate. Moreover, as a result of the reforms in public administration and the universities over the previous decade, many of the public servants who had been allies of the movement were now consultants, dependent on their business clients for continued employment. Similarly, in universities, the increased emphasis on obtaining consultancies and research funds made it difficult to find dissenting intellectuals who would put their expertise to work for the movement. Many were doing well-funded research or held consultancies paid for by big business.

## Globalisation

While governments in Australia were adopting the neo-liberal policies emanating from New Right think-tanks, international developments were encouraging a free-trade agenda which reinforced this economic rationalist trend. Therefore, while conservationists' campaigns were pushing governments to take a stronger regulatory role on the environment, domestic and international pressures were forcing governments to question the efficacy of regulation itself. The goal of environmentalists—to incorporate environmental protection into the very fabric of Australian political culture—was within reach by 1990, but at a time when the Australian Settlement itself was coming apart.

The General Agreement on Tariffs and Trade was moving steadily through the late 1980s and 1990s to persuade member countries to reduce and eliminate barriers to trade. Australia was in the forefront, eliminating the policy of industry protection that had been a pillar of the Australian Settlement since Federation. When Australia helped set up the Asia–Pacific Economic Cooperation (APEC) meetings in 1989, it accepted the APEC agenda of increased privatisation, structural adjustment and decreased public expenditure, reduced government control of business activity, and rapid economic growth. Therefore, it was not surprising that the Keating government's reluctance to implement a strong interventionist role on the environment[45] was followed by an even stronger aversion by the Howard government. Not only did the federal Coalition government relinquish its mineral export control powers in May 1997, but it also refused to put conditions on grants from the Natural Heritage Trust Fund so that recipients of money from the fund were prevented from clearing native vegetation.

Attempts by some green organisations to reverse this trend by encouraging the Coalition to adopt a stronger position on environmental regulation resulted in public acrimony and bitter in-fighting. The hostility of many conservationists to the Goss government in Queensland prompted the Queensland Greens Party to encourage the Coalition to move to the political middle ground and adopt reformist policies on the environment. The Greens gave preferences to Coalition candidates over Labor in a handful of seats at the 1995 state election and this prompted a furious outburst from some conservation groups. In a similar manoeuvre TWS, angry at the Keating government's stand on forests, attempted to encourage the Coalition to adopt a better stance on this issue and gave it some support in the 1996 federal election. This decision was strongly opposed by other conservation groups, such as the ACF, who felt that forest campaigners were hijacking the movement's broader campaign for the election. In both cases a Coalition government came to power and implemented policies that were significantly worse than those of Labor in government.

### Sustainability

There is no easy way for Australian environmentalists to make *ecologically* sustainable development, which requires government to play a directive role on economic development, part of a new national consensus for the twenty-first century. There is, in the late 1990s, a card that the environment movement can play. The pollster, Rod Cameron, in a paper to a Minerals Council seminar, identified industry policy as 'a major sleeping issue that is about to break through and become a dominant theme in Australian community and political life'.[46] With strong support in the community for governments to *plan* for jobs, the possibility exists for promoting a strong regulatory framework, including environmental regulation and this would, in turn, give greater encouragement to the environmental management industries sector. However, political forces other than the populist Right would need to take advantage of this support in the community.

The movement will need to maintain its professional, routinised approach that takes well-researched, clearly thought-out policy positions into the public arena and decision-making forums. At the same time, it will need to launch militant campaigns on important environmental issues that mobilise new generations of activists and dramatise environmental concerns. The movement will also need to form alliances that counter the anti-environmental, economic rationalist, free-trade agenda. The last two decades have seen green groups forge strong alliances with indigenous groups and sections of the trade union movement. The next decade should see these links strengthened and social justice groups added to the alliance.

This alliance will probably be extended to the international level to combat the most destructive effects of the international free-trade push. To a certain extent, this has already happened. Approximately 600 representatives from non-government organisations from around the Asia–Pacific met in Manila in early 1997 during the APEC leaders' summits. These representatives discussed how such concerns as development with justice, human rights, women's issues, indigenous people, and the environment could be addressed in the region. They also discussed how this could be achieved in the context of the debilitating pressures for deregulated trade and investment regimes, increased power of multinational corporations, dismantling of social infrastructure, and rapid economic growth that was largely reliant on exploitation of non-renewable resources and increased pollution.[47]

# Epilogue

The environment movement, like most social movements, contains a wide spectrum of political and ethical positions. Eco-socialists, eco-feminists, deep ecologists, liberal pragmatists, and even conservatives work together for common goals with utilitarians, animal rightists, and ecocentrists. Outsiders often look at this diversity and proclaim that it could not possibly work; yet the green movement's record, in spite of many reverses, shows that it does. Perhaps the main reason for this is that the Australian movement has never been torn apart by ideological disputes. It has, instead, focused on strategic objectives, and major debate and disputation has usually centred on objectives and strategy rather than on theory. These disputes have sometimes been fierce, but nowhere near as divisive as ones based on ideological differences; because they are disputes about strategic direction, they are based on the need to respond to a concrete situation that is apparent to all. Even where there have been fights between, for example, the liberal progressive leaderships of mainstream groups and the more anarchistic direct actionists, these have usually been over the efficacy of particular approaches to direct action rather than over politics or culture. In the end, each side has usually been prepared to acknowledge the value of the other's contribution.

This is not to argue that there is no recognisable green political alternative. However, it does mean that green politics is inchoate and its outlines emerge in the context of struggle. Most campaigners, for example, have never taken a position explicitly hostile to the market or private property. Nevertheless, the logic of environmental struggle has resulted in some of the most militant campaigns being directed against particular sections of industry and, as with woodchipping in native forests, conservationists have devoted themselves to destroying the industry itself. Secondly, greens are not necessarily opposed to experts but, in the context of struggle, the anti-ecological and anti-democratic orientation of many experts have become obvious and a critique of technocracy has emerged within the movement. Thirdly, conservationists have followed the traditional liberal progressive path of seeking a stronger regulatory role for government, but they have also been sceptical of the state. Calls for increased regulation are usually accompanied by demands for public participation, such as third-party rights in legislation, public consultation in planning, and freedom-of-information and right-to-know legislation. A significant minority probably supports radical decentralisation measures. Finally, conservationists have had to confront social justice issues, not necessarily out of any strong ideological commitment, but because an environmental victory at the expense of a group like Aborigines, who are already disadvantaged, would be hollow.

Analysts of environmental politics have examined the relatively low green vote in the 1993 federal election (which was dominated by debate over a tax on goods and services), the decreased membership of conservation groups during the 1990s, and the declining interest of the media in environmental issues. They usually advance one of three main arguments to explain these phenomena.

The first is that environmental issues have declined in popularity as other issues have arisen to take their place. This view is almost a truism and popular in the media; it is based on the belief that environmental conflicts are not embedded in the nature of the system of industrial capitalism but are instead a fad brought about by skilful media manipulation. Environmentalism might return as a fad, but that will come about as the result of the cyclical and arbitrary nature of politics. The exponents of this view have probably never looked at Worldwatch Institute publications detailing the inexorable loss of species, destruction of crucial habitat like tropical rainforests, and the drift toward global warming, or pondered on the possibility that significant minorities around the world might undertake sustained effort to reverse such trends. Media interest might attract larger numbers into movement activities, but it does not create the organisational basis that is the necessary precondition for such mass mobilisation.

The second view is that the green movement is less relevant now because all major parties have environmental policies. Senator Robert Hill, environment minister in the Howard government, attempted to put this view in an angry address to a meeting in May 1997:

I say [Bob Brown is] in a timewarp ... twenty years ago there was sort of a select group of environmentalists who were the high-profile lobby ... made their name on confrontation. Basically jumping in front of bulldozers and the like ... What's happened since then of course is that the whole environment debate has changed ... Everyone now is an environmentalist.[1]

The challenge for the movement, according to this view, is to improve communication with government so that its agenda will be properly implemented. This theory is expounded by one of the most influential observers of Australian environmental politics, Elim Papadakis.[2] It is dependent on the validity of the assumption that ecological crises can be resolved without major changes to social structures or, at least, that existing political forces are capable of making the necessary adjustments without bitter social conflict. This assumption is questionable, especially given the record of both Labor and Coalition governments in Australia during the 1990s when they have faced the task of making hard environmental decisions that are opposed by major resource industries. Labor governments have mediocre to bad records in this area; conservative governments have been disastrous.

The third argument is that the decade of the 1980s was a successful period for environmental politics, with big campaigns around major issues, but the movement in the 1990s has become more of a lobby group within a well-defined institutional framework for policy development. This argument looks at the increasingly bureaucratic nature of major conservation groups like the Australian Conservation Foundation, The Wilderness Society, Greenpeace and the Worldwide Fund for Nature; the degree to which they are incorporated into the workings of government; and their emphasis on careful research and skilful lobbying. It makes a Weberian analysis about the logic of social movement development beyond its early phase of mass mobilisation into the routinisation and bureaucratisation of a mature movement.

There is much to this argument. Many people looking at these activists at work would say the movement seemed to be operating in just the way that a conservative approach, like resource mobilisation theory, says it should. People arrange their strategies at reasonably well-organised meetings, write letters, raise funds, lobby decision-makers, issue press releases, and generally mobilise their resources as efficiently as possible to achieve their goals. They usually do not espouse fundamentalist views about the relationship between human beings and the environment and, more often than not, frame their arguments about environmental protection to emphasise the need for wise and efficient resource use. They rarely point to conflicts that cannot be resolved within current institutional frameworks.

In many ways this approach avoids the problems of social movement theory that sees the green movement as possessing post-materialist values that are in conflict with mainstream values. Writers like Inglehart[3] and Offe[4] see environmental activists as the standard-bearers of a new, revolutionary system of values that can lead us into an ecologically sustainable future with systems of governance that are genuinely democratic. There are undoubtedly many people in Australia with post-materialist values, with a long-term vision of ecological sustainability and democratic structures; but these values are unlikely to provide the basis for an enduring and difficult struggle with a state dedicated to short-term political survival and large sections of industry determined on short-term economic viability.

Nevertheless, there is a dynamic that drives the environment movement into a radical confrontation with industrialism. This does not depend on movement activists maintaining a moral purity that enables a post-materialist challenge to win final victory; nor does it depend on the whims of the media. It is a dynamic that pits such goals as endless economic growth against the goal of ecological sustainability. Despite the many international conferences and conventions and the increased prominence of environmental issues, all the major indicators show a worsening of global environmental health. Whether one looks at atmospheric pollution, loss of biodiversity and habitat, population growth, desertification or water pollution, the signs are that they are all rapidly worsening. For Beck this is the material base for a green politics that is broad-based and revolutionary. He sees the concept of 'risk' becoming manifest to people whose welfare is increasingly threatened by pollution and the 'technocratic challenge to democracy' and says that such fears will prompt large numbers of people into action for radical social change.[5]

This is part of the reason why the environment movement will continue to be a major challenge to modern industrial society. More importantly, it brings us to the realisation that only the imposition of *limits* to activity that is not ecologically sustainable can avert or mitigate ecological crises. In an era when the major ideological response of elites around the world to contemporary economic problems is to resurrect neo-liberalism and to reassert technocratic approaches to decision-making, a worldwide movement emphasising the need to limit resource usage and the generation of wastes is a revolutionary challenge indeed. As the earth approaches its 'limits to growth', the options for further resource extraction and waste absorption by the natural environment are reduced, the capacity for technological fixes is stretched, and the contradictions between the economic and ecological imperatives become more apparent and more severe. In this context the environment movement should be seen more as a 'self-limiting' movement along the lines of Polish Solidarity than a mass movement that has

become institutionalised. In other words, it focuses on the key problems
that are its *raison d'être*, not the social system that might be the cause of
those problems. If the social system can successfully address those
problems, well and good. If it cannot, and the issues are fundamental to
human welfare, then the system will fall under the weight of its own
contradictions.

The environment movement might often operate as little more than
a slightly eccentric lobby group, but it is involved in a conflict that will
not be resolved without major social change. The struggles will probably
be even more intense than those of the previous thirty years and will
increasingly require co-operative action with politically compatible
social movements and with movements in other countries.

When Judith Wright said of the story of the Great Barrier Reef campaign that it had 'no real beginning and no one knows where its end will
be', she might well have been describing the modern environment
movement itself. It is seldom that the movement has won a major victory
and felt confident that it would not have to be defended again one day.
The one constant theme in the history of the environment movement in
this country has been its attempt to make environmental protection a
pillar of the Australian Settlement and of the national political culture.
If ecologically sustainable development becomes part of the national
consensus, past achievements can be consolidated and future environmental disasters averted by a prevailing ethic that enshrines such goals
as protecting species diversity, ensuring that future generations inherit
the same beauty and diversity that this generation has enjoyed, and
refusing to adopt practices and technologies that might undermine
ecological integrity. Until that situation is reached, there will be the
need for a strong environment movement that is involved in conflicts
over land and resource use.

# Notes

## Abbreviations

| | |
|---|---|
| AAAS | Australasian Association for the Advancement of Science |
| *ADB* | *Australian Dictionary of Biography* |
| AHA | Australian Historical Association |
| ANU | Australian National University |
| ANUP | Australian National University Press |
| CQU | Central Queensland University |
| CUP | Cambridge University Press |
| EUP | Edinburgh University Press |
| *HS* | *Australian Historical Studies* |
| NBAC | Noel Butlin Archives Centre |
| NSWUP | New South Wales University Press |
| OUP | Oxford University Press |
| *JRAHS* | *Journal of the Royal Australian Historical Society* |
| SUP | Sydney University Press |
| *Trans. RSSA* | *Transactions and Proceedings and Report of the Royal Society of South Australia* |
| UNE | University of New England |
| UQP | University of Queensland Press |
| UWAP | University of Western Australia Press |

## *Introduction*

1 Malcolm Saunders and Ralph Summy, *The Australian Peace Movement: A Short History*, Canberra, Peace Research Centre, ANU, 1986, p. 5.
2 Sara Parkin, *The Life and Death of Petra Kelly*, London, Pandora, 1994, p. 81.
3 Jan Pakulski, *Social Movements: The Politics of Moral Protest*, Melbourne, Longman Cheshire, 1991, p. xvi.

4 G. C. Bolton, *Spoils and Spoilers: Australians Make Their Environment*, Sydney, Allen & Unwin, rev. edn, 1992 (1st pub. 1981); R. L. Heathcote, 'The Visions of Australia 1770–1970' in Amos Rapoport (ed.), *Australia as Human Setting*, Sydney, Angus & Robertson, 1972, pp. 77–98; J. M. Powell, *Environmental Management in Australia, 1788–1914: Guardians, Improvers and Profit*, Melbourne, OUP, 1976; J. M. Powell, *A Historical Geography of Modern Australia: The Restive Fringe*, Cambridge, CUP, 1988.

5 See Touraine's comments about May 1968 in Alain Touraine, 'An Introduction to the Study of Social Movements', *Social Research*, vol. 52, no. 4, Winter 1985, p. 771; A. Jamison, R. Eyerman, J. Cramer and J. Laessoe, *The Making of the New Environmental Consciousness: A Comparative Study of the Environmental Movements in Sweden, Denmark and the Netherlands*, Edinburgh, EUP, 1990, p. x.

6 See Pakulski's discussion of Touraine's work in *The Politics of Moral Protest*, Melbourne, Longman Cheshire, 1991, pp. 24–5.

7 Alberto Melucci, 'The Symbolic Challenge of Contemporary Movements', *Social Research*, vol. 52, no. 4, Winter 1985, p. 810.

8 See for example Karl Werner Brandt's discussion of symbolic challenges in 'New Social Movements as a Metapolitical Challenge; The Social and Political Impact of a New Historical Type of Protest', *Thesis Eleven*, no. 15, 1986, pp. 66–7.

9 Melucci, 'Symbolic Challenge ...', pp. 794–5; see also Jean Cohen, 'Strategy or Identity: New Theoretical Paradigms and Contemporary Social Movements', *Social Research*, vol. 52, no. 4, Winter 1985, pp. 663–716.

10 Sidney Tarrow, *Power in Movement: Social Movements, Collective Action and Politics*, New York, CUP, 1994, p. 3.

11 Jamison *et al.*, *Making of the New ...*, pp. 5–6.

12 Charles Tilly, 'Models and Realities of Popular Collective Action', *Social Research*, vol. 52, no. 4, Winter 1985, pp. 717–18.

13 Pakulski, *Politics of Moral Protest*, p. 33.

14 Cohen, 'Strategy or Identity', pp. 685–95, esp. p. 694.

15 For an overview of the Australian debate on this issue, see Verity Burgmann, *Power and Protest: Movements for Change in Australian Society*, Sydney, Allen & Unwin, 1993, pp. 115–17. Also Gisela Kaplan, 'Women in Europe and Australia: Feminisms in Parallel?' in Norma Grieve and Ailsa Burns (eds), *Australian Women: Contemporary Feminist Thought*, Melbourne, OUP, 1994, pp. 40–52.

16 For a critical discussion of the relationship between intellectuals and social movements, see Burgmann, *Power and Protest*, pp. 6–7.

17 Pakulski, *Politics of Moral Protest*, pp. 42–3; see also Touraine's discussion on the opposition between social movements and revolutionary outcomes in 'Study of Social Movements', pp. 755–9, 762.

18 Alain Touraine, François Dubet, Michel Wieviorka and Jan Strzelecki, *Solidarity The Analysis of a Social Movement: Poland 1980–1981*, Cambridge, CUP, 1983.

19 Cohen, 'Strategy or Identity', pp. 668–9.

20 Roberta Garner, *Contemporary Movements and Ideologies*, New York, McGraw-Hill, 1996, p. 385.

21 Claus Offe, 'New Social Movements: Challenging the Boundaries of Institutional Politics', *Social Research*, vol. 52, no. 4, Winter 1985, pp. 849–56; Klaus Eder, 'The "New Social Movements": Moral Crusades, Political Pressure Groups, or Social Movements?', *Social Research*, vol. 52, no. 4, Winter 1985, p. 879.

22   Brandt, 'New Social Movements ...', pp. 66–7.
23   Weak totalitarian regimes also facilitate social movement formation. Pakulski discusses the relationship between different types of state and social movement activity in *Politics of Moral Protest*, pp. 55–8.
24   Ferdinand Muller-Rommel and Thomas Poguntke (eds), *New Politics*, Aldershot, Dartmouth, 1995, p. xiv; Wolfgang Rudig, 'Peace and Ecology Movements in Western Europe', *West European Politics*, vol. 2, January 1988, pp. 28–9; Thomas Poguntke, *Alternative Politics: The German Green Party*, Edinburgh, EUP, 1993, pp. 26–8.
25   Offe, 'Challenging the Boundaries', pp. 831–2.
26   Pakulski, *Politics of Moral Protest*, pp. 15–17, 70–3.
27   Brandt, 'New Social Movements', pp. 63–4.
28   Desley Deacon, *Managing Gender: The State, the New Middle Class and Women Workers 1830–1930*, Melbourne, OUP, 1989; Kereen Reiger, *The Disenchantment of the Home: Modernizing the Australian Family 1880–1940*, Melbourne, OUP, 1985.
29   Pakulski discusses the different positions in *Politics of Moral Protest*, pp. 69–71.
30   See Pakulski's discussion on sociopolitical blockage and relative closure in *Politics of Moral Protest*, pp. 54–6.
31   Jean Cohen discusses the relationship between social movements and civil society in 'Strategy or Identity', esp. pp. 699–705.
32   Melucci, 'Symbolic Challenge ...', p. 810.
33   Tamar Hermann, 'From Unidimensionality to Multidimensionality', *Research in Social Movements, Conflicts and Change*, vol. 15, 1993, pp. 181–202.
34   Sharon Beder, *Global Spin: The Corporate Assault on Environmentalism*, Melbourne, Scribe, 1997; Rudig, 'Peace and Ecology Movements ...', p. 35.
35   Offe, 'Challenging the Boundaries', p. 829; Cohen, 'Strategy or Identity ...', p. 673; Melucci, 'Symbolic Challenge ...', pp. 800–1.
36   Mario Diani, *Green Networks: A Structural Analysis of the Italian Environmental Movement*, Edinburgh, EUP, 1995, p. 6.
37   Jamison, *et al.*, *Making of the New*, pp. 57–63.

## Part I   The First Wave: 1860s to World War II

1   Alain Touraine, 'An Introduction to the Study of Social Movements', *Social Research*, vol. 52, no. 4, Winter 1985, p. 784.
2   J. M. Powell, 'The Genesis of Environmentalism in Australia' in Don Garden (ed.), *Created Landscapes: Historians and the Environment*, Carlton, History Institute Vic., 1992, pp. 8–9.
3   Marilyn Lake, 'The Politics of Respectability: Identifying the Masculinist Context', *HS*, vol. 22, no. 86, 1986, pp. 116–31; Katie Spearritt, 'New Dawns: First Wave Feminism 1880–1914' in Kay Saunders and Raymond Evans (eds), *Gender Relations in Australia: Domination and Negotiation*, Marrickville, NSW, Harcourt Brace Jovanovich, 1992, pp. 325–49.
4   Marilyn Lake, 'Between Old World "Barbarism" and Stone Age "Primitivism": The Double Difference of the White Australian Feminist' in Norma Grieve and Ailsa Burns (eds), *Australian Women: Contemporary Feminist Thought*, Melbourne, OUP, 1994, pp. 80–91.
5   E.g. Richard H. Grove, *Green Imperialism: Colonial Expansion, Tropical Island Edens and the Origins of Environmentalism*, Cambridge, CUP, 1995.

6    Tom Griffiths, *Hunters and Collectors: The Antiquarian Imagination in Australia*, Cambridge, CUP, 1996, ch. 6. (Also published as 'The Natural History of Melbourne: The Culture of Nature Writing in Victoria, 1880–1945', *HS*, vol. 23 no. 93, October 1989, pp. 339–65.)

7    For examples of some of these criticisms, see J. M. Powell, *Environmental Management in Australia, 1788–1914*, Melbourne, OUP, 1976, pp. 171–2; Elim Papadakis, *Politics and the Environment: The Australian Experience*, Sydney, Allen & Unwin, p. 68; Peter Christoff, 'Environmental Politics' in Judith Brett, James Gillespie and Murray Goots (eds), *Developments in Australian Politics*, Melbourne, Macmillan, 1994.

8    Sandra Bardwell, 'National Parks in Victoria, 1866–1956: "For all the people for all time"', PhD thesis, Dept of Geography, Monash University, 1974, p. 351 (also ch. 1, p. 71).

9    R. B. Walker, 'Fauna and Flora Protection in New South Wales, 1866–1948', *Journal of Australian Studies*, no. 28, 1991, pp. 27–8; Gerard Castles, 'Handcuffed Volunteers: A History of the Scenery Preservation Board in Tasmania 1915–71', Hons thesis, University of Tasmania, 1986.

10    Verity Burgmann, *Power and Protest: Movements for Change in Australian Society*, Sydney, Allen & Unwin, 1993, pp. 187–8.

11    The classic text on this topic is Henry Reynolds, *The Other Side of the Frontier*, Ringwood, Vic., Penguin, 1982.

12    Verity Burgmann offers a concise history of the modern land rights movement in *Power and Protest*, ch. 1.

13    W. H. Selway, 'The National Parks and Forest Reserves of Australia', *Trans. RSSA*, vol. XXXIV, 1910, pp. 279–305; W. F. Gates, 'Reservations' in Sir James Barrett (ed.), *Save Australia: A Plea for the Right Use of our Flora and Fauna*, Melbourne, Macmillan, 1925, p. 21.

14    William Lines, *Taming the Great South Land: A History of the Conquest of Nature in Australia*, Sydney, Allen & Unwin, 1981, p. 149.

15    Stephen Fox, *John Muir and his Legacy: The American Conservation Movement*, Boston, Little Brown, 1981, pp. 110–11.

16    Samuel P. Hays, *Conservation and the Gospel of Efficiency: The Progressive Conservation Movement, 1890–1920*, Cambridge, Mass., Harvard University Press, p. 141.

17    See the introduction to Michael Roe, *Nine Australian Progressives*, St Lucia, UQP, pp. 1–21.

18    *Emu*, vol. VII, October 1907, pp. 81, 4.

19    Von Mueller cited in Powell, *Environmental Management*, pp. 71–2.

20    Arthur Groom, *One Mountain After Another*, Sydney, Envirobook, 1992 (3rd edn), p. 201.

21    Bernard O'Reilly, *Green Mountains*, Sydney, Envirobook, 1968, p. 87.

22    *Emu*, vol. VII, October 1907, p. 4.

23    Jan Pakulski, *Social Movements: The Politics of Moral Protest*, Melbourne, Longman Cheshire, 1991, p. 55. This point is discussed in the Introduction.

*1   Professors, Learned Assessors*

1    For these three paragraphs and paragraph following, see reports in *Emu*, vol. VI , January 1907, pp. 95–103; vol. VII, January 1908, pp. 126–36; vol. VIII, October 1908, pp. 86–91.

2    *Emu*, vol. X, December 1910; Michael Roe, *Nine Australian Progressives*, St Lucia, UQP, 1984, p. 1.

3   Paul Kelly, *The End of Certainty: Power, Politics and Business in Australia*, Sydney, Allen & Unwin, 1994 (rev. edn), pp. 1–16; Roberta Garner, *Contemporary Movements and Ideologies*, New York, McGraw-Hill, 1996, pp. 378–80.

4   Richard H. Grove, *Green Imperialism: Colonial Expansion, Tropical Island Edens and the Origins of Environmentalism*. Cambridge, CUP, 1995. For more detailed discussion concerning imperial science and Australia, see Tom Griffiths and Libby Robin (eds), *Ecology and Empire: Environmental History of Settler Societies*, Melbourne, MUP, 1997.

5   For examples of romantic responses to the Australian environment, see Stephen Martin, *A New Land: European Perceptions of Australia 1788–1850*, Sydney, Allen & Unwin, 1993, esp. chs 4, 6.

6   For a brief overview of animal protection and anti-pollution developments in Britain in 1820–40s see John McCormick, *The Global Environmental Movement*, Chichester, John Wiley, 1995 edn, pp. 4–5. On the impact of the evangelical reform movement on indigenous issues and land rights and on the convict system see respectively Henry Reynolds, *The Law of the Land*, Ringwood, Vic., Penguin, 1992; John Hirst, *Convict Society and its Enemies*, Sydney, Allen & Unwin, 1983.

7   Alec H. Chisholm, *The Joy of the Earth*, Sydney, Collins, 1969, p. 43.

8   William J. Lines, *An All Consuming Passion: Origins, Modernity and the Australian Life of Georgiana Molloy*, Sydney, Allen & Unwin, 1994, p. 279.

9   P. E. de Strzelecki, *Physical Description of New South Wales and Van Diemen's Land*, London, Longman, Brown, Green & Longman, 1845 (facs. edn, 1967), pp. 355–6.

10  Colin Finney, *Paradise Revealed: Natural History in Nineteenth-Century Australia*, Melbourne, Museum of Victoria, 1993, pp. 17, 35.

11  Martin, *New Land*, p. 97; H. M. Whittell, 'The Visits of John Gilbert, Naturalist to Swan River Colony', Battye Library.

12  In *Mammals of Australia*, published in 1863.

13  Finney, *Paradise Revealed*, pp. 63, 160, fn 37, 161 fn 58; Anne Allingham, 'Omnium Gatherum: A Naturalists' Tradition in Tropical Queensland' in *Peripheral Visions*, pp. 144–51; Judith McKay, *Brilliant Careers: Women Collectors and Illustrators in Queensland*, South Brisbane, Queensland Museum, 1997; Margaret Swann, 'Mrs Meredith and Miss Atkinson, Writers and Naturalists', *JRAHS*, vol. XV, part I, 1929, pp. 1–29; *Trans. RSSA*, vol. XXIII, 1898–99, p. 319.

14  Lines, *An All-Consuming Passion*.

15  *ADB*, vol. 11, pp. 465–6.

16  Report of the Native Fauna and Flora Committee, *Trans. RSSA*, vol. XL, 1916, p. 623.

17  'George Crommelin', *ADB*, vol. 3, p. 496.

18  Finney, *Paradise Revealed*, pp. 105–8, 113.

19  Finney, *Paradise Revealed*, pp. 131–3.

20  Tom Griffiths, *Hunters and Collectors: The Antiquarian Imagination in Australia*, Cambridge, CUP, 1996, p. 132.

21  'Presidential Address, October 6, 1891', *Trans. RSSA*, vol. XIV, 1890–91, p. 374.

22  Finney, *Paradise Revealed*, pp. 89–92.

23  Chisholm, *Joy of the Earth*, p. 150. The Woodlanders are discussed in more detail in Griffiths, *Hunters and Collectors*, pp. 127–36, also published as 'The Natural History of Melbourne: The Culture of Nature Writing in Victoria, 1880–1945', *HS*, vol. 23, no. 93, October 1989.

24   Lorna McDonald, *Rockhampton: A History of City and District*, St Lucia, UQP, 1981, pp. 403–13.
25   Finney, *Paradise Revealed*, p. 128.
26   *North Queensland Naturalist*, vol. 1, 1933; Ross Fitzgerald, *From 1915 to the early 1980s: A History of Queensland*, St Lucia, UQP, 1984, pp. 81–2.
27   *ADB*, vol. 8, pp. 544–5; W. Catton Grasby, 'Preservation of Flora and Fauna in Western Australia' in Barrett (ed.), *Save Australia*, p. 202; Judith McKay, *Ellis Rowan: A Flower Hunter in Queensland*, South Brisbane, Queensland Museum, 1990, p. 59, fn. 20; Western Australian Sub-committee of the Australian Academy of Science Committee on National Parks, *National Parks and Reserves in Western Australia*, Perth, Australian Academy of Science and the National Parks Board of WA, [1963?], pp. 13–21; Bryce Moore, 'Tourists, Scientists and Wilderness Enthusiasts' in B. K. de Garis (ed.), *Portraits of the South West: Aborigines, Women and the Environment*, Nedlands, UWAP, 1993, pp. 119–31.
28   Elizabeth N. Marks, 'A History of the Queensland Philosophical Society and the Royal Society of Queensland from 1859 to 1911', *Proceedings of the Royal Society of Queensland*, vol. 71, no. 2, 1959, p. 29.
29   Finney, *Paradise Revealed*, pp. 131–6. See Marks, 'History of the Queensland Philosophical Society', p. 35.
30   E.g. Skertchley, F. M. Bailey, Dr Shirley and Henry Tryon: Marks, 'History of the Queensland Philosophical Society ...', p. 33; White, 'Henry Tryon First Honorary Secretary, Royal Society of Queensland, and His Place in Queensland Science'; *Proceedings of the Royal Society of Queensland*, vol. 56, no. 8, 1945, p. 79.
31   J. Keith Jarrott, *History of Lamington National Park*, Beaudesert, Jarrott & NPAQ Inc, 1990, pp. 3–4.
32   *Sydney Mail*, 5 March 1919; Groom, *One Mountain*, pp. 74–89, 92–7, 125.
33   Jarrott, *Lamington National Park*, pp. 53–9.
34   For examples, see Alec H. Chisholm, 'The Great National Parks Movement', Romeo Watkins Lahey Memorial Lecture, *NPA News*, March 1972, p. 8.
35   R. B. Walker, 'Fauna and Flora Protection in New South Wales, 1866–1948', *Journal of Australian Studies*, no. 28, 1991, p. 22.
36   Powell, *Environmental Management*, pp. 90–1; *ADB*, vol. 4, pp. 108–9; Allen Strom, 'Impressions of a Developing Conservation Ethic, 1870–1930' in *Australia's 100 Years of National Parks*, Sydney, National Parks and Wildlife Service, 1979, pp. 48–50.
37   Finney, *Paradise Revealed*, p. 126; Bolton, *Spoils and Spoilers*, p. 99; Hazel Rowley, *Christina Stead: A Biography*, Melbourne, Heinemann, 1993, p. 4. The Natural History Association evolved into the Field Naturalists Society of New South Wales in 1890: Finney, *Paradise Revealed*, p. 126.
38   J. H. Prince, *The First 100 Years of the Royal Zoological Society of NSW 1879 to 1979*, p. 21; Strom, 'Developing Conservation Ethic', p. 50; Walker, 'Fauna and Flora Protection ...', p. 22.
39   Finney, *Paradise Revealed*, pp. 48–61, 157 fn. 66; Powell, *Environmental Management*, p. 114; Gerard Castles, 'Handcuffed Volunteers: A History of the Scenery Preservation Board in Tasmania, 1915–71', Hons thesis, University of Tasmania, 1986, p. 20.
40   Castles, 'Handcuffed Volunteers', p. 25; Powell, *Environmental Management*, p. 114; Geoff Mosley, 'The Tasmanian National Park System', *Tasmanian Tramp*, no. 17, January 1966, p. 38.
41   Finney, *Paradise Revealed*, pp. 80–5, 93; Powell, *Environmental Management*, p. 44.

42  Finney, *Paradise Revealed*, pp. 124–5; 'Barrett', *ADB*, vol. 7, p. 185; 'Chisholm', *ADB*, vol. 13, pp. 422–3.

43  E.g. Geelong and Ballarat: Finney, *Paradise Revealed*, pp. 127–8.

44  *Conservation Council of Victoria Newsletter*, May 1980.

45  W. H. Selway, 'The National Parks and Forest Reserves of Australia', *Trans. RSSA*, vol. XXXIV, 1910, pp. 286–7.

46  Sandra Bardwell, 'National Parks in Victoria, 1866–1956', PhD thesis, Geography Dept, Monash University, 1974, p. 448; 'Highlights of 100 Years of National Parks in Victoria', *Parkwatch*, no. 129, Winter 1982, pp. 6–7; Stephen Johnston, 'Profile of a Parks Pioneer', *Park Watch*, no. 169, June 1992, pp. 9–11; Jane Lennon, 'Cornerstone of the Continent: A History of Wilsons Promontory', *Park Watch*, no. 172, March 1993, p. 5.

47  'Annual Report' and 'The Anniversary Address of the President Professor Ralph Tate', *Trans. RSSA*, vol. XIX, 1894–95, pp. 264–5, 266. A Natural History Society of South Australia was also reported to have been established as early as 1839. Finney, *Paradise Revealed*, p. 63; 'Sixteenth Annual Report of the Field Naturalists Section', *Trans. RSSA*, vol. XXIII, 1898–99, p. 318; W. H. Selway, 'The National Parks and Forest Reserves of Australia', *Trans. RSSA*, vol. XXXIV, 1910, p. 283; Reports of the Native Fauna and Flora Protection Committee of the Field Naturalists Section, *Trans. RSSA*, vols XIV–LII, 1890–1928; Samuel Dixon, 'The Effects of Settlement and Pastoral Occupation in Australia upon the Indigenous Vegetation', *Trans. RSSA*, vol. XV, 1892, pp. 195–206.

48  Selway, 'The National Parks and Forest Reserves of Australia', pp. 284–6; Report of the Native Fauna and Flora Protection Committee, *Trans. RSSA*, vol. XXXV, 1911, p. 245; Capt S. A. White, 'The Movement for Protection in South Australia' in Barrett (ed.), *Save Australia*, pp. 185–7; Warren Bonython, 'The Origins and History of the Conservation Movement' in *Pollution and Conservation: Selected Papers*, Dept of Adult Education, University of Adelaide, 1972, p. 65.

49  C. French, 'A Naturalist's Health Trip to Northern Queensland', *Victorian Naturalist*, vol. XXIV, no. 11, March 1908, pp. 167–8; *ADB*, vol. 5, pp. 306–8; Powell, *Environmental Management*, pp. 70–2.

50  Finney, *Paradise Revealed*, pp. 137–9.

51  Powell, *Environmental Management*, pp. 121–2.

52  Jack Thwaites, 'John Watt Beattie', *Tasmanian Tramp*, no. 23, June 1979, p. 77; Geoff Mosley, 'The Tasmanian National Park System', *Tasmanian Tramp*, no. 17, January 1966, p. 38.

53  Bonython, 'Origins and History ...', p. 65; Selway gives the year as 1896. Selway, 'The National Parks and Forest Reserves of Australia', p. 284.

54  Bolton, *Spoils*, p. 99.

55  Chisholm, *Joy of the Earth*, p. 103; Allen Strom, 'Impressions of a Developing Conservation Ethic, 1870–1930' in *Australia's 100 Years of National Parks*, Sydney, NPWS, 1979, p. 50; F. I. Norman and A. D. Young, '"Short-sighted and doubly short-sighted are they ...": Game Laws of Victoria, 1858–1958', *Journal of Australian Studies*, no. 7, 1980, pp. 4–5. The exception was Tasmania, which introduced closed seasons for a range of native animals from 1860: Bolton, *Spoils*, p. 98.

56  Donald McDonald and Charles Barrett were both members of the BOC. For their masculinist and militarist orientations see Griffiths, *Hunters*, pp. 136–41; Bolton, *Spoils*, p. 99; NF&FPC, *Trans. RSSA*, vol. XXIII, 1898–99; *Emu*, vol. VI, July 1906, p. 38; Chisholm, *Joy of the Earth*, p. 161.

57  Cited in Chisholm, *Joy of the Earth*, p. 170. See also NF&FPC Field Naturalists Section, *Trans. RSSA*, vol. XLIII, 1919.
58  *Emu*, vol. X, December 1910.
59  Report of the Native Fauna and Flora Protection Committee of the Field Naturalists Section, *Trans. RSSA*, vol. XXIX, 1905.
60  *Emu*, vol. VIII, October, 1908.
61  *Emu*, vol. VI, January 1907; *ADB*, vol. 11, pp. 491–2; McKay, *Ellis Rowan*, p. 1.
62  *Emu*, vol. XIII, April 1909.
63  Barrett, *Save Australia*, pp. 2–4; Fitzgerald, *From 1915 to the Early 1980s*, pp. 73–7; Prince, *First One Hundred Years*, pp. 13–14.
64  Walker, 'Fauna and Flora Protection ...', p. 25.
65  Finney, *Paradise Revealed*, pp. 141–3, 119–24.
66  C. Turney, 'W. Catton Grasby—Harbinger of Reform' in C. Turney (ed.), *Pioneers of Australian Education*, vol. 2, Sydney University Press, 1972, pp. 196–7, 225–6.
67  Turney, 'W. Catton Grasby', p. 222; Chisholm, *Joy of the Earth*, p. 151.
68  History of the Gould League, Gould Society of NSW Records, Mitchell Library; White, 'Henry Tryon', pp. 77–80.
69  Western Australian Sub-committee, *National Parks and Reserves in Western Australia*, pp. 23–4.
70  Central Queensland Native Birds Protection Society, Nature Notes, Patrick V. Maloney Collection, Rockhampton and District Historical Society; MacDonald, *Rockhampton*, pp. 410–13.
71  The National Association of Audubon Societies was the amalgamation of state-based Audubon Societies which was formed in 1905: Fox, *Muir and His Legacy*, pp. 151–2.
72  Fox, *Muir and His Legacy*, pp. 173–82.
73  A. H. Chisholm, 'Birds of a Feather Flock ...?', *Australian Zoologist*, vol. 3, part 8, January 1925, pp. 300–5.
74  Chisholm, 'Birds of a Feather Flock ...?', p. 305.
75  Eric Rolls, *They All Ran Wild: The Animals and Plants that Plague Australia*, Sydney, Angus & Robertson, 1969.
76  Paul Stevens, 'Plants, Forests and Wealth: Vegetation Conservation in Queensland, 1870–1900' in B. J. Dalton (ed.), *Peripheral Visions: Essays on Australian Regional and Local History*, Dept of History and Politics, James Cook University, 1991, pp. 182–3, 184; J. M. Powell, 'A Baron under Siege: Von Mueller and the Press in the 1870s', *Victorian Historical Journal*, vol. 50, no. 1, 1979, pp. 18–35.
77  See for example Walker, 'Fauna and Flora Protection ...', p. 19.
78  E.g. Tower Hill, Portland, Ballarat and Rockhampton. Finney, *Paradise Revealed*, p. 127; MacDonald, *Rockhampton*, pp. 405–6; Bolton, *Spoils*, p. 97. Western Australia's Acclimatisation Committee was established with government support in 1898. Moore, 'Tourists, Scientists ...', p. 124.
79  R. Wright, 'The Fight for Phillip Island, 1861–1868', *Journal of Australian Studies*, no. 7, November 1980, pp. 25–32; R. Wright, *Bureaucrats' Domain: Space and the Public Interest in Victoria 1836–84*, Melbourne, OUP, 1989, pp. 200–2.
80  Wright, 'The Fight ...', p. 27; Bolton, *Spoils*, p. 46.
81  P. A. O'Shanesy, *Contributions to the Flora of Queensland*, Rockhampton, 1880, Capricornia Collection, CQU, preface and pp. 23, 36.
82  McDonald, *Rockhampton*, p. 404.

83 A. Thozet, *Notes on Some of the Roots, Tubers, Bulbs and Fruits used as Vegetable Food by the Aboriginals of Northern Queensland*, Rockhampton, W. H. Buzacott, 1866.

84 Carolyn Pettigrew and Mark Lyons, 'Royal National Park—A History' in *Australia's 100 Years of National Parks*, pp. 15–28; Selway, 'The National Parks and Forest Reserves of Australia', pp. 289–90. The title 'Royal' was not added until 1954.

85 Rowley, *Christina Stead*, p. 9.

86 Rowley, *Christina Stead*, pp. 5, 19–22, 24–5, 40, 43, 45–6; 'Stead', *ADB*, vol. 12, pp. 57–8.

87 David Stead, *Fishes of Australia*, 1906; David Stead, *Edible Fishes of New South Wales*, 1908.

88 Strom, 'Developing Conservation Ethic', p. 50.

89 Powell, *Environmental Management*, pp. 54–5, 59–64.

90 Cited in Powell, *Environmental Management*, pp. 71–2.

91 Powell, *Environmental Management*, pp. 90–1. Woolls continued to decry the destruction of eucalypts and published an article on it in *Victorian Naturalist* in 1891. See Lines, *Great South Land*, p. 133.

92 Paul Stevens, 'Plants, Forests and Wealth: Vegetation Conservation in Queensland, 1870–1900' in Dalton (ed.), *Peripheral Visions*, pp. 176–8; Kevin Frawley, 'Early Rainforest Management in Queensland', *Habitat*, vol. 9, no. 4, 1981, pp. 6–7.

93 Jane Lennon, 'Victoria's Hidden Inheritance: Historic Sites on Public Land' in *Created Landscapes*, p. 37.

94 L. T. Carron, 'A History of Forestry and Forest Product Research in Australia', *Historical Records of Australian Science*, vol. 5, no. 1, 1980, p. 38; Bolton, *Spoils*, pp. 47–8.

95 Reports of the Native Fauna and Flora Protection Committee of the Field Naturalists Section in *Trans. RSSA*, vols XXIII–XLIII, 1890–1919.

96 John Dargavel, 'Constructing Australia's Forests in the Image of Capital' in Stephen Dovers (ed.), *Australian Environmental History: Essays and Cases*, Melbourne, OUP, 1994, p. 83.

97 Powell, *Environmental Management*, pp. 121–5; Norman and Young, '"Short-sighted and doubly short-sighted ..."', p. 22 fn. 11.

98 Gill cited in Powell, *Environmental Management*, p. 123.

99 'John Ednie Brown', *ADB*, vol. 3, pp. 261–2; Walker, 'Fauna and Flora Protection ...', p. 21.

100 H. Bodinner, 'Forestry in Western Australia', 1967, Battye Library, WA.

101 Len Webb, 'The Rape of the Forests' in A. J. Marshall (ed.), *The Great Extermination*, London, Heinemann, 1966, pp. 209, 218.

102 Stevens, 'Plants, Forests and Wealth ...', pp. 177–8.

103 Jarrott, *Lamington National Park*, pp. 9–10; *Australia's 100 Years of National Parks*, p. 133.

104 Selway, 'The National Parks and Forest Reserves of Australia', p. 298.

105 Desley Deacon, *Managing Gender*, Melbourne, OUP, 1989, pp. 168–9; 'Swain', *ADB*, vol. 12, pp. 145–6; Peter Taylor, *Growing Up: Forestry in Queensland*, Sydney, Allen & Unwin, 1997, pp. 58–60.

106 Cited by Webb, 'The Rape of the Forests', pp. 219–20.

107 Ross Fitzgerald, *From 1915 to the Early 1980s: A History of Queensland*, St Lucia, UQP, 1984, pp. 79–83.

108 Kevin Frawley, 'Rainforest Management in Queensland after 1900', *Habitat*, vol. 13, no. 5, October 1985; *ADB*, pp. 145–6.

109 Carron, 'Forestry and Forest Products ...', p. 11.
110 Stevens, 'Plants, Forests and Wealth ...', p. 191; Walker, 'Fauna and Flora Protection ...', p. 21.
111 See for example Aynsley Kellow, *Is the Rest of the World Watching: Prospects for Environmental Politics in Australia?*, Griffith University, n.d., pp. 5–6.
112 Powell, *Environmental Management*, p. 19; Bolton, *Spoils*, p. 37.
113 Strzelecki, *Physical Description of New South Wales*, pp. 373–4.
114 Samuel Dixon, 'The Effects of Settlement and Pastoral Occupation in Australia upon the Indigenous Vegetation', *Trans RSSA*, vol. XV, part II, December 1892.
115 Bolton, *Spoils*, p. 139.
116 See contributions by Owen Jones and E. G. Ritchie in Barrett (ed.), *Save Australia*, chs VI, XIII.
117 J. M. Powell, *A Historical Geography of Modern Australia*, Cambridge, Cambridge University Press, 1988, pp. 48–54; Fitzgerald, *From 1915*, pp. 62–5.
118 Interview with Milo Dunphy, 6 July 1993; C. M. Hall, *Wasteland to World Heritage: Preserving Australia's Wilderness*, Melbourne, MUP, 1992, pp. 114–15; see also the discussion of tensions between the Victorian Forests Commission and State Rivers and Water Supply Commission in the late 1930s in Bardwell, 'National Parks in Victoria', pp. 421–3.
119 Bolton, *Spoils*, p. 136.
120 Bardwell, 'National Parks in Victoria', pp. 426–7.
121 Francis Ratcliffe, *Flying Fox and Drifting Sand*, Sydney, Angus & Robertson, 1963 (2nd edn).
122 Introduction in Jock H. Pick, *Australia's Dying Heart*, Melbourne, MUP, 1944 (2nd edn).
123 Jan McDonald, 'Not as Dry as Dust', AHA conference paper, 1994.
124 J. G. Mosley, 'Towards a History of Conservation in Australia' in *Australia as Human Setting*, pp. 141–2.
125 Powell, *A Historical Geography*, pp. 129–37; J. M. Powell, *The John Murtagh Macrossan Memorial Lecture*, St Lucia, UQP, 1993, pp. 15–38.
126 Interview with John McCabe, Rockhampton, 1993.

## 2  Sane Citizens and Sanitarians

1 Penny Russell, 'Paradise Lost: Sir John and Lady Jane Franklin', and Marguerite Hancock, 'A Marriage of Opposites: Charles Joseph and Sophie La Trobe' in Penny Russell (ed.), *For Richer, for Poorer: Early Colonial Marriages*, Melbourne, MUP, 1994, pp. 50–72, 73–93.
2 Chisholm, 'The Great National Parks Movement', p. 3.
3 Chisholm, 'The Great National Parks Movement', pp. 7, 11.
4 James Bowen, 'The Great Barrier Reef: Towards Conservation and Management' in Dovers (ed.), *Australian Environmental History*, p. 237.
5 Chisholm, 'The Great National Parks Movement', p. 3. Francis Ratcliffe also noted that another Queensland governor with a party of eight hunters reputedly killed 800 birds in one week in the late 1920s: *Flying Fox and Drifting Sand*, Sydney, Angus & Robertson, 1963 (2nd edn), p. 20.
6 S. Elliott Napier, *On the Barrier Reef: Notes from a No-Ologist's Pocket-book*, Sydney, Angus & Robertson, 1934 (6th edn), pp. 4–8.
7 *ADB*, vol. 4, p. 108; Strom, 'Developing Conservation Ethic', p. 46.
8 'Ellis Rowan', *ADB*, vol. 11, pp. 465–6.

9   E. J. Banfield, *The Confessions of a Beachcomber*, Pymble, Angus & Robertson, 1968 (rev. edn).

10  Pettigrew and Lyons, 'Royal National Park', p. 18.

11  Myles Dunphy, *Selected Writings*, compiled and annotated by Patrick Thompson, Sydney, Ballagirin, 1986, pp. 129, 3–4, 6–8, 22; Strom, 'Impressions of a Developing Conservation Ethic', p. 46.

12  Dunphy, *Selected Writings*, pp. 7–9.

13  'Bushwalkers' Conservation Movement's Schemes 1914–64', p. 28 in Myles Dunphy, *Bushwalking Conservation Movement 1914–64, Book 1*, mss 4457, Mitchell Library.

14  Journal, vol. 4, cited in Dunphy, *Selected Writings*, p. 123

15  On the changing attitudes and sympathy of conservationists to Aboriginal people in the interwar period, see Jennifer MacCulloch, 'Ghosts: Aboriginal People as Animals 1890s to 1920s', AHA conference paper, 1994.

16  Dunphy, *Selected Writings*, pp. 55–9.

17  Dunphy, *Selected Writings*, 'Introduction' and p. 14; Myles Dunphy, 'The Bushwalking Conservation Movement, 1914–1965' in *Australia's 100 Years of National Parks*, p. 56.

18  'The New Conservators', p. 13 and 'Bushwalkers' Conservation Movement's Schemes 1914–64', p. 36 in Myles Dunphy, *Bushwalking Conservation Movement 1914–64, Book 1*, mss 4457, Mitchell Library.

19  Dunphy, 'Bushwalkers' Conservation Movement's Schemes 1914–64', p. 39; *Selected Writings*, pp. 32–9.

20  Dunphy, 'Bushwalkers' Conservation Movement's Schemes 1914–64', pp. 22, 30–2.

21  Dunphy, *Selected Writings*, p. 184; 'Marie Byles', *ADB*, 1940–80, pp. 325–6.

22  Dunphy, 'Bushwalkers' Conservation Movement's Schemes 1914–64', p. 35.

23  Dunphy, *Selected Writings*, pp. 175–7; 'Bushwalkers' Conservation Movement's Schemes 1914–64', p. 32.

24  Chisholm, 'The Great National Parks Movement', pp. 6–7.

25  Amy Eastwood, Isabel Eastwood and Hazel Merlo, *Uphill After Lunch: Melbourne Women's Walking Club*, Melbourne Women's Walking Club Inc, n.d. See also Sandra Bardwell, 'The Changing Face of the Victorian Countryside—Bushwalking in the Past, Present and Future', *Park Watch*, no. 150, September 1987, p. 12.

26  'Marie Byles', *ADB*, vol. 13, pp. 325–6; Rowley, *Christina Stead*, p. 58.

27  'Cyril Tennison White', *ADB*, vol. 12, pp. 463–4; J. K. Jarrott, 'The First Fifty Years', *NPA News*, vol. 50, no. 5, August 1980, p. 9.

28  Jarrott, *History of Lamington National Park*, p. 82.

29  'Albert Heber Longman' and 'Irene Maud Longman', *ADB*, vol. 10, pp. 138–40.

30  *Tasmanian Tramp*, no. 23, June 1979.

31  Sandra Bardwell, 'National Parks in Victoria', 1866–1956, PhD thesis, Geography Dept, Monash University, 1974, pp. 451–5; 'Highlights of 100 Years of National Parks in Victoria', pp. 6–7.

32  Groom, *One Mountain*, pp. 109, 125–6; Jarrott, *History of Lamington National Park*, pp. 23, 85–6.

33  O'Reilly, *Green Mountains*.

34  Groom, *One Mountain*, pp. 129–30.

35  R. Allen Clelland, 'R. W. Lahey Memorial Lecture', *Supplement to PA News*, October 1970, pp. 4–5; Jarrott, 'The First Fifty Years', pp. 4–5; Jarrott, *History of Lamington National Park*, p. 10.

36  Fairy Bower near Rockhampton was degazetted as a national park as a result of wartime degradation by the military authorities: Jarrott, 'The First Fifty Years', pp. 5–7; Groom, *One Mountain*, pp. 176–7, 191–7.

37  'Samuel White', *ADB*, vol. 12, pp. 472–3; Colin R. Harris, 'The National Parks and Reserves of South Australia', MA thesis, Dept of Geography, University of Adelaide, 1974, pp. 27, 29, 36–42; Derek Whitelock, *Conquest to Conservation: History of Human Impact on the South Australian Environment*, Netley, SA, Wakefield, pp. 130–1.

38  Moore, 'Tourists, Scientists ...', pp. 114–19.

39  Western Australian Sub-committee AASCNP, *National Parks and Reserves in Western Australia*, Australian Academy of Science and National Parks Board of Western Australia, n.d., pp. 21–3, 31–3, 37–40.

40  Gerard Castle, 'Handcuffed Volunteers: A History of the Scenery Preservation Board in Tasmania, 1915–1971', BA Hons thesis, University of Tasmania, 1986, pp. 25–32.

41  'As It Was In the Beginning', *Tasmanian Tramp*, no. 1, February 1933, pp. 4–5; J. B. Thwaites, 'Club Founder—E. T. Emmett', *Tasmanian Tramp*, no. 9, December 1949, pp. 9–10; Jessie Luckman, 'The Club's Role in Conservation', *Tasmanian Tramp*, no. 21, January 1974, pp. 4–10; Peter Allnutt, 'The Club's Foundation Fifty Years Ago', *Tasmanian Tramp*, no. 23, 1979, pp. 1–4; Castle, 'Handcuffed Volunteers', pp. 58–74.

42  Mosley, 'The Tasmanian National Park System', pp. 38–9; Castle, 'Handcuffed Volunteers', pp. 21–3.

43  J. B. Thwaites, 'Club Founder—E. T. Emmett'.

44  Citations from Jack Thwaites, 'John Watt Beattie', *Tasmanian Tramp*, no. 23, June 1979, pp. 72–80; 'Beattie', *ADB*, vol. 7, pp. 232–3.

45  Castle, 'Handcuffed Volunteers', p. 88.

46  Turney, 'W. Catton Grasby ...', pp. 196–7.

47  Chisholm, *Joy of the Earth*, p. 151.

48  'The Junior Tree Warden', Stead Papers, Box 25, Mitchell Library.

49  Rowley, *Christina Stead*, p. 18.

50  Dunphy, *Selected Writings*, p. 9.

51  Enid Barclay, 'Fevers and Stinks: Some Problems of Public Health in the 1870s and 1880s', *Queensland Heritage*, vol. 2 no. 2, May 1971, p. 4; Michael Cannon, *Life in the Cities*, Melbourne, Nelson, 1975, p. 128.

52  Katie Spearritt, 'New Dawns: First-Wave Feminism, 1880–1914' in Kay Saunders and Raymond Evans (eds), *Gender Relations in Australia: Domination and Negotiation*, Sydney, Harcourt Brace Jovanovich, 1992, p. 326.

53  David Dunstan, 'Dirt and Disease' in Graeme Davison, David Dunstan and Chris McConville (eds), *The Outcasts of Melbourne*, Sydney, Allen & Unwin, 1985, pp. 159–62.

54  Shirley Fisher, 'The Pastoral Interest and Sydney's Public Health', *HS*, vol. 20, no. 78, April 1982, pp. 74, 80–4; Cannon, *Life in the Cities*, p. 171.

55  Dunstan, 'Dirt and Disease', p. 155. The motion was put by Adelaide's Dr Joseph Verco, an active member of the Royal Society of South Australia.

56  E.g. Royal Commission on the Sanitary Condition of Melbourne, Victoria 1888–90; Royal Commission on Noxious Trades, Victoria 1870–71; Select Committee on Condition of the Working Class of the Metropolis, NSW 1860; Royal Commission for the Improvement of Sydney and its Suburbs, NSW 1909; Report on the Prevalence of Typhoid Fever in Brisbane and Suburbs, Qld 1884; *Sanitary Aspects of the Deep-Drainage System of Adelaide*, SA 1888; Health of Hobart, Tasmania 1896.

57   Cited in Barclay, 'Fevers and Stinks', pp. 3, 7.

58   John Lack, '"Worst Smelbourne": Melbourne's Noxious Trades' in Graeme Davison, David Dunstan and Chris McConville (eds), *The Outcasts of Melbourne: Essays in Social History*, Sydney, Allen & Unwin, 1985, p. 197; see also Fisher, 'The Pastoral Interest and Sydney's Public Health', pp. 73–89.

59   Lack, '"Worst Smelbourne" ...', pp. 190–1; see also Barclay, 'Fevers and Stinks', pp. 6–7.

60   Bolton, *Spoils*, p. 171; Barclay, 'Fevers and Stinks', pp. 5–6.

61   Louisa Meredith, *Over the Straits: A Visit to Victoria*, London, Chapman & Hall, 1861, pp. 186–208.

62   Cannon, *Life in the Cities*, pp. 27–8.

63   Victoria 1871, New South Wales 1873, South Australia 1875, Queensland 1876 and again in 1883, Tasmania 1878. Elinor White, *Lesser Lives*, Brisbane, 1937, pp. 16, 123–4.

64   Jennifer MacCulloch, 'Animals in Sydney c. 1880–1930', *Sydney Gazette: Organ of the Sydney History Group*, vol. 6, no. 6, 1984, pp. 33, 37–8.

65   R. Wright, *The Bureaucrats' Domain: Space and the Public Interest in Victoria, 1836–84*, Melbourne, OUP, pp. 243–5.

66   Cannon, *Life in the Cities*, p. 154; Michael Roe, *Nine Australian Progressives*, St Lucia, UQP, 1984, p. 174; Anne Wood, 'The Evolution and Growth of Women's Organisations in Queensland 1859–1958', *Journal of the Royal Historical Society of Queensland*, vol. 6, no. 1, 1959, p. 196; Strom, 'Some Events in Nature Conservation ...', p. 66; W. F. Gates, 'Reservations' in Barrett, *Save Australia*, pp. 19–22.

67   Dunstan, 'Dirt and Disease', p. 167; Peter Curson and Kevin McCracken, *Plague in Sydney: The Anatomy of an Epidemic*, Kensington, NSWUP, n.d., pp. 154–5; Roe, *Nine Australian Progressives*, pp. 185–90.

68   Powell, *Environmental Management*, p. 159; J. M. Freeland, 'People in Cities' in Amos Rapoport (ed.), *Australia as Human Setting*, Sydney, Angus & Robertson, 1972, p. 117.

69   Cited in Bardwell, 'National Parks in Victoria', p. 359.

70   Roe, *Nine Australian Progressives*, pp. 66–7; *ADB*, vol. 7, pp. 187–8; Barrett, *Save Australia*, pp. 1–15; Bardwell, 'National Parks in Victoria', pp. 355–9, 449–51.

71   Powell, *Environmental Management*, pp. 164–6; Robert Freestone, '"The New Idea": The Garden City as an Urban Environmental Ideal, 1910–1930', *JRAHS*, vol. 73, part 2, October 1987, pp. 100–3.

72   Freeland, 'People in Cities', p. 118; Walker, 'Fauna and Flora Protection', p. 25; Roe, *Nine Australian Progressives*, pp. 169, 202.

73   Freeland, 'People in Cities', p. 121; David Saunders, 'Man and the Past' in Rapoport, *Australia as Human Setting*, p. 128. Queensland was the last to form in 1963.

74   Walker, 'Fauna and Flora Protection', p. 25; Roe, *Nine Australian Progressives*, p. 202; Beryl Cook, Dr Thomas Price and Public Health, unpub. paper, USQ archives; Chisholm, 'The Great National Parks Movement', pp. 9–10; Lord Horder, 1935 cited by S. Murray-Smith in *ADB*, vol. 7, p. 188; W. F. Gates, 'Reservations' in Barrett, *Save Australia*, pp. 19–23.

75   See discussion in John Docker, *The Nervous Nineties: Australian Cultural Life in the 1890s*, Melbourne, OUP, 1991, pp. 214–20.

76   Bardwell also notes that Victorian conservation groups such as the Field Naturalists and the Town Planning Association described themselves as part

of a movement in this period. See her discussion in 'National Parks in Victoria', p. 468.

77  *Emu*, vol. IX, January 1910.
78  Bernard O'Reilly, *Green Mountains*, Sydney, Envirobook, 1968, pp. 127–8. The public feeling for national parks was experienced directly by the O'Reilly family, who took up the last land selection on the McPherson Range before Lamington National Park was declared, encircling them in a roadless wilderness.

## Part II  The Second Wave Builds: World War II to 1972

1  See discussion in the Introduction.
2  Patricia Grimshaw *et al.* (eds), *Creating a Nation*, Ringwood, Vic., McPhee Gribble, 1994, pp. 268–70; Malcolm Saunders and Ralph Summy, *The Australian Peace Movement: A Short History*, Canberra, Peace Research Centre, ANU, 1986, pp. 32–3.
3  S. Alomes, 'The Social Context of Postwar Conservatism' in A. Curthoys and J. Merritt (eds), *Australia's First Cold War 1945–1953: Society, Communism and Culture*, vol. 1, Sydney, Allen & Unwin, 1984.
4  Rachel Carson, *Silent Spring*, London, Penguin, 1962.
5  Stephen Fox, *John Muir and His Legacy: The American Conservation Movement*, Little Brown, Boston, 1981, pp. 292–9.
6  The first deaths due to mercury poisoning occurred at Minamata Bay in the 1950s. See Leonard J. Webb, *Environmental Boomerang*, Brisbane, Jacaranda, 1973, pp. 43–4.

### 3  Old Meets New

1  Patricia Grimshaw *et al.* (eds), *Creating A Nation*, Ringwood, Vic., McPhee Gribble, 1994, p. 263; Geoffrey Bolton, *Oxford History of Australia*, vol. V: *The Middle Way, 1942–88*, Melbourne, OUP, 1990, pp. 20–2.
2  Arthur Groom, *One Mountain After Another*, Sydney, Envirobook, 1992 (3rd edn), pp. 188–9.
3  Groom, *One Mountain*, p. 191. Groom's scenic rim vision was not implemented for another fifty years.
4  Stephen Johnston, 'Profile of a Parks Pioneer', *Park Watch*, no. 169, June 1992, pp. 8–12.
5  Bardwell, 'National Parks in Victoria, 1866–1956: for all the people, for all time', Dept of Geography, Monash University, 1974, pp. 544–7, 554.
6  Gerard Castles, 'Handcuffed Volunteers: A History of the Scenery Preservation Board in Tasmania, 1915–71', BA Hons thesis, University of Tasmania, 1986, pp. 58–74; Jessie Luckman, 'The Club's Role in Conservation', *Tasmanian Tramp*, no. 21, Jan. 1974, pp. 4–10.
7  Luckman, 'The Club's Role in Conservation', p. 7.
8  Castles points out that the HEC had no plans for Lake Pedder when this decision was made but the board did not even consider the uncertainty of the HEC's plans.
9  Allen Strom, 'Some Events in Nature Conservation Over the Last Forty Years' in *Australia's One Hundred Years of National Parks*, Sydney, NP&WS, 1979, pp. 67–72.
10  Bardwell, 'National Parks in Victoria', pp. 424–5, 551.

11    Ralph Summy and Malcolm Saunders, 'The 1959 Melbourne Peace Congress: Culmination of Anti-Communism in Australia in the 1950s' in Ann Curthoys and John Merritt (eds), *Better Dead Than Red: Australia's First Cold War, 1945–1959*, vol. 2, Sydney, Allen & Unwin, 1986, pp. 74–95.

12    Stephen Fox, *John Muir and His Legacy: The American Conservation Movement*, Little, Brown, Boston, 1981, pp. 292–9.

13    Kathleen McArthur, *Living on the Coast*, Kangaroo Press [1989], p. 100; Veronica Brady, *South of My Days: A Biography of Judith Wright*, Sydney, Angus & Robertson, 1998, p. 237.

14    Early in its formation the South Australian Trust took up unique natural features as well, as discussed later in this chapter: interview with Warren Bonython, 10 December 1993. Some of the trusts were also active on rural landscape preservation. New South Wales National Trust first met in 1945 and incorporated in 1950; South Australia, 1955; Victoria, 1956; and Western Australia, 1959: David Saunders, 'Man and the Past' in Amos Rapoport (ed.), *Australia as Human Setting*, Sydney, Angus & Robertson, 1972, p. 128.

15    Prince, *First One Hundred Years*, p. 34.

16    Graham Chittleborough, *Shouldn't Our Grandchildren Know?*, Fremantle Arts Centre Press, 1992, pp. 40–4.

17    A. J. Marshall (ed.), *The Great Extermination*, London, Panther, 1966.

18    Interview with Len Webb, December 1997.

19    Leonard J. Webb, *Environmental Boomerang*, Brisbane, Jacaranda, 1973, p. 1; J. G. Mosley, 'Towards a History of Conservation in Australia' in Rapoport (ed.), *Australia as Human Setting*, p. 152; Milo Dunphy, 'Emergence of the Australian Environmental Conscience' in Rob Dempsey (ed.), *The Politics of Finding Out: Environmental Problems in Australia*, Melbourne, Cheshire, 1974, p. 271.

20    Patricia Clare, *The Struggle for the Great Barrier Reef*, London, Collins, 1971, pp. 62–72; Judith Wright, *The Coral Battleground*, West Melbourne, Nelson, 1977, p. 2.

21    Wright, *Coral Battleground*, pp. 1–3; Judith McKay (ed.), *Brilliant Careers: Women Collectors and Illustrators in Queensland*, South Brisbane, Queensland Museum, 1997, pp. 60–1.

22    Clare, *The Struggle*, p. 91; Wright, *Coral Battleground*, p. 43.

23    Clare, *The Struggle*, p. 87; Wright, *Coral Battleground*, p. 19.

24    Wright, *Coral Battleground*, pp. 19–24.

25    The Australian Littoral Society evolved into the Australian Marine Conservation Society in the mid-1990s.

26    Wright, *Coral Battleground*, pp. 9–12.

27    Wright gives the figure of 80,920 square miles: *Coral Battleground*, pp. 32, 28–30.

28    Clare, *The Struggle*, p. 98; Wright, *Coral Battleground*, pp. 30–1; Brady, *South of My Days*, p. 226.

29    James Bowen, 'The Great Barrier Reef: Towards Conservation and Management' in Stephen Dovers (ed.), *Australian Environmental History: Essays and Cases*, Melbourne, OUP, 1994, pp. 240–2.

30    Wright, *Coral Battleground*, p. 31.

31    Wright, *Coral Battleground*, pp. 83–6, 88–9.

32    Wright, *Coral Battleground*, pp. 45–6, 51.

33    Wright, *Coral Battleground*, pp. 54, 84, 92, 119.

34 Australian Academy of Science, *National Parks and Reserves in Australia*, Canberra, 1968, p. 38; Wright, *Coral Battleground*, pp. 50, 59, 84, 122, 45, 54, 137.
35 In this period, more than two decades before the High Court judgments on Wik and Mabo, there was no legal consideration of indigenous title to the reef.
36 Wright, *Coral Battleground*, pp. 40, 42, 79, 118, 179; Bowen, 'The Great Barrier Reef ...', p. 248.
37 Wright, *Coral Battleground*, pp. 110–16, 121, 134–5, 141–2, 160–1.
38 Bowen, 'The Great Barrier Reef ...', pp. 251–2; Wright, *Coral Battleground*, p. 188.
39 Bowen, 'The Great Barrier Reef ...', p. 248; Geoff Mosley, 'Laying the Foundations: ACF in the Sixties', *Habitat*, vol. 24, no. 6, December 1996; Wright, *Coral Battleground*, pp. 49, 60–2.
40 Wright, *Coral Battleground*, pp. 62–6.
41 Francis Ratcliffe, *Flying Fox and Drifting Sand*, Sydney, Angus & Robertson, 1963 (2nd edn); Frank Fenner, 'Francis Ratcliffe: The Australian Conservation Pioneer', *ACF Newsletter*, February 1971, pp. 4–5; Francis Ratcliffe, 'The Australian Conservation Foundation', presented at the Wildlife Conservation seminar, UNE, 22–25 January 1965, ACF Council Meeting Papers, 1965–72, NBAC; Wright, *Coral Battleground*, pp. 4–5.
42 Ratcliffe, 'The Australian Conservation Foundation', p. 4; Francis Ratcliffe, 'Policy and Programme: Some General Considerations', Meeting of Council, 18–19 September, 1965, ACF Council Meeting Papers 1965–72, NBAC.
43 John Warhurst, 'The Australian Conservation Foundation: Twenty Five Years of Development' in Ronnie Harding (ed.), *Ecopolitics V: Proceedings*, Kensington, UNSW, 1992, p. 47.
44 Interview with Milo Dunphy, 6 July 1993.
45 F. N. Ratcliffe, 'Notes for Members of Executive and Council on Problems of Staffing, Finance and General Policy, (Confidential), May 1968', ACF Council Meeting Papers 1965–72, NBAC; Wright, *Coral Battleground*, p. 135.
46 ACF press release, 8 October 1971; ACF Council Meeting Papers, 1965–72, NBAC; *Bulletin*, 11 November 1972, pp. 11–12 in ACF Woodchips File, NBAC.
47 Derek Whitelock, *Conquest to Conservation: History of Human Impact on the South Australian Environment*, Netley, Wakefield, 1985, pp. 133, 138–9; interview with Warren Bonython, 10 December 1993.
48 J. M. Powell, '"Action Analysis" of Resource Conflicts: the Little Desert Dispute, 1963–72' in J. M. Powell (ed.), *The Making of Rural Australia: Environment, Society and Economy: Geographical Readings*, Melbourne, Sorrett, 1974, pp. 165–7.
49 Powell, '"Action Analysis" ...', pp. 165, 168–9.
50 Powell, '"Action Analysis" ...', pp. 169–70.
51 Libby Robin, 'Of Desert and Watershed: The Rise of Ecological Consciousness in Victoria, Australia' in Michael Shortland (ed.), *Science and Nature: Essays in the History of the Environmental Sciences*, Oxford, British Society for the History of Science, 1993, p. 127; Powell, '"Action Analysis" ...', p. 171.
52 Robin, 'Of Desert and Watershed', p. 124.
53 Powell, '"Action Analysis" ...', pp. 165–7; J. M. Powell, *A Historical Geography of Modern Australia: The Restive Fringe*, Cambridge, CUP, 1988, pp. 236–42;

NOTES (PAGES 110–122) 283

'Development of the Little Desert', ACF Little Desert Files. NBAC; R. D. Piesse, 'The Little Desert Land Settlement Scheme (Western Victoria)', ACF Little Desert Files, NBAC.
54 Robin, 'Of Desert and Watershed ...', pp. 146–7.
55 Robin, 'Of Desert and Watershed ...', p. 133 and esp. fn. 67. The group soon split and a more radical student group was formed.
56 Powell, *A Historical Geography*, p. 244; 'Development of the Little Desert', ACF Little Desert Files, NBAC; Transcript and SOBAC, *Conservation* in ACF Little Desert Files, NBAC; R. D. Piesse, 'The Little Desert Land Settlement Scheme'.
57 See Robin's evidence from participants in the Little Desert campaign, although her interpretation of these developments is from a different perspective: 'Of Desert and Watershed ...', pp. 141–5.
58 Milo Dunphy, 'Map Me a Coast and You Map My Childhood', *Habitat*, vol. 9, no. 2, 1981, p. 5; G. Piper, *My One Fourteen Millionth Share*, West Ryde, NSW, Temnor, 1980, pp. 76–8.
59 Piper, *One Fourteen Millionth*, pp. 76–8.
60 Merike Johnson, 'Environmental Policy Making—The Myall Lakes Experience', unpublished paper, 1988, TEC, pp. 3–5; National Trust of Australia (NSW), *Submission to an Inquiry held by Mr Walter Bunning*, 1973; Piper, *One Fourteen Millionth*, p. 86; interview with Milo Dunphy.
61 *The Colong Story*, Sydney, Colong Committee, n.d., pp. 7–9; 'The Colong Scandal', Colong Committee pamphlet; interview with Milo Dunphy, 6 July 1993.
62 *Colong Story*, p. 11; *Save Colong Bulletin*, no. 15.
63 *Colong Story*, pp. 11–12, 20–1, 32.
64 *Colong Story*, pp. 16–19.
65 *Colong Story*, pp. 15, 22.
66 *Colong Story*, pp. 21–9.
67 Kevin Kiernan, 'I Saw My Temple Ransacked' in Cassandra Pybus and Richard Flanagan (eds), *The Rest of the World is Watching: Tasmania and the Greens*, Sydney, Pan Macmillan, 1990, p. 21; Roger Green, *Battle for the Franklin*, Melbourne, Fontana and ACF, 1981, pp. 44–5; Dick Johnson, *Lake Pedder: Why a National Park Must be Saved*, Melbourne, LPAC Vic. and Tas. and Australian Union of Students, 1972, pp. 56–8.
68 Kiernan, 'I Saw My Temple ...', pp. 23–4; Green, *Battle for the Franklin*, pp. 51–2, 67; J. G. Mosley, 'Conservation Case Study 3: South-West Tasmania', *Tasmanian Conservation Trust Circular*, September 1970, p. 20.
69 Reece and the attorney-general are cited in Pamela Walker, 'The United Tasmania Group', Hons thesis, Political Science Dept, University of Tasmania, 1986, p. 20; Johnson, *Lake Pedder*, pp. 45–53, 58, 70–5; Keith McKenry, 'A History and Critical Analysis of the Controversy concerning the Gordon River Power Scheme' in *Pedder Papers: Anatomy of a Decision*, Parkville, ACF, 1972, pp. 9–30; interview with Milo Dunphy; Kiernan, 'I Saw My Temple ...', pp. 24–6, 32.
70 Green, *Battle for the Franklin*, pp. 54–6.
71 Green, *Battle for the Franklin*, pp. 70–1; Kiernan, 'I Saw My Temple ...', pp. 27–8.
72 Green, *Battle for the Franklin*, p. 67; Kiernan, 'I Saw My Temple ...', pp. 31–2.
73 *ACF Newsletter*, February 1972, p. 3; Report and Minutes of the Sixth Annual General Meeting of the ACF, *ACF Newsletter*, December 1972, pp. 4–5;

interview with Geoff Mosley, 5 February 1994; R. D. Piesse, 'Functions and Future of the Australian Conservation Foundation', *Tasmanian Conservation Trust Circular*, no. 23, June 1970; Green, *Battle for the Franklin*, pp. 61–5.

74  Mosely, 'Towards a History of Conservation', p. 152.
75  Interview with Milo Dunphy.
76  Green, *Battle for the Franklin*, pp. 76–8.
77  Wright, *Coral Battleground*, p. 103.

### Part III  The Campaigning Movement: 1973–1983

1  D. H. Meadows *et al.*, *The Limits to Growth: A Report for the Club of Rome's Project on the Predicament of Mankind*, London, Pan Books, 1974.
2  Elim Papadakis, *The Green Movement in West Germany*, London, Croom Helm, 1984. Fritjof Capra and Charlene Spretnak, *Green Politics: the Global Promise*, London, Hutchinson, 1984.
3  Pakulski, *Social Movements*, p. 186. See also Tamar Hermann, 'From Unidimensionality to Multidimensionality', *Research in Social Movements, Conflicts and Change*, vol. 15, 1993, pp. 181–202.

#### 4  Taking to the Streets

1  Manuel Castells, *The City and the Grassroots: A Cross-Cultural Theory of Urban Social Movements*, University of California, 1983.
2  For more detailed accounts of these campaigns, see Jack Mundey, *Green Bans and Beyond*, Sydney, Angus and Robertson, 1981; Richard J. Roddewig, *Green Bans: The Birth of Australian Environmental Politics*, Sydney, Hale and Iremonger, 1978; Marion Harding and Peter Manning, *Green Bans: The Story of an Australian Phenomenon*, Melbourne, ACF, 1975.
3  Interview with Jack Mundey, 25 April 1996.
4  For the political context within which the New South Wales BLF decided to undertake the Green Bans, see the film *Rocking the Foundations*, produced, directed and narrated by Pat Fiske, Sydney, Bower Bird Films, 1985.
5  Interview with Jack Mundey, 25 April 1996.
6  The first Green Ban was actually imposed by the Federated Engine Drivers' and Firemen's Association.
7  The calling of a public meeting became a necessary step for a community group to take before any BLF ban was imposed.
8  Mundey, *Green Bans and Beyond*, p. 82.
9  Mundey, *Green Bans and Beyond*, p. 105.
10  *Rocking the Foundations*.
11  Mundey, *Green Bans and Beyond*, p. 127.
12  Relations between Dunphy and Mundey, both ACF councillors, became strained when Milo directed preferences to the Democrat candidate, Richard Jones, ahead of Jack in the 1988 NSW Legislative Council elections. As a result Jones, not Mundey, was elected.
13  Harding and Manning, *Green Bans*.
14  Mundey, *Green Bans and Beyond*, p. 121.
15  Jack Mundey, 'Urban Development and the Common Man', *The Developer*, vol. 12, no. 1, 1974, p. 115, quoted in Richard J. Roddewig, *Green Bans*, p. 75.
16  See T. Powell, 'National Urban Strategy', *RAPI Journal*, vol. 12, no. 1, 1974.

17 Roddewig, *Green Bans*, p. 88.
18 Roddewig, *Green Bans*, p. 91.
19 Committee of Inquiry into the National Estate, *Report on the National Estate*, Canberra, AGPS, 1974.
20 Roddewig, *Green Bans*, pp. 109–12.
21 M. Wilcox, 'Conservation and the Law', *Habitat*, vol. 8, no. 3, June 1980, p. 30.
22 Interview with Moss Cass, 6 February 1997.
23 Dick Jones in Roger Green, *Battle for the Franklin*, Melbourne, Fontana/ACF, 1981, pp. 56–7.
24 Interview with Moss Cass, 6 February 1997.
25 Interview with Milo Dunphy, 6 July 1993.
26 Green, *Battle for the Franklin*, p. 61.
27 *ACF Newsletter*, July 1973, p. 1.
28 John Sinclair and Beverley Broadbent, 'Coming of Age: ACF in the 1970s', *Habitat*, vol. 24, no. 5, December 1996, p. 9.
29 John Warhurst, 'The Australian Conservation Foundation: Twenty-Five Years of Development' in Ronnie Harding (ed.), *Ecopolitics V: Proceedings*, University of NSW, 1992, p. 47.
30 Chittleborough later rejoined ACF.
31 See 'How the ACF Was Taken Over' by H. G. Andrewartha, C. Warren Bonython, A. Dunbavin Butcher, R. G. Chittleborough, D. F. Dorward, Patricia Mather and J. S. Turner, April 1974. Also statement by the ACF, 8 August 1974, ACF files.
32 Interview with Milo Dunphy. Also see 'The Election of the 1972–1975 Council and Consequent Changes in the Australian Conservation Foundation', statement by the ACF Council, 1974, for details of these payouts.
33 William Lines, *Taming the Great South Land: A History of the Conquest of Nature in Australia*, Sydney, Allen & Unwin, 1991, pp. 213–15.
34 Jim Falk, *Global Fission: The Battle over Nuclear Power*, Melbourne, OUP, 1982, p. 261. Acid mine drainage, not radioactive waste material, is the major pollution problem at the Rum Jungle site.
35 Cited in Falk, *Global Fission*, p. 258.
36 *Chain Reaction*, no. 1, 1976.
37 Ranger Uranium Environmental Inquiry, *First Report*, Canberra, AGPS, 1976.
38 The Communist Party of Australia had been able, under Aaron's leadership, to get over the illusion shared by many other Marxist groups that nuclear power was acceptable if used under socialism.
39 *Chain Reaction*, September 1975, p. 4.
40 It should be noted that the connections between the mainstream conservation movement and the anti-uranium movement were not seamless. Some people were anti-uranium for reasons that had little to do with the natural environment, and some well-known conservationists were not opposed to uranium. The ACF, for example, had a number of resignations over its anti-uranium stance, and one of its presidents, Sir Marcus Oliphant, was pro-uranium, a fact which made his term as president difficult.
41 *Chain Reaction*, no. 4, November 1975, p. 6.
42 *Chain Reaction*, no. 1, 1976, p. 39.
43 *Chain Reaction*, vol. 2, no. 2, 1976, p. 10.
44 *Chain Reaction*, vol. 2, no. 2, 1976, p. 14.

45  Malcolm Saunders and Ralph Summy, *The Australian Peace Movement: A Short History*, Canberra, Peace Research Centre, Australian National University, 1986, pp. 32–5.
46  Roger Moody, *The Gulliver File*, London, Minewatch, p. 597.
47  *First Ranger Report*, p. 185.
48  *First Ranger Report*, p. 177.
49  See Joseph Camilleri, 'The Uranium Debate and the First Ranger Report', *Habitat*, vol. 4, no. 5, April 1977, pp. 3–7.
50  *First Ranger Report*, p. 185
51  *First Ranger Report*, pp. 34–5.
52  See Barbara James in *Habitat*, vol. 4, no. 5, April 1977, pp. 13–20, for a discussion of energy alternatives to nuclear power, including the prediction of an enhanced greenhouse effect from fossil fuels.
53  *First Ranger Report*, p. 6.
54  Falk, *Global Fission*, p. 264.
55  Jim Falk, 'Movement Against Uranium', *Arena*, no. 46, 1977, pp. 31–3.
56  Falk, *Global Fission*, p. 265.
57  Falk, *Global Fission*, p. 265.
58  *CANP Newsletter*, November 1977, p. 1.
59  *Chain Reaction*, vol. 2, no. 4, 1977.
60  Interview with David Allworth, 2 May 1996.
61  *Chain Reaction*, vol. 3, no. 1, 1977, p. 3.
62  Cited in Falk, *Global Fission*, p. 267.
63  Falk, *Global Fission*, p. 268.
64  Ranger Uranium Environmental Inquiry, *Second Report*, Canberra, Australian Government Publishing Service, 1977, p. 9.
65  See *Chain Reaction*, vol. 4, nos 2–3, 1979.
66  See Falk, *Global Fission*, p. 385 fn. 42.

## 5  *Taking to the Bush*

1  Drew Hutton, 'From the Moral High Ground to Political Power', *Social Alternatives*, vol 11, no. 3, October 1992, p. 15.
2  Tim Bonyhady, *Places Worth Keeping: Conservationists, Politics and the Law*, Sydney, Allen & Unwin, 1993, pp. 3–4.
3  See John Sinclair (with Peter Corris), *Fighting for Fraser Island*, Alexandria, NSW, Kerr Publishing, 1994, p. 191. Bonyhady says the real reason FIDO did not use direct action was lack of resources: *Places Worth Keeping*, p. 148 fn. 2.
4  Sinclair, *Fighting for Fraser Island*, p. 31.
5  The group was called the Fraser Island Defenders Organisation after 1976.
6  Sinclair, *Fighting for Fraser Island*, pp. 147–54.
7  Bonyhady, *Places Worth Keeping*, p. 3
8  Bonyhady, *Places Worth Keeping*, p. 2.
9  Sinclair, *Fighting for Fraser Island*, p. 108.
10  Sinclair, *Fighting for Fraser Island*, p. 110.
11  Bonyhady, *Places Worth Keeping*, p. 9.
12  Bonyhady, *Places Worth Keeping*, p. 16.
13  Although this did not include the whole Great Sandy Region, as the conservation movement wanted.
14  This is a term that we have used a number of times. See further discussions in this chapter and in Chapter 8. There is a considerable body of literature

on regulatory capture in Australia. See, for example, John Dargavel, *Fashioning Australia's Forests*, Melbourne, OUP, 1995; Elim Papadakis, *Environmental Politics and Institutional Change*, Cambridge, CUP, 1996; Neil Gunningham, 'Negotiated Non-Compliance: A Case Study of Regulatory Failure', *Law and Policy*, vol. 9, no. 1, January 1987, pp. 69–95; Parliament of New South Wales, *Fifty-Second Report of the Public Accounts Committee: Inquiry pursuant to Section 57(1) of the Public Finance and Audit Act 1983, concerning the Forestry Commission*, 1990–91.

15  L. T. Carron, *A History of Forestry in Australia*, Canberra, ANUP, 1985, pp. 41–2.

16  Ian Watson, *Fighting over the Forests*, Sydney, Allen & Unwin, 1990, p. 8.

17  Interviews with Alex Colley, 9 July 1993, and Milo Dunphy, 6 July 1993.

18  Colong Committee, *The Colong Story*, Sydney, n.d., p. 12; Carron, *A History of Forestry*, p. 53.

19  R. and V. Routley, *The Fight for the Forests*, Canberra, Research School of Social Sciences, 1974.

20  Colong Committee, *How the Rainforest Was Saved*, Sydney, 1983, p. 3.

21  Colong Committee, *How the Rainforest ...*, p. 13.

22  Colong Committee, *How the Rainforest ...*, p. 17. The park proposal was derisively called Snake Park by conservationists because of its unnecessarily contorted shape. Also see Joseph Glascott 'Hopes Betrayed', *Sydney Morning Herald*, 3 May 1978.

23  Nan Nicholson, *Terania Creek*, 1982.

24  See Peter Prineas and Elizabeth Elenius, 'Why Log Terania Creek?', n.d., Sydney, NPA.

25  Ros Taplin, 'Environmental Policy and Policymaking in New South Wales', PhD thesis, Griffith University, Queensland, 1989, p. 83.

26  See 'The Role of the Forestry Commission', Big Scrub Environment Centre (Terania Creek file), September (year not available). Also Nicholson, *Terania Creek*, p. 23.

27  Ian Cohen, *Green Fire*, Sydney, Angus & Robertson, 1996, p. 18. Griff Foley, 'Terania Creek: Learning in A Green Campaign', *Journal of Adult and Community Education*, vol. 31, no. 3, November 1991, pp. 164–5.

28  Interview with Nan and Hugh Nicholson, 17 April 1993; Cohen, *Green Fire*, p. 19.

29  Taplin, p. 94.

30  Cohen, *Green Fire*, p. 29.

31  Interview with Jeni Kendall and Paul Tait, 17 April 1993.

32  Interview with Nan and Hugh Nicholson; Cohen, *Green Fire*, p. 22; Foley, *Terania Creek*, p. 166.

33  Interview with Jeni Kendall and Paul Tait.

34  Interviews with Nan and Hugh Nicholson, and with Dudley Leggett, 15 April 1993.

35  Interview with Ian Cohen, 15 April 1993.

36  Well-known environmentalist Joan Staples first came to prominence in this campaign.

37  Colong Committee, *How the Rainforest ...*, p. 31.

38  Vividly described in Cohen's *Green Fire*. Also interview with Cohen.

39  Colong Committee, *How the Rainforest ...*, p. 38. John Corkhill from northern NSW would continue to take the Forestry Commission to court for its failure to demand EISs before logging took place.

40  Colong Committee, *How the Rainforest ...*, Epilogue.

41  Watson, *Fighting over the Forests*, p. 116.
42  Watson, *Fighting over the Forests*, p. 121.
43  Green, *Battle for the Franklin*, p. 61.
44  Kevin Kiernan in Green, *Battle for the Franklin*, pp. 88–9.
45  Bob Brown spent a week fasting on the top of Mt Wellington in protest against the visit of the USS *Enterprise* to Hobart.
46  Phillip Toyne, *The Reluctant Nation: Environment, Law and Politics in Australia*, Sydney, ABC Books, 1994, p. 37.
47  Interview with Chris Harris, 27 February 1997.
48  Hutton, 'From the Moral High Ground ...', p. 15.
49  Geoff Lambert, known as a raconteur in The Wilderness Society, tells the story of a Tasmanian public servant who saved the Franklin by persuading Premier Lowe to sign the nomination for the South-West for World Heritage listing just before going off to the Labor caucus meeting that overthrew him as leader.
50  Toyne, *The Reluctant Nation*, pp. 38–9. Thompson in Green, *Battle for the Franklin*, p. 146.
51  Green, *Battle for the Franklin*, p. 147. Bob Brown illustrates how even a negative, defensive campaign can be pursued in a manner that presents an affirmative world view. He was stopped in the street by an old lady who told him how much she loved the 'no dams' slogan—'It's so positive, Dr Brown.'
52  When Milo Dunphy ran against John Howard in Bennelong in the March 1983 federal election, Howard was surprised to find several of his Liberal friends handing out how-to-vote cards for Milo who was, of course, giving his preferences to Labor.
53  Advice from the federal Attorney-General's Department that the Commonwealth had the powers to stop the dam was leaked to the *Age* and published 1 July 1982. It also pointed out that any decision not to intervene would be based on political not constitutional grounds.
54  Interview with Geoff and Judy Lambert, 3 July 1993.
55  Green, *Battle for the Franklin*, p. 262; interview with Milo Dunphy.

### Part IV  The Professional Movement: 1983–1990

1  Robert Leach, 'Australia, Asia and Pacific Integration: The Return of Radical Nationalism', *Dyason House Papers*, vol. 6, December 1980, pp. 7–8.
2  Paul Kelly, *The End of Certainty*, Sydney, Allen & Unwin, 1992. See Chapter 1 for a discussion of the meaning of these terms.
3  See Pakulski, *Social Movements*, p. 21.

### 6  *Fighting for Wilderness*

1  Cheryl Saunders, 'The National Implied Power and Implied Restrictions on Commonwealth Power', *Federal Law Review*, vol. 14, nos 3–4, March 1984, p. 274.
2  Wilderness Action Group, *The Trials of Tribulation*, p. 1; Toyne, *Reluctant Nation*, p. 65.
3  Cairns and Far North Environment Centre, Notice of meeting for 13 March 1981.
4  Benny Zable came to the Far North during this time. He taught the group the importance of theatre, especially spectacular banner-making.

5   A. Keto and K. Scott, *Tropical Rainforests of North Queensland: Their Conservation Significance*, Australian Heritage Commission, 1986, p. 1.
6   Quoted in Wilderness Action Group, *Trials of Tribulation*, p. 1.
7   Interview with Rosemary Hill and Mike Graham, 8 June 1992.
8   Toyne, *Reluctant Nation*, p. 207n.
9   *Courier-Mail*, 19 March 84.
10  Interview with Hill and Graham; Wilderness Action Group, *Trials of Tribulation*, p. 5.
11  Wilderness Action Group, *Trials of Tribulation*, p. 11.
12  *Canberra Times*, 3 February 1984, p. 9.
13  Interview with Hill and Graham.
14  *Age*, 31 October 1985, p. 3.
15  Jo Vallentine, 'Greening the Peace Movement' in Drew Hutton (ed), *Green Politics in Australia*, Sydney, Angus & Robertson, 1987.
16  Interview with Phillip Toyne, 8 June 1995.
17  Toyne, *Reluctant Nation*, p. 76. One of the problems of campaigning on wilderness issues is that, almost always, support for conservation is strongest in far-away metropolitan areas and weakest among locals who have most exposure to the beauty of these areas.
18  Graham Richardson, *Whatever It Takes*, Sydney, Bantam Books, 1994, ch. 10.
19  *Sydney Morning Herald*, 17 September 1986.
20  Toyne, *Reluctant Nation*, p. 128.
21  Toyne, *Reluctant Nation*, p. 128.
22  Interview with Michael Krockenberger, 4 February 1994.
23  Richardson, *Whatever It Takes*, p. 259.
24  Interview with Michael Krockenberger, 4 February 1994.
25  Michael Krockenberger, 'Kakadu: Unleashing the Wrath of Bula', *Habitat*, vol. 17, no. 1, February 1989.
26  Resource Assessment Commission, *Kakadu Conservation Zone: Final Report*, vol 1, April 1991.
27  Logging was also a major threat to forests but woodchipping, being more profitable than logging, was able to subsidise loggers to go into areas that were otherwise not profitable for exploitation.
28  Bill Hare, *Habitat*, vol. 14, no. 2, April 1986, p. 7; *Wilderness News*, vol. 6, no. 5, July 1985, p. 6.
29  *Wilderness News*, vol. 5, no. 1, March 1984.
30  Hare, *Habitat*, vol. 14, no. 2, April 1986.
31  *Wilderness News*, vol. 5, no. 1, March 1984, pp. 7–9.
32  *Wilderness News*, vol. 5, no. 3, July 1984, p. 4.
33  Robin Gray, *Hansard*, 23 April 1985.
34  *Habitat*, vol. 16, no. 4, August 1988, p. 7.
35  *Habitat*, vol. 14, no. 2, April 1986, p. 9.
36  *Wilderness News*, vol. 6, no. 5, July 1985, p. 3.
37  *Wilderness News*, vol. 6, no. 8, October–November 1985, p. 2.
38  *Habitat*, April 1986.
39  Interview with Bob Brown, 6 October 1995.
40  Interview with Bob Brown.
41  *Weekend Australian*, 8–9 March 1986, p. 1.
42  Interview with Bob Brown.
43  *Weekend Australian*, 8–9 March 1986, p. 1.
44  Interview with Bob Brown.
45  *Habitat*, April 1986, p. 10.

46   *Habitat*, vol. 14, no. 6, December 1986, pp. 17–18.
47   Richardson, *Whatever It Takes*, p. 216.
48   There are moves afoot to give this area its Aboriginal name of Kooparina Niara.
49   Joan Staples, *Habitat*, vol. 16, no. 4, August 1988, p. 4.
50   Toyne, *Reluctant Nation*, p. 78; *Age*, 25 August 1987.
51   Paul Kelly, *The End of Certainty*, p. 355.
52   Kelly, *The End of Certainty*, p. 243. Ian McAllister and John Warhurst (eds), *Australia Votes: The 1987 Federal Elections*, Melbourne, Longman Cheshire, 1988, p. 41.
53   McAllister and Warhurst, pp. 71–2.
54   Joan Staples, *Habitat*, vol. 16, no. 4, August 1988, p. 5.
55   Richardson, *Whatever It Takes*, p. 230.
56   Richardson, *Whatever It Takes*, p. 234.
57   Geoff Law, *Habitat*, vol. 16, no. 6, December 1988, p. 9.
58   Toyne, *Reluctant Nation*, p. 103.
59   *Australian*, 30 November 1988.
60   See Ian Penna, *Habitat*, vol. 14, no. 3, June 1986, pp. 30–1.
61   Jeff Angel, *Habitat*, vol. 15, no. 1, February 1987, p. 38.
62   *Wilderness News*, vol. 7, no. 5, June 1986, p. 7.
63   *Sydney Morning Herald*, 25 March 1986.
64   *Wilderness News*, vol. 8, no. 2, March 1987, p. 6.
65   Bonyhady, *Places Worth Keeping*, pp. 88–9.
66   Sue Salmon, *Habitat*, vol. 17, no. 4, August 1989, p. 7.
67   Linda Parlane, *Habitat*, vol. 14, no. 3, June 1986, p. 9.
68   *Environment Victoria*, March 1984, p. 7.
69   *Environment Victoria*, October 1984, p. 9.
70   P. Christoff and M. Blakers, *Jobs in East Gippsland*, 1985.
71   *The Sun Easterly*, 21 February 1985, p. 1.
72   *Environment Victoria*, December 1986.
73   *Wilderness News*, vol. 8, no. 5, June 1987, p. 6.
74   *ACF Newsletter*, December 1987, p. 1.
75   *Jarrah Forests or Bauxite Dollars? A Critique of Bauxite Mine Rehabilitation in the Jarrah Forests of Southwestern Australia*, Campaign to Save Native Forests (WA) and ACF, 1985.
76   *Greener Times*, November–December 1992, p. 20.
77   Interviews with Peter Brotherton, 7 April 1994, and Barbara Churchward, 10 April 1994.
78   Bonyhady, *Places Worth Keeping*, p. 60.
79   See articles on Antarctica by J. Broady and G. Mosley in *Habitat*, October and December 1983.
80   B. Brewster, *Antarctica: Wilderness At Risk*, Melbourne, published for Friends of the Earth by Sun Books, 1980; Doyle and Kellow, *Environmental Politics and Policymaking*, p. 248.
81   Geoff Mosley, 'Peace Out of the Cold', *Peace Studies*, vol. 48, 1986.
82   See Stuart Harris, *Australia's Antarctic Policy Options*, Centre for Resource and Environmental Studies, ANU, 1984.
83   Margaret Moore, *Habitat*, vol. 16, no. 4, August 1988, p. 21.

### 7   *Urban Issues and Pollution*

1   J. West, 'Goals, Strategy and Structure: How the Conservation Movement

Organised for Victory in the 1980s' in Ian Marsh (ed.), *The Environmental Challenge*, Melbourne, Longman Cheshire, 1991. West uses the term 'preservationist' to mean preserving wilderness in its pristine state, while the term 'conservation' often connotes creating a balance between the needs of humans and the natural environment.

2  Roger Moody, *The Gulliver File*, London, Minewatch, p. 824.
3  Moody, *The Gulliver File*, p. 824.
4  Interview with Angela Jones, 8 March 1996.
5  Interview with Ciaron O'Reilly, 10 March 1996.
6  Interview with Angela Jones.
7  Interview with Ciaron O'Reilly.
8  Gavin Gilchrist, *The Big Switch*, Sydney, Allen & Unwin, 1994, p. 44. Since then, despite the existence of certain well-known scientific heretics, the consensus among mainstream atmospheric scientists has been that significant global warming is occurring.
9  Gilchrist, *The Big Switch*, p. 11.
10 P. Graboski and J. Braithwaite, *Of Manners Gentle: Enforcement Strategies of Australian Business Regulatory Agencies*, Melbourne, OUP, 1986.
11 Jane Elix, *Habitat*, vol. 15, no. 3, June 1987, p. 11.
12 Garry Smith, *Toxic Cities*, Sydney, UNSWP, 1990, pp. 97–8.
13 James McClelland, former Whitlam government minister and chief justice of the NSW Land and Environment Court in the early 1980s, was critical of the Wran government's preparedness to override the court's decisions on issues. He writes in his autobiography, *Stirring the Possum*, that Wran reacted to McClelland's Parramatta Park decision by saying, 'We'll show old Jim who is boss.'
14 Quoted in Toyne, *Reluctant Nation*, p. 115.
15 Richardson, *Whatever It Takes*, p. 239.
16 Richardson, *Whatever It Takes*, p. 116.
17 Toyne, *Reluctant Nation*, p. 117.
18 Cassandra Pybus and Richard Flanagan (eds), *The Rest of the World Is Watching*, Sydney, Pan Books, 1990, p. 58.
19 N. Economou, 'Problems in Environmental Policy Creation: Tasmania's Wesley Vale Pulp Mill Dispute' in K. Walker (ed.), *Australian Environmental Policy*, Sydney, UNSWP, 1990, p. 141.
20 Criminal Justice Commission, *Report on Public Hearings into the Improper Disposal of Liquid Waste in South-East Queensland*, Brisbane, 1994.
21 Sharon Beder, *Toxic Fish and Sewer Surfing: How Deceit and Collusion Are Ruining Our Great Beaches*, Sydney, Allen & Unwin, 1989, p. 108.
22 Beder, *Toxic Fish*, pp. 112–13. Beder had a number of friends in STOP, which she joined in 1989; she subsequently became one of its spokespersons.
23 Sharon Beder, 'Sewerage Treatment and the Engineering Establishment' in Brian Martin (ed.), *Confronting the Experts*, Albany, NY, State University of New York Press, 1996, p. 38.
24 Peter Brotherton, 'Intractable Waste: The Problem that Won't Go Away', *Habitat*, vol. 18, no. 5, December 1990, p. 16.
25 Brotherton, 'Intractable Waste'.
26 Interviews with Peter Christoff, 5 May 1996, and Arnold Ewald, 7 May 1996.
27 Sharon Beder, *Bulletin*, 30 July 1991, p. 94.
28 Kate Short, *Quick Poison, Slow Poison: Pesticide Risk in the Lucky Country*, Sydney, Envirobook, 1994, p. 243.

29   Short, *Quick Poison, Slow Poison*, p. 243.
30   K. P. Sheridan, 'Forward to Pesticides Act 1978: What you Need to Know',
     Department of Agriculture, NSW, May 1979, in Short, *Quick Poison, Slow
     Poison*, pp. 238–9.
31   Short, *Quick Poison, Slow Poison*, p. 227.
32   Interview with John Pollak, 8 May 1996.
33   Interview with John Pollak.
34   Interview with Naomi Segal, 7 May 1996.
35   Queensland Government, *Official Opening of Mt Taylor Park*, Kingston, 1989.
36   Interview with Thelma Towers, 6 October 1990.
37   This campaign is ably analysed by Tim Bonyhady, *Places Worth Keeping*, ch. 6.
38   Bonyhady, *Places Worth Keeping*, p. 106.
39   See Grabosky and Braithwaite, *Of Manners Gentle*, and CJC, *Liquid Waste
     Inquiry*.
40   Peter Newman, 'Towards a More Sustainable City in Australia', paper
     delivered at the Royal Australian Planning Institute, 18th Biennial
     Congress, Perth, n.d.
41   Peter Newman and Jeffrey Kenworthy, *Cities and Automobile Dependence: An
     International Sourcebook*, Aldershot, Gower, 1989.
42   At about the same time the Brisbane City Council had begun an inner
     western ring road known as Hale Street, which almost tore apart the
     small, historic inner suburb of Petrie Terrace. See Nathalie Haymann,
     *Resumed in Protest: The Human Cost of Roads*, Grays Point, NSW, Bungoona
     Books, 1994.
43   Beder, 'Sewerage Treatment and the Engineering Establishment'.
44   *Sydney Harbour Tunnel Environmental Impact Statement: Teachers Guide*,
     Environmental Education Project, University of Sydney, n d.
45   *Environment Victoria*, no. 72, September 1989.
46   *Habitat*, vol. 15, no. 3, June 1987.


### 8  *Greenies and Numbers Men*

1    Peter Christoff, *Arena*, no. 70, 1985, p. 10.
2    *Peace Studies*, August–September, 1985, p. 25.
3    Christoff, *Arena*, no. 70, 1985, p. 15.
4    Interview with Bob Brown.
5    Several newsletters were put out by the Getting Together organising
     committee.
6    For the best analysis of green political theory in Australia, see Robyn
     Eckersley, *Environmentalism and Political Theory: Toward An Ecocentric
     Approach*, London, UCL Press, 1992.
7    Joseph Camilleri, 'Reshaping Australian Politics', *Social Alternatives*, vol. 6,
     no. 4, 1987, pp. 29–32.
8    *Australian Journal of Politics and History*, vol. 35, no. 3, 1989, pp. 459–64.
9    Pybus and Flanagan, *The Rest of the World is Watching*, p. 134.
10   Interview with Bob Brown.
11   *Habitat*, vol. 17, no. 4, 1989, p. 2.
12   Marcus Haward and Peter Larmour (eds), *The Tasmanian Parliamentary
     Accord: Public Policy 1989–92*, Canberra, Federalism Research Centre, ANU,
     1992, pp. 21–9.
13   Rosemary Sandford, 'The Salamanca Process' in Haward and Larmour
     (eds), *The Tasmanian Parliamentary Accord*, p. 129.

14   Bob Burton, *Ecopolitics V: Proceedings* edited by Ronnie Harding, University of NSW, p. 109 (abstract only).
15   ACF/TWS leaflet in C. Bean, I. McAllister and John Warhurst (eds), *The Greening of Australian Politics: The 1990 Federal Election*, Melbourne, Longman Cheshire, 1992, p. 53.
16   C. Bean *et al.*, *The Greening of Australian Politics*, p. 41; *Australian*, 8 March 1990.
17   Elim Papadakis, *Politics and the Environment: The Australian Experience*, Sydney, Allen & Unwin, 1992, pp. 173–8.
18   See Bean, McAllister and Warhurst, *Greening of Australian Politics*, ch. 7.
19   Bean, McAllister and Warhurst, *Greening of Australian Politics*, p. xiv; *Australian*, 28 March 1990.
20   Interview with Jack Mundey.
21   Penny Figgis, 'Lobbying—Persuasion and Pressure in the Political System', *Habitat*, vol. 13, no. 4, 1985, pp. 10–12; interview with Penny Figgis, 2 February 1994.
22   Interview with Penny Figgis.
23   *ACF Newsletter*, July 1986, p. 8.
24   See *ACF Newsletter*, May 1986, pp. 14–15.
25   *ACF Newsletter*, May 1986, p. 14.
26   *ACF Newsletter*, March 1986, p. 7.
27   *ACF Newsletter*, June 1986, p. 14.
28   Interview with Phillip Toyne.
29   The advent of the skilful NGO chief executive was exemplified in 1989 when Toyne and that other 'political carrier' Rick Farley from the NFF forged their partnership—see *Habitat*, February 1990, p. 13.
30   Richardson, *Whatever It Takes*, p. 214.
31   Interview with Phillip Toyne; *Habitat*, vol. 15, no. 5, 1987, p. 7.
32   *Habitat*, vol. 15, no. 5, 1987, p. 7.
33   Timothy Doyle, 'The Green Elites and the 1987 Federal Election', *Chain Reaction*, nos 63–64, 1991.
34   Timothy Doyle, 'The Myth of the Common Goal: The Conservation Movement in Queensland', *Social Alternatives*, vol. 6, no. 4, 1987.

### Part V   Dancing in the Dark: The Movement in the 1990s

1   Alberto Melucci, *Challenging Codes: Collective Action in the Information Age*, Cambridge, CUP, 1996.

### 9   Counter-Moves

1   W. L. Hare (ed.), *Ecologically Sustainable Development: Submission to the Federal Government on behalf of the ACF, Greenpeace Australia, The Wilderness Society and Worldwide Fund for Nature Australia*, Melbourne, ACF, 1990.
2   Mark Diesendorf and Clive Hamilton (eds), *Human Ecology, Human Economy*, Sydney, Allen & Unwin, 1997, p. 286.
3   Diesendorf and Hamilton, *Human Ecology, Human Economy*, p. 295.
4   Diesendorf and Hamilton, *Human Ecology, Human Economy*, p. 290. This 'bureaucracy-industry complex' is often commented upon by scholars. See M. Jänicke, *State Failure: The Impotence of Politics in Industrial Society*, Cambridge, Polity Press, 1990, quoted in Papadakis, *Environmental Politics and Institutional Change*, pp. 29–30.

5 Peter Kinrade, 'Turning Down the Heat: Australia's Greenhouse Obligations and Options', *Habitat*, vol. 23, no. 1, February 1995.

6 Jim Downey, Letter to the Editor, *Australian*, 16 May 1997. Peter Fries, 'Smoke and Mirrors', *Australian*, 21 May 1997.

7 The National Heritage Trust was one of the coalition's policy promises in the lead-up to the 1996 federal election. It would be funded from the one-third sale of the government's telecommunications carrier, Telstra.

8 Bob Brown, 'Federal Government—Greenhouse Deception', press release, 22 May 1997.

9 Peter Newman, 'Freeway Frenzy: The Last Gasp?', *Habitat*, vol. 23, no. 1, February 1995, pp. 48–52.

10 Sue Jackson and David Cooper, 'Coronation Hill Pay-back: The Case of McArthur River', *Arena*, October–November 1993.

11 See Toyne, *The Reluctant Nation*, pp. 151–74; 'Fast-Tracking and the McArthur River Mine', *Conservation News*, vol. 26, no. 2, May 1994, p. 1. Also documents obtained under Freedom of Information regarding Impact Assessment Study for the Ernest Henry mine.

12 Ralph Lindsey, 'Shoalwater–Byfield: National Estate Built on Sand', *Habitat*, vol. 19, no. 1, February 1991, pp. 4–7.

13 Wayne Sanderson, 'Greens Call for Inquiry into Mining', *Courier-Mail*, 11 April 1997.

14 Jim Downey and Helen Rosenbaum, 'What Was Yours Is Now Mines', *Habitat* Supplement, vol. 25, no. 7, February 1997.

15 *Australian*, 15 February 1996.

16 'Keep the Dirt on Australia's Uranium', *Chain Reaction*, no. 75, July 1996, pp. 9–118; David Sweeney, 'Unclean, Unsafe and Unwanted', *Habitat* Supplement, June 1996. Brian Williams, 'Prospect of New Uranium Mine As CRA Starts Search', *Courier-Mail*, 21 May 1997, p. 2.

17 Bob Phelps, 'Genetic Engineering: Fast Track for False Promises', *Habitat*, vol. 22, no. 1, February 1994, p. 40.

18 Interview with Bob Phelps, 4 February 1994.

19 Bob Phelps, 'Genetic Engineering'; interview with Bob Phelps.

20 The Colong Committee's long-cherished hope of World Heritage listing for the Blue Mountains is one that has been held up for years, not through a lack of proper assessment but because of a lack of political will, especially from the federal government. See *Colong Bulletin*, no. 150, May 1995, and no. 155, February–March 1996.

21 Jim Downey, 'Protecting Areas of Significance', *Habitat*, vol. 24, no. 3, June 1996, p. 10.

22 Mark Horstman, 'Cape York Peninsula: Forging a Black-Green Alliance', *Habitat*, vol. 20, no. 2, April 1992.

23 Horstman, 'Cape York Peninsula', p. 24.

24 This statement is called *Sharing the Land, Healing the Land*.

25 *Habitat*, vol. 24, no. 3, June 1966, p. 10.

26 Horstman, 'Cape York Peninsula', p. 20.

27 Keith Muir, 'Aboriginal Reconciliation and Wilderness', *Colong Bulletin*, no. 62, May 1997, p. 5.

28 Richard Ledger, 'Rangelands Pastoralism: Is it Sustainable?', *Habitat*, vol. 24, no. 1, February 1995, p. 44.

29 This was an estimate of the Australian Nature Conservation Agency in 1990. Other estimates put the figure much higher. For example, one report from the Department of Primary Industry in Queensland put the number of

cleared hectares in that state at 700,000, and some even talked about a figure of more than one million hectares per annum.

30   'A Freeholding Response to Wik Would Be the Biggest Land Grab since 1788', *Ecosphere*, vol. 18, no. 1, March 1997.

31   Resource Assessment Commission, *Australian Forest and Timber Inquiry: Final Report*, Canberra, 1992.

32   *Conservation News*, February 1993, p. 12.

33   Kevin Parker, 'Woodchip Debacle', *Wilderness News*, February–March 1995, p. 6.

34   Parker, 'Woodchip Debacle'.

35   Ted Mack, *North Shore Times*, 8 February 1995, quoted in *Colong Bulletin*, no. 149, March 1995, p. 3.

36   *Colong Bulletin*, no. 150, May 1995, p. 5.

37   Peter Wright and Carisa Triola, 'East Gippsland Countdown', *Habitat*, vol. 24, no 4, August 1996, p. 29.

38   *Colong Bulletin*, May 1995, p. 5.

39   Interview with Virginia Young,  4 June 1997.

40   See Bob Burton, 'Mothers Opposing Pollution: All Washed Up', *Chain Reaction*, no. 76, December 1996, pp. 28–31.

41   According to a Wilderness Society activist in the United States, 'they claim to lead a grassroots movement, but they are in fact speaking for industry and their grass is well watered with corporate money': quoted in Bob Burton, 'Nice Names—Pity about the Policies: Industry Front Groups', *Chain Reaction*, no. 70, January 1994, p. 17.

42   Roberta Garner, *Contemporary Movements and Ideologies*, New York, McGraw-Hill, 1996, pp. 356–8.

43   Doug McEachern, 'Business and the Environment' in *Business Mates: Power and Politics in the Hawke Era*, Sydney, Prentice Hall, 1991.

44   See Business Council of Australia, *Achieving Sustainable Development: A Discussion Paper by the Business Council of Australia*, 1990.

45   See Toyne, *The Reluctant Nation*, ch. 10, 'The New Federalism'.

46   Michael Gordon, 'Compromise We Had To Have', *Weekend Australian*, 7–8 June 1997, p. 21.

47   Anna Reynolds and Mark Horstman, 'APEC: Fast Track or Log Jam?', *Habitat*, vol. 25, no. 1, February 1997. These two well-known environmentalists participated in the Manila People's Forum.


*Epilogue*

1   Transcript of a speech to the Committee for the Economic Development of Australia, 15 May 1997.

2   Elim Papadakis, *Environmental Politics and Institutional Change*, Cambridge, CUP, 1996.

3   R. Inglehart, *Cultural Shift in Advanced Industrial Society*, Princeton, NJ, Princeton University Press, 1990.

4   C. Offe, 'New Social Movements: Challenging the Boundaries of Institutional Politics', *Social Research*, no. 52, 1985.

5   Ulrich Beck, *Ecological Politics in An Age of Risk*, Oxford, Polity Press, 1995.

# Bibliography

## Books, Articles and Theses

Allingham, Anne, '*Omnium Gatherum*: A Naturalist's Tradition in Tropical Queensland', in J. B. Dalton (ed.), *Peripheral Visions: Essays on Australian Regional and Local History*, Department of History and Politics, James Cook University, 1991.

Angel, Jeff, Letter to the Editor, *Habitat Australia* vol. 15, no. 1, February 1987.

Anon., 'A Freeholding Response to Wik Would Be the Biggest Land Grab Since 1788', *Ecosphere*, vol. 18, no. 1, March 1997.

Anon., 'Keep the Dirt on Australia's Uranium', *Chain Reaction*, no. 75, July 1996, pp. 9–18.

Australian Academy of Science, *National Parks and Reserves in Australia*, Canberra, 1968.

Australian Conservation Foundation, *Newsletter*, 1967–82.

Australian Conservation Foundation, 'Reports and Minutes of the Sixth Annual General Meeting of the ACF', *Newsletter*, December 1972.

*Australian Dictionary of Biography*, vols. 3–11.

*Australia's 100 Years of National Parks*, Sydney, National Parks and Wildlife Service, 1979.

Banfield, E. J., *Confessions of a Beachcomber*, Sydney, Angus & Robertson, 1968, rev. edn.

Barclay, Enid, 'Fevers and Stinks: Some Problems of Public Health in the 1870s and 1880s', *Queensland Heritage*, vol. 2, no. 2, May 1971, pp. 3–12.

Bardwell, Sandra, 'The Changing Face of the Victorian Countryside—Bushwalking in the Past, Present and Future', *Park Watch*, no. 150, September 1987, pp. 12–14.

Bardwell, Sandra, '100 Years of National Parks in Victoria: Themes and Trends', *Park Watch*, no. 129, Winter 1982, pp. 4–7.

Bardwell, Sandra, 'Queensland Pioneers', *Park Watch*, no. 120, Autumn 1980, pp. 14–15.

Bardwell, Sandra, 'National Parks in Australia', *Park Watch*, no. 116, March 1979, pp. 3–6.

Bardwell, Sandra, 'National Parks in Victoria, 1866–1956: "For All the People for All Time"', PhD thesis, Dept of Geography, Monash University, 1974.

Barrett, James (ed.), *Save Australia: A Plea for the Right Use of Our Flora and Fauna*, Melbourne, Macmillan, 1925.

Bean, C., McAllister, I., and Warhurst, John (eds), *The Greening of Australian Politics: The 1990 Federal Election*, Melbourne, Longman Cheshire, 1990.

Beck, Ulrich, *Ecological Politics in an Age of Risk*, Oxford, Polity Press, 1995.

Beder, Sharon, *Global Spin: The Corporate Assault on Environmentalism*, Melbourne, Scribe Publications, 1997.

Beder, Sharon, 'Sewerage Treatment and the Engineering Establishment', in Brian Martin (ed.), *Confronting the Experts*, Albany, NY, State University of New York Press, 1996.

Beder, Sharon, *Toxic Fish and Sewer Surfing: How Deceit and Collusion Are Ruining Our Great Beaches*, Sydney, Allen & Unwin, 1989.

Bodinner, H., 'Forestry in Western Australia', Perth, Battye Library, 1967.

Bolton, Geoffrey, *Spoils and Spoilers: A History of Australians Shaping Their Environment*, Sydney, Allen & Unwin, 1992 , 2nd edn.

Bolton, Geoffrey, *The Oxford History of Australia, vol. 5: The Middle Way*, Melbourne, OUP, 1990.

Bonyhady, Tim, *Places Worth Keeping: Conservationists, Politics and the Law*, Sydney, Allen & Unwin, 1992.

Bonython, Warren, 'The Origins and History of the Conservation Movement', in *Pollution and Conservation: Selected Papers*, Adelaide, Department of Adult Education, University of Adelaide, 1972.

Bowen, James, 'The Great Barrier Reef: Towards Conservation and Management', in Stephen Dovers (ed.), *Australian Environmental History Essays and Cases*, Melbourne, OUP, 1994.

Brandt, Karl-Werner, 'New Social Movements as a Metapolitical Challenge: The Social and Political Impact of a New Historical Type of Protest', *Thesis Eleven*, no. 15, 1986, pp. 60–8.

Brewster, B., *Wilderness at Risk*, Melbourne, Sun Books for Friends of the Earth, 1980.

Broady, Paul, 'Antarctic Wilderness—Will It Survive?', *Habitat Australia*, vol. 13, no. 3, June 1985, pp. 16–19.

Brotherton, Peter, 'Intractable Waste: The Problem that Won't Go Away', *Habitat Australia*, vol. 18, no. 5, December 1990, pp. 16–19.

Brown, Bob, and Singer, Peter, *The Greens*, Melbourne, Text Publishing Co., 1996.

Burgmann, Verity, *Power and Protest: Movements for Change in Australian Society*, Sydney, Allen & Unwin, 1993.

Burgmann, Verity, and Milner, Andrew, 'Intellectuals and the New Social Movements', in Rick Kuhn and Tom O'Lincoln (eds), *Class and Conflict in Australia*, Melbourne, Longman, 1996.

Burton, Bob, 'Mothers Opposing Pollution: All Washed Up', *Chain Reaction*, no. 76, December 1996, pp. 28–31.

Burton, Bob, 'Nice Names—Pity about the Policies: Industry Front Groups', *Chain Reaction*, no. 70, January 1994, pp. 16–19.

Business Council of Australia, *Achieving Sustainable Development: A Discussion Paper by the Business Council of Australia*, 1990.

Camilleri, Joseph, 'Reshaping Australian Politics', *Social Alternatives*, vol. 6, no. 4, 1987, pp. 29–32.

Camilleri, Joseph, 'The Uranium Debate and the First Ranger Report', *Habitat Australia*, vol. 4, no. 5, April 1977, pp. 3–8.

Cannon, Michael, *Life in the Cities*, Melbourne, Nelson, 1975.
Carron, L. T., *A History of Forestry in Australia*, Canberra, ANUP, 1985.
Carron, L. T., 'A History of Forestry and Forest Product Research in Australia',
    *Historical Records of Science*, vol. 5, no. 1, 1980, pp. 7–57.
Castells, Manuel, *The City and the Grassroots: A Cross-Cultural Theory of Urban Social
    Movements*, University of California, 1983.
Castles, Gerard, 'Handcuffed Volunteers: A History of the Scenery Preservation
    Board in Tasmania, 1915–71', BA Honours thesis, University of Tasmania, 1986.
Chisholm, A. H., 'Birds of a Feather Flock ...?', *Australian Zoologist*, vol. 3, part 8,
    January 1925, pp. 300–5.
Chisholm, Alec H., 'The Great National Parks Movement', Romeo Watkins
    Lahey Memorial Lecture, *NPA News*, March 1972.
Chisholm, Alec H., *The Joy of the Earth*, Sydney, Collins, 1969.
Chittleborough, Graham, *Shouldn't Our Grandchildren Know: An Environmental
    Life Story*, Fremantle, Fremantle Arts Centre Press, 1992.
Christoff, Peter, 'Environmental Politics', in Judith Brett, James Gillespie
    and Murray Goots (eds), *Developments in Australian Politics*, Melbourne,
    Macmillan, 1994.
Christoff, Peter, 'The Nuclear Disarmament Party', *Arena*, no. 70, 1985,
    pp. 9–20.
Christoff, P., and Blakers, M., *Jobs in East Gippsland*, ACF, 1985.
Clare, Patricia, *The Struggle for the Great Barrier Reef*, London, Collins, 1971.
Clelland, R. Allen, 'R. W. Lahey Memorial Lecture', *Supplement to NPA News*,
    October 1970, pp. 2–11.
Cohen, Ian, *Green Fire*, Sydney, Angus & Robertson, 1996.
Cohen, Jean, 'Strategy or Identity: New Theoretical Paradigms and Con-
    temporary Social Movements', *Social Research*, vol. 52, no. 4, Winter 1985,
    pp. 663–716.
Colong Committee, *The Colong Story*, Sydney, n.d.
Committee of Inquiry into the National Estate, *Report on the National Estate*,
    Canberra, Australian Government Publishing Service, 1974.
Commoner, B., *The Closing Circle: Nature, Man and Technology*, New York, Knopf,
    1971.
Cook, Beryl, 'Dr Thomas Price and Public Health', unpublished paper, USQ
    Archives.
Cotgrove, S., *Catastrophe or Cornucopia: The Environment, Politics and the Future*,
    Chichester, Wiley, 1982.
Criminal Justice Commission, *Report on Public Hearings into the Improper Disposals
    of Liquid Waste in South-East Queensland*, Brisbane, 1994.
Curson, Peter and McCracken, Kevin, *Plague in Sydney: The Anatomy of an
    Epidemic*, Kensington, NSWUP, n.d.
Davis, B. W., 'Characteristics and Influence of the Australian Conservation
    Movement: An Examination of Selected Conservation Controversies', PhD
    thesis, University of Tasmania, 1981.
Davison, Graeme, Dunstan, David, and McConville, Chris, *The Outcasts of
    Melbourne*, Sydney, Allen & Unwin, 1985.
de Strzelecki, P. M., *Physical Description of New South Wales and Van Diemen's Land*,
    London, Longman, Brown, Green and Longman, 1845; 1967, facs. edn.
Deacon, Desley, *Managing Gender: The State, the New Middle Class and Women
    Workers, 1830–1930*, Melbourne, OUP, 1989.
Diani, Mario, *Green Networks: A Structural Analysis of the Italian Environmental
    Movement*, Edinburgh, EUP, 1995.

Diesendorf, Mark, and Hamilton, Clive (eds), *Human Ecology, Human Economy*, Sydney, Allen & Unwin, 1997.

Dixon, Samuel, 'The Effects of Settlement and Pastoral Occupation in Australia upon the Indigenous Vegetation', *Transactions and Proceedings and Report of the Royal Society of South Australia*, vol. XV, 1892, pp. 195–206.

Docker, John, *The Nervous Nineties: Australian Cultural Life in the 1890s*, Melbourne, OUP, 1991.

Dovers, Stephen (ed.), *Australian Environmental History: Essays and Cases*, Melbourne, OUP, 1994.

Downey, Jim, Letter to the Editor, *Australian*, 16 May, 1997.

Downey, Jim, 'Protecting Areas of Significance', *Habitat Australia*, vol. 24, no. 3, June 1996, p. 10.

Downey, Jim, and Rosenbaum, Helen, 'What Was Yours is Now Mines', *Habitat Australia*, Supplement, vol. 25, no. 7, February 1997, pp. 17–24.

Doyle, T. J., 'Antarctica and the Science of Exploitation', *Habitat Australia*, vol. 13, no. 3, June 1985, pp. 12–15.

Doyle, Timothy, 'The Green Elites and the 1987 Federal Election', *Chain Reaction*, nos 63–4, April 1991, pp. 26–31.

Doyle, Timothy, 'The Myth of the Common Goal: The Conservation Movement in Queensland', *Social Alternatives*, vol. 6, no. 4, 1987, pp. 33–6.

Doyle, Timothy, and Kellow, Aynsley, *Environmental Politics and Policy-Making in Australia*, South Melbourne, Macmillan, 1995.

Dunphy, Milo, 'Map Me a Coast and You Map My Childhood', *Habitat Australia*, vol. 9, no. 2, 1981, p. 5.

Dunphy, Milo, 'Emergence of the Australian Environmental Conscience', in Rob Dempsey (ed.), *The Politics of Finding Out: Environmental Problems in Australia*, Melbourne, Cheshire, 1974.

Dunstan, David, 'Dirt and Disease', in Graeme Davison, David Dunstan and Chris McConville (eds), *The Outcasts of Melbourne: Essays in Australian History*, Sydney, Allen & Unwin, 1985.

Eastwood, Amy, Eastwood, Isobel, and Merlo, Hazel, *Uphill After Lunch*, Melbourne, Melbourne Women's Walking Club, n.d.

Eckersley, Robyn, *Environmentalism and Political Theory: Toward an Ecocentric Approach*, London, UCL Press, 1992.

Eckersley, Robyn (ed.), *Markets, the State and the Environment*, South Melbourne, Macmillan Education Australia, 1995.

Economou, N., 'Problems in Environmental Policy Creation: Tasmania's Wesley Vale Pulp Mill Dispute', in K. Walker (ed.), *Australian Environmental Policy*, Sydney, NSWUP, 1990.

Eddy, Elizabeth, 'The Green Movement in Southeast Queensland: The Environment, Institutional Failure, and Social Conflict', PhD thesis, University of Queensland, 1996.

Eder, Klaus, 'The New Social Movements: Moral Crusades, Political Pressure Groups, or Social Movements?', *Social Research*, vol. 52, no. 4, Winter 1985, pp. 869–90.

Ehrlich, Paul, *The Population Bomb*, New York, Ballantyne, 1968.

Elix, Jane, 'Kurnell Peninsula: Still in the Danger Zone', *Habitat Australia*, vol. 15, no. 3, June 1987, pp. 11–12.

*ESD Discussion Paper*, Commonwealth Government, Australian Government Publishing Service, 1990.

ESD Working Groups, *Final Report*, Australian Government Publishing Service, 1991.

Falk, Jim, *Global Fission: The Battle Over Nuclear Power*, Melbourne, OUP, 1982.
Falk, Jim, 'Movement Against Uranium', *Arena*, no. 46, 1977, pp. 31–3.
Fenner, Frank, 'Francis Ratcliffe: The Australian Conservation Pioneer', *ACF Newsletter*, February 1971, pp. 4–6.
Figgis, Penny, 'Lobbying—Persuasion and Pressure in the Political System', *Habitat Australia*, vol. 13, no. 4, August 1985, pp. 10–12.
Finney, Colin, *Paradise Revealed: Natural History in Nineteenth-Century Australia*, Melbourne, Museum of Victoria, 1993.
Fisher, Gillian, *Half-Life: The NDP: Peace, Protest and Party Politics*, Sydney, State Library of New South Wales Press, 1995.
Fisher, Shirley, 'The Pastoral Interest and Sydney's Public Health', *Australian Historical Studies*, vol. 20, no. 78, 1982, pp. 73–89.
Fitzgerald, Ross, *From 1915 to the Early 1980s: A History of Early Queensland*, St Lucia, UQP, 1984.
Foley, Griff, 'Terania Creek: Learning in a Green Campaign', *Journal of Adult and Community Education*, vol. 31, no. 3, November 1991.
Fox, Stephen, *John Muir and his Legacy: The American Conservation Movement*, Boston, Little Brown, 1981.
Frawley, Kevin, 'An Ancient Assemblage: The Australian Rainforests in European Conceptions of Nature', *Continuum*, vol. 3, no. 1, 1990, pp. 137–67.
Frawley, Kevin, *Exploring Some Australian Images of Environment*, Australian Defence Force Academy, 1987.
Frawley, Kevin, 'Rainforest Management in Queensland after 1900', *Habitat Australia*, vol. 13, no. 5, October 1985, pp. 4–7.
Frawley, Kevin, 'Early Rainforest Management in Queensland', *Habitat Australia*, vol. 9, no. 4, 1981, pp. 6–7.
Freeland, J. M., 'People in Cities', in Amos Rapoport (ed.), *Australia as Human Setting*, Sydney, Angus & Robertson, 1972.
Freestone, Robert, 'The New Idea: The Garden City as an Urban Environmental Ideal, 1910–1930', *Journal of the Royal Australian Historical Society*, vol. 73, part 2, October 1987, pp. 94–108.
French, C., 'A Naturalist's Health Trip to Northern Queensland', *Victorian Naturalist*, vol. XXIV, no. 11, March 1908, pp. 167–75.
Garner, Roberta, *Contemporary Movements and Ideologies*, New York, McGraw-Hill, 1996.
Gates, W. F., 'Reservations', in Sir James Barrett (ed.), *Save Australia: A Plea for the Right Use of our Flora and Fauna*, Melbourne, Macmillan, 1925.
Gilchrist, Gavin, *The Big Switch: Clean Energy for the Twenty-First Century*, Sydney, Allen & Unwin, 1994.
Glascott, Joseph, 'Hopes Betrayed', *Sydney Morning Herald*, 3 May 1978.
Goldsworthy, Lyn, 'World Park on Ice', *Chain Reaction*, vol. 37, pp. 36, 40.
Gooding, Janda, *Wildflowers in Art*, Perth, Art Gallery of Western Australia, 1991.
Gordon, Michael, 'Compromise We Had to Have', *Weekend Australian*, 7–8 June 1997.
Green, Roger (ed.), *Battle for the Franklin*, Melbourne, Fontana and ACF, 1981.
Greenpeace Australia, 'Behind the Fronts: The Anti-Environment Movement Unmasked', *Greenpeace Australia News*, vol. 4, no. 8, Summer 1994, pp. 4–5.
Griffiths, Tom, *Hunters and Collectors*, Cambridge, CUP, 1996.
Griffiths, Tom, 'The Natural History of Melbourne: The Culture of Nature Writing in Victoria, 1880–1945', *Australian Historical Studies*, vol. 23, no. 93, October 1989, pp. 339–65.

Griffiths, Tom, and Robin, Libby (eds), *Ecology and Empire: Environmental History of Settler Societies*, Melbourne, Melbourne University Press, 1997.

Grimshaw, Patricia, Lake, Marilyn, McGrath, Ann, and Quartly, Marian, *Creating a Nation*, Ringwood, Vic., McPhee-Gribble, 1994.

Groom, Arthur, *One Mountain after Another*, Sydney, Envirobook, 1992, 3rd edn.

Grove, Richard, H., *Green Imperialism: Colonial Expansion, Tropical Island Edens and the Origins of Environmentalism*, Cambridge, CUP, 1995.

Guy, Kevin, '"Sanctuaries" and Environmental Justice', *Chain Reaction*, no. 71, pp. 28–9.

Hall, Colin Michael, *Wasteland to World Heritage: Preserving Australia's Heritage*, Melbourne, Melbourne University Press, 1992.

Hancock, Marguerite, 'A Marriage of Opposites: Charles Joseph and Sophie La Trobe', in Penny Russell (ed.), *For Richer for Poorer: Early Colonial Marriages*, Melbourne, Melbourne University Press, 1994.

Harding, Marion, and Manning, Peter, *Green Bans: The Story of an Australian Phenomenon*, Melbourne, ACF, 1975.

Hare, Bill, 'The Tasmanian Woodchip Sellout: Hawke's Lake Pedder', *Habitat Australia*, vol. 14, no. 2, April 1986, pp. 4–11.

Hare, W. L. (ed.), *Ecologically Sustainable Development: Submission to the Federal Government on behalf of the Australian Conservation Foundation, Greenpeace Australia, The Wilderness Society and Worldwide Fund for Nature Australia*, Melbourne, ACF, 1990.

Harris, Colin R., 'The National Parks and Reserves of South Australia', MA thesis, Dept of Geography, University of Adelaide, 1974.

Harris, Stuart (ed.), *Australia's Antarctic Policy Options*, Canberra, Centre for Resource and Environmental Studies, Australian National University, 1984.

Haward, Marcus, and Larmour, Peter (eds), *The Tasmanian Parliamentary Accord: Public Policy, 1989–92*, Canberra, Federalism Research Centre, Australian National University, 1992.

Hay, P. R., 'The Environment Movement and Historical Scholarship: Patterns of Interpenetration', *Tasmanian Historical Research Association Papers and Proceedings*, vol. 40, no. 4, December 1993, pp. 154–64.

Haymann, Nathalie, *Resumed in Protest: The Human Cost of Roads*, Grays Point, NSW, Bungoona Books, 1994.

Hays, Samuel, P., *Conservation and the Gospel of Efficiency: The Progressive Conservation Movement, 1890–1920*, Cambridge Mass., Harvard University Press, 1959.

Heathcote, R. L., 'The Visions of Australia, 1770–1970', in Amos Rapoport (ed.), *Australia as Human Setting*, Sydney, Angus & Robertson, 1972.

Hermann, Tamar, 'From the Unidimensionality to Multidimensionality', *Research in Social Movements, Conflicts and Change*, vol. 15, 1993, pp. 181–202.

Hill, Senator Robert, Transcript of a Speech to the Committee for the Economic Development of Australia, 15 May 1997.

Hirst, J. D., *Convict Society and Its Enemies: A History of Early New South Wales*, Sydney, Allen & Unwin, 1983.

Holloway, G., 'The Wilderness Society: The Transformation of a Social Movement Organisation', BA Honours thesis, University of Tasmania, 1985.

Horstman, Mark, 'Cape York Peninsula: Forging a Green–Black Alliance', *Habitat Australia*, vol. 20, no. 2, April 1992, pp. 18–25.

Hutton, Drew, 'From the Moral High Ground to Political Power', *Social Alternatives*, vol. 11, no. 3, October 1992, pp. 13–16.

Hutton, Drew (ed.), *Green Politics in Australia*, Sydney, Angus & Robertson, 1987.

Jackson, Sue, and Cooper, David, 'Coronation Hill Pay-back: The Case of McArthur River', *Arena*, October–November 1993, pp. 20–2.

James, Paul (ed.), *Technocratic Dreaming: Of Very Fast Trains and Japanese Designer Cities*, Sydney, Left Book Club, 1990.

Jamison, A., Eyerman, R., Cramer, J., and Laessoe, J., *The Making of the New Environmental Consciousness: A Contemporary Study of the Environmental Movements in Sweden, Denmark and the Netherlands*, Edinburgh, EUP, 1990.

Jänicke, M., *State Failure: The Impotence of Politics in Industrial Society*, Cambridge, Polity Press, 1990.

*Jarrah Forests or Bauxite Dollars? A Critique of Bauxite Mine Rehabilitation in the Jarrah Forests of Southwestern Australia*, Campaign to Save Native Forests (WA) and ACF, 1985.

Jarrott, J. Keith, *History of Lamington National Park*, Beaudesert, Jarrott and NPAQ Inc., 1990.

Jarrott, J. Keith, 'The First Fifty Years', *NPA News*, vol. 50, no. 5, August 1980.

Johnson, Dick, *Lake Pedder: Why a National Park Must Be Saved*, Melbourne, LPAC Victoria and Tasmania, and Australian Union of Students, 1972.

Johnson, Merike, 'Environmental Policy Making: The Myall Lakes Experience', unpublished paper, Sydney, Total Environment Centre, 1988.

Johnston, Stephen, 'Profile of a Parks Pioneer', *Park Watch*, no. 169, June 1992, pp. 8–12.

Kaplin, Gisela, 'Women in Europe and Australia: Feminisms in Parallel?', in Norma Grieve and Ailsa Burns (eds), *Australian Women: Contemporary Feminist Thought*, Melbourne, OUP, 1994.

Kelly, Paul, *The End of Certainty*, Sydney, Allen & Unwin, 1992.

Keto, A., and Scott, K., *Tropical Rainforests of North Queensland: Their Conservation Significance*, Australian Heritage Commission, 1986.

Kiernan, Kevin, 'I Saw My Temple Ransacked', in Cassandra Pybus and Richard Flanagan (eds), *The Rest of the World Is Watching*, Sydney, Pan Books, 1990.

Kinrade, Peter, 'Turning Down the Heat: Australia's Greenhouse Obligations and Options', *Habitat Australia*, vol. 23, no. 1, February 1995, pp. 27–34.

Krockenberger, Michael, 'Kakadu: Unleashing the Wrath of Bula', *Habitat Australia*, vol. 17, no. 1, February 1989, pp. 4–8.

Lack, John, 'Worst Smellbourne: Melbourne's Noxious Trades', in Graeme Davison, David Dunstan and Chris McConville (eds), *The Outcasts of Melbourne: Essays in Australian History*, Sydney, Allen & Unwin, 1985.

Law, Geoff, 'Still Getting It Wrong on Tasmania's Forests', *Habitat Australia*, vol. 16, no. 6, December 1988, pp. 8–9.

Leach, Robert, 'Australia, Asia and Pacific Integration: The Return of Radical Nationalism', *Dyason House Papers*, vol. 6, December 1980.

Ledger, Richard, 'Rangelands Pastoralism: Is it Sustainable?', *Habitat Australia*, vol. 24, no. 1, February 1995, pp. 42–6.

Lennon, Jane, 'Cornerstone of the Continent: A History of Wilsons Promontory', *Park Watch*, no. 172, March 1993, pp. 5–8.

Lindsey, Ralph, 'Shoalwater–Byfield: National Estate Built on Sand', *Habitat Australia*, vol. 19, no. 1, February 1991, pp. 4–8.

Lines, William J., *An All-Consuming Passion: Origins, Modernity and the Australian Life of Georgiana Molloy*, Sydney, Allen & Unwin, 1994.

Lines, William J., *Taming the Great South Land: A History of the Conquest of Nature in Australia*, Sydney, Allen & Unwin, 1991.

Marks, Elizabeth, N., 'A History of the Queensland Philosophical Society and the Royal Society of Queensland from 1859 to 1911', *Proceedings of the Royal Society of Queensland*, vol. 71, no. 2, 1959.

Marshall, A. J. (ed.), *The Great Extermination*, London, Heinemann, 1966.

McAllister, I., and Warhurst, John (eds), *Australia Votes: The 1987 Federal Elections*, Melbourne, Longman Cheshire, 1988.

McClelland, James, *Stirring the Possum*, Ringwood, Vic., Viking, 1988.

McCormick, John, *The Global Environment Movement*, Chichester, UK, John Wiley, 1995, 2nd edn.

MacCulloch, Jennifer, 'Animals in Sydney c.1880–1930: Dogs, Cats and Horses', *Sydney Gazette: Organ of the Sydney History Group*, vol. 6, no. 6, 1984, pp. 31–41.

McDonald, Lorna, *Rockhampton: A History of City and District*, St Lucia, UQP, 1981.

McEachern, Doug, *Business Mates: The Power and Politics of the Hawke Era*, Sydney, Prentice Hall, 1991.

McKay, Judith, *Ellis Rowan: A Flower Hunter in Queensland*, South Brisbane, Queensland Museum, 1990.

McKay, Judith (ed.), *Brilliant Careers: Women Collectors and Illustrators in Queensland*, South Brisbane, Queensland Museum, 1997.

McKenry, Keith, 'Parks for the People', *Victorian Historical Journal*, vol. 49, no. 1, February 1978, pp. 23–36.

McKenry, Keith, 'A History and Critical Analysis of the Controversy Concerning the Gordon River Power Scheme', *Pedder Papers: Anatomy of a Decision*, Parkville, Vic., ACF, 1972.

Martin, Stephen, *A New Land: European Perceptions of Australia, 1788–1850*, Sydney, Allen & Unwin, 1993.

Meadows, D. H., Meadows, J., Randers, J., and Behrens, W. W. III, *The Limits to Growth: A Report for the Club of Rome's Project on the Predicament of Mankind*, London, Pan Books, 1974.

Melucci, Alberto, *Challenging Codes: Collective Action in the Information Age*, Cambridge, CUP, 1996.

Melucci, Alberto, 'The Symbolic Challenge of Contemporary Movements', *Social Research*, vol. 52, no. 4, Winter 1985, pp. 789–816.

Meredith, Louisa, *Over the Straits: A Visit to Victoria*, London, Chapman and Hall, 1861.

Moody, Roger, *The Gulliver File*, London, Minewatch, 1992.

Moore, Bryce, 'Tourists, Scientists and Wilderness Enthusiasts: Early Conservationists of the South West', in B. K. de Garis (ed.), *Portraits of the South West: Aborigines, Women and the Environment*, Nedlands, UWAP, 1993.

Mosley, [J.] Geoff, 'Laying the Foundations: ACF in the Sixties', *Habitat Australia*, vol. 24, no. 6, December 1996, Supplement, pp. 4–7.

Mosley, [J.] Geoff, 'Peace Out of the Cold', *Peace Studies*, no. 2, April–May 1986, pp. 2–7.

Mosley, [J.] Geoff, 'Antarctica: How Can We Save It?', *Habitat Australia*, vol. 11, no. 6, December 1983, pp. 2–7.

Mosley, J. G[eoff], 'Towards a History of Conservation in Australia', in Amos Rapoport (ed.), *Australia as Human Setting*, Sydney, Angus & Robertson, 1972.

Mosley, J. G[eoff], 'Conservation Case Study 3: South-West Tasmania', *Tasmanian Conservation Trust Circular*, September 1970.

Mosley, [J.] Geoff, 'The Tasmanian National Park System', *Tasmanian Tramp*, no. 17, January 1966, pp. 37–49.

Muir, Keith, 'Aboriginal Reconciliation and Wilderness', *Colong Bulletin*, no. 162, May 1997, pp. 1, 4–5.

Muller-Rommel, Ferdinand, and Poguntke, Thomas (eds), *New Politics*, Aldershot, UK, Dartmouth, 1995.

Mundey, Jack, *Green Bans and Beyond*, Sydney, Angus & Robertson, 1981.

Mundey, Jack, 'Urban Development and the Common Man', *The Developer*, vol. 12, no. 1, 1974.

Napier, S. Elliott, *On the Barrier Reef: Notes from a No-Ologist's Pocket-Book*, Sydney, Angus & Robertson, 1934, 6th edn.

Nash, Roderick, *Wilderness and the American Mind*, New Haven and London, Yale University Press, 1967.

National Trust of Australia (NSW), *Submission to an Inquiry held by Mr Walter Bunning*, 1973.

Newman, Peter, 'Freeway Frenzy: The Last Gasp?', *Habitat Australia*, vol. 23, no. 1, February 1995, pp. 48–52.

Newman, Peter, 'Towards a More Sustainable City in Australia', paper delivered at the Royal Australian Planning Institute, 18th Biennial Congress, Perth, n.d.

Newman, Peter, and Kenworthy, Jeffrey, *Cities and Automobile Dependence: An International Sourcebook*, Aldershot, UK, Gower, 1989.

Nicholson, Nan, 'Terania Creek', unpublished paper, 1982.

Norman, F. I., and Young, A. D., '"Short-sighted and doubly short-sighted are they ..."': Game Laws of Victoria, 1858–1958', *Journal of Australian Studies*, no. 7, 1980, pp. 25–32.

Offe, Claus, 'New Social Movements: Challenging the Boundaries of Institutional Politics', *Social Research*, vol. 52, no. 4, Winter 1985, pp. 817–68.

O'Reilly, Bernard, *Green Mountains*, Sydney, Envirobook, 1968.

O'Shanesy, P. A., *Contributions to the Flora of Queensland*, Rockhampton, Capricornia Collection, CQU, 1880.

Pakulski, Jan, *Social Movements: The Politics of Moral Protest*, Melbourne, Longman Cheshire, 1991.

Papadakis, Elim, *Environmental Politics and Institutional Change*, Cambridge, CUP, 1996.

Papadakis, Elim, *Politics and the Environment: The Australian Experience*, Sydney, Allen & Unwin, 1992.

*Papers Delivered at the Weekend Conference on National Parks Held at Cunningham's Gap National Park, Australia, 27–28 June 1964*, Brisbane, NPAQ, n.d.

Parker, Kevin, 'Woodchip Debacle', *Wilderness News*, February–March 1995.

Parkin, Sara, *The Life and Death of Petra Kelly*, London, Pandora, 1994.

Parlane, Linda, 'D-Day Arrives in East Gippsland's Woodchip War', *Habitat Australia*, vol. 14, no. 3, June 1986, pp. 9–10.

Penna, Ian, 'Eden Woodchipping: A Management Bind Over Fire and Wildlife', *Habitat Australia*, vol. 14, no. 3, June 1986, pp. 30–1.

Phelps, Bob, 'Genetic Engineering: Fast Track for False Promises', *Habitat Australia*, vol. 22, no. 1, February 1994, pp. 39–43.

Piesse, R. D., 'Functions and Future of the Australian Conservation Foundation', Tasmanian Conservation Trust Circular, no. 23, June 1970.

Piper, G., *My One Fourteen Millionth Share*, West Ryde, NSW, Temnor, 1980.

Poguntke, Thomas, *Alternative Politics: The German Green Party*, Edinburgh, EUP, 1993.

Powell, J. M., 'The Genesis of Environmentalism in Australia', in Don Garden (ed.), *Created Landscapes: Historians and the Environment*, Carlton, History Institute Victoria Inc., 1992.

Powell, J. M., *Plains of Promise, Rivers of Destiny: Water Management and the Development of Queensland, 1824–1990*, Brisbane, Boolarong, 1991.

Powell, J. M., *Watering the Garden State: Water, Land and Community in Victoria, 1834–1988*, Sydney, Allen & Unwin, 1989.

Powell, J. M., *An Historical Geography of Modern Australia: The Restive Fringe*, Cambridge, CUP, 1988.

Powell, J. M., 'A Baron Under Seige: Von Mueller and the Press in the 1870s', *Victorian Historical Journal*, vol. 50, no. 1, 1979, pp. 18–35.

Powell, J. M., *Environmental Management in Australia, 1788–1914: Guardians, Improvers and Profit*, Melbourne, OUP, 1976.

Powell, J. M., '"Action Analysis" of Resource Conflicts: The Little Desert Dispute', in J. M. Powell (ed.), *The Making of Rural Australia: Environment, Society and Economy: Geographical Readings*, Melbourne, Sorett, 1974.

Powell, T., 'National Urban Strategy', *Royal Australian Planning Institute Journal*, vol, 12, no. 1, 1974, pp. 8–10.

'Presidential Address, October 6, 1891', in *Transactions and Proceedings and Report of the Royal Society of South Australia*, vol. XIV, 1890–1, pp. 368–75.

Prince, J. H., *The First One Hundred Years of the Royal Zoological Society of New South Wales*, Sydney, Royal Zoological Society, 1979.

Prineas, Peter, and Elenius, Elizabeth, 'Why Log Terania Creek?', Sydney, National Parks Association, n.d.

Public Interest Research Group, *Legalised Pollution*, St Lucia, UQP, 1973.

Pybus, Cassandra, and Flanagan, Richard (eds), *The Rest of the World Is Watching*, Sydney, Pan Books, 1990.

*Queensland Museum Memoirs*, 1912–27.

Ranger Uranium Environmental Inquiry, *First Report*, Canberra, Australian Government Publishing Service, 1976.

Ranger Uranium Environmental Inquiry, *Second Report*, Canberra, Australian Government Publishing Service, 1977.

Rapoport, Amos (ed.), *Australia as Human Setting*, Sydney, Angus & Robertson, 1972.

Ratcliffe, Francis, *Flying Fox and Drifting Sand*, Sydney, Angus & Robertson, 1963, 2nd edn.

Reece, R. H. W., *Aborigines and Colonists: Aborigines and Colonial Society in New South Wales in the 1830s and 1840s*, Sydney, SUP, 1974.

Reid, G. S., and Oliver, M. R., *The Premiers of Western Australia, 1890–1982*, Nedlands, UWAP, 1982.

Reiger, Kerreen, *The Disenchantment of the Home: Modernising the Australian Family, 1880–1940*, Melbourne, OUP, 1985.

Reports of the Native Fauna and Flora Protection Committee of the Field Naturalists Section, *Transactions and Proceedings and Report of the Royal Society of South Australia*, vols XIV–LII, 1890-1928.

Resource Assessment Commission, *Australian Forest and Timber Inquiry: Final Inquiry*, Canberra, 1992.

Resource Assessment Commission, *Kakadu Conservation Zone: Final Report*, vol. 1, April 1991.

Reynolds, Anna, and Horstman, Mark, 'APEC: Fast Track or Log Jam?', *Habitat Australia*, vol. 25, no. 1, February 1997, pp. 13–15.

Reynolds, Henry, *The Law of the Land*, Ringwood, Vic., Penguin, 1987.

Reynolds, Henry, *The Other Side of the Frontier*, Ringwood, Vic., Penguin, 1981.

Richardson, Graham, *Whatever It Takes*, Sydney, Bantam Books, 1994.

Robin, Libby, 'Of Desert and Watershed: The Rise of Ecological Consciousness in Victoria, Australia', in Michael Shortland (ed.), *Science and Nature: Essays in the History of the Environmental Sciences*, Oxford, British Society for the History of Science, 1993.

Roddewig, Richard J., *Green Bans: The Birth of Australian Environmental Politics*, Sydney, Hale and Iremonger, 1978.

Roe, Michael, *Nine Australian Progressives*, St Lucia, UQP, 1984.

Rolls, Eric, *They All Ran Wild: The Animals and Plants that Plague Australia*, Sydney, Angus & Robertson, 1969.

Routley, R., and Routley, V., *The Fight for the Forests*, Canberra, Research School of Social Sciences, 1974.

Rowley, Hazel, *Christina Stead: A Biography*, Melbourne, Heinemann, 1993.

Rudig, Wolfgang, 'Peace and Ecology Movements in Western Europe', *West European Politics*, vol. 11, January 1988, pp. 26–39.

Russell, Penny, 'Paradise Lost: Sir John and Lady Jane Franklin', in Penny Russell (ed.), *For Richer, For Poorer: Early Colonial Marriage*, Melbourne, Melbourne University Press, 1994.

Salmon, Sue, 'The Last Stand: NSW Forest Battle Hots Up', *Habitat Australia*, vol. 17, no. 4, August 1989, pp. 4–8.

Sanderson, Wayne, 'Greens Call for Inquiry into Mining', *Courier Mail*, 11 April 1997.

Sandford, Rosemary, 'The Salamanca Process,' in Marcus Haward and Peter Larmour (eds.) *The Tasmanian Parliamentary Accord: Public Policy 1989–92*, Canberra, Federalism Research Centre, Australian National University, 1992.

Saunders, Cheryl, 'The National Implied Power and Implied Restrictions on Commonwealth Power', *Federal Law Review*, vol. 14, nos 3–4, March 1984, pp. 267–73.

Saunders, David, 'Man and the Past', in Rapoport, Amos (ed), *Australia as Human Setting*, Sydney, Angus and Robertson, 1972.

Saunders, Malcolm and Summy, Ralph, *The Australian Peace Movement: A Short History*, Canberra, Peace Research Centre, Australian National University, 1986.

Selway, W. H., 'The National Parks and Forests Reserves of Australia', *Transactions and Proceedings and Reports of the Royal Society of South Australia*, vol. XXXIV, 1910, pp. 279–305.

Sheridan, K. P., 'Forward to Pesticides Act 1978: What You Need to Know', Department of Agriculture, New South Wales, May 1979.

Short, Kate, *Quick Poison Slow Poison: Pesticide Risk in the Lucky Country*, Sydney, Envirobook, 1994.

Sinclair, John and Broadbent, Beverley, 'Coming of Age: ACF in the Seventies, *Habitat Australia*, vol. 24, no. 5, December, 1996, Supplement, pp. 8–14.

Sinclair, John and Corris, Peter, *Fighting for Fraser Island*, Alexandria, New South Wales, Kerr Publishing Pty Ltd, 1994.

Smith, Gary, *Toxic Cities*, Sydney, University of New South Wales Press, 1990.

Smith, James, *Contributions to the Geology of Central Queensland*, Rockhampton Municipal Library, 1892.

South Australian Sub-Committee of Australian Academy of Science National Parks Committee, *Report of South Australian Sub-Committee*, Canberra, AAS.

Spearritt, Katie, 'New Dawns: First Wave Feminism 1880–1914', in Kay Saunders, and Ray Evans, (eds), *Gender Relations in Australia: Domination and Negotiation*, Sydney, Harcourt Brace Jovanovich, 1992.

Spender, Lynne (ed.), *Her Selection: Writings by Nineteenth-Century Australian Women*, Ringwood, Penguin, 1988.

Staples, Joan, 'Getting It Wrong on Tasmania's Forests', *Habitat Australia*, vol. 16, no. 4, August 1988, pp. 3–6.

Stevens, Paul, 'Plants, Forests and Wealth: Vegetation Conservation in Queensland, 1870–1900', in B. J. Dalton (ed.), *Peripheral Visions: Essays on Australian Regional and Local History*, Department of History and Politics, James Cook University, 1991.

Strom, Allen, 'Impressions of a Developing Conservation Ethic, 1870–1930,' in *Australia's 100 Years of National Parks*, Sydney, National Parks and Wildlife Service, 1979.

Summy, Ralph and Saunders, Malcolm, 'The 1959 Melbourne Peace Congress: Culmination of Anti-Communism in the 1950s' in Ann Curthoys and John Merritt, *Better Dead than Red, Australia's First Cold War 1945–1959*, vol. 2, Sydney, Allen and Unwin, 1986.

Swann, Margaret, 'Mrs Meredith and Miss Atkinson, Writers and Naturalists', *Journal of the Royal Australian Historical Society*, vol. XV, part 1, 1929, pp. 1–29.

Sweeney, Dave, 'Unclean, Unsafe and Unwanted', *Habitat Australia*, June 1996, Supplement, pp. 17–24.

*Sydney Harbour Tunnel Environmental Impact Statement: Teachers Guide*, Environmental Education Project, University of Sydney, n.d.

*Sydney Mail*, March 1919.

Taplin, Ros, 'Environmental Policymaking in New South Wales: Wran and the Rainforests', PhD Thesis, Griffith University, Nathan, Qld, 1989.

Tarrow, Sidney, *Power in Movement: Social Movements, Collective Action and Politics*, New York, Cambridge University Press, 1994.

Taylor, Peter, *Growing Up: Forestry in Queensland*, Sydney, Allen and Unwin, 1997.

Thorpe, Bill, 'A Social History of Colonial Queensland: Towards a Marxist Analysis', PhD thesis, History Department, University of Queensland, 1986.

Thozet, A., *Notes on Some of the Roots, Tubers, Bulbs and Fruits used as Vegetable Food by the Aboriginals of Northern Queensland*, Rockhampton, W. H. Buzacott, 1866.

Thwaites, Jack, 'John Watt Beattie', *Tasmanian Tramp*, no. 23, June 1979, pp. 72–80.

Tilly, Charles, 'Models and Realities of Popular Collective Action', *Social Research*, vol. 52, no. 4, Winter 1985, pp. 717–47.

Touraine, Alain, 'An Introduction to the Study of Social Movements', *Social Research*, vol. 52, no. 4, Winter 1985, pp. 749–87.

Touraine, Alain, Dubet, François, Wieviorka, Michel, and Strzelecki, Jan, *Solidarity: The Analysis of a Social Movement, Poland 1980–81*, Cambridge, Cambridge University Press, 1985.

Touraine, Alain, *The Voice and the Eye*, Cambridge, Cambridge University Press, 1981.

Townend, Christine, *A Voice for the Animals: How Animal Liberation Grew*, Kenthurst, NSW, Kangaroo Press, 1981.

Toyne, Phillip, *The Reluctant Nation: Environment, Law and Politics in Australia*, Sydney, ABC Books, 1994.

Vallentine, Jo, 'Greening the Peace Movement', in Drew Hutton, (ed.), *Green Politics in Australia*, Sydney, Angus and Robertson, 1987.

Walker, K. J. (ed.), *Australian Environmental Policy*, Sydney, University of New South Wales Press, 1992.

Walker, Pamela, 'The United Tasmania Group', BA Hons thesis, Political Science Department, University of Tasmania, 1986.

Walker, R. B., 'Fauna and Flora Protection in New South Wales, 1866–1948', *Journal of Australian Studies*, no. 28, 1991, pp. 17–28.

Warhurst, John, 'The Australian Conservation Foundation: Twenty Five Years of Development' in Ronnie Harding (ed.) *Ecopolitics V: Proceedings*, Kensington, University of New South Wales, 1992, pp. 46–54.

Watson, Ian, *Fighting Over the Forests*, Sydney, Allen and Unwin, 1990.

Webb, Leonard J., *Environmental Boomerang*, Brisbane, Jacaranda Press, 1973.

Webb, L. J., Whitelock, D. and le Gay Brereton, J. (eds), *The Last of Lands: Conservation in Australia*, Brisbane, Jacaranda Press, 1969.

Webb, Len, 'The Rape of the Forests' in A. J. Marshall (ed.), *The Great Extermination*, London, Heinemann, 1966.

West, J., 'Goals, Strategy and Structure: How the Conservation Movement Organised for Victory in the 1980s' in Ian Marsh (ed.), *The Environmental Challenge*, Melbourne, Longford Cheshire, 1991.

Western Australian Sub-committee of the Australian Academy of Science Committee on National Parks, *National Parks and Reserves in Western Australia*, Perth, Australian Academy of Science and the National Parks Board of Western Australia, n.d.

White, C. T., 'Henry Tryon—First Hon. Secretary, Royal Society of Queensland, and His Place in Queensland Science', *Proceedings of the Royal Society of Queensland*, vol. 56, no. 8, 1945, pp. 77–80.

White, Elinor, *Lesser Lives*, Brisbane, 1937.

Whitelock, Derek, *Conquest to Conservation: History of Human Impact on the South Australian Environment*, Netley, SA, Wakefield Press, 1985.

Whittell, H. M., 'The Visits of John Gilbert, Naturalist, to Swan River Colony', in Battye Library.

Wilcox, M, 'Conservation and the Law', *Habitat Australia*, vol. 8, no. 3, June 1980, pp. 26–31.

Williams, Brian, 'Prospect of New Uranium Mine as CRA Starts Search', *Courier Mail*, 21 April 1997.

Wood, Anne, 'The Evolution and Growth of Women's Organisations in Queensland 1859–1958', *Journal of Royal Historical Society of Queensland*, vol. 6, no. 1, 1959, pp. 184–213.

World Commission on Environment and Development, *Our Common Future*, Melbourne, Oxford University Press, 1990.

Wright, Judith, *The Coral Battleground*, West Melbourne, Nelson, 1977.

Wright, Peter, and Triola, Carisa, 'East Gippsland Countdown', *Habitat Australia*, vol. 24, no. 4, August 1996, p. 29.

Wright, R., *The Bureaucrats' Domain: Space and Public Interest in Victoria, 1836–84*, Melbourne, Oxford University Press, 1989.

Wright, R., 'The Fight for Phillip Island, 1861–1868', *Journal of Australian Studies*, no. 7, November 1980, pp. 25–32.

## Interviews

Allworth, David, Friends of the Earth, Toowoomba, 2 May 1996.

Angel, Jeff, Total Environment Centre, Sydney, 8 July 1992.

Beresford, Marcus, South Australian Conservation Council, Adelaide, 8 December 1993.

Bonython, Warren, Australian Conservation Council and South Australian Conservation Council, Adelaide, 10 December 1993.

Brotherton, Peter, Australian Conservation Council, Melbourne, 7 February 1994.

Brown, Bob, The Wilderness Society and Australian Greens, Brisbane, 21 April 1996.

Cass, Moss, Minister for the Environment, Whitlam Government 1972–75, Melbourne, 6 February 1997.

Churchward, Barbara, Conservation Council of Western Australia, Perth, 5 December 1993.

Cohen, Ian, NSW: Nightcap campaign and Australian Greens, Broken Head Beach, 15 April 1993.

Colley, Alex, Colong Foundation, Sydney, 9 July 1993.

Diesendorf, Mark, Australian Conservation Foundation, Canberra, 10 June 1995.

Dunphy, Milo, Total Environment Centre, Sydney, 6 July 1993.

Falk, Jim, Friends of the Earth and Australian Conservation Foundation, Wollongong, 29 June 1993.

Figgis, Penny, Australian Conservation Foundation, Melbourne, 8 July 1993.

Graham, Mike, Cairns and Far North Environment Centre, Kuranda, 8 June 1992.

Harris, Chris, The Wilderness Society, Sydney, 27 February 1997.

Hardy, Craig, Capricorn Conservation Council, Rockhampton, 27 November 1992.

Hill, Rosemary, Cairns and Far North Environment Centre, Kuranda, 8 June 1992.

Jeffreys, Adrian, The Wildlife Preservation Society of Queensland, Brisbane, 30 June 1992.

Jones, Angela, Roxby Downs campaign, Brisbane, 8 July 1994.

Kendell, Jeni, Terania Campaign, Nimbin, 17 April 1993.

Krockenberger, Mike, Australian Conservation Foundation, Melbourne, 4 February 1994.

Lambert, Geoff, The Wilderness Society, Sydney, 3 July 1993.

Lambert, Judy, The Wilderness Society, Sydney, 3 July 1993.

Leggett, Dudley, Terania Native Forest Action Group, Byron Bay, 15 April 1993.

Luckman, Jessie, interviewed by Greg Borschmann, Environmental Awareness in Australia, Oral History Project, NLA.

McCabe, John, Capricorn Conservation Council and Queensland Conservation Council, Rockhampton, 28 November 1992.

Mosley, Geoff, Australian Conservation Foundation, Melbourne, 5 February 1994.

Mundey, Jack, Builders Labourers' Federation and Australian Conservation Foundation, Sydney, 25 April 1996.

Nicholson, Hugh, Terania Native Forest Action Group, Terania Creek, 17 April 1993.

Nicholson, Nan, Terania Native Forest Action Group, Terania Creek, 17 April 1993.

O'Brien, Pat, Wildlife Preservation Society of Queensland, Rockhampton, 27 November 1992.

O'Reilly, Ciaron, Roxby Downs campaign, Brisbane, 9 July 1994.
Phelps, Bob, Australian Conservation Foundation, Melbourne, 4 February 1994.
Pollak, John, Toxic Chemicals Committee, Sydney, 8 May 1996.
Robertson, Margaret, The Wilderness Society, Perth, 4 December 1993.
Robertson, Peter, The Wilderness Society, Perth, 4 December 1993.
Segal, Naomi, Greenpeace and Householders for Safe Pesticide Use, Brisbane and Perth, 19 February 1994.
Short, Kate, Toxic Chemicals Committee, St. Albans, 6 May 1996.
Silby, John, South Australian Conservation Council, Adelaide, 10 December 1993.
Strom, Alan, The Wildlife Preservation Society of Australia and Sydney Bushwalkers, Sydney, 10 July 1993.
Towers, Thelma, Residents Against Toxic Substances, Kingston, Brisbane, April–May 1990.
Toyne, Phillip, Australian Conservation Council, Canberra, 8 June 1995.
Valentine, Peter, James Cook University, Townsville, 12 June 1996.
Walker, Sid, Nature Conservation Council of New South Wales, Sydney, 25 April 1996.
Webb, Len, December 1997.
Wilkie, S., Wilderness Action Group, Cairns, 10 June 1992.
Wright, Judith, interviewed by Greg Borschmann, Environmental Awareness in Australia, Oral History Project, NLA.
Young, Virginia, The Wilderness Society, Brisbane, 4 June 1997.


### Archives and newsletters

Australian Conservation Foundation: Council Meeting Papers 1965–83, NBAC, ANU.
Australian Conservation Foundation: Councillors' Files, NBAC, ANU.
Australian Conservation Foundation: *Habitat Australia.*
Australian Conservation Foundation: History File, NBAC, ANU.
Australian Conservation Foundation: Legal Files, NBAC, ANU.
Australian Conservation Foundation: Letters to the Editor, NBAC, ANU.
Australian Conservation Foundation: Little Desert File, 1969, NBAC, ANU.
Australian Conservation Foundation: Little Desert File, Cuttings, 1964–69, NBAC, ANU.
Australian Conservation Foundation: *Newsletter,* 1967–82.
Australian Conservation Foundation: Newspaper Cutting Books—Conservation, ACF office, Melbourne.
Australian Conservation Foundation: Submissions, ACF office, Melbourne.
Australian Conservation Foundation: Woodchip Files, 1969–76, 1979–80, NBAC, ANU.
Australian Conservation Foundation: Wingecarribee 1968–69, NBAC, ANU.
Barwick, Sir Garfield, *Economic Growth and the Environment,* Occasional Publication no. 7, Australian Conservation Foundation, September 1971.
Barwick, Sir Garfield, *The Preservation of Diversity,* Occasional Publication no. 5, Australian Conservation Foundation, n.d.
Big Scrub Environment Centre, 'The Role of the Forestry Commission' (Terania Creek file), September (year not available).
Cairns and Far North Environment Centre, Archival material on Mt Windsor and Wet Tropics.

Campaign Against Nuclear Power (Qld), *Newsletter*, 1976–79.
Campaign to Save Native Forests, file, Battye Library, 1975.
Capricorn Conservation Council: Minute Book, 1978–87.
Capricorn Conservation Council: Minutes of AGMs 1973, 1975–76.
Central Queensland Native Birds Protection Society, *Nature Notes 1901–1954*, The Patrick V. Maloney Collection, Rockhampton and District Historical Society.
*The Colong Bulletin.* (Colong Foundation)
*Conservation and Mining in Modern Australia*, Viewpoint no. 6, Australian Conservation Foundation, August 1971.
Conservation Council of South Australia, *Annual Reports*, 1982–93.
Conservation Council of South Australia, Roxby Downs Files.
Conservation Council of South Australia, Lead Toxicity Files.
Conservation Council of South Australia, Submissions 1982–92.
Conservation Council of South Australia, *Environment South Australia*, 1992–93.
Conservation Council of Victoria (later Environment Victoria), *Environment Victoria*, 1981–89.
Conservation Council of Victoria, *Environment News*, 1976–77.
Conservation Council of Western Australia Inc., *Annual Report*, 1977–93.
Conservation Council of Western Australia Inc., *The Greener Times*, 1991–93.
Conservation Council of Western Australia Inc., 'Historical Review', Battye Library, n.d.
*The Emu*, vols. VI–X, 1907–10.
Friends of the Earth, *Chain Reaction*, 1976–97.
Friends of the Earth and Project Jonah, *Whale Campaign Manual*, Melbourne, FOE, n.d.
Getting Together conference, Newsletters and ephemera, program and associated papers.
*Mangroves and Man*, Viewpoint no. 7, Australian Conservation Foundation, September 1972.
*North Queensland Naturalist*, vol. 1, 1933.
National Parks Association of Queensland, *NPA News*.
National Parks Association of Victoria, *Park Watch*, 1979–93.
Project to Stop the Concorde, *The Concorde Crisis*, Sydney, Ecology Action, n.d.
Ratcliffe, Francis, 'The Australian Conservation Foundation', presented at the Wildlife Conservation Seminar, University of New England, 22–25 January 1965. (NBAC)
Western Australian Forest Alliance, *The Real Forest News*, 1993.
Tasmanian Conservation Trust, *Circular*, 1968–82.
Tasmanian Environment Centre, Wesley Vale Files.
*Tasmanian Tramp*, 1933–79.
Total Environment Centre, Botany Bay–Kurnell Peninsula Files.
Total Environment Centre, Myall Lakes File.
*Transactions and Proceedings and Report of the Royal Society of South Australia*, XIV–LII, 1890–1928.
*Transactions of the Natural History Society of Queensland*, vol. 1, 1892–94.
*Victorian Naturalist*, 1908.
*Wilderness Conservation*, Viewpoint, Australian Conservation Foundation, n.d.
Wright, Judith, *Conservation as an Emerging Concept*, Occasional Publication no. 2, Australian Conservation Foundation, n.d.

### Personal papers

Dunphy, Myles Joseph, Conservation Conferences.
Dunphy, Myles Joseph, Miscellaneous Conservation Correspondence Files.
Dunphy, Myles Joseph, 'The Bushwalking Conservation Movement, 1914–64'.
Dunphy, Myles Joseph, 'The New Conservators'.
Dunphy, Myles Joseph, 'The Incidence of Major Parklands in New South Wales',
    Book 1.
Stead, David George, and Harris, Thistle Yolette, Papers, 1887–1989, Boxes 2,
    25, ML.
Wright, Judith, Papers, 1962–92, Folders 102–7, 117, 121, 125, 386, 387, 400,
    NLA.

# Index